Rationality and Irrationality
in Economics

Maurice Godelier

Rationality and Irrationality in Economics

Translated from the French by Brian Pearce

Monthly Review Press
New York and London

First published as *Rationalité et Irrationalité*
en économie by François Maspero, Paris, France.
Copyright © 1966 by François Maspero.

Library of Congress Cataloging in Publication Data
Godelier, Maurice.
　　　　Rationality and irrationality in economics.
　　　　Translation of Rationalité et irrationalité en économie.
　　　　Includes bibliographical references.
　　　　1. Economics—History.　　2. Comparative economics.
3. Marxiam economics.　　I. Title.
HB75.G5613　　1973　　330.09　　72-92033
ISBN 0-85345-276-8
ISBN 0-85345-349-7 pbk.

Monthly Review Press
62 West 14th Street, New York, N.Y. 10011
47 Red Lion Street, London WC1R 4PF

Manufactured in the United States of America

10　9　8　7　6　5　4　3

Foreword to the English edition
(1972)

Functionalism, Structuralism and Marxism

When this book was published in 1966 it offered an interim report on a task of research that had been begun in 1958, with the aim of finding the answer to two questions which are really only a single question: 'What is the rationality of the economic systems that appear and disappear throughout history – in other words, what is their hidden logic and the underlying necessity for them to exist, or to have existed: and what are the conditions needed for a rational understanding of these systems – in other words, for a fully-developed comparative economic science?'

Here was a question that, though precise, led me into a field of research that seemed unlimited, being defined by no boundaries either *de jure* or *de facto*; a question the vastness of which showed clearly enough that it had been advanced by a philosopher – that is, by a mind given to focusing directly upon basic truths, concerned with the foundations of reality and of how we know them. At the same time, however – and here the philosopher who put forward this huge question showed that he was no longer a philosopher of the traditional sort, but a Marxist – the answer to this question was *not* sought *in philosophy or by philosophical means*, but in and through examining the knowledge accumulated by the sciences, and a variety of theoretical methods. Hence the strange journey from philosophy to economics, and then to anthropology, the stages of which are indicated by the texts assembled in this book.

I thus had twice to apply myself to learning a new theoretical method, and to endeavouring to find out if the question of rationality still meant something, and what the new forms were in which it presented itself. If, however, it proved necessary to go beyond political economy to anthropology, this was because the former, as it exists today, restricts *itself* to analysing two contemporary economic systems, and for it the question of economic 'rationality' leads ineluctably to the assertion, increasingly supported by 'proofs', of the *superiority* of one system over the other, and the *necessity* for one of them (this one or that) to *vanquish* the other in the course of historical development. I therefore had to subject to critical examination the 'evidence' adduced by the advocates of each system and to seek the *conditions* needed if this evidence was to contribute scientific and not ideological proof.

In this search for the epistemological conditions of a rigorous proof, one conclusion became obvious at an early stage, namely, that the question of the 'rationality' of a system means primarily the question of the 'historical necessity' for its existence – in other words, in order to think out this question one has to construct the theory of the conditions for the system's appearance and development, something that is usually excluded from, or kept outside, the field of research of political economy and left to the 'historians' of economic life. A second conclusion emerges, as an extension of the first: the conditions for the rise, functioning and evolution of any system are twofold, some belonging to the sphere of men's intentional activity, while others, of more decisive importance, give expression to the unintentional properties inherent in social relations, properties that do not belong to men's consciousness, having neither their origin nor their basis in that sphere, and that are latent with the possibility of transforming these social relations.

If, however, economic and social systems are mutually contradictory, and if each of them develops and changes and eventually vanishes from history, this is because no system exists or can reproduce itself elsewhere than within definite *limits*, by way of transformations that are compatible with the unintentional properties of its inner structures – these limits being merely the ways in which these unintentional properties, and the relations of functional compatibility and incompatibility determined by them, are manifested. It was therefore necessary to bring these concepts of compatibility, incompatibility and limits into relation with the concept of contradiction and the concepts of systems-theory and cybernetics. This was how I started on my investigation of the concepts of correspondence and contradiction between structures, and my criticism of ideas derived either from Hegel or from Marx as he has been misrepresented by dogmatic Marxism.

The ultimate question still stood, however: is there an *ultimate* reason, an *ultimate* basis for the transformations that economic systems undergo, transformations that are governed by the relations of compatibility and incompatibility between the structures composing these systems? And since (unless we are to assume that history is given meaning from outside itself and is driven by some *a priori* purpose) this basis has to be looked for *within* the various types of relations that obtain among men, the question then becomes: which, among these relations, are the ones that bear primary responsibility for the major transformations that occur in the history of mankind, determining them in the last *analysis*? Among the possible answers to this question, we know the one offered by Marx: the relations that men form among themselves in order to carry out, and in the process of carrying out, the production of the material conditions of their existence determine, in the last analysis, the relations of compatibility and incompatibility *between* all levels of social life – and, therefore, it is the major transformations that take place in the material conditions of their existence that determine, in the last analysis, the outstanding transformations that occur in the forms and functions of the other levels of social life (political, ideological, etc.).

There seemed, however, to be an unavoidable objection to this answer offered by Marx. How could this hypothesis be reconciled with the fact for example, that within many primitive societies it is relations of kinship between men that dominate social organization (Radcliffe-Brown, Evans-Pritchard), or that religious relations seem to dominate Indian society, dividing men into a hierarchy of castes in accordance with an ideology of purity and impurity (Louis Dumont)?

Thus, unless facts were to be dogmatically denied and treated as hallucinations, the Marxist problematic in the sphere of economic and social science, concerned with accounting for the existence and variety of societies and their history, became: how are we to conceive the relations between the determining structure and the dominant one, and what determining power in economic relations is it that dictates that there shall be dominance by kinship-relations or by politico-religious relations? *This* question could not be answered, or even asked, by dogmatic Marxism and the other forms of that vulgar materialism to which dogmatic Marxism belongs, even though it denies the affinity. For vulgar materialism, the economy, which it reduces to the relations between technology and environment, 'produces' the given society, giving rise to it as an epiphenomenon. This means refusing to see the irreducible differences between the levels and structures of social life, the reason for the relative autonomy with which they operate, and reducing all levels to so many functions, either apparent or concealed, of economic activity. One example will suffice to show the dead-end that vulgar materialism plunges into, thus enabling various idealist theories of society and history to triumph over its helplessness. In kinship-relations, whatever form they may take, there is an *element* that can never be reduced to a mere economic relation or deduced exclusively from such a relation. This is the relation between individuals of opposite sexes who cooperate, in a socially regulated relationship, namely, marriage, to ensure the biological reproduction of society. Clearly, it depends on definite conditions of the production of material existence whether the division between the sexes is or is not the dominant form of the division of labour, and whether it is relations of consanguinity within a group or marriage-relations between groups that constitute the means of direct cooperation in production or indirect cooperation in the circulation of goods: but, from the outset, kinship relations are not reduced to the effecting of these functions alone, and for this reason it is not possible simply to 'deduce' then from the latter. It therefore seems clear to me that only if we radically reject vulgar materialism can we hope to tackle correctly the task of analysing the relations between determination and dominance, and so to establish, so far as some societies are concerned, the working of the structural causality of their various modes of production in relation to their organization and evolution.

These theoretical conclusions, and the need to apply them to modes of production and forms of society different from the ones examined by political economy, inevitably led me towards that scientific activity which, of all the 'humane' sciences, deals with *the largest number* of *living* economic and social systems which still retain, despite the varying extent of the transformations in them dictated by the intervention, direct or indirect, of the capitalist and socialist systems, some *essential* elements of their earlier way of functioning. For this reason – the survival within a number of contemporary societies of non-capitalist elements which are alive but which seem, at first sight, to the European investigator to be odd or even absurd – I was drawn towards a scientific activity that requires of the researcher from the outset a degree of detachment from the facts, history and ideology of his own society much greater than that required of the historian or economist studying Western societies, in so far as these investigators have the impression (usually illusory) of possessing greater familiarity with what they are studying, a prior knowledge of their field of work which causes them to effect not so much cognition as recognition, comparable to the cognition of essences in Plato's philosophy.

This scientific activity exists and is called 'anthropology'. I therefore became an anthropologist. I was unable, however, given my wish to analyse economic and social systems in such a way that their unintentional social structures should become apparent, to adopt the standpoint of structural anthropology, since I realized that structuralism was no more competent than functionalism, though for different reasons, to work out the theory of the conditions needed for the historical appearance and disappearance of the systems it studies: that is, to form a conception of history. From the outset I rejected the dilemma of 'anthropology versus history', as put forward in differing forms by Boas, Lowie, Goldenweiser, Leach or Lévi-Strauss.

In association with Professor Lévi-Strauss, who took a close interest in my project and obtained for me all the facilities I needed in order to carry it out, I therefore undertook to initiate myself into anthropology, while devoting special attention to what is called 'economic anthropology', the field that it seemed ought to include the data of my theoretical problems, and perhaps the elements for their solution. This meant, apparently, turning away from analysis of the realities and problems of our own society; but very soon I rediscovered these realities present at the very heart of the theory and practice of anthropology.

After completing an initial survey of the methodological problems of economic anthropology,[1] I set forth to serve my apprenticeship 'in the field', among the Baruya, a tribe living in the interior of New Guinea who had seen a white man for the first time only in 1951 and had been brought under effective supervision by the Australian administration so recently as 1960, six years before my arrival among them. I remained there from 1967 to 1969.[2] The Baruya are a tribe of slash-and-burn cultivators who had, in about 1950, given up using their former tools of

---

[1] M. Godelier, 'Objet et méthodes de l'anthropologie économique', in *l'Homme*, V, no. 2, 1965 (see below, pp. 249 et seq.).

[2] This research was financed by the Conseil National de la Recherche Scientifique and the Wenner Gren Foundation, which twice awarded me a research grant and to which I express my gratitude.

stone and bamboo in favour of axes and matchets made of steel, which came to them through the channels of their old-established inter-tribal trade, from those parts of the island where the white men were already present and dominant. This replacement of factors of production had been undertaken of their own free will, without pressure from white administrators or missionaries, since they had not yet been discovered by the latter.

History thus presented itself, by way of exception, with a remarkable case of 'abridgement', cancelling before our very eyes, in a few isolated valleys amid the mountains of New Guinea, the enormous distance that separates, in space and time, two extreme forms of historical development – a primitive society which had hardly emerged from the neolithic stage when it found itself confronted by foreigners who claimed the 'right', in the name of the 'superiority' of their social system and their values, to 'pacify' this society by military means, to 'civilize' it and to turn it into matter for anthropological study: in short, to subject it thenceforth to the order of the European world not of Herodotus or of Cortes, but of lunar exploration and imperialist war. Straight away the question of the 'rationality' of economic and social systems and of history arose in its entirety, but now in the setting of the live and painful coming-together of two of these systems, grasped through the field-work which is the craft of the anthropologist, a craft that had to be performed as it actually exists, *inevitably* surrounded from the start and *from within* by the problems that are dictated by history – the history of today, but also that of yesterday.

Once again the 'question of rationality' arose as one which science cannot 'dodge' in any way, and which *does not disengage* the work that produces scientific knowledge from the present or from reality, and does not sever the close link that binds together today, yesterday and tomorrow, like the near and the far.

This was the theoretical scope of my investigation of economic rationality and these were the courses I followed in investigating it. I appreciate that what I have accomplished is only a few very short journeys, resulting in isolated discoveries in a vast area the systematic exploration of which calls for cooperation between great numbers of researchers.

There is something, though, which matters more than the number of researchers, and which at the same time promises to attract these in ever-growing numbers, namely, the need to carry out a theoretical revolution in the humane sciences, a revolution that becomes daily more urgent if we are to rescue these sciences from the dead-ends of functionalist empiricism or the helplessness of structuralism in face of history. It seems to me that such a revolution must today proceed by way of the reconstruction of these sciences on the basis of a Marxism that has been radically purged of all traces of vulgar materialism and dogmatism. If this revolution is accomplished, the unsolved problems that are piling up will find their solution, and while it is the chief purpose of a revolution to solve problems, we must nevertheless not overlook the fact that one of the means, and effects, of this transformation is the subjection to criticism from the new point of view of the old approaches and methods that are still dominant in the field of the humane sciences. The remainder of this foreword will be devoted to outlining some of these essential criticisms.

SOME CRITICAL EFFECTS OF QUESTIONING THE RATIONALITY
OF ECONOMIC AND SOCIAL SYSTEMS

These critical effects necessarily take three directions: criticism of Hegel's dialectics, criticism of empiricism (above all, functionalist empiricism), and criticism of structuralism.

The need to conceptualize the relations of incompatibility between structures, to find out why there are limits to the possible transformations of these structures, limits beyond which the reproduction of a system becomes compromised or even impossible, necessarily led me to reflection about dialectics, and above all about Hegel's dialectics, since for many Marxists the dialectics of Marx and of Hegel are identical at the level of principles, with their different bases (materialist or idealist) merely changing their application without changing their laws.

As a result of my analysis I think I have shown that the basis of Hegelian idealism, the postulate that matter *is* thought-in-itself which does not conceive itself, and so, thought which is both itself and its opposite, which was directly expressed in the first principle of Hegelian dialectics – the postulate of the identity of opposites – does not belong to science but to metaphysics. All that belongs to the realm of scientific thought is the principle of the *unity* of opposites, which enables us to grasp at once their complementarity (their compatibility) and their necessary conflict (their incompatibility), and the capacity that exists for reproduction of this unity within certain limits.[3]

[3] Cf. Karl Marx, *Contribution to the Critique of Political Economy* (Lawrence and

Far from contradicting the recent discoveries of cybernetics or systems-theory, Marxist dialectics, stripped of its equivocal and distorting affinity to Hegel's, appears as an abstract tool of positive value which has now been enriched, in a sense, by mathematical research on the theory of systems and their internal regulation. Without this radical criticism of the connexion between principle and content in Hegel's dialectics, dialectics must remain what it has been up to now, a 'device for proving anything and everything', alien to and repudiated by science. This has obliged me to come out against the ambiguous formulations of Lenin, Mao Tse-tung or such Marxists as Lucien Sève, and to consider the thesis of Louis Althusser (according to which the basic difference between Hegel's dialectics and the dialectics of Marx lies in the fact that in the former, contradiction is always simple, but in the latter is 'overdetermined') as an achievement that is positive but secondary – positive in so far as it implies and shows that it is impossible to reduce the different instances of society one to another, but secondary in that it does not bring out the radically 'metaphysical' and non-scientific nature of the first principle of the *Wissenschaft der Logik*: the principle of the identity of opposites. The master *is not* the slave, the employer *is not* the worker, even if the one cannot exist without the other; and this relation even opposes them one to the other just as much as it unites them.

Was it necessary, then, in order to get back to the facts of reality, to return to empiricism? But to what kind of empiricism? To abstract empiricism or to functionalist empiricism, whether in its idealist form (e.g. in anthropology, the trend called 'cultural anthropology') or its materialist form (e.g. the 'cultural ecology' upheld by Marvin Harris)?

The essential weakness of abstract empiricism is well known. The individual is taken as the starting-point of science, but in fact it is easy to show that this principle is violated as soon as formulated. We need only mention Walras's model of a pure economy, which serves as paradigm of the neo-classical theory of the optimum conditions for the functioning of a market economy that maintains itself in a state of equilibrium. This analysis proceeds from the existence of abstract individuals endowed with certain

---

Wishart edn, London, 1971): 'After this, nothing is simpler for a Hegelian than to assume that production and consumption are identical' (p. 199). . . . 'The conclusion which follows from this is not that production, distribution, exchange and consumption are *identical*, but that they are links of a single *whole*, different aspects of one *unit*' (p. 204).

scales (whether transitive or intransitive) of subjective preferences and with a psychology, simple but 'natural', that consists of a tendency to maximize their satisfactions. It is then assumed that these individuals, who are so many embodiments of a theoretical fetish, the eternal *homo oeconomicus*, live in a world where they cannot but compete with each other. It then remains to be ascertained how these individuals, who are assumed (and this is another fantastical assumption) to face each other with equal resources and information, will have to go about exchanging their labour and their products so as to maximize their satisfactions.

It is clear from this summary that to start from the individual is always to make a false start, giving oneself a false picture, for one has immediately, even though surreptitiously, placed these individuals in a universe which, though certainly abstract, possesses the very form of capitalist economy, being formally determined and organized by certain principles which are those of the capitalist mode of production: (a) every product, including labour-power, is an exchangeable commodity; (b) relations between all the individuals are relations of commodity exchange; (c) exchange-relations are relations of competition.

The dispute between formalists and substantivists in economic anthropology, about the subject-matter of political economy, now becomes understandable. For the former,[4] who follow Lionel Robbins and Samuelson,[5] and so are linked with the conservative majority of the economists of the capitalist countries, economics studies merely the forms of behaviour of individuals seeking to maximize their satisfactions; for the latter, following Karl Polanyi,[6] economics deals with social relations that are bound up with the production of material means of existence, social relations of which capitalist commodity economy is only one example among others. This definition reproduces that given by the classical economists, and opposes the marginalists' definition, but it is the one that, *in reality*, all economists apply in their *practice*. This is why the dispute about the definition of what is economic has only a limited significance, since, as soon as they have left behind them the discussion

[4] E.g. Leclair, Bunting, Salisbury. Cf. *Economic Anthropology*, ed. by Leclair and Schneider, Holt, Rinehart and Winston, 1968.

[5] Lionel Robbins, *The Subject Matter of Economics*, 1932, chapter 1, section 4: 'Economics and the exchange economy'.

[6] K. Polanyi, Arensberg, Pearson, *Trade and Market in the Early Empires*, Glencoe, 1957, and K. Polanyi, 'Primitive, Archaic and Modern Economics', in *Essays of Karl Polanyi*, ed. George Dalton, Anchor Books, 1968.

about this definition, both substantivists and formalists can find themselves *in agreement* on the *essential definitions* of non-Marxist political economy, concerning the concepts of value, wages, profit, price, etc. And it is about *these* definitions that the basic disputes are carried on in economic science, and in relation to them that non-Marxist and Marxist assumptions and analyses confront each other.

This analysis could be pursued, to show how Pareto came on the scene to make Walras's model more effective by eliminating one of its weak points, namely, the restrictive assumption of equality in information and in means of production possessed by all the individuals who come face to face in a competitive market. By showing that an optimum could be attained even in a situation where there was inequality in appropriation of the means of production, Pareto[7] introduced into Walras's model the very form of the fundamental social relation of the capitalist mode of production, which is not merely a generalized commodity economy, in which every product is exchanged as a commodity, but a *capitalist* commodity economy, that is, one that assumes the fundamental inequality between a class which owns money and means of production and another class which is without these, and has regularly to sell to the former the use of its labour-power.

An economic doctrine which sought to be the 'pure' science of the fundamental laws of the economy was able to develop – by a paradox that was perfectly predictable – only through jettisoning its point of departure, namely, the existence of abstract and equal individuals, so as to re-introduce clandestinely the existence of concrete social relations – the *necessary* relation of inequality between two classes: necessary in two ways, because it is how the system functions and is reproduced, and because it is dictated by a history which economic science is incapable or not desirous of analysing.

Pure neo-classical economics is thus a *committed* economics through and through, both in the questions it asks and in those it fails to ask: committed to legitimizing and reproducing the capitalist system—and the

[7] Vilfredo Pareto, *Manuel d'Economie Politique*, 2nd edn, Giard, Paris, 1927: chapter VI, pp. 32–51. See in this connexion: A. Marshall, *Principles of Economics*, 8th edn, Macmillan, London, 1920, book IV, chapter 13, and A. C. Pigou, *The Economics of Welfare*, Macmillan, 1932, chapters 9 to 11. Pareto had indeed opened the way to what has been called the 'New Welfare Economics', which was explored by men so diverse as Allais, Barone, Hicks, Kalder, Lange, Arrow, Debreu, etc., and was conceived primarily as a way of bringing order into the functioning of the capitalist system.

refinements of econometry and mathematical research can never change this in the least. This was recognized in his own way by one of the greatest of the econometricians, T. C. Koopmans, when he wrote, with lucidity and prudence, commenting on the apologetical discourses of some of his colleagues:

A competitive equilibrium, even if it is also a Pareto optimum, may involve a more unequal distribution of income than is regarded as desirable from a *social* point of view. The concept of a Pareto optimum is *insensitive* to this consideration, and in that respect the term 'optimum' is a misnomer.[8]

Actually, this discussion is not only of interest to economists. What is fundamental to the debate is that there is no *direct* experience between individuals except *through* the social relations that 'mediate' them, and this is why it is of interest to all the humane sciences alike. The concept of 'immediate' experience is scientifically meaningless, and this is why science cannot take the individual and his 'immediate' experience of the world and of other people as its point of departure. This principle is explicitly acknowledged by functionalism, by structuralism and by Marxism. The work of such anthropologists as Mary Douglas[9] or Colin Turnbull[10] shows clearly enough that we have to push analysis to the point where it explains the *form* that the relations existing among men and between men and nature assumes in the consciousness of individuals, and also that this form, far from explaining these relations, itself needs to be explained on the basis of them, by means of a method that enables one *at the same time* to compare various societies and their symbolical systems.

Functionalist empiricism, however, starts not from individuals but from the relations between them. These relations are not taken one by one, but together, and this group of relations is regarded as an 'integrated' whole to the extent that these different relations are functionally com-

---

[8] T. C. Koopmans, *Three Essays on the State of Economic Science*, McGraw Hill, 1957, p. 49. My emphasis, M.G.

[9] Mary Douglas, *Purity and Danger*, Routledge and Kegan Paul, 1966. See the important preface by Professor Luc de Heusch to the French translation of this work, *De la souillure* (p. 9), in which he analyses the difficulty of establishing a comparative theory of religions without criticizing the principles of functionalism, which asserts that 'the symbolical order of every society is a prisoner of its own sociological specificity'.

[10] Colin M. Turnbull, *Wayward Servants*, New York, 1965; and, especially, his excellent *The Forest People* (1961).

plementary. These functions determine the role and status of individuals in their social system, and this system constantly tends towards a state of equilibrium. Study of a society thus means study of a system, of a totality that is functionally integrated and that reproduces itself as such. Knowing the history of this system does not help one to know how it functions. History itself appears as 'a succession of accidental events', which are left to the ethnologist or the historian, while theoretical analysis of the systems is reserved for the anthropologist or the sociologist. These views are well known, and it is unnecessary to do more than refer the reader to the classical writings of Radcliffe-Brown and Nadel, or, for sociology, to the work of Talcott Parsons.[11]

What structuralism and Marxism alike reject is not, of course, the principle that science must take as its subject of analysis the *relations* between men, or the principle that relations must be analysed in their unity within a whole, or the principle that priority must be given to studying the logic of these relations and this whole before studying their origin and evolution. Malinowski and Radcliffe-Brown were right to turn away from that pseudo-history, the evolutionism of the nineteenth century which saw in a given society a collection of customs inherited from a past period that one reconstituted by means of assumptions that were unverified and often unverifiable, and instead to study the facts themselves as they presented themselves before their eyes.

I have shown elsewhere that Marx, turning his back on the 'historicist' method, dealt with the origin of the capitalist mode of production only after studying its internal logic and establishing his theory of value and surplus-value, and have shown that this methodological principle of priority for the analysis of a structure over that of its origin is the principle of modern linguistics and of Lévi-Strauss, even though the latter, unlike Marx, accepts the empiricist view that history is a 'succession of accidental events'.

What both structuralists and Marxists reject are the empiricist definitions of what constitutes a social structure. For Radcliffe-Brown and Nadel, a social structure is an aspect of *reality* itself; it is order, the ordering of the *visible* relations between men, an ordering that explains the

[11] A. R. Radcliffe-Brown, *Structure and Function in Primitive Society*, Cohen and West, 1952: see the introduction; F. Nadel, *The Theory of Social Structure*, Cohen and West, London, 1957: see 'Preliminaries'; Talcott Parsons, *Essays in Sociological Theory, Pure and Applied*: see chapter 10, 'The Social System'.

logic of the complementariness of these visible relations.[12] For others – and, despite his criticisms of functionalism, Leach is the best example of these – the structure is an *ideal* order which the mind introduces into things by reducing the multiform flux of reality to simplified images that give one a hold upon reality and make possible social action, social practice.[13]

For Marx as for Lévi-Strauss a structure is *not* a reality that is *directly* visible, and so directly observable, but a *level of reality* that exists *beyond* the visible relations between men, and the functioning of which constitutes the underlying logic of the system, the subjacent order by which the apparent order is to be explained.

Let me recall the insistence with which Lévi-Strauss returns to this essential point, combating the idealistic and formalistic interpretations to which his ideas are commonly subjected. In his reply to Maybury-Lewis, he emphasizes the fact that: 'Of course the final word should rest with experience. However, the experiment suggested and guided by deductive reasoning will not be the same as the unsophisticated ones with which the whole process started. . . . The ultimate proof of the molecular structure of matter is provided by the electronic microscope, which enables us to see *actual* molecules. This achievement does not alter the fact that henceforth the molecule will not become any more visible to the naked eye. Similarly, it is hopeless to expect a structural analysis to change our way of perceiving concrete social relations. It will only *explain* them better.'[14]

Introducing to the public the first volume of *Mythologiques*, Lévi-Strauss again declared categorically: 'I have thus completed my demonstration of the fact that, whereas in the public mind there is frequently

[12] Radcliffe-Brown, in D. Forde and A. R. Radcliffe-Brown, eds. *African Systems of Kinship and Marriage*, Oxford University Press, 1950, p. 43. The elements of the social structure are human beings, 'what is meant by social structure' being 'any arrangement of persons in institutionalized relationships'.

[13] E. Leach, *Political Systems of Highland Burma*, Harvard University Press, 1954; reprinted Bell and Sons, 1964, pp. 4–5: 'I hold that social structure in practical situations (as contrasted with the sociologist's abstract model) consists of a set of ideas about the distribution of power between persons and groups of persons.' Then, referring to the models constructed by sociologists and anthropologists, Leach adds this definition of an orthodox functionalism: 'Social structure . . . the principles of organization that unite the component parts of the system', and concludes with a subjectivist pirouette: 'The structures which the anthropologist *describes* are models which *exist only* as logical constructions in his own mind.'

[14] Lévi-Strauss, 'On manipulated sociological models', in *Bijdragen tot de taal-, land- en volkenkunde*, The Hague, 1960, p. 53. My emphasis, M.G.

confusion between structuralism, idealism and formalism, structuralism has only to be confronted with true manifestations of idealism and formalism for its own *deterministic and realistic* inspiration to become clearly manifest.'[15]

The idealist and formalist interpretations of structuralism are based on the opening sentence of the well-known passage that Lévi-Strauss devoted to the concept of social structure:

Passing now to the task of defining 'social structure', there is a point which should be cleared up immediately. The term 'social structure', has nothing to do with empirical reality but with models which are built up after it (*d'après celle-ci*)[16]

This sentence, taken out of his context, conveys the illusion that the theoretical positions of Lévi-Strauss and of Leach are identical, or at least are fundamentally linked. But Lévi-Strauss's sentence cannot be interpreted correctly unless it is taken in relation to the sentence that follows:

Social relations consist of the raw material out of which the models making up the social structure are built (*qui rendent manifeste la structure sociale elle-même*).[16]

To make a structure '*manifeste*' does not mean creating it out of nothing or assuming that it exists only in the human mind, either in the form of models indigenous to social reality or in that of the abstract models of the sociologists.

To sum up this complex group of theoretical positions and oppositions as simply as possible, let me say that Lévi-Strauss affirms, like Radcliffe-Brown, the 'reality' of social structures as existing outside the human mind, and so opposes Leach. But Lévi-Strauss at the same time opposes Radcliffe-Brown, since for him the reality of a social structure is not the 'ordering' of the social relations that are directly observable by the informant or the anthropologist.[17] He is thus led to criticize functionalism for its inability to grasp the order underlying visible social relations and

[15] Lévi-Strauss, *Le Cru et le Cuit*, Plon, 1964, p. 35. My emphasis, M.G. (English translation, *The Raw and the Cooked*, London, 1970, p. 27). See my article, 'Système, structure et contradiction dans le *Capital*' in *Temps Modernes*, 1966, pp. 828–64 (English translation, 'System, Structure and Contradiction in *Capital*', in *Socialist Register*, 1967, pp. 91–119).

[16] Lévi-Strauss, in *Anthropologie structurale*, Plon, 1957, pp. 305–6 (English translation, *Structural Anthropology*, London, 1968, p. 279).

[17] This is a criticism that Meyer Fortes directed at Radcliffe-Brown when he wrote in 1949 in the Radcliffe-Brown Festschrift: 'Structure is not immediately visible in the

construct a solid basis for a comparative science of societies. Consequently he finds himself side by side with Leach, who also criticises the truisms of functionalism, but moves in the opposite direction from Lévi-Strauss, towards a formalism that keeps intact the empiricist view of reality as a multiform, unstructured flux. It is understandable that such an interplay of agreement and disagreement at different levels should naturally give rise to confusions and misconceptions in the social science field which make it both difficult and necessary for researchers to undertake a critical analysis of the epistemological conditions and principles of their methods of cognition.[18] This is why a thorough analysis of the relations between structuralism and Marxism presents itself as a fundamental task, since it is possible for a radical difference and opposition to exist beneath and within a common acceptance of certain methodological principles and a common affirmation that science must be materialistic and deterministic.

Let us recall once again what these points of agreement are. There is first the methodological principle that social relations must be analysed as forming '*systems*'. Then there is the principle that the inner *logic* of these systems must be analysed *before* their *origin* is analysed. We see at once that, as regards these two principles, Marxism is not opposed either to structuralism or to functionalism.

These two principles are set forth in Marx's methodological *Introduction* to his *Contribution to the Critique of Political Economy*, where he defines the order in which it is necessary to study and expound the way the capitalist mode of production works: 'Rent cannot be understood without capital, but capital *can* be understood without rent. Capital is the economic power that dominates everything in bourgeois society. It must form both the point of departure and the conclusion and it has to be expounded before landed property. After analysing capital and landed property separately, their interconnection must be examined.

It would be inexpedient and wrong therefore to present the economic categories successively in the order in which they have played their dominant role in

"concrete reality" . . . When we describe structure . . . we are, as it were, in the realm of grammar and syntax, not of the spoken word' (in *Social Structure : Studies presented to A. R. Radcliffe-Brown*, Oxford, 1949, p. 56).

[18] This is how it is that Edmund Leach appears in the eyes of his Anglo-American colleagues as the isolated but turbulent representative of structuralism, and he himself declares his 'sympathy with his (Lévi-Strauss's) general point of view' and his 'obvious debt' to him (in *Rethinking Anthropology*, 1961, preface, p. vi).

history. *On the contrary, their order of succession is determined by their mutual relation in modern bourgeois society and this is quite the reverse of what appears to be natural to them or in accordance with the sequence of historical development.* The point at issue is not the role that various economic relations have played in the succession of various social formations appearing in the course of history; even less is it their sequence 'as concepts' (Proudhon) (a nebulous notion of the historical process), but their *position* within modern bourgeois society.[19]

Marx thus does not make the question of the origin or the history of social relations the key question or principal question for science, as did the evolutionists and diffusionists of the nineteenth century; his thinking on this point converges with that of Malinowski or of Lévi-Strauss.[20] This accounts for the existence of a text such as *Pre-Capitalist Economic Formations* in which Marx, after having discovered the true, hidden nature of surplus-value, turns back to the history of Antiquity and the Middle Ages and analyses the differences between various archaic or ancient modes of production and the capitalist mode.

This is the underlying reason for the internal structure of *Capital*, as well as for the existence of texts like *Pre-Capitalist Economic Formations* and also the drafts of Marx's letter to Vera Zasulich (8 March 1881). In *Capital*, it is only *after* establishing that the content of the exchange-value of commodities is socially-necessary labour-time, and that capital is not a thing but a social relation between two classes, one of which appropriates the value created by the other (surplus-value), that Marx turns to the problem of the origins of capitalism, and deals with it under the title of 'the primitive accumulation of capital'. In *Pre-Capitalist Economic Formations* he had gone beyond the question of the origins of capitalism

[19] Karl Marx, *Contribution to the Critique of Political Economy* (Lawrence and Wishart edn, p. 213). My emphasis, M.G.

[20] Compare Lévi-Strauss in *Les Structures élémentaires de la parenté*, Mouton, 1968, p. 449 (English translation, *Elementary Structures of Kinship*, p. 390): 'A functional system, e.g. a kinship system, can never be interpreted in an integral fashion by diffusionist hypotheses. The system is bound up with the total structure of the society employing it, and consequently its nature depends more on the intrinsic characteristics of such a society than on cultural contacts and migrations.' And again, on p. 165 (English translation, p. 142): 'We have been careful to eliminate all historical speculation, all research into origins, and all attempts to reconstruct a hypothetical order in which institutions succeeded one another.' And Evans-Pritchard, similarly: 'A history of the legal institutions of the England of today will only show us how they have come to be what they are and not how they function in our social life' (*Social Anthropology*, London, 1951, p. 48).

and outlined, writing as historian and anthropologist, a remarkable analysis of the original logics of the functioning of certain ancient and archaic modes of production, endeavouring to imagine some of the conditions of their internal transformations and their history. Marx's method in relation to history can be grasped very clearly in the passage he devoted to defining the nature of money as a commodity *specialized in the function* of expressing the value of other commodities, as 'universal equivalent'. When Marx says that he is going to show 'the genesis of the money-form' of exchange-value, what he does is to determine at one and the same time the *specific function* of one particular category of commodities in relation to all the others, the *'form'* that a commodity has to assume in order to fulfil this specialized function as universal equivalent, and the practical *conditions* that make both necessary and possible the specialization of a certain category of commodities in this function. And Marx emphasizes that this theoretical procedure which he calls the 'ideal genesis' of money is not at all a 'history' of the different forms of money that are encountered in human societies. Such a 'history' is possible, and can be scientific, only on the basis of results won by preliminary structural research, and the results of these historical researches will also contribute to the development of structural research. In this circular movement of cognition, the starting-point of which is always analysis of functions and of the structures that realize them in defined conditions, a single science of man is constituted, which does not isolate in closed fetishized compartments, or oppose to each other, ethnology and anthropology, history and theory, etc.

A method like this which aims at grasping simultaneously the basis, the *raisons d'être* of the *functions*, the *form* and the *conditions* of existence (and so of the rise and evolution of social relations, which thereby exist *only* as *structures* endowed with objective properties) lays down rigorous lines for a new and fruitful relation between scientific disciplines, both the different departments of history (economic, political, social, ideological, cognitive activities, etc.), and what are called the theoretical disciplines (anthropology, sociology, political economy, etc.). After that has been established the functionalists' view may cease to be true, or to seem true, according to which: 'the historian can *only* provide us with the succession of *accidental* events which have *caused* a society to become what it is.'[21]

[21] This is how Evans-Pritchard sums up the attitude of the functionalists towards history, without, however, endorsing it himself. See the next note.

But the functionalists' criticism of the historian's work, a criticism to which Marx subscribed in advance when he himself criticized the 'historians' of capitalism or of Antiquity, goes further than a mere criticism of the present state of a theoretical method, a situation that one may still hope and endeavour to improve. Beyond the criticism of history as a craft (*Historie*, historiography) there is the empiricist view that history as reality (*Geschichte*) is only a succession of 'events', and of events that are themselves only 'accidents'. On this fundamental point concerning not just the epistemological conditions of a *science* of history but the nature of the *actual process* of human history, Marx is opposed both to Radcliffe-Brown[22] and to Leach or Lévi-Strauss. I shall come back to this point. Before doing so, however, let me recall a third methodological principle which opposes Marxism and structuralism to functionalist empiricism, namely, that what is visible is a *reality* concealing *another*, deeper reality, which is hidden and the discovery of which is the very purpose of scientific cognition.

We are here at the very heart of Marx's method as displayed in *Capital* – at the point of origin of the theoretical revolution he effected in political economy and in the humane sciences.[23] What is this method? Marx shows the absurd, falsely 'obvious' character of the conceptions that individuals *spontaneously* form regarding the nature of commodities and of economic relations in commodity societies: 'A commodity appears at first sight a very trivial thing, and easily understood.'[24]

Marx shows that the reason why a commodity is a complex and obscure reality is that what makes a product of labour a commodity, namely, its value, is social labour that does not *appear* as such.

The existence of the things *qua* commodities, and the value relation between the products of labour which stamps them as commodities, have absolutely no connexion with their physical properties and with the material relations arising therefrom. There it is a definite social relation between men, that assumes, in their eyes, the fantastic form of a relation between things. In order, therefore,

[22] Let me recall that on this crucial point there is disagreement among the functionalists. Evans-Pritchard stresses, for instance, that: 'History is not merely a succession of changes but . . . a growth . . . Furthermore . . . history alone provides a satisfactory experimental situation in which the hypotheses of functional anthropology can be tested' (*Social Anthropology*, p. 60).

[23] See my article: 'Economie marchande, fétichisme, magie et science', in 'Objets du fétichisme', *Nouvelle Revue de Psychanalyse*, Autumn 1970, no. 2.

[24] Marx, *Capital*, I, 1938, Allen and Unwin edn, p. 41.

to find an analogy, we must have recourse to the mist-enveloped regions of the religious world. In that world the productions of the human brain appear as independent beings endowed with life, and entering into relation both with one another and the human race.[25]

The fetishizing of commodities is not the effect of the alienation of con-sciousnesses but the effect *in* and *for* consciousnesses of the disguising of social relations *in* and *behind* their appearances. Now these appearances are the *necessary* point of departure of the representations of their econo-mic relations that individuals *spontaneously* form for themselves. Such images thus constitute a more or less coherent body of illusory beliefs concerning the social reality within which these individuals live, and serve them as means of *acting* within and upon this social reality.

We see the full implication for the social sciences of Marx's demonstra-tion of the existence of a process of fetishization of social relations, a demonstration carried out on the basis of the particular example pro-vided by the fetishizing of commodity relations of production.[26] In showing that, by his labour, the worker creates *not only the equivalent* of the value represented by his wages but also *additional* value for which he is not paid, and which constitutes the origin and essence of surplus value, Marx shows at the same time that, in practice, the wage-relation 'makes the actual relation invisible and, indeed, shows the direct opposite of that relation'. Thus, at the level of visible social relations, everything happens, in the eyes of both the capitalists and the workers, as though wages paid for all the labour contributed by the worker and profit were not produced by labour but by capital. The economic categories of wages, profit, inter-est on capital, etc., therefore express quite well the visible relations of the capitalist system, and as such they have *pragmatic utility*, being of service in management and the taking of decisions; but they possess no scientific value, for they do not reflect the true, underlying logic of the system. No econometrical refinements can alter this fact – which does not at all signify that the use of mathematics does not increase the pragmatic *utility* of the categories of vulgar economics, in so far as, at the level of

---

[25] ibid., p. 43.

[26] I have tried to analyse other forms of fetishism connected with non-commodity modes of production in 'Fétichisme, religion et théorie générale de l'idéologie chez Marx', in *Annali*, Feltrinelli, 1970, pp. 22–40, and in an article devoted to Lévi-Strauss's *La Pensée sauvage* and *Mythologiques*, 'Mythe et histoire, réflexions sur les fondements de la pensée sauvage', in *Annales*, May–August 1971, pp. 541–58.

the day-to-day practice of business management of enterprises and competition, what is essential is not to have a scientific theory of the real functioning of the system in its totality, but to anticipate the functioning of variables – wages, investments, profits – which must and can be treated *separately*.

The final pattern of economic relations as *seen* on the surface in their real existence and consequently in the conceptions by which the bearers and agents of these relations seek to understand them, is very much different from, and indeed quite the *reverse*, of *their inner but concealed essential pattern and the conception corresponding to it.*[27]

It is therefore impossible for scientific cognition to be built up from the spontaneous representations formed by individuals of their social relations, and this radically refutes empiricism in all the fields where it operates. There is no fundamental difference between the spontaneous models of their society that individuals make for themselves, 'the set of ideas' they have regarding their 'social structure in practical situations' (Leach), and the learned models constructed by sociologists and economists who start from the same spontaneous representations and whose models 'exist only as logical constructions in [their] own mind' (Leach). On this point Marx and Lévi-Strauss are agreed, and the latter's analysis of the mechanisms by which mythical representations of reality are constructed is an essential scientific gain. However, Marx requires of science that it not merely discover the mechanisms of mythical thought but also the mechanisms which, existing *outside of* thought, impose upon the latter the illusory conceptions which it forms of reality – that is to say, both their content and their historical *necessity*.

It is, in reality, much easier to discover by analysis the earthly core of the misty creations of religion than, conversely, it is to develop from the actual relations of life the corresponding celestialized forms of those relations. The latter method is the only materialistic, and therefore the only scientific one.[28]

It is the actual significance of the structural analysis of myths and of all ideology that is called in question by this reflection of Marx's on the history of religion.

Before pursuing our analysis of the difference and opposition between Marxism and structuralism, let me mention an important consequence of

[27] Marx, *Capital*, III, FLPH edn, p. 205.
[28] Marx, *Capital*, I, 1938, Allen and Unwin edn. p. 367.

the Marxist criticism of 'bourgeois' political economy and of its empiricist premisses. The most abstract categories of political economy, those which seem the most innocent of any ideological content, constitute only abstract cognition of the determinations that are common to all societies, and not real cognition of the specific structures of these societies.

The establishment of the individual as a mere *worker* is itself a product of historical development.

Labour is quite a simple category. The idea of labour in that sense, as labour in general, is also very old. Yet 'labour' thus defined by political economy is as much a modern category as the conditions which have given rise to this simple abstraction. . . . This example of labour strikingly shows how even the most abstract categories, in spite of their applicability to all epochs – just because of their abstract character – are by the very definiteness of the abstraction a product of historical conditions as well, and are fully applicable only to and under those conditions.[29]

This analysis, which would not be repudiated by any anthropologist[30] shows well enough the extent to which abstract categories such as 'economy', religion, politics, seen as so many sub-systems of a social system (Talcott Parsons), contain strictly the *apparent form* of the social relations of capitalist society. In the latter, the economy seems to function in a purely autonomous way, independently of political and religious relations which are seen as 'exogenous' variables. Authentic Marxism, however, does not pre-judge the form and content of real economic relations in the various societies known to history. Their modes of production are not objects available for direct cognition through experience, but realities which have to be 'recognized' by discovering them where the vulgar and abstract conceptions of economy and society do not accompany them – that is, also in the functioning of political or religious or kinship relations. A mode of production is not reducible to the subsistence activities of a society, but a complex reality that has to be 'reproduced' reconstructing its content by thought. We can now appreciate better the ridiculous and

---

[29] From Marx's *Grundrisse der Kritik der Politischen Ökonomie*: English translation of these passages in *Marx's Grundrisse*, David McLellan, London, 1971, pp. 37, 39.

[30] Marshall Sahlins, *Tribesmen*, Prentice Hall, 1968, p. 80: 'A man works, produces in his capacity as a social person, as a husband and father, brother and lineage mate, member of a clan, a village. Labour is not implemented apart from these existences as if it were a different existence. "Worker" is not a status in itself nor "labour" a true category of tribal economics.'

ideologically-marked nature of the advice given to English-speaking apprentice anthropologists in that little manual of instruction, *Notes and Queries on Anthropology*:

If the investigator has been trained in *ordinary* economic theory but has no anthropological training, he should remember continually the importance of the social setting of the economic institutions he is studying, *otherwise he will not grasp* the value system upon which the economic organization depends. If he has had no economic training he is recommended to study the *fundamental principles* expounded in one of the *recognized* economic textbooks.[31]

Poorly concealed behind the look of innocent common sense are the contradictions of an empiricism that simultaneously declares and denies that it suffices to use 'ordinary economic theory', that of the 'recognized textbooks', in order to analyse original economic systems that *cannot be conceived* otherwise than in their *inner* relation with a definite 'social setting'. It is clear that for conceiving this inner relation, 'ordinary economic theory', even the theory of 'fundamental principles', does not offer an adequate instrument. Actually – and this is the radical originality of Marx's thought, which opposes it both to structuralism and to functionalism – Marxism assumes that this inner relation, which provides the underlying logic of the functioning of societies and of their history, is determined, in the last analysis, by the conditions of *production and reproduction* of their material basis, or, to use his terminology, their mode of production.

Marxism is not a philosophy of history, or a 'model of history'. History is not a concept that explains, but that one explains. Marxism is above all a theory of society, a hypothesis regarding the articulation of its internal levels and the specific hierarchical causality of each of these levels. Marxism assumes both the relative autonomy of social structures and their reciprocal relation in a specific way of *referring back* to a system of *constraints* which determine in the last analysis, but which are never directly visible, and which express the conditions of production and reproduction of the material basis of social existence. Developing the theory of these structures, their articulations, their causality, and the conditions necessary for them to appear and to disappear, signifies making history a

---

[31] *Notes and Queries on Anthropology*, revised and rewritten by a committee of the Royal Anthropological Institution of Great Britain and Ireland, Routledge, 1960. My emphasis, M.G.

science and developing it as such, as provisional synthesis and conclusion, as 'reproduction of the concrete by means of thought'.[32]

From the moment, however, when one accepts the assumption of the existence of necessary conditions for the appearance and disappearance of social structures, for their specific articulation and causality, history as reality can no longer be reduced to a succession of purely accidental events. Events have their own necessity, and accidents are seen to impose a necessity which ultimately does not depend on them since it expresses the objective properties of social relations, properties of compatibility and incompatibility, which underlie the limited system of their possible transformations. There is no point in counterposing the internal causes of the transformations of societies to the external ones since in the end it is the same unintentional properties of the social structures that are expressing themselves. It is pointless to bring forward as an objection to Marxism the dominance of kinship relations in this case or politico-religious relations in that, for Marxism does not deny these facts, declines to reduce structures one to another as epiphenomena of material life, but undertakes precisely to *explain* this dominance by *seeking* the reasons for it in specific determinations of different modes of production.[33] Faced

[32] Cf. Marx: 'The concrete concept is concrete because it is a synthesis of many definitions, thus representing the unity of diverse aspects. It appears therefore in reasoning as a summing-up, a result, and not as the starting-point, although it is the real point of origin, and thus also the point of origin of perception and imagination' (*Contribution to the Critique of Political Economy*, Lawrence and Wishart edn, p. 206).

[33] 'In the estimation of [a critic of Marx], my view that each special mode of production and the social relations corresponding to it, in short, that the economic structure of society, is the real basis on which the juridical and political superstructure is raised, and to which definite social forms of thought correspond: that the mode of production determines the character of the social, political and intellectual life generally, all this is very true for our own times, in which material interests preponderate, but not for the Middle Ages, in which Catholicism, nor for Athens and Rome, where politics, reigned supreme. In the first place it strikes one as an odd thing for anyone to suppose that these well-worn phrases about the Middle Ages and the Ancient World are unknown to anyone else. This much, however, is clear, that the Middle Ages could not live on Catholicism, nor the Ancient World on politics. On the contrary, it is the mode in which they gained a livelihood that explains why here politics and there Catholicism played the chief part. . . . On the other hand, Don Quixote long ago paid the penalty for wrongly imagining that knight errantry was compatible with all economical forms of society' (*Capital*, I, 1938, Allen and Unwin edn, p. 54n). Marx gave only fragments of 'explanations' of these different dominances, but his thought is very clear, and does not justify the criticisms made by Louis Dumont of his alleged utilitarian and Victorian

with these facts of dominance, British anthropology has proved incapable of doing anything more than repeat that the dominant structures 'serve' to 'integrate' the various parts of the social whole, while failing to explain why it is that in one case kinship and in another politics or religion fulfilled the role of integrator.

The British social anthropologists were less concerned about total configurations of cultural knowledge than about the functional integration of institutions which supported and maintained society. . . . The key to the complex and beautiful unity of society was conceived to be its structure based on kin, marital and political relations. . . . Here were hidden elaborate networks and subtle symmetries to be discovered, whereas subsistence activities were considered simple, undifferentiated and boringly repetitive wherever one found them.[34]

And yet, on many occasions in their practical work, British anthropologists have contradicted[35] this common doctrine of the older functionalism (as against the neo-functionalism of cultural ecology), without drawing radical conclusions from their having done so.

Thus, Leach, in his work *Political Systems of Highland Burma*, when he analyses the concepts of 'Property and Ownership', states:

The concepts which are discussed in the present section are of the *utmost importance* for my general argument for they provide the categories in terms of which social relations are linked with economic facts. In the *last analysis* the power relations in any society must be *based* upon the control of real goods and the primary sources of production, but this Marxist generalization *does not carry us very far.*[36]

---

conception of man: 'Marx shut himself within the confines of the modern view of man as an individual . . . Marx fully shared the outlook of the scholars of the Victorian age . . .', in 'La civilisation indienne et nous', *Cahiers des Annales*, Armand Colin, Paris, 1964, p. 39.

[34] Robert McC. Netting, 'The Ecological Approach in Cultural Study', *A McCaleb Module in Anthropology*, 1971, pp. 3–4.

[35] E.g. R. Firth, in *Primitive Polynesian Economy*, p. 7: 'W. L. Wagner argued that the Murngin did not create a separate economic structure . . . but were dependent on their other institutions, primarily their kinship system, to regulate indirectly their technology and control their distribution and consumption of goods and services (*A Black Civilisation*, 1937, p. 138). But the lack of what may be classed as specifically economic *institutions* does not mean the lack of economic *process*' (emphasis by R. Firth).

[36] E. Leach, *Political Systems of Highland Burma*, Bell and Sons, 1964, p. 141. My emphasis, M.G.

One cannot but wonder at the inconsequence of the conclusion, a pirouette by which the author shrugs off an hypothesis 'of the utmost importance', and applicable to 'any society', so as not to seem to be casting doubt on the non-Marxist theses of the functionalists.

Much more seriously, however, R. Firth says in the preface to the second edition of his *Primitive Polynesian Economy*:

After publishing an account of the social structure, in particular the kinship structure (*We, the Tikopia*, London, 1936), I analysed the economic structure of the society, because so many social relationships were made more manifest in their economic content. Indeed, the *social structure* in particular the political structure. was clearly *dependent on specific economic relationships arising out of the system of control* of resources. With these relationships in turn were linked the religious activities and institutions of the society.[37]

Throughout his work Firth encouraged the development of economic anthropology, 'for a deeper understanding of social conditions and structures in the communities the anthropologist studies'.[38] But he did not cease to show confidence in the general principles of non-Marxist political economy, as the theoretical framework needed in order to analyse the economic systems of primitive and peasant societies.[39]

However, is not functionalism engaged in ridding itself of its inconsistencies and its traditional theoretical hesitations, thanks to the efforts of the American school known as that of 'cultural ecology'?[40] This school declares itself to be resolutely materialist, and aims to reinterpret all human cultures on the basis of the material conditions of the adaptation of

[37] Firth, op. cit., chapter XI. Among other valuable works by Anglo-American anthropologists on primitive economic systems should be mentioned Nadel's excellent book *Black Byzantium*, devoted to the Nupe of Nigeria, and *The Nuer*, by Evans-Pritchard.

[38] In *Primitive Polynesian Economy*, p. 14. His evaluation of Herskovits's work, *Economic Anthropology*, 1952, which was for a long time one of the few textbooks available to anthropologists on the subject, should be called to mind: 'Herskovits examines material from a wide range of sources dealing with "non-literate" economic systems. His treatment tends to be eclectic rather than rigorously theoretical and it is difficult to discern what is the general framework of his analysis' (in *Economics of the New Zealand Maori*, Owen, Wellington, 1959, p. 32).

[39] R. Firth, 'A viewpoint from economic anthropology', in *Capital, Saving and Credit in Peasant Studies*, ed. R. Firth and B. S. Yamey, Allen, 1964, pp. 15–35.

[40] Andrew P. Vayda and Roy A. Rappaport, 'Ecology, Cultural and Non-Cultural', in J. A. Clifton, ed., *Introduction to Cultural Anthropology*, 1968, Boston, Houghton Mifflin, pp. 477–97.

man to definite environments.[41] Every society is studied as a subsystem of a wider totality, the ecological system within which it lies, and the functioning and conditions of reproduction of this ecological system are analysed by means of systems-theory and communication-theory (feedback mechanisms, entropy, etc.). The whole of functionalism seems to have recast, in its orientation (materialistic), its method (modern systems theory) and its theoretical possibilities and aspirations (comparison of societies and construction of a multilinear schema of social evolution). Are we not here in the theoretical universe, if not of Marx himself, then at least of Marxism as it is generally understood and practised?

I do not here propose to draw up a survey, even a provisional one, of the works of the anthropologists who adhere to the doctrine of cultural materialism. Robert Netting has recently done this, very firmly and perceptively, by compiling a list of the positive discoveries that were quickly made as soon as *detailed* study was undertaken of the ecological environment and conditions of production of the peoples who live by hunting and food-gathering (Richard Lee, De Vore, Steward), the Indians of the North-West Coast (Suttles), the pastoral societies of East Africa (Gulliver, Deshler, Dyson-Hudson), and slash-and-burn cultivators (Geertz, Roy, Rappaport). Confronted by facts, the theses that had been repeated over and over again by 'cultural anthropology', and which every anthropology student had accepted as gospel truth, gradually collapsed – the 'hardship' of the life of the hunters and food-gatherers, the potlatch 'excesses' of the North-West Coast Indians, the 'cattle complex' and 'love for their cows' of the African herdsmen, and the 'irrational practices' of slash-and-burn agriculture.[42] To the work of the anthropologists must be added that of archaeologists such as Braidwood, Flannery, McNeish, etc., who have devoted themselves since the 1950s to reconstituting in minute detail the ecological conditions of existence of the pre-neolithic populations of Mesopotamia and Mesoamerica, and have transformed our knowledge of the processes of domestication of plants and animals and of the appearance of new economic and social systems

[41] 'The tendency in social anthropology has been to study societies as if they were isolated, self-sufficient systems, subsisting on thin air, with no visible roots in the soil. The guiding principle, derived in large part from Durkheim and more explicitly from Radcliffe-Brown, has been that social facts require sociological explanations' (in *The Family Estate in Africa*, ed. R. F. Gray and P. H. Gulliver, London, 1964, p. 6).

[42] See the collection of articles by A. P. Vayda, *Environment and Cultural Behaviour*, The Natural History Press, New York, 1969.

based on agriculture and stockbreeding. Here too an old-established and respected idea, that of the 'neolithic revolution' (Childe), had to be called in question and profoundly revised.[43]

It was inevitable that these positive results should be obtained as soon as a systematic effort was devoted to analysing essential aspects of the functioning of primitive or ancient societies which had been dogmatically neglected or wrongly handled, except by brilliant exceptions like Malinowski, Firth and Evans-Pritchard, on the pretext that they were 'undifferentiated and boringly repetitive'. Nevertheless, what is called the ecological approach, as soon as it tries to become a *general* theory of social life and history, comes to grief in so far as, on such essential points as the causality of the economy and/or the environment, the nature of the functional relations between social structures, and the driving-forces of the evolution of systems, it relies upon the dogmas of vulgar materialism, which ultimately prove to be not merely helpless in face of the idealism that is widespread in the social sciences but even to justify this idealism and contribute to reproducing it.

Let me briefly review some of the weaknesses of this new form of vulgar materialism.

The economy, as a system of social relations between men engendered in and from the process of producing their material conditions of existence, is reduced to technology and the relation between men and nature. Instead of determination, in the last analysis, by the economy, we have determination, in the last analysis, by the ecological environment, to which man *adapts himself* by inventing the appropriate techniques. Social structures are seen as so many means that are functionally necessary for this ecological adaptation.[44] Their hidden, latent rationality lies in providing adaptive, selective advantages which are disguised under forms that appear to be irrational, non-economic, etc. Thus, Marvin Harris, wishing, so to speak, to 'desacralise' the sacred cattle of India, writes:

I have written this paper because I believe the irrational, non-economic and exotic aspects of the Indian cattle complex are greatly overemphasized at the

---

[43] Cf. P. J. Ucko and C. W. Dimbleby, *The Domestication and Exploitation of Plants and Animals*, Aldine, 1969, and the collection of articles edited by Stuart Struever, *Prehistoric Agriculture*, The Natural History Press, New York, 1971.

[44] I refer the reader to the cuttingly-written, de-bunking paper by Jonathan Freedman, 'Marxism, structuralism and vulgar materialism', Congress of the American Anthropological Association, 1971.

expense of the rational, economic and mundane interpretations. . . . Insofar as the beef-eating taboo helps discourage growth of beef-producing industries it is part of an ecological adjustment which maximizes rather than minimizes on the calorie and protein output of the productive process.[45]

Here we recognize empirical materialism, the 'economism' that *reduces* all social structures to nothing but epiphenomena of the economy which is itself reduced, through technique, to a function of adaptation to the environment. With this view of the matter, the problems presented by the dominance and the plurality of functions of kinship relations or politico-religious relations remain inaccessible to materialist analysis; it is impossible to conceive the specific articulation of structures; and reciprocal causality is reduced to probabilist correlation and history to a series of events of greater or less frequency.

Dependent as we are on the unfolding of the natural continuum of events our generalisations must be couched in probabilistic terms derived from the observation of the frequencies with which predicted or retrodicted events occur.[46]

Actually, as Lévi-Strauss had already commented, invoking the secret rationality of adaptive advantages in order to explain distinct forms of social organization leads one very quickly into either truisms or absurdities.[47] As soon as a society exists, it functions, and it is tautological to say that a variable is adaptive because it fulfils a necessary function in the total system.

Proof that a certain trait or cultural arrangement has positive economic value is not an adequate explanation of its existence or even of its presence. The *problématique* of adaptive advantage does not specify a uniquely correct answer. As principle of causality in general and economic performance in particular, adaptive advantage is indeterminate: stipulating grossly what is impossible but rendering suitable anything that is possible.[48]

[45] M. Harris, 'The cultural ecology of India's sacred cattle', in *Current Anthropology*, Vol. 7, no. 1, Feb. 1966, pp. 51–66. See the same writer's critique of historical materialism in *The Rise of Anthropological Theory*, Crowell, New York, 1968, pp. 4–5.

[46] M. Harris, *The Rise of Anthropological Theory*, p. 614.

[47] Lévi-Strauss: 'To say that a society functions is a truism, but to say that everything in a society functions is an absurdity' (*Anthropologie structurale*, p. 17: English translation, *Structural Anthropology*, p. 13).

[48] M. Sahlins, 'Economic anthropology and anthropological economics', in *Social Sciences Information*, VIII (5), Oct. 1969, pp. 29–30. See his *Essays in Stone-Age Economics*, Aldine, 1972: I am grateful to Mr. Sahlins for having allowed me to read the manuscript of this book.

We see, then, that a materialism like this is unable to explain the reasons why, the fundamental necessity of what exists, i.e. the reasons why the history of societies that are not always completely 'integrated' totalities, but totalities whose unity is the provisionally stable effect of a structural compatibility that enables different structures to reproduce themselves until they reach the point at which the internal (and external) dynamic of these systems forbids this totality to go on existing as such.

The 'new materialism' seems analytically innocent of any concern for contradiction – although it sometimes figures itself a client of Marxism (minus the dialectical materialism). So it is unmindful of the barriers opposed to productive forces by established cultural organizations each congealed by its adaptive advantages in some state of fractional effectiveness.[49]

The limitations and failures to which functionalism is subject are thus still due to the same theoretical basis, to the axioms of a reductionist and abstract empiricism, whether this be idealistic or materialistic.[50] What, then, in relation to history and to the problem of the relation between economy and society, are the positions taken up by Lévi-Strauss, who, as we have seen, rejects from the outset empiricism in all its forms?

For Claude Lévi-Strauss, 'It is tedious, as well as useless, . . . to amass arguments to prove that all societies are in history and change: that this is so is patent.'[50] History is not merely a 'cold' history in which 'societies which create the minimum of that disorder which the physicists call 'entropy' . . . tend to remain indefinitely in their initial state'.[51] It is also made up of these 'non-recurrent chains of events whose effects accumulate to produce economic and social upheavals.'[52]

In order to explain these fundamental historical transformations, Lévi-Strauss accepts 'the undoubted primacy of infrastructures'.[53]

---

[49] This does not mean that analysis of functional relations between elements of a social structure or other social structures is not a scientific task. See, e.g., P. Collins, 'Functional analyses', in the symposium *Man, Culture and Animals*, ed. A. Leeds and A. P. Vayda, Washington, D.C., 1965.

[50] Lévi-Strauss, *La Pensée sauvage*, p. 310 (English translation, *The Savage Mind*, p. 234).

[51] Lévi-Strauss, *Entretiens avec Georges Charbonnier*, Plon, 1961, p. 38 (English translation, *Conversations with Claude Lévi-Strauss*, ed. G. Charbonnier, London, 1969, p. 33).

[52] Lévi-Strauss, *La Pensée sauvage*, p. 311 (English translation, p. 235).

[53] ibid., p. 173 (English translation, p. 130).

I do not at all mean to suggest that ideological transformations give rise to social ones. Only the reverse is in fact true. Men's conception of the relations between nature and culture is a function of modifications of their own social relations. . . . We are however merely studying the shadows on the wall of the cave. . . .[54]

Lévi-Strauss himself states: 'It is to this theory of superstructures, scarcely touched upon by Marx, that I hope to make a contribution.'[55]

One cannot but note that this theory of society, of the 'law of order' of the relation between economy and society, has *vanished* when Lévi-Strauss, in the conclusions to *Du Miel aux Cendres* sees in the fundamental historical upheaval at the end of which, 'at the frontiers of Greek thought, mythology gave way to a philosophy that emerges as the preliminary condition for scientific reflection, . . . an historical *occurrence* whose *whole significance* lies in having happened in that place at that time'.[56]

History, even though endowed with a 'law of order', is thus deprived of any necessity, and the births of Western philosophy and science are seen as mere accidental events. 'Neither here nor there was the transition necessary, and if *history* retains its position *in the front rank*, this position is the one that *rightfully* belongs to *irreducible contingency*.'[57] The Claude Lévi-Strauss who had put as epigraph to his *Elementary Structures of Kinship* Tylor's statement that 'the tendency of modern inquiry is more and more towards the conclusion that if law is anywhere, it is everywhere',[58] thus finds himself in the end in agreement with the empiricism that sees in history a succession of accidental events.

To go back to ethnology, it was one of us, E. R. Leach, who commented that 'the evolutionists have never discussed in detail – still less observed – what actually happened when a society in Stage A changed into a society at Stage B: it was merely argued that all Stage B societies must somehow have evolved out of Stage A societies'.[59]

We are back at the positions held by functionalist empiricism: 'History

---

[54] ibid., p. 155 (English translation, p. 117).
[55] ibid., p. 173 (English translation, p. 130).
[56] Lévi-Strauss, *Du Miel aux Cendres*, p. 407.
[57] ibid., p. 408.
[58] Tylor, *Primitive Culture*, London, 1871, p. 22.
[59] Cf. Lévi-Strauss, 'Les limites de la notion de structure en ethnologie', in *Sens et Usages du Terme 'Structure'*, ed. Roger Bastide, Mouton, 1962, p. 45; Leach, *Political Systems of Highland Burma*, p. 283.

is concerned with changes, ethnology with structures' – and this because changes, 'processes, are not analytical objects but the particular way in which a temporality is *experienced* by a *subject*',[60] an empiricist view that is profoundly contrary to the thesis of the 'law of order' of social changes which Lévi-Strauss took from Marx.

We thus see before us a theoretical method which, underneath the apparently harmonious character of the author's work, is based upon two opposed systems of theoretical principles – one of which affirms the necessity of historical transformations while the other affirms their irreducibly contingent nature. (Incidentally, Marx did not contrast necessity and contingency as two irreducible realities.) The question arises whether Lévi-Strauss's theoretical method leads necessarily from the first conclusion to the second. What he was aiming to do in *Elementary Structures of Kinship* was to explain the reasons for the prohibition of incest and the different marriage-systems which constitute modalities of this,[61] or, at least, systems with elementary structures, that is, systems which 'while defining all members of the society as relatives, divide them into two categories, viz., possible spouses and prohibited spouses.'[62]

From this standpoint, the systems prescribing marriages between cross cousins and proscribing marriages between parallel cousins became particularly good examples of these elementary structures of kinship, and study of them constituted a special and crucial part of the analysis.

The method used consisted first, negatively, of eliminating 'all historical speculation, all research into origins, and all attempts to reconstruct a hypothetical order in which institutions succeeded one another'.[63] Not that for Lévi-Strauss the different features of a kinship system could not have different origins and their own histories, but they never form entities that can be isolated and treated as independent of the rest, and they are never merely juxtaposed, but always combined in a specific way, forming 'a structural phenomenon'.[64] The method thus consisted, positively, of treating in every case the rules of marriage, the nomenclatures, the systems of privileges and of prohibitions as 'indissociable aspects of

---

[60] ibid., p. 44.
[61] Lévi-Strauss, *Structures élémentaires de la parenté*, Mouton, 1968, p. 68 (English translation, *Elementary Structures of Kinship*, London, ch. 5).
[62] ibid., p. ix (English translation, p. xxiii).
[63] ibid., p. 165 (English translation, p. 142).
[64] ibid., p. 145 (English translation, p. 124).

one and the same reality', and showing that this reality was the actual structure of the systems under examination.[65]

This was how Lévi-Strauss showed, in opposition to Frazer, that in the case of cross-cousin systems, parallel cousins are excluded from marriage 'for the same reason' that cross cousins are approved.[66] Prohibition and prescription are effects of one and the same principle, which, though it shows itself particularly clearly in the case of the marriage of cross cousins, is 'present' in all systems: the principle of reciprocity.[67]

But this principle means one thing only, namely, the fundamental nature of marriage as a 'form of exchange'.[68] The prohibition of incest then appears not as an arbitrary or mysterious rule of social life, but as one of the conditions necessary for marriage to take place as a socially regulated exchange of women between groups. The women that one group forbids itself to marry are available for marriage to other groups, and reciprocally. Seen in this way, the practices of endogamy and exogamy are clarified, together with the existence of dual organizations and different systems of kinship, since these are based on a form of exchange, whether this be restricted or generalized. Hence the very plan of Lévi-Strauss's work, which leads us from the simple forms of restricted exchange to the complex forms of generalized exchange, to come to a halt at the threshold of the 'complex structures' of kinship which 'limit themselves to defining the circle of relatives and leave the determination of the spouse to other mechanisms, economic or psychological'.[69]

A huge table of 'forms' of kinship systems is gradually built up, all being linked together in an immense system of transformations, a sort of Mendeleyev's table of kinship relations: from the kinship systems of the tribes of Australia and Melanesia to others found in South-East Asia, China, Tibet and India, and stopping, for the time being, at the door of the American, African and European systems.

Two results of this theoretical work seem to me to be fundamental. On the one hand, an *order* has been discovered in a vast number of kinship systems that appeared to have little in common, and that belong to societies which in most cases had no contact with each other, and this

[65] ibid., p. lx (English translation, p. xxiii).
[66] ibid., p. 151 (English translation, p. 129).
[67] ibid., p. 166 (English translation, p. 144).
[68] ibid., p. 80 (English translation, p. 69).
[69] ibid., p. ix (English translation, p. xxiii).

order of forms is an order of transformations. On the other, the analysis has brought out the presence of an invariant in all these varied forms: the fact that marriage is an exchange of women, that kinship relations are relations between groups before they are relations between individuals, and that these social relations employ different forms of the same principle, namely, reciprocity in exchange. Lévi-Strauss has thus brought to light a 'fundamental fact of social and mental reality', a fact that is at the same time a norm of all social life, and which, because it is *present in* every form of kinship relations, appears as a *meta-historical* 'fact-principle' which must be found on pain of falling into the traps of historicism and empiricism.

What we regard as the means of escaping from cultural history, he [Frazer] attempted to interpret as cultural history. The very thing we see as a necessary condition of society (*la condition de la société*), he sought to analyse into stages of social evolution.[70]

In my view, matrimonial exchange is *a* condition rather than *the* condition of society. It is, of course, always possible to read Lévi-Strauss in an idealist spirit, interpreting this *meta*-historical condition as a *supra*-historical condition with its source in a reality or in principles transcending history. This would mean denying what Lévi-Strauss has himself emphasized with the greatest clearness, that this meta-historical condition is nothing to do with either 'irrational events' or human 'intentions' or with 'the design of the legislation', but is merely 'the experimental discovery of the immanence of a relation'[71] between men that is unintentional and which makes of them a society.

Why, then, does Lévi-Strauss's structural analysis, although it does not deny history or tear itself away from history, yet never 'meet' history in its concrete diversity and reality? My analysis enables me to answer this question precisely.

Structural analysis does not meet history because, from the outset, it has separated analysis of the form of kinship relations from analysis of their functions. It is not that these functions are denied, but they are never explored as such. As a result, the problem of the *real articulation* of kinship relations and the other social structures that characterize concrete,

[70] ibid., p. 157 (English translation, p. 136).
[71] ibid., pp. 116–17 (English translation, p. 100).

historically determined societies – concrete realities within which Lévi-Strauss limits himself to distinguishing the 'formal system' of kinship relations to be studied in itself and compared with other 'forms' of kinship, similar or contrasting – is never analysed either. Of course Lévi-Strauss is not unaware of these problems,[72] but he has not tackled them. And yet these are fundamental problems, the solution of which will enable us not merely to understand the form but also the content of social relations, the conditions for their appearance and for their disappearance and so, the history of mankind through their history. Thus, in connexion with 'the correlation established by Murdock between patrilinear institutions and the highest levels of culture',[73] Lévi-Strauss says: 'It is true that in societies where political power *takes precedence* over other forms of organization the duality which would result from the masculinity of political authority and the matrilineal character of descent could not subsist. Consequently, societies attaining this level of political organization tend to generalize the paternal right.'[74]

A structural morphology without analysis of functions, without 'physiology', is incomplete, and only joint development of these two fields of investigation can enable us to pose correctly the problems of the transformation and evolution of systems, the problems of history.

A functional system, e.g., a kinship system, can never be interpreted in an integral fashion by diffusionist hypotheses. The system is bound up with the *total structure* of the society employing it, and consequently its nature *depends* more on the *intrinsic characteristics* of such a society than on cultural contacts and migrations.[75]

It is therefore necessary to take up the task where it has been abandoned, and go beyond structural analysis of the forms of kinship or the

[72] ibid., p. 162 (English translation, p. 139): 'Actually there is nothing in the exchange of women faintly resembling a reasoned solution to an economic problem (although it can acquire this function in societies which have already learnt in some other way what purchase and sale are).' I do not think that kinship relations acquire economic functions only when an economy of buying and selling (a market economy) has been established.

[73] G. P. Murdock, 'Correlation of matrilineal and patrilineal institutions', in *Studies in the Science of Society presented to A. G. Keller*, New Haven, 1937. See on this subject the conclusions of H. Driver and K. Schuessler, 'Correlational analysis of Murdock's 1957 ethnographic sample', in *American Anthropologist*, vol. 69, 1967, pp. 332–52.

[74] Lévi-Strauss, *Structures élémentaires*, p. 36. My emphasis, M.G. (English translation, pp. 116–17).

[75] ibid., p. 144. My emphasis, M.G. (English translation, p. 390).

compilation of a formal grammar of the myths of the American Indians.

In my article 'Mythes et histoire, réflexions sur les fondements de la pensée sauvage',[76] I showed that Lévi-Strauss, *in the same way* as he had brought out, through his study of kinship forms, a relation that is immanent in society, an unvarying feature of kinship, namely, the fact that marriage is an 'exchange', has also brought out through his study of the myths of the American Indians a meta-historical invariant, namely, thought *in the savage state*, i.e. the formal structure of thought as 'a direct expression of the structure of the mind (and behind the mind, probably, of the brain)' (in Lévi-Strauss, *Le Totémisme aujourd'hui*, p. 130: English translation, *Totemism*, London, 1969, p. 163).

At the same time Lévi-Strauss has brought out in great detail all the elements of ecological, economic and social reality which are *transposed* in myths and make these myths no longer thought in the savage state but the thought of savages, i.e. the thought of men living in historically-determined social relations.

Once again, what is lacking is analysis of the precise functions of these forms of thought, of the articulation of these forms of ideology with the other levels of social reality, and of the conditions of their transformation. What is lacking above all is a theory of the foundations and forms of the fetishization of social relations, of the necessity of this fetishization.

Every history of religion, even, that fails to take account of this material basis is uncritical. It is, in reality, much easier to discover by analysis the earthly core of the misty creations of religion than, conversely, it is to develop from the actual relations of life the corresponding celestialized forms of those relations. The latter method is the only materialistic, and therefore the only scientific one.[77]

To go further than a structural morphology means, therefore, trying to account for the forms, functions, mode of articulation and conditions of transformation of the social structures within the concrete societies studied by the historian and the anthropologist. It is precisely in order to accomplish this complex task, which presupposes a combination of several theoretical methods, that Marx's hypothesis of the determination, in the last analysis, of the forms and the evolution of societies by the conditions of production and reproduction of their material life is needed as the central hypothesis. And I have shown that, despite appearances

[76] English translation in *New Left Review*, 69, September-October 1971.
[77] See note 28.

and assertions to the contrary, it is to this central hypothesis that we are inevitably brought by a rigorous functionalism and structuralism when these try to penetrate more deeply into the logic of the facts and societies they analyse.[78]

From this standpoint it will no longer be possible to go on counterposing anthropology to history or to sociology as three fetishized separate domains, nor to present economic anthropology or economic history as mere specialized lines of research belatedly added to other specialized domains that are more advanced. What is involved in the study of societies on the basis of their mode of production and reproduction is the complete and radical re-working of all the theoretical methods that have been developed in the process of man's cognition in his social life and his historical evolution. What is involved is the crisis, latent or overt, which prevails today in the humane sciences, the problem of their unity and their progress.

The question of the 'rationality' of economic and social systems is thus at the same time the critical question of the 'rationality' of the various theories that have been put forward by the humane sciences, together with the forms of action and the objectives of the social groups representing the different economic and social systems that confront each other on the scene of history. There is thus no way of 'disengaging' science from history, thought from action, and a theoretical revolution in the humane sciences will necessarily furnish a theory that will be more effective for revolutionary practice.

[78] Cf. Marx in the famous 'sixth chapter' of *Capital*, long unpublished, which has recently appeared in French in the 'Collection 10/18', Plon, Paris, 1971, as *Un chapitre inédit du 'Capital'* (the original, with a Russian translation, was published in 1933 in *Arkhiv Marksa i Engelsa*, vol. II (VII), under the title: *Erstes Buch. Der Produktionsprozess des Kapitals. Sechstes Kapitel. Resultate des unmittelbaren Produktionsprozess*): 'My conception differs fundamentally from that of the bourgeois economists who, prisoners of capitalist conceptions, see indeed how production takes place *within* capitalist relations, but now not how these *relations* are themselves produced, at the same time creating the material conditions for their own dissolution—abolishing with the same stroke their *historical justification*, as a *necessary form* of economic development and production of social wealth' (translation from the original, p. 176).

I
The Theme

*All science would be superfluous if the outward appearance
and the essence of things directly coincided.*

Karl Marx, *Capital*, III, FLPH edn, p. 797

When, in 1958, I set about examining ideas concerning 'rationality and irrationality in economics', this was the effort of a philosopher who was trying, at one and the same time, to move beyond the limits of philosophy and, in doing this, to extirpate in himself every speculative form of philosophical thinking.

Those were the days when people were proclaiming, in the name of Marx, of Nietzsche, or of Science, the death of all kinds of philosophy and when many were preaching at the crossroads that the useless carcass which had sustained them ought to be abandoned there and then, so that they might be free to move off along the solid road of 'useful' experiments, which might be scientific, political or aesthetic in character. For me, too, going beyond philosophy meant going into a particular field of experience, that of economic reality, and finding a foothold there by learning to locate the problems that arise in it and to think them out with the aid of the categories, assumptions and doctrines that are offered by economic theory. For others, though, going beyond philosophy meant giving it up altogether and never going back to it, because there was nothing more to be done with it. In my view, there *was* still something to be done in philosophy, something that required precisely this, that one should enter a different field in order to get to know it from the inside, in the hope of being able, one day, both to change to some extent the state of economic knowledge and to produce new philosophical knowledge. In this twofold task that I assumed, was there not, though, some danger of confusing philosophy with science, and returning to the speculative forms of that former philosophical consciousness with which all of us wished to settle accounts?

Settling accounts meant, above all, eradicating the ancient claim of the philosopher, whether materialist or idealist, to have special access to the world of those first and last truths without which, in his view, practice is blind and the sciences remain suspended over an inner void, lacking foundation. From Plato to the young Marx, from Hegel to Sartre, the philosopher claimed to bring back from his 'great detour' that missing basis, that 'almost nothing' which completes everything, because it can enable the whole of practice and of knowledge to be grasped anew in the light of the fundamental truths of philosophy. In claiming to fill the gaps in scientific knowledge with truths deduced from some fundamental knowledge, it was hard to avoid that speculative fusion, and confusion, of philosophy and science in which philosophies take shape as world-systems built around a truth that is itself established by an ideological act of dictation as the most primary of all truths, as a dogma.

It was thenceforth necessary to sacrifice the claim made by the traditional philosopher, to break the ancient speculative alienation; this sacrifice meant, for some, the abolition of philosophy, but for others its renewal. This sacrifice implied rejection of the religious philosophies, of Hegel's absolute idealism, of Husserl's transcendental idealism, of Heidegger's fundamental ontology, and of Marxism. At this point everything that was starting to become clearer grew dark and chaotic again. This was largely due to the paradoxical situation of the Marxism of that time, torn between its founders and its continuators. Around this Marxism contradictions and conflicts were pushed to extreme lengths.

It seemed that everyone, whether he was announcing the death of philosophy or only that of speculative forms of philosophy, found what he needed to find by way of support for his view in the Marx of the *juvenilia* or of the *1844 Manuscripts*, or even in the Marx of the *Theses on Feuerbach*.

Confronting these 'Marxes' were the Marxist philosophers of the twentieth century. These philosophers were to be seen claiming the right, on the basis of the general principles of historical and dialectical materialism, to settle out of hand questions of biology and physics, to reject psychoanalysis, and to denounce mathematical formalism. With the theory of the successive stages of mankind's evolution, history assumed the appearance of being subject to the external authority of a few laws by means of which the Marxist philosopher would decipher the secrets of historical necessity. True, the facts showed themselves stubborn, and the societies of Africa, Asia or pre-Columbian America fitted badly, or even refused to fit at all, into these conclusions arrived at in advance, and the rebellion of these facts gave rise to disputes about the 'periodization' of history into the stages of primitive communism, slave-owning society, feudalism, etc. Thus, at the end of the Stalin era and of the first experience of socialism, Marxism had become a closed set of dogmas and recipes. It had suffered the fate of all the speculative philosophies known to history, and was thus open to the radical criticism of Marx himself.

Ultimately, all these contradictions took us back to Marx and to the question: who was the Marx of *Capital*? Had he, like Rimbaud, accomplished in his twenties a philosophical work of exceptional importance, to which thereafter he referred only jokingly, satisfied to become, not, in his case, a trader in Abyssinia, but the leading economist of his age? Was he only a scientist or was he also a philosopher? If his philosophy was to be found buried in *Capital*, had it anything in common with the great texts of his youth?

This crucial question determined my starting point – an attempt to study the method of *Capital* (my articles of 1960–61). It was against this theoretical background, dominated by the need to clarify the nature of the relation between philosophy and science, that I undertook to analyse the rationality of the economic theories of Marx and of the classical economists. At the same time, through and behind this epistemological analysis, what was at issue was the rationality of capitalism and of socialism, that is to say, ultimately, the question of the comparative rationality of economic systems, and this was to lead me later on to seek for evidence in the field of economic anthropology.

In the meantime, in 1963, when the opportunity was presented by the publication of Volume III of Auguste Cornu's great work on Marx and Engels, I went back to the problem of the relationship between philosophy and economics in the *1844 Manuscripts*, the work that resulted from Marx's first major encounter with classical political economy, and therefore a work of particular interest for my investigation. Now, in my article 'Political Economy and Philosophy', I came to the conclusion that, in this first encounter with economics, Marx's approach had not permitted him to go beyond the old way of thinking of speculative philosophy, or to alter the state of the economic science of his time, or to produce any new scientific knowledge – because at that time he still repudiated Ricardo's theory of value, in which he was later to perceive the fundamental contribution to science made by bourgeois political economy.

This double failure seemed to me to have a single root in the idea which Marx then held as to the philosopher's role. He had just worked out a philosophy that made labour the 'true' essence of man and of history, the self-creation of man through praxis. From this basic assumption Marx drew two critical conclusions. Revolution was necessary in order to put an end to the alienation of the producers, destroy the régime of private property, and restore to man his lost essence, his humanity. The communist revolution would be the instrument of 'positive humanism'.

For Marx it was necessary to criticize political economy because, while stressing the essential part played by labour in the formation of value, this science had presented labour, in the alienated form characteristic of capitalism, as the 'natural' and 'rational' form of labour. It was thus lacking in critical awareness of its own approach and ignorant of its own foundations.

Thus, in the *1844 Manuscripts*, Marx, as possessor of the 'true' image of man's essence, sees himself as holding the keys to the present and to the future, to practice and to theory. This ideal image functions as a 'normative model' enabling him both to criticize bourgeois society and economic science and to deduce the content of the rational society of the future. Possession of this normative image is the basis and justification of the right assumed by philosophy to wield jurisdiction over practice and its theoretical expressions, including political economy. This jurisdiction will cease when, the essence of man having become existence and the rational become real, philosophy dies in that moment of triumph when it becomes the 'world' of practice. Accordingly, the philosopher thinks he has given a complete answer to the question of the rationality and irrationality of political economy and of the capitalist system, when he claims:

(1) to have established the 'true essence of man' and found out what is 'rational',

(2) to show that the contradictions of society arise from the contradiction between Man's essence and the historical reality of the capitalist system, which is based upon the alienation of human labour, and so upon the de-humanization of the producers,

(3) to bring into economic science the theoretical rationality it lacks, critical awareness of its own approach and an adequate knowledge of its own foundation, and

(4) to show grounds for the practical necessity of the communist revolution, which will abolish private property and reconcile man with himself by realizing what is rational and rationalizing what is real.

I have dwelt at some length on analysis of the relationship between philosophy and economic science in the *1844 Manuscripts* because this shows that if the question of the rationality or irrationality of economic science and of economic realities is tackled from the angle of an *a priori* idea, a speculative definition of what is rational, then the entire answer found can only be ideological, that is, a theory (whatever the intentions of its author and whatever the refinements he may contribute to it) which will still be based upon misunderstanding of the reality and its problems. But perhaps the question itself fails to correspond to any real problem at all, and is not a scientific problem but a question of ideology? I sense from the outset that the question, if it is to be scientific, must refer to a necessity governing the appearance and disappearance of social and economic systems in history which does not depend for its meaning upon any final cause that precedes and transcends it, any teleology of a true essence of man accessible to philosophy alone. Such a necessity must be wholly internal to the concrete structures of social life and must be explicable by those who study these structures scientifically.

Already knowing fairly well, then, how *not* to present the problem of economic rationality, I set out in 1961–62 to come to grips with this theme by way of the writings, specialized or otherwise, that had been devoted to it. I will briefly describe the places where I came upon the problem of rationality and the forms, both ideological and scientific, in which it appeared to me.

THE RATIONALITY OF ECONOMIC SYSTEMS: A QUESTION OF IDEOLOGY OR A SCIENTIFIC PROBLEM?

Consequently, those who have asserted that all is well have talked nonsense : they ought to have said that all is for the best – (Pangloss, in Voltaire's *Candide*).

I have sought the theme of economic rationality first and foremost in those places where it appears most plainly in the writings of contemporaries: Allais, Alschner, Arrow, Barber, Baudin, Becker, Bross, Divisia, Fey, Hutchison, Kantorovitch, Katona, Lange, Marschak, Nove, Pagani, Parsons, Robbins, Rothschild, Savage, Schuetz, Simon, Taylor, Von Mises, Von Neumann, Weber.[1]

[1] M. Allais, 'Le comportement de l'homme rationnel devant le risque. Critique des postulats et axiomes de l'école américaine' in *Econometrica*, vol. 21, Oct. 1953, pp. 503–46; 'La psychologie de l'homme rationnel devant le risque: la théorie et l'expérience', in *Journal de la Société de Statistique de Paris*, 1953.

G. Alschner, 'Rationalität und Irrationalität in der Wirtschaftlichen Handlungen und ihre Erfassung durch die Wirtschaftstheorie', in *Schmollers Jahrbuch für Gesetzgebung*, 1957.

When we consider the expression 'economic rationality', other expressions at once spring to mind in connexion with it, as belonging to the same field of meaning: effectiveness, efficiency, profitability, return,

K. Arrow, 'Le principe de rationalité dans les décisions collectives', in *Economie appliquée*, 1952, no. 4.

W. Barber, 'Economic rationality and behaviour patterns in an underdeveloped area', in *Economic Development and Cultural Change*, April, 1960.

L. Baudin, 'Irrationality in economics', in *Quarterly Journal of Economics*, vol. 68, Nov. 1954.

G. Becker, 'Irrational behaviour and economic theory', in *Journal of Political Economy*, vol. 70, Feb. 1962.

I. Bross, *Prévision et décisions rationnelles*, Dunod, 1961.

F. Divisia, *Economie rationelle*, Paris, 1928.

A. Fey, *Der Homo Oeconomicus in der Klassichen Nationalökonomie*, Limburg, 1936.

T. Hutchison, *The Significance and Basic Postulates of Economic Theory*, Kelly, 1960.

L. Kantorovitch, *Calcul économique et utilisation des ressources*, Dunod, 1963.

G. Katona, 'Rational behaviour and economic behaviour', in *Psychological Review*, 1953, no. 5.

O. Lange, *Economic politique*, vol. I, P.U.F., 1962 (English version, *Political Economy*, vol. I, Pergamon, 1963).

J. G. March and H. A. Simon, *Les Organisations*, Dunod, 1964 (trans. of *Organisations*, New York, 1958).

J. Marschak, 'Rational behaviour, uncertain prospects and measurable utility', in *Econometrica*, vol. 18, 1950.

A. Nove, 'Economic rationality and Soviet growth', in *I.S.E.A.*, 1960, no. 104.

A. Pagani, 'La razionalità del comportamento economico', in *Antologia di Scienze Sociali*, Bologna, 1963.

T. Parsons and N. J. Smelser, *Economy and Society*, London, 1957.

L. Robbins, *Essai sur la nature et la signification de la science économique*, Paris, 1947 (trans. of *An Essay on the Nature and Significance of Economic Science*, London, 1932).

K. Rothschild, 'The meaning of rationality: a note on Professor Lange's article', in *Review of Economic Studies*, no. 14, 1946–7.

L. Savage, 'An axiomatisation of reasonable behaviour in the face of uncertainty', in *Colloque C.N.R.S.*, 1953.

A. Schuetz, 'The problem of rationality in the social world', in *Economica*, 10, 1943.

H. Simon, 'A behavioural model of rational choice', in *Quarterly Journal of Economics*, 1955, 69: 'Rational choice and the structure of the environment', in *Psychological Review*, 1956–63; 'Rationality and administrative decision-making', in *Models of Man, Social and Rational*, Wiley, 1957.

F. Taylor, *Scientific Management*, New York, 1947.

L. Von Mises, *Human Action*, 1949.

J. Von Neumann and O. Morgenstern, *Theory of Games and Economic Behaviour*, 1947.

Max Weber, *Wirtschaft und Gesellschaft*, 1922, vol. I.

productivity, minimization of cost, maximum profit, maximum satisfaction, optimum decision, choice, calculation, forecasting, management
and organization (of labour, of an enterprise, of a branch of industry, of
the national economy), development, balanced growth, progress, distribution, justice, etc. It is easy to see the link between these themes of
effectiveness, return, profit, satisfaction, welfare and so on, but a break
appears in this chain as soon as we ask: 'effectiveness for *whose* profit is
being aimed at in a given instance ?' When the themes of the legitimacy of
profit and of how to define individual satisfaction and collective benefit
are considered, it would seem that any sort of scientific rigour must go
by the board, to be replaced by an open clash between ideologies concerning welfare, justice and so on. On the other hand, *once* an objective
has been chosen, the problems of effectiveness, return and minimum cost
arise, and these seem to require theoretical working-out that is carried
to the point of numerical calculation. Is the question of economic rationality a question, then, to which there are two answers – one, the fundamental answer that relates to the choice of objectives and the determining
of ends, being dependent upon ideology, whereas the other, belonging
more or less to the sphere of science, is confined to determining the
means of realizing these ends ?

If these are the problems that are involved, explicitly or implicitly, in
the theme of 'economic rationality', they call in question the status of
political economy as a science, they affect the scientific validity of the
theses which, from Adam Smith to Kantorovitch and from Marx to
Pareto, have been counterposed to each other in order to explain the
nature of profit, the functioning of capitalist economy, the potentialities
of this economy as compared with the economies of the *ancien régime*
or of socialism, and so on. The question of economic rationality is thus at
the same time an epistemological question, concerning political economy
as a science.

In its content, however, the theme of rationality goes well beyond the
limits of political economy, and crops up in very different fields of
thought and in many and varying epochs. We find it in the disputes
among scholastic theologians about the just price (*justum pretium*)[2] in the

---

[2] St Thomas Aquinas, *Summa*, II–2, Quaest. LXXVII, 'De fraudulentia'. On the
development of this theme down to the 16th century by the theologians Mercado,
De Soto, etc, see Schumpeter, *History of Economic Analysis*, New York, 1954, pp. 82–
107.

capitularies and polyptychs of the Middle Ages,[3] in which the description of lords' demesnes from the business standpoint is accompanied by models of 'good management' for the instruction of their administrators, in the thirteenth-century English treatises on farming,[4] and, in remoter times, in the writings of Varro, Posidonius and Columella,[5] or in Xenophon's *Oeconomicus*. For its part, ethnology, long before Morgan, found it hard not to accuse of irrationality whatever feature it observed in different societies that was not 'civilized' but had got stuck at the stages, now left behind, of barbarism or even savagery. And philosophy, from Montesquieu's *Lettres Persanes* to Rousseau's *Discours sur l'Origine de l'Inégalité*, is full of reflections on these contrasts, some valid and some not, with other societies. Today, in order to advance technical progress, in which the promise of social progress is seen to lie, political economy turns to ethnology, history and sociology, in the hope of deciphering, in the structures of non-Western 'traditional' societies, the secret of that absence of the spirit of enterprise which is regarded as the basis of their poverty, dependence and 'under-development'.[6] These many dimensions that have been added to the theme of economic rationality seem to have deprived it of any clear-cut outline, and removed it from the grasp of theory. If we are to get anywhere with this theme we must go back to the texts in which it is expounded explicitly, so as to see if there is any connexion between the problems that underlie it such as may, bit by bit, account for the way these problems crop up in many different fields, and explain the transition from one problem to another.

Rationality of agents and rationality of systems

In current writing the theme of economic rationality is presented in the form of two questions:

[3] *Polyptique de l'Abbé Irminon*, ed. Guérard, vol. 2, pp. 313–14; *Capitulare de villis et curtis*, ed. Boretius, pp. 83–9; and the *Brevium exempla ad describendas res ecclesiasticas et fiscales*, ed. Boretius, pp. 254–5. See G. Duby, *L'Economie rurale et la vie des campagnes dans l'Occident médiéval*, Paris, Aubier, 1962, vol. I, documents.

[4] *Walter of Henley's Husbandry*, ed. Lomont, and other treatises, see G. Duby, op. cit., vol. I, pp. 311–15.

[5] *Les Agronomes latins*, trans. Nizard, ed. Didot, 1877.

[6] See H. Leibenstein, *Economic Backwardness and Economic Growth*, Wiley, 1957, chapter 9: 'Growth incentives, agents and activities and the minimum effort thesis', pp. 112–46.

(1) How, in a given economic system, must economic agents behave in order to secure the objectives they set themselves?

(2) What is the rationality of the economic system itself, and can it be compared with that of other systems?

The first question aims at making explicit a rationality of intention that is adhered to by individuals, the second at throwing light on an unintended rationality – the capacity, for example, possessed by a number of systems to ensure growth of the means of production, improvement in the standard of living, and so on. Two quotations will show how one of these questions leads to the other.

We cannot approach the peasantry of the Ivory Coast, at the present stage, with the techniques, structures, statutes and administrative methods that have been worked out for the peasantry of France, who are at a *different stage* of economic and intellectual *development*, closer to *rational behaviour*.[7]

It has become clear that we have not always appreciated in their entirety the complexity and duration of the processes of transition from individual small-scale cultivation to the *large-scale agricultural enterprise* which is *required* if modern technique is to be given *rational* application.[8]

On the one hand, forms of behaviour are being contrasted (that of the Ivory Coast peasant with that of the French peasant), and, through these, 'stages of development' (that is, economic and social structures), while on the other, contrast is made between structures (small-scale ownership, large-scale cultivation) and, through these, between forms of behaviour in relation to modern technique. I shall show how, eventually, any analysis of rational economic behaviour must lead to the contrasting of different economic systems and of the various doctrines that claim to explain the mechanisms and potentialities of these systems. The major contrast in our own day is that between the capitalist and socialist systems, and, on the theoretical plane, between neo-classical and marginalist political economy, on the one hand, and Marxist political economy, on the other.

What is meant by rational behaviour?

Maurice Allais provides us with a clear definition, generally accepted by economists:

---

[7] René Dumont: *Afrique Noire: développement agricole* (*Etudes Tiers Monde*, Paris, P.U.F., 1962), p. 134. My emphasis, M.G.

[8] J. Triomphe and P. Noirot, 'De la supériorité de l'agriculture socialiste', *Démocratie nouvelle*, no. 10, October 1961, p. 43.

We have to have recourse to the definition which seems to emerge from scientific logic, by which a man is considered rational when:
(a) he pursues ends that are mutually coherent, and
(b) he employs means that are appropriate to the ends pursued.[9]

Analysis of rational behaviour is thus seen as a theoretical investigation aimed at discovering the conditions under which it is possible to attain a certain objective, taking into account a certain set of constraints. Since any activity in pursuit of an end potentially possesses a logic that will ensure its effectiveness in face of a series of constraints, the theory of rational behaviour necessarily takes the form, if the content of the activity being analysed remains indeterminate, of a formal theory of all purposive action, a logic of action, or, to use the expression used by Slutsky,[10] Kotarbinski[11] and Von Mises,[12] 'praxiology'.[13]

Can this theory of the general forms of purposive action constitute a science and avoid being merely a jejune and pointlessly complicated reflexion upon such general concepts as 'the end', 'the means', 'the act', 'the level', 'effectiveness', 'correction', etc.? In order to escape from this empty formalism, the theory must take account of the concrete forms of purposive action, whether it be economic, political, religious, military, etc. This raises the problem of the relation between this formal theory and the various theories, including economics, that deal with these special kinds of activity. Here, however, we come upon a paradox, since the very subject-matter of economics as defined by the majority of present-day economists is nothing else than the subject-matter of the formal theory of

---

[9] M. Allais, *Fondements d'une théorie positive des choix comportant un risque*, 1955, p. 31.

See also J. Bénard, 'Problèmes et instruments de synthèse d'un plan indicatif', *I.S.E.A.*, 1958, p. 9: 'The quest for an economic optimum consists in *choosing the best means* of arriving at *ends that are regarded as the best*. If we speak of an optimum this means, therefore, that we agree that choices are possible, that is, that several procedures exist for arriving at the same end, and that these can be arranged in order of preference. There must, in other words, be in existence, at one and the same time, *alternatives* that can be substituted one for another, and *criteria* of choice. Determination of the optimum will result from combining these two series of elements.'

[10] E. Slutsky, *Ein Beitrag zur formal-praxeologischen Grundlegung der Ökonomik*, Kiev, 1926, quoted by Lange, op. cit., p. 216.

[11] Kotarbinski: *Traktat o dobrej robocie* ('Treatise on good work'), 1955: cf. Lange, p. 215.

[12] L. Von Mises, op. cit., p. 3.

[13] M. Weber, 'Die Grenznutzenlehre und das psychologische Grundgesetz', in *Gesammelte Aufsätze zur Wissenschaftslehre*, p. 372.

purposive action. Economics, according to Robbins's famous formulation,[14] taken over by Von Mises, Samuelson, Burling, etc, is 'the science which studies human behaviour as a relationship between ends and scarce means which have alternative uses'.

A formal and a material definition of the economy

What is the meaning of this coincidence between the two definitions? Economics ceases to be a special sphere of social life and now appears as an aspect of every human activity in so far as this activity seeks to 'economize' its means. Every kind of purposive activity thus has the right to be regarded as 'economic', or is at least so in essence, so that no kind of activity is left as actually economic, and economics becomes dissolved in a general theory of action in which nothing distinguishes it from theories of politics, religion and so on. Let us leave it to Burling to show the absurdity of his own thesis:

> If all behaviour involving allocation is economic then the relationship of a mother to her baby is just as much an economic one, or rather has just as much of an economic aspect, as the relationship of an employer to his hired labourer. ... There are no specifically economic techniques or economic goals.[15]

This position logically leads him to see in the Freudian theory of the personality dominated by the pleasure-principle, Lasswell's theory of power, and Zipf's essay[16] on 'least effort', so many statements that are equivalent to the 'economic' principle of the optimum use of scarce means.

Let us proceed further. Proof of the basic impotence of the formal theory of purposive action to define what is economic, as such, is to be found in the very fruitfulness of that Operational Research which has in recent years done so much to perfect the practical instruments of business management. The formal theory sees this as evidence of its own clearly-established correctness and usefulness; but operational research is not a branch of political economy, it is a set of mathematical procedures that

---

[14] Robbins, op. cit., p. 6 (English original, p. 15).

[15] R. Burling, 'Maximization theories and the study of economic anthropology', in *American Anthropologist*, vol. 64, August 1962, p. 811.

[16] G. Zipf, *Human Behaviour and the Principle of Least Effort*, Cambridge, Mass., 1949.

enable one to maximize or minimize the value of an objective function. Whether this objective be the maximum destruction of the military-strategic apparatus of an enemy, the 'rational' management of the stock of a department store, or a game of chess, the mathematical procedures remain 'indifferent' to the objects that they are manipulating, and the logic of the calculation remains the same in every case. Thus, operational research does not define what is economic, any more than it defines the art of war or the theory of information. On the contrary, in order to be applied, it has to assume that these 'objects' already exist and have been defined, and that manipulating them will present the type of problems that it is able to solve. Now, the principle of operational research practice, that of achieving the best combination of limited means that can realize a quantifiable purpose, is precisely the formal principle used by Robbins, Samuelson and Burling to define specifically the subject-matter of economics. While operational research itself cannot define the objects which it manipulates, the principle underlying it is no better able to do this, as has been admitted by one of the best-known econometricians, Pierre Massé, who declared in 1958:

Koopmans has defined the activity of production as the 'best utilization of limited means in order to achieve desired ends'. However *different* our *respective ends* may be, it seems to me that this *definition* could apply *just as well* to the art of war.[17]

We are thus confronted with a formal definition of 'the economic' which is good for nothing, and a principle of rationality which, in order to elucidate something in the economy, has to assume that the latter has already been correctly defined. This means that nothing can be *deduced* from the general principle of rational action, and that three conditions are needed for the investigation of economic rationality to result in scientific cognition:

(1) That what is in general 'economic' be defined in real and not formal terms, in terms of structure, not behaviour;

(2) That the specific structure of a particular economic system be known or assumed, so that the rationality of the behaviour of an economic agent within this system may be analysable; and

(3) Finally, and a condition that I shall for the time being put on one

[17] P. Massé, in *Operational Research in Practice: Report of a NATO Conference*, edited by Max Davies and Michel Verhulst, Pergamon, 1958, p. 114.

side, that a certain structure of the needs of the members of a society, that is, a definite hierarchy of ends (objectives), be given and known.

In order to be able to obtain positive knowledge the advocates of the formal definition of what is economic, as we shall see, surreptitiously re-introduce these three conditions, and are thus able to imagine that they have deduced this knowledge from a formal general principle. Let us dwell a little longer on the consequences of these attempts to bind the laws of political economy and the properties of historical economic systems to the formal properties of purposive action.

What is described as 'rational economic behaviour', from this stand-point? It is behaviour which applies the general principle of rationality under conditions in which the end and the means of the action are quantified. Let Oskar Lange define it:

> This principle [the principle of economic rationality] asserts that the maximum degree of realization of the end is achieved by proceeding in such a way that either for a given outlay of means the maximum degree of realization of the end is achieved, or that for a given degree of realization of the end the outlay of the means is minimal. The first variant of this procedure is called the *principle of greatest effect* or the *principle of greatest efficiency*. The second variant is called *the principle of the minimum outlay of means* or *the principle of economy of means* . . . These are thus two equivalent variants of the principle of economic rationality.[18]

A question therefore arises: whence do we get the general principle of rational action?

Two ideological answers to the problem : Adam Smith and Oskar Lange

Answers of two sorts have been given to this question, both of them leading to the same dead end. The rationality principle is presented as being a constant feature of human nature, an everyday and commonplace fact of experience derived from some non-historical or trans-historical '*a priori*'. How does one proceed from recognizing this universal feature of human nature to analysing a particular economic system and the behaviour of individuals within this system? The classical economists offer

[18] O. Lange, op. cit., pp. 191–2 (English version, pp. 167–8). Lange quotes Quesnay: 'When the greatest possible increase in pleasure for the greatest possible economy in expenses has been achieved, then economic behaviour has reached perfection' (*Sur les Travaux des Artisans*) (Eng. trans. of Lange's book, p. 172, n. 26).

us, with their doctrine of liberalism, a typical example of a pseudo-deduction carried out on the basis of this generality. From Quesnay and Smith onward, economic theory has preached *laissez-faire* and denounced any intervention by the state in economic life. If only the state will refrain from interfering, the artificial obstacles raised by history and ignorance against the freedom of the individual will vanish, and human nature – 'unshackled',[19] so to speak – will lead individuals, moved solely by the mere incentive of their private self-interest, to create a system of perfect competition that will benefit the whole community. Guided by this 'invisible hand', the capitalist system appears as the 'natural order' of society, the rise of which was delayed until the progress of the Enlightenment[20] had at last dispersed the darkness accumulated by the ignorance that prevailed during mankind's early ages and under the *ancien régime*. Capitalist market economy is thus deduced by way of an ideal pseudo-origin of capitalism, in which this economic system appears as the best of all possible worlds, and worthy of our full confidence as a means of ensuring human progress. As Adam Smith says:

All systems either of preference or of restraint, therefore, being thus completely taken away, the obvious and simple system of natural liberty establishes itself of its own accord. Every man, as long as he does not violate the laws of justice, is left perfectly free to pursue his own interest his own way, and to bring both his industry and capital into competition with those of any other man, or order of men. The sovereign is completely discharged from a duty, in the attempting to perform which he must always be exposed to innumerable delusions, and for the proper performance of which no human wisdom or knowledge could ever be sufficient; the duty of superintending the industry of private people, and of directing it towards the employments most suitable to the interest of the society.

With the coming of capitalism, mankind, restored to its true nature, emerges at last from savagery and barbarism and enters the age of civilization:

Among civilized and thriving nations, on the contrary [in contrast to 'savage nations'], though a great number of people do not labour at all, many of whom consume the produce of ten times, frequently of a hundred times, more labour than the greater part of those who work; yet the produce of the whole labour

[19] J. Marchal, *Le Mécanisme des prix*, 1951, pp. 426, 427, 432.

[20] Kant, 'Réponse à la question: Qu'est-ce que les Lumières?', in *La Philosophie de l'histoire*, Aubier, 1947, pp. 83–92.

of the society is so great that all are often abundantly supplied, and a workman, even of the lowest and poorest order, if he is frugal and industrious, may enjoy a greater share of the necessaries and conveniences of life than it is possible for any savage to procure.[21]

Deducing the economic system of free competition from the general principle of rationality, assumed to be an inherent characteristic of human nature, is thus an ideological approach to the problem which results in an apologia for this system. Other writers, however, try to present the rationality principle not as an eternal fact but as a product of history. The best-known attempt in this direction is that made by Oskar Lange, who develops certain theses first advanced by Max Weber.

For Lange, the principle of economic rationality is an historical product of capitalism:

The most important case of the application of the principle of economic rationality is that of the capitalist enterprise. This principle shows itself here in full for the first time in the history of the development of human economic activity. It could not show itself earlier, i.e. in natural economy. For in natural economy there is a multiplicity of aims of economic activity, quantified in various degrees and not commensurable with each other, nor are the means commensurable either. In these conditions activity follows the customary and traditional paths, traditionally established aims are realized with the aid of traditional means.[22]

Here we see outlined a curious conception of the history of humanity. Like Rostow,[23] Lange thrusts indiscriminately into the concept of 'traditional economy' all the social and economic formations, starting with primitive societies, which preceded the rise of capitalism. This concept is, moreover, defined by the *absence* of something, namely, of commodity and monetary forms of exchange, and their absence is seen as both effect and cause of tradition and habit. In order to justify this view, Lange makes a cursory appeal to ethnology and Herskovits, and to the interpretations of pre-capitalist economic history offered by Sombart[24] and Max Weber,[25] which he vaguely backs up with a quotation from Marx. The conclusion he draws is therefore not surprising:

[21] Adam Smith, *The Wealth of Nations*, Everyman edition, vol. II, p. 180, and vol. I, p. 2.

[22] Lange, op. cit., pp. 193–4 (Eng. trans., p. 169).

[23] W. Rostow, *The Stages of Economic Growth*, 1960.

[24] W. Sombart, *Der moderne Kapitalismus*, 1902, vol. I, pp. 37–8.

[25] M. Weber, *Wirtschaftsgeschichte*, 1924, pp. 302–3.

Economic activity [under natural economy] realizes goals established by tradition with the help of means established by tradition, without carrying out a reasoned analysis of either. [Its aims] are established by custom and morality, approved by religion and sometimes also sanctioned by legislation.[26]

The reign of reason thus begins with the appearance of capitalism. By a different path we have arrived at the same result that was attained by those who make of the rationality principle a permanent characteristic of human nature. But let us take the matter further. How did the rationality principle first appear in history? The development of commodity and money relations made it necessary to seek maximum gain, and so led to book-keeping, to economic calculations. 'Gainful activity becomes an activity based on reasoning, a *rational activity*.'[27]

The birth of rationality thus coincides with the birth of capitalist commodity production, and the first reasonable men are the chief characters in bourgeois society: the merchant, the banker and, above all, the entrepreneur. We thus arrive at an apologia for capitalism which differs not at all from that of the incense-bearers of economic liberalism, of Charles Gide, for example, who declared:

The disposition to compare immediate toil with remote gratification – a faculty which is called foresight – belongs only to civilized races, and, among these, only to the wealthier classes. The savage and the poor are equally improvident.[28]

However, Lange's ambition aims higher than this. Unlike the spokesmen of liberalism, for whom the general principle of rationality was realized in a particular, unique system, he wants to show how the special principle of capitalist rationality has become, historically, a general principle of behaviour. Like Schumpeter,[29] Lange postulates simultaneously a pseudo-explanation along materialist lines and an historical pseudo-origin. He assumes, indeed, that the principle of rationality, having first arisen from capitalist economic practice, has spread gradually outward from this its place of birth and apprenticeship, to invade the other aspects of social practice:

[26] Lange, op. cit., p. 173 (Eng. trans., p. 151).

[27] op. cit., p. 173 (Eng. trans., p. 157).

[28] *Principes d'économie politique*, p. 87 [*Principles of Political Economy*, 8th edition, trans. Veditz, 1904, p. 83].

[29] See his *Capitalism, Socialism, Democracy*, London, 1943.

Economic activity is the widest field for the application of the economic principle and is the sphere in which the principle first appeared, although not the only one. Moreover, the economic principle has entered and is continually taking over new fields for its application (technology, military strategy, scientific research, etc.).[30]

Here we are well and truly sunk in 'economism'. Economic (and so, material) practice is presented as being the source, the matrix of all rationality. The rational approach progressively conquers all the other aspects of social practice. The ultimate result of this progressive rationalization of the world is the establishment of the socialist mode of production. This thesis allows Lange to counterbalance the apologia for capitalism implicit in his 'historical' origin of the rationality principle with a critique of capitalism's inability to apply this principle thoroughly, on the scale of the entire economic activity of society:

The first historical triumph of the principle of economic rationality thus takes place in the capitalist enterprise, but it is a limited and distorted triumph.[31]

Limited, because economic rationality is achieved within enterprises that are the private property of capitalists, and is the instrument for maximizing their private profit and not for an end that is in the general interest of society. Distorted, because the antagonistic character of capitalist production-relations means that the striving for maximum private profit makes it necessary to regard as rational the exploitation and poverty of the working class, and results in a wastage of productive forces at the level of society as a whole.

Full and coherent application of the rationality principle is thus impossible within the framework of capitalism: for this, socialism, 'the social ownership of the means of production is indispensable'.[32]

Socialism is in this way invested with a degree of rationality higher than that of capitalism. The comparative rationality of the two systems is theoretically defined and established, and, with the coming of socialism, individuals are at last offered the chance to develop rational behaviour in all their activities. Planning on the scale of society as a whole must necessarily have the effect of 'strengthening the trend towards rational behaviour in all fields of human activity'.[33] Disencumbered, in so far as its

[30] Lange, op. cit., p. 214 (Eng. trans., p. 187).
[31] ibid., p. 197 (Eng. trans., p. 173).   [32] ibid., p. 198 (Eng. trans., p. 173).
[33] ibid., p. 215 (Eng. trans., p. 188).

infrastructure is concerned, of household economy, the last islet where tradition held out, and disencumbered, in its superstructure, of the state and religion, 'irrational or even anti-rational elements' that will have become useless through the disappearance of the exploiting classes, the future socialist society will see the final triumph of reason, freedom and truth.

In the end we have arrived once again at an apologia, but one that this time takes the dual form of a limited apologia for capitalism serving to reinforce a total apologia for socialism. We thus see before us a vast ideological construction aimed at proving the superiority of a certain economic system over all those that preceded it. The fact that Lange's ideology is 'progressive' confers upon it no scientific quality and justifies no-one in regarding it as constituting scientific knowledge of the history of mankind, or as a Marxist theory. In fact, this alleged historical and materialistic origin of the rationality principle is exploded immediately one looks at the contradictions and absurdities to which the idea leads. Lange, indeed, is inconsistent when he declares that:

Behaviour guided by the economic principle, the principle of economic rationality, is thus the product of historical development, a feature of a certain historical stage in the development of economic relations. It is not, as is sometimes falsely stated, a universal property of human activity . . .[34]

Clearly, then, if economic rationality is defined as seeking for maximum profit by way of commodity or monetary exchange, then, in every case where economic activity is not directed towards a market and gain in money terms, there is no economic rationality – but elsewhere Lange states:

Thus it can be seen that the economic principle is the principle of all rational human behaviour directed to the maximum realization of a given end.[35]

Here Lange is making use of the very thesis that he has just rejected, the view taken by those who see in the rationality principle the universal and eternal principle of all purposive action. This principle is thus no longer seen as the historical product of capitalist economic practice, and its materialist pseudo-origin is exposed as a myth the implications of which are absurd, since to suppose that this principle, having arisen from economic practice, then gradually takes over technology, the art of war

[34] ibid., p. 196 (Eng. trans., p. 172).   [35] ibid., p. 214 (Eng. trans., p. 187).

and the other aspects of social life is implicitly to claim that all the technical progress accomplished by mankind before the rise of capitalism was *not* the result of activity consciously striving to discover and adapt means for attaining ends. Mankind, according to this view, waited for the coming of capitalism before learning to economize effort and get the best out of the means at its disposal. And this applies with equal force to the history of all social structures, the conditions in which there appeared new forms of kinship, political and religious organization, and so on.

In reality, everything that we know of ethnology and history shows that, in all societies, individuals and groups have tried to maximize certain objectives, the content and order of priority of which expressed the dominance of certain social relations (kinship, religion) as compared with others, and were rooted in the very structure of each type of society. For instance, in primitive societies, competition for the control of women was not due to the needs or preferences, sexual or otherwise, of individual men, but to the central importance of kinship in these societies. Analysing the reason why one structure rather than another should have been accorded this central importance means working towards the discovery of a 'social rationality' of which, as we shall see, economic rationality is only one aspect. When we expose the unscientific character of this theory of the historical origin of the formal principle of the rationality of purposive action, do we find ourselves back at the position of those who see in this a characteristic inherent in human nature?

No, because when we state that this principle is a universal one we merely record a fact which, as such, *explains nothing* about the multiple content of human activity or the reasons for the rise and fall, in the course of history, of various economic and social systems.

Let us, then, draw the methodological conclusions that necessarily follow: in order to obtain scientifically-valid knowledge regarding any real economic behaviour it is essential that, *quite independently of this commonplace recognition* of the general *form* of intelligent behaviour on the part of individuals, the *real* subject-matter of economic science (that is, what differentiates what is economic from what is political, religious, etc.) be defined, that the specific features of the various economic systems that have appeared in history be known, together with the hierarchy of values in a given society. Otherwise, theoretical reflection upon the idea of economic rationality merely knocks together, out of a few superficial facts and appearances, a pseudo-deduction which the author can use at will to 'justify' some economic system or other. At best, it serves to construct a coherent ideology, an apologetic. We shall show later on that the rationality of socialism, as of any other economic system, can and must be established without resort to any hypothesis about the formal structure of the behaviour of individuals, and that the necessity of the transition to socialism is in no way the ultimate and conclusive application of a formal principle of action and the will to maximize individual objectives.[36]

Therefore, if I am to work out, step by step, the scientific problematic of the idea of economic rationality, I am now obliged by the conclusions of my twofold criticism of the liberal ideology of the classical economists and of the socialist ideology of Lange, to define the real subject-matter of political economy. What line am I to take, since the formal definition of the economy as a *form* of behaviour, as the will to 'economize' means, offers no possibility, no criterion for distinguishing what is economic from what is political, religious, etc.?

Should I adopt the common view, the old 'realistic' definition which, from Plato to Adam Smith and Alfred Marshall, has reduced what is economic to the material wealth of societies? This definition is vulnerable because it provokes an objection that has become classical. When a musician receives fees for a concert, or a priest accepts offerings to himself and his God, these men have produced no material goods but only ideal 'objects' for consumption, they have rendered 'services'. The economic sphere therefore embraces the production and exchange of services – but the 'realistic' definition of the classical economists fails to include this huge domain. (By services we do not mean, of course, merely the services needed for the functioning of the economy.) Should I then simply complete the classical definition by writing that economic activity means the production, distribution and consumption of goods and services? It is easy to see that I should then fall, though for different reasons, into the same embarrassment as the formal theory finds itself in. If the production of services is economic, then the economic sphere absorbs and explains the whole of social life, religion, kinship, politics, the acquiring of knowledge. Once more, everything becomes 'economic', by rights, while nothing actually remains as economic.

Where, then, does the difficulty lie?

The realistic definition, completed in this way, is wrong not because,

[36] This rules out any attempt on psychologistic or culturalistic lines to define 'social rationality'.

as in its original form, it leaves out the economic reality of services, but because it ascribes to the economic sphere the production of services *in its entirety*, all the aspects of a service, whereas *only one* aspect of any service belongs to the economic sphere. What is this aspect? A service, a non-economic activity, has an economic aspect when the realization of this service involves, directly or indirectly, the use of material means. In archaic societies the establishment of kinship-bonds between a clan that gave wives and a clan that received them implied the mutual supplying of labour and products; in Tibet the spread of Buddhism implied a vast economic organization centred on the lamaseries. Consequently, that which is economic is an aspect of the operation of activities that are non-economic – kinship, religion, politics, the acquisition of knowledge, and so on.

The 'economic' appears as a complex social reality because it is both a *particular field* of activity, directed towards the production, distribution and consumption of material objects, and at the same time, through the mechanisms of this production, distribution and consumption, a *particular aspect* of all non-economic activities. This way of describing the economic sphere enables us, as we shall see, to present in fresh terms the fundamental problem of needs and their order of priority, and so of the purposiveness of economic activities. Since economic activity is at one and the same time a specific activity which defines a particular field of social relations *and* an activity involved in the functioning of the other social structures, that which is economic does not possess, at its *own* level, the *whole* of its meaning and purpose, but only a part. For the advocates of the formal definition of the economy, any purposive activity is economic by virtue of its very *form*, or at least has an economic aspect, since the individual tries to 'economize' his means. For me, on the contrary, any purposive activity *may have* an economic aspect by virtue of its *content*, that is, if its realization implies, directly or indirectly, the use of material means.

What consequences does this definition of the economy entail for the problematic of economic rationality? It implies that we are trying to define the specific structures of the production, distribution and consumption of material goods within a particular society, that is, the economic system of this society and its internal relations with the other social structures. It obliges us to look for the reasons for the rise, evolution and disappearance of these systems in history. This signifies that economic rationality, seen in its twofold content – at once the rationality of economic systems and the rationality of the behaviour of economic agents within these systems – *is revealed only through cognition of the laws of functioning* and evolution of these systems, and this cognition is the outcome of theoretical research not only by economists but also by specialists in other social sciences, in so far as what is economic is partly determined by the functioning of the non-economic structures of social life.

Economic rationality and the rationality of economic science

Economic rationality thus reveals itself only through the epistemological rationality of economic science, that is to say, through the truth of the theoretical explanations constructed by this science. I have shown that economic rationality and the rationality of economic science are *one and the same question* and that cognition of economic rationality *wholly depends* on the truth of the hypotheses worked out by the economists (and the other specialists in social sciences).

To bring out the rationality of economic systems and economic agents thus means measuring the scientific validity of the hypotheses put forward in order to explain the functioning, origin and evolution of these systems and these forms of behaviour. This can easily be illustrated by the example which is closest to us and which gave rise to the birth of economic science, namely, the example of capitalism. The latter undeniably presents itself as the most highly developed form of commodity economy, in which individuals act with the aim of obtaining maximum profit from the sale of commodities. This profit itself appears as a part of the exchange value of these commodities, the difference between their cost of production and their selling price.

The question of the rationality of the capitalist system and of the economic practice of individuals within this system is thus entirely dependent on how economic science explains the nature and origin of the exchange value of any commodity (product or labour-power), of money, prices, profits (entrepreneur's profit, ground rent, interest, merchant's profit, etc.) and wages. It therefore depends on the *validity of the definitions of the fundamental categories* of the economic theory of capitalism, and, going beyond economic theory, it leads us back to *scientific cognition of the historical conditions* for the rise and evolution of this system.

Now, these fundamental categories are nowadays defined from two theoretical standpoints that are basically opposed to each other.

One school starts from the confrontation of individuals' preferences in a market situation, in order to account for the 'rates' that they observe in exchanging with each other their goods and their labour. These rates are expressed through prices, and it is these that determine the value of products and of factors of production. The subjective utility of goods for each consumer is thus taken as the basis for explaining how the capitalist economy works, and for determining, one after another, the content of the categories and laws of this economy. This doctrine, which is to-day the predominant one, is to some extent the heir of the classical theories: it finds its most fully-worked-out expression in contemporary marginalism.

The other school starts, on the contrary, from the technical and social conditions of the production of material goods in capitalist society in order to explain the origin and nature of the value of commodities *even before* they have been offered on the market, and then analyses the mechanism of price-formation in accordance with the structures of the market. Finally, the school analyses capitalist profit, and, by way of profits and wages, the structure of consumers' effective demand.

This second school is Marxism, which has inherited the essential theories of the classical economists on the origin and nature of the exchange value of commodities.

The question of the economic rationality of capitalism is thus entirely bound up with the question of the scientific validity of marginalism or of Marxism; and the question, still more fundamental than that, of the *comparative* rationality of capitalism and socialism, or other systems, depends on the *possibility* that one or the other of these theories has of *constituting itself a general theory* of the economy.

I can now try to draw up a first general balance-sheet of my analysis. I think I have, in fact, determined the general nature of our problem and defined, to some extent, the negative and positive conditions for a scientific solution of it.

Subject-matter and theoretical conditions of this inquiry

The idea of economic rationality involves a twofold problem: studying the economic behaviour of individuals within particular economic systems and studying the objective capacities for evolution possessed by these systems themselves. We know that these two problems are connected, even though they are not on the same plane, for in order to understand the rationality of the economic behaviour of individuals we need to know the structure of the economic and social system in which they act. This twofold content of the idea of economic rationality explains why this theme has many dimensions, and why it reappears in different epochs and a variety of forms. What Xenophon's work, the treatises of Columella and of Walter of Henley, and a manual of industrial management all have in common is the same concern to determine what the rules are for 'good' management, good government, whether of a slave-worked estate, a feudal lord's demesne, or a capitalist enterprise. The discussions on the just price and the just profit engaged in by the scholastic theologians have their echo nowadays, but they make us think, first and foremost, of Aristotle's criticism of 'money-making', of the economy gone mad through working for the market. The need to accumulate money indefinitely, the possibility of becoming rich without any limit, seemed to Aristotle to be irrational phenomena which contradicted the ancient Greek ideal of family autarky. And ethnologists' and historians' theories about the evolution of societies and their 'progress' from primitive savagery to 'civilization' remain, at bottom, reflections on the origin and nature of '*under*-development' and on the need for the underdeveloped countries to adopt more rational systems, choosing between capitalism and socialism.

Having determined the nature of the problem, I have indicated, in the course of my critique of classical liberalism and of Lange, some of the negative and positive conditions for solving it. We have seen:

(a) that it is not possible to start from individuals and the general form of purposive behaviour in order to analyse the content of the rationality of economic systems and economic agents;

(b) that no scientific knowledge can be deduced from observing the existence of this general form of behaviour, and that any such deduction is merely an ideological construction;

(c) that we cannot make any progress without defining what is economic, and that this definition cannot be a formal one;

(d) that it is not possible to analyse the economic sphere in all its aspects by means of economic science alone, because what is economic is implied by the functioning of the non-economic structures, which thus to some extent determine its significance.

I have suggested a positive definition of 'economics' by bringing out its complex nature, as at once a particular field of social relations, governed by the production, distribution and consumption of material goods, and, thereby, also a particular aspect of the functioning of the other social structures.

I have shown that the decisive question is that of the possibility of analysing scientifically the comparative rationality of economic systems, and that, in the last analysis, the answer to this question depends entirely on the scientific character, the epistemological rationality, of the different theoretical hypotheses put forward to explain the functioning, origin and evolution of economic systems.

In order to bring out the theoretical difficulties presented by the task of determining the rationality of economic systems, and to indicate a general method making it possible to overcome them, let us now get more closely to grips with an example. I will choose the example of capitalist economic rationality, which has been the chief subject-matter of political economy from its beginning.

We know already that this implies measuring the scientific validity of all the theories put forward to explain the many aspects of the functioning, origin and evolution of capitalism. Such an undertaking is obviously beyond my powers, and is inseparable from the development of full scientific cognition of capitalism, which is a task for many persons, and one not yet completed. I must therefore confine myself to an aspect which though essential, does not exhaust the subject. Since my aim is to construct a rigorous general problematic, I will restrict myself to a rapid analysis of how present-day writing on economic matters (principally, the work of the marginalists) has dealt with the problem of capitalist economic rationality. So as to prevent any misunderstanding, I will briefly sum up my conclusions.

The specialist reader will already have perceived that the marginalist approach does not satisfy the negative conditions for a rigorous solution of the problem. Marginalism, indeed, takes as its point of departure the behaviour of individuals, sets forth a formal definition of what is economic, eliminates the problem of scientific analysis of social needs by contenting itself with statistical cognition of individual preferences, all added together, among which it seeks to isolate a collective scale of satisfactions, so as to define the conditions for an economy of social welfare. Finally, and most important, marginalism, with the theory of 'factorial incomes', breaks down before the central problem of capitalist economic rationality – the problem of the origin and essence of capitalist profit and of the value of commodities.

Marginalism, which fails in relation to these essential points, is not the general scientific theory of the capitalist system that it claims to be, but forms an enormous, coherent ideological construction founded upon the theory of the marginal income of the factors of production and crowned by the theory of the equilibrium of perfect competition.

Nevertheless, despite its inadequacy as a general theory, marginalism has succeeded in solving a certain number of real problems. We must therefore take note of these positive partial results and not dodge the difficult task of explaining how these successes could be realized within the framework of a non-scientific general theory. I offer three explanations, which are different but convergent:

(1) Some economic problems have a structure such that certain marginalist hypotheses can account for some of their aspects. For example, marginalism gives special attention to the effect of the relations between supply and demand on the formation of prices in situations of competition. Inasmuch as the category of price is more complex than that of value, because it reflects both cost of production and the relation between supply and demand, marginalism gives us some knowledge of part of the mechanism of price-formation, in the short (and middle) term.

(2) Certain problems can be partly dealt with by employing the economic concepts of profit, price, wages, as these are used in everyday practical life, though they provide no scientific indication of the essence and origin of the phenomena referred to. Or, rather, these concepts contain indications which relate to that everyday practice in which it *seems obvious* that wages are the price of labour and profit is the product of capital, that is, in which the exploitation of labour by capital *never directly appears* and in which everything happens *as though* this did not exist. One can, by means of these concepts and on the basis of a given set of prices, calculate the optimum proportions of the volume of stocks and of the amount of capital tied up, and the minimum delay of capital-rotation, and in this way determine the conditions for realizing a maximum rate of profit – that is, certain norms of rational behaviour by the capitalist entrepreneur, for the optimum management of his capital. It is equally possible to deal with the problems of the national economy by bringing out, through the use of input-output matrices, certain conditions of equilibrium that can become the principles of government economic

policy in relation to prices, credit, etc. At these two levels, the problems of economic optimum present tasks of calculating the extreme variations of the variables that contribute to maximizing the rate of profit of the enterprise or the rate of growth of the national economy. Marginalism apparently has positive results to its credit in these fields, and this for three reasons: (a) because marginalism itself starts from the vulgar concepts of current economic practice, and systematizes them; (b) because it focuses upon the extreme situations in which producers and consumers may be placed, and thereby seems to provide grounds for the use of marginal calculation and the legitimacy of its own concepts; (c) because, by excluding, through the theory of factor income, any hypothesis of an exploitation of labour by capital that would constitute the structure of capitalism, it provides the general theoretical framework in and by which the ideological content of vulgar economic concepts can be taken up and systematized, and the 'appearances' of everyday business practice legitimized and given a grounding in scientific truth.

(3) Finally, and here is a mechanism that it needs more subtlety to perceive, many writers who appeal to the authority of marginalism, nevertheless, when analysing certain special problems, abandon, for the time being, the general hypotheses which they explicitly accept, in favour of special hypotheses which are theoretically incompatible with marginalism. For example, research on optimum management of an enterprise usually assumes that the enterprise in question is unable to modify market prices but can only adapt itself to these prices – though this contradicts the general marginalist assumption that each economic agent contributes by his supply and his demand to the formation of prices.

Having concluded this critique of marginalism we must go further and outline the answer to the problems that this doctrine can neither formulate nor solve, and which relate to the fundamental aspects of the way capitalism works, the rationality of this system. The road to follow, as we shall see, can only be the road of Marxism, but this must be a Marxism that can definitely satisfy two conditions. On the one hand it must be able to take in all the partial knowledge produced by the neo-classical and marginalist doctrine, and at the same time account for this knowledge on a Marxist basis, and develop it further. This implies that Marxist theory itself is developed and tackles those problems of competition and the role played by supply and demand which Marx, as we know, chose to leave outside his field of analysis. On the other hand, and above all, Marxism, in order to come to grips with the problem of the comparative rationality of capitalism and socialism, and to become a general theory, must offer a scientific explanation of the rise and evolution of economic systems. Such an explanation demands a definition of the idea of contradiction applicable to the social sciences. I will quickly demonstrate that, though Marxism is now facing up to these theoretical tasks, it is far from satisfying the two conditions mentioned, and I will suggest a new definition of the idea of contradiction.

CAPITALIST ECONOMIC RATIONALITY

Analysing capitalist economic rationality means first of all analysing the rationality of the economic agents who appear in this system. For the sake of simplicity I will reduce the categories concerned to three: entrepreneur, worker and consumer. The category of entrepreneur here includes those of industrialist, banker and trader, and the category of worker includes both those of manual worker and office worker, but I do not intend to extend my analysis to investigate such distinctions further. We observe, merely by glancing through specialist writings on these matters, a number of typical facts. Entrepreneurs and workers are two categories of agents who fulfil distinct and complementary functions in the process of production or in the circulation of commodities. But both entrepreneurs and workers are consumers. There are in reality, therefore, only two categories of agents, who carry on, either simultaneously or successively, two kinds of activity, those of production (and trade) and those of consumption.

As a general rule one assumes that these individuals pursue, in their economic activities, ends that are mutually coherent, and that they employ means that are appropriate to these ends. Their economic behaviour becomes rational when they organize it so as to obtain the *maximum income* from the use of their means, and so as to use this income in the optimum way, securing the *maximum satisfaction* desired.

The entrepreneur's income presents itself as income from his capital, or profit, that of the worker as income from his work, or wages. The entrepreneur may use his income in two different ways: he may invest part of his profit, thus transforming it into capital (and, therefore, into wages), or he may transform it into consumer goods. The worker can use his income in one way only, by transforming it into consumer goods.

The rational entrepreneur

We now perceive a profound difference between these economic agents, since one of the categories controls the use of capital and the factors of social production – raw materials, intermediate products, labour. The entrepreneur, or his representative, the manager, thus assumes the decisive functions of economic activity within a capitalist system. The behaviour of entrepreneurs, that is, the totality and succession of acts of decision-making and management by which they direct the activity of the enterprises, makes up the essential aspect of economic practice under this system, or, at least, the essential aspect of the intended content of this practice. And this practice is dominated by the problem of investment-choice, that is, the problem of measuring the efficiency of investments.[37]

The theory of rational behaviour for entrepreneurs thus undertakes to *break down* into its elements the series of strategic acts that are the entrepreneur's prerogative – determination of investment possibilities, forecasting of the consequences bound up with each of these, choice between alternatives, ways of carrying out investment[38] – and to determine for each of these the *optimum conditions* for its accomplishment. Knowledge of these conditions therefore supplies the *norms*, principles or recipes for maximizing profit of enterprise. These norms determine the *forms of behaviour and forms of organization* (institutions, structures) that are best adapted to the end that is aimed at. The conditions are not merely economic but also psychological, sociological, legal, etc., and in order to analyse them we must enlist the help of psychologists, sociologists, lawyers, and, above all, mathematicians. The decisive acts of management then become mathematical problems the solutions of which, set out logically and in numerical terms, seem to drive back, or even drive out altogether, the uncertainty attached to subjective or *a priori* (*ex-ante*) estimates. By taking the form of *calculation*, the economic practice of the entrepreneur seems to have attained its most completely *rational form*.

I shall merely refer to the contribution made by psychologists and

[37] Bross, op. cit., chapter 6, 7, 8.
[38] See 'L'entreprise, ses techniques et son gouvernement', in *Economie Appliquée*, vol. xvii, 1964, no. 2, 'Aspects sociaux de l'entreprise' and in particular the following articles: R. J. Monsen, B. O. Saxberg and R. A. Sutermeister, 'Les motivations sociologiques de l'entrepreneur dans l'entreprise moderne'; M. Haire, 'Aspects psychologiques de la gestion industrielle'; and H. Koontz, 'La formation des directeurs pour le profit'.

sociologists. They have begun to study the motivations[39] and aptitudes of the head of an enterprise, and shown that desire for 'gain' is not the only motive behind his actions, this often being combined with appetite for power.[40] They have dealt at length with the forms of authority, command-structure and organization that are most advantageous for the running of an enterprise, and we shall come upon this problem again when we consider the rational behaviour of the worker and the 'scientific' organization of labour. The most important results in relation to rational management of an enterprise have come, however, from economists who are mathematicians or engineers making use of the potentialities for analysis offered by a certain number of mathematical tools, some of them old (infinitesimal calculus) and some of them new (linear programming, non-linear programming, statistics and games-theory, cybernetics). I shall briefly describe their approaches to the subject and the results they have achieved.

The task before them is that of calculating the level of employment of the factors of production that will maximize the profit of an enterprise. The classical solution to this problem is that the profit is at its maximum when the marginal cost of a product is equal to its selling-price.[41]

So long as an enterprise has not reached this situation, at which its marginal costs and its selling prices are equal, or when it has gone beyond this situation, though it may certainly be making profits, yet these will not be maximum profits, and in each case it will be suffering a *failure to gain*.[42] Managing an enterprise rationally thus amounts to solving a two-fold problem:

(1) Choosing a programme of activity that enables a profit to be made, and which is practicable;

(2) Choosing among all the acceptable programmes the one that maximizes profits or minimizes costs for the enterprise.

Many programmes are impracticable because of the constraints to which the given enterprise is subject (physical production-capacity,

[39] ibid.

[40] See F. Perroux, *Economie et Société*, p. 107, who quotes Henri de Man and recalls Schumpeter's concept of the dynamic entrepreneur (*Unternehmer*) as against the concept of the 'man in charge' (*Wirt*) in a stationary circuit.

[41] See March and Simon, op. cit., and the extensive bibliography to this work: also Tannenbaum, 'The manager concept: a rational synthesis', in *Journal of Business*, 1949, no. 22, pp. 225–41.

[42] See Samuelson, *L'Economique* [French trans. of *Economics*], ch. xxxiv, p. 480.

financial capacity, costs, etc.). These constraints can be expressed in the form of equations, or inequations, in which the unknowns represent the quantities of means used. One then has to determine which programmes are compatible with the constraints, and this determination can be effected through input-output analysis.

Next, the optimum programme has to be found from among all the practicable programmes. Two methods are possible: either maximizing the objective function subject to given balance relationships, or minimizing the outlay function for a given value of the objective function. The two methods produce the same result, and are based on the 'duality' of the solutions to the problem of choosing an optimum programme.

The consequences of this duality are fundamental, for while the 'initial' problem that is to be solved involves determining the levels of activity of an enterprise, the 'final' problem involves determining a system of prices. This means that the problem of optimum management of an enterprise can be approached equally well from the angle of allocation of resources or from that of prices.

This phenomenon, the parallelism and inseparability of the valuation and allocation problems, has been called the 'dualism of pricing and allocation'.[43]

What has to be done, then, is to calculate the increase in the objective function which is brought about by using one additional unit of an available means, or the decrease in this function which is brought about by reducing by one unit the use being made of this means. If this increase or decrease is a constant magnitude, linear programming is used to calculate it. If the magnitudes are variable, then the classical infinitesimal calculus is used. The maximum of the objective function is then attained when the marginal increases are the same whatever the outlay of means. When the marginal substitution-rates keep diminishing, non-linear programming can be used, but in this case 'we are deprived of the most powerful tool used in the linear case',[44] namely, the fact that the optimum must occur at one of the peaks (the number of which is finite) of the polygon of possible solutions. The problem of the optimum nevertheless has a solution, the conditions of which have been defined by Kuhn and Tücker.[45] These

[43] See R. Dorfman, P. A. Samuelson and R. M. Solow, *Linear Programming and Economic Analysis*, New York, 1958, pp. 177–8. [44] ibid., p. 189.

[45] H. Kuhn, A. Tücker: 'Non-linear Programming', in J. Neyman, *Proceedings of the Second Berkeley Symposium on Mathematical Statistics and Probability*, Berkeley, 1951, pp. 481–92.

various calculation-procedures are employed given the setting, which is exceptional, of a perfect forecast. When uncertainty arises in the estimation of possibilities of profit, what has to be done is to calculate the probability that the hoped-for gain will occur. Rational decision then takes the form of a calculation of risks, and amounts to choosing a strategy that 'brings chance under control'. The task amounts to reducing the uncertain to the probable and then maximizing the sum of the mathematical expectation of future results, reduced to present value. The difficulty then consists in determining the magnitude of the rate that will make this 'discounting' possible.

When the interest rate is known, the criterion of the total discounted profit solves the problem of investment choice.[46]

Thus, the search for a management optimum in a case where there are circumstances of risk necessitates resort to the theory of probability, the theory of information and cybernetics, to the extent that, for example, the carrying-out of a decision entails consequences which will have to be taken into account when making the next decision in the total series of decisions needed in order to realize a strategy for producing and selling.[47] Finally, in so far as the situation of each entrepreneur is such that the success of his management activity is subordinated to the combined actions of all his competitors and of himself, the theory of games can carry further the analyses of which classical statistical theory is capable. In the case of a strictly determined game, contests are settled when there is equality of the max-min and the min-max.

In the case of games involving a non-constant sum, and games in which several persons participate, games theory has shown that the only way in which the opponents can maximize their profits is by coming to an agreement among themselves.

The theory of many-person games in the hands of Von Neumann and Morgenstern is essentially a theory of coalitions, their formation and revision. ... The concept of coalitions maintained by side payments among the members is an excellent theoretical counterpart to cartels and similar institutions.[48]

We have here situations of monopolistic competition. Already, the use of non-linear programming was related to situations of this type, since it

[46] P. Massé, *Le Choix des investissements*, pp. 11–13 (Eng. trans., *Optimal Investment Decisions*, Prentice-Hall, 1962, p. 23).

[47] Guilbaud, *What is Cybernetics?*, 1960. [48] Dorfman, op. cit., pp. 444–5.

dealt with cases of non-constant increase and decrease of the objective functions of the enterprise, cases that no longer correspond to perfectly competitive market situations, in which enterprises can take as constants the prices of what they produce and what they consume. Dropping the assumption of a perfectly competitive market means dropping the assumption of an enterprise that is passive in relation to the market, and brings to notice all the possibilities that exist for interfering with the environment: technical innovation, influencing customers, differentiation of products, and so on.[49]

I shall discuss later on the significance of the results achieved by the mathematical economists. For the moment, let me just point out the nature of the economic concepts which they employ. Profit, for example, is defined as the income of capital and measured by the difference between the selling price and the cost of production of commodities.

The rate of interest (i) is defined on the basis of the practice of the finance market, where '"one franc right now" can be exchanged for $1 + i$ francs in a year',[50] and is seen as the price of the transfer in time of the power to dispose of an asset. In other words, these concepts reflect the way in which economic realities *appear* and are *manipulated* in the *current practice* of capitalist economy. In the same way, the concept of wages is presented as the price or income of labour. Optimum management of an enterprise implies determining an optimum rate of wages and of employment of labour. With this problem, however, we touch on the question of analysing the rationality of workers' behaviour.

The rational worker

The worker is seen as a factor of production, which has a cost and a return, and which has to be combined with the other factors of production in order to obtain some product or other. The problem of the rational use of the worker consists, therefore, in (1) determining the optimum rate of wages and of employment which will maximize the profits of the enterprise, allowing for the productivity of this factor, and (2) determining the factors that affect the productivity of the worker, and influencing these factors.

[49] F. Perroux, preface to French trans. of *Monopoly and Competition* (1954) by E. Chamberlin.

[50] P. Massé, *Le Choix des investissements*, p. 8 (Eng. trans., p. 10).

Solution of the problem of the optimum employment of labour is governed by the general principle of equalizing the price and the marginal-revenue-product of the labour concerned. The marginal-revenue-product of labour depends on the marginal productivity of labour and the marginal costs of output.[51] It is therefore necessary to isolate the marginal productivity of labour and of capital and to measure them separately. Discussion has not ended on the procedure to be followed for this calculation: we shall see later on the fundamental reasons for this.

Drawing up a policy on wages and employment is merely one aspect of the rational utilization of capital, since wages are a fraction of capital before they become the income of a worker. Such a policy is, therefore, essentially an aspect of the rationality of the capitalist who transforms into labour-power one fraction of his capital and tries to get the best results from this. Getting the best results from labour-power means influencing the factors that increase its productivity. Analysis of these factors is the concern of what is called 'scientific labour management' or 'rational organization of labour'. With Taylor,[52] at the beginning of this century, rationalization of labour took the form of study aimed at eliminating all waste of time in the worker's movements and determining the movements and speeds of motion best adapted to the machine – in short, as a predominantly physiological adaptation of the human mechanism to the mechanics of industry. Taylor's axiom was that, for every operation a worker has to carry out there is a 'one best way'. The rational worker is thus the one who does his work in accordance with the 'best norms', thereby economizing motion, and so time, and so, in turn, the money of the enterprise. In order to encourage him to conform to the norms and to foster emulation, the worker is offered a system of bonuses. Scientific labour-management seeks in this way to establish the conditioned reflex most profitable for the enterprise, to produce a human production-automaton physically conditioned and 'stimulated' by the psychological spring of prestige and the material spring of the bonus.[53]

The behaviourist outlook of Watson,[54] Tolman,[55] etc., was soon questioned, for it was perceived that, precisely in order to achieve the

[51] Samuelson, *L'Economique* [*Economics*], ch. 28, pp. 587–606.

[52] Taylor, *Principes d'organisation scientifique des usines*, ch. 1.

[53] Cf. the 22 principles of economy of motion by the worker, in Barnes, *Motion and Time Study*, 1949, pp. 556–7.   [54] Watson, *Machines and Man*, London, 1935.

[55] Tolman, *Purposive Behaviour in Animals and Man*, Berkeley, 1932.

best use of the workers' productive capacity, one needs to take into consideration also their feelings, motivations, desires and personal relations. From Mayo's famous experiments[56] to the recent research into group dynamics, psychology, social psychology and sociology have done much work on workers' aptitudes and attitudes and on the forms of organization and authority that encourage them to increase their productivity and their initiative, or which, on the contrary, have an inhibiting effect upon them. At the end of an extensive inquiry Elmo Roper concluded that the hierarchical order of the desires of the workers he had studied was as follows:[57]

(1) Security: work at a *reasonable* wage and free from *fear* of being dismissed;

(2) Hope of promotion;

(3) 'Consideration' in labour-relations;

(4) Dignity.

This work by psychologists, etc., has often brought us new knowledge on previously unknown aspects of the functioning of industrial labour and the social behaviour of workers in the setting of capitalist production-relations, and criteria have been formulated for rational behaviour on the part of the worker. But what kind of rationality is meant here?

In general the worker is said to be 'rational' when he *participates* actively and totally in the functioning of the enterprise, and identifies his interest with the interest of the enterprise, which is to make the maximum profit. The rationality so defined is thus a *complementary, derivative and dependent* rationality, which the worker needs to possess in order that the capitalist's rationality may be *fully* effective and that, over the head of the individual capitalist, the capitalist system may function without any insurmountable contradictions. Psychology and sociology study the conditions for this active participation, this adhesion or integration on the part of the worker, and they may discover ways of mitigating the conflicts and stresses that can arise between the worker and the enterprise, threatening to interrupt the very functioning of the latter. Contrariwise, one has to know how to create optimum stress:

By stress is meant the discrepancy between the level of aspiration and the level of achievement. According to this hypothesis, if achievement too easily

---

[56] Mayo, 'Reverie and industrial fatigue', in *Journal of Personnel Research*, 1924, pp. 274–81.   [57] In J. A. Brown, *The Social Psychology of Industry*, 1954.

exceeds aspiration, apathy results; if aspiration is very much above achievement, frustration or desperation result, with consequent stereotypy. In the first case, there is no motivation for innovation; in the second case, neurotic reactions interfere with effective innovation. Optimal 'stress' results when the carrot is just a *little* way ahead of the donkey – when aspirations exceed achievement by a small amount.[58]

The extreme case of the resolute adversary who wants to destroy the capitalist system appears as a 'deviant', in need of psycho-therapy and socio-therapy to improve his human relationships. Thus, if the worker is not willing to become rational, or 'reasonable', on his own initiative, science provides part of the means needed to bring him to this condition in spite of himself. As Michel Crozier observes in his preface to the French edition of March and Simon:

A new danger that the theoreticians and practitioners of human relations have both come up against is the risk of manipulating people. As soon, indeed, as we have grasped that man is also a creature with emotions, and that scientific investigation enables us to know what factors determine his emotions, it becomes difficult not to make use of this knowledge for the purpose of manipulating him.[59]

These researches on the rationality of the worker's behaviour[60] thus

[58] In March and Simon, *Organizations*, p. 184.
[59] March and Simon, *Les Organisations*, [French trans. of *Organizations*], p. ix.
[60] Let me put before the reader for his consideration this admirable text on 'practical rationality', from Varro, *On Agriculture*, Book I, chapter 17:
'Now I turn to the means by which land is tilled. Some divide these into two parts: men, and those aids to men without which they cannot cultivate; others into three: the class of instruments which is articulate, the inarticulate, and the mute; the articulate comprising the slaves, the inarticulate comprising the cattle, and the mute comprising the vehicles. All agriculture is carried on by men – slaves, or freemen, or both; by freemen, when they till the ground themselves, as many poor people do with the help of their families; or hired hands, when the heavier farm operations, such as the vintage and the haying, are carried on by the hiring of freemen; and those whom our people called *obaerarii* (those who work off a debt by labour), and of whom there are still many in Asia, in Egypt and Illyricum. With regard to these in general, this is my opinion: it is more profitable to work unwholesome lands with hired hands than with slaves; and even in wholesome places it is more profitable thus to carry out the heavier farm operations, such as storing the products of the vintage or harvest. As to the character of such hands Cassius gives this advice: that such hands should be selected as can bear heavy work, are not less than twenty-two years old, and show some aptitude for farm labour. You may judge of this by the way they carry out their other orders, and, in the case of new

presuppose in general that this rationality coincides with that of the capitalists, or at least that it is derived from the latter and depends upon it. It is therefore necessary to demonstrate that the capitalist's interest coincides with that of the worker, and of society as a whole. This demonstration, as we shall see, is undertaken by the theories of general equilibrium and welfare. Let us say straight away that all that needs to be done in order to sweep away this fine apologetic construction, this 'Identikit' picture of the Rational Worker, is to recall that improvements in wages and working conditions have been effected not by capitalists spontaneously concerned about the welfare of society but as a result of the trade-union and political struggles of the working class, which has gradually, since the last century, forced the capitalists to make these concessions.

---

hands, by asking one of them what they were in the habit of doing for their former master.

'Slaves should be neither cowed nor high-spirited. They ought to have men over them who know how to read and write and have some little education, who are dependable and older than the hands whom I have mentioned; for they will be more respectful to these than to men who are younger. Furthermore, it is especially important that the foremen be men who are experienced in farm operations; for the foreman must not only give orders but also take part in the work, so that his subordinates may follow his example, and also understand that there is good reason for his being over them – the fact that he is superior to them in knowledge. They are not to be allowed to control their men with whips rather than with words, if only you can achieve the same result. Avoid having too many slaves of the same nation, for this is a fertile source of domestic quarrels. The foremen can be made more zealous by rewards, and care must be taken that they have a bit of property of their own, and mates from among their fellow-slaves to bear them children; for by this means they are made more steady and more attached to the place. Thus, it is on account of such relationships that slave families of Epirus have the best reputation and bring the highest prices. The good will of the foremen should be won by treating them with some degree of consideration; and those of the hands who excel the others should also be consulted as to the work to be done. When this is done they are less inclined to think that they are looked down upon, and rather think that they are held in some esteem by the master. They are made to take more interest in their work by being treated more liberally in respect either of food, or of more clothing, or of exemption from work, or of permission to graze some cattle of their own on the farm, or other things of this kind; so that, if some unusually heavy task is imposed, or punishment inflicted on them in some way, their loyalty and kindly feeling to the master may be restored by the consolation derived from such measures' (Cato and Varro, *De Re Rustica*, trans. Hooper and Ash, Harvard U.P., 1934, pp. 225–9).

The rational consumer

At the end of the production-process in which they fulfil functions that are distinct, unequal and complementary, the entrepreneur and the worker meet again, confronting the totality of consumer goods available. They possess unequal amounts of income enabling them to acquire these goods. The problem then arises for them of behaving as 'rational consumers', that is, of securing maximum satisfaction from the use of their incomes. Each individual has his own special preferences; consumer goods possess different degrees of utility for each individual. It is assumed that each arranges his preferences in an order of priority and makes his choice accordingly. It has also been assumed, since Pareto,[61] that several different combinations of goods and services bring the same individual equivalent satisfactions, which can be expressed in an indifference-curve.[62] Finally, it is assumed that individuals' scales of preference are separate and unique and do not overlap. These preferences and needs are not subject to discussion, and the problem of the rationality of ends is not raised. Maurice Allais emphasizes this strongly:

> It cannot be stressed too much that, *apart from the condition of coherence, there is no criterion for judging the rationality of ends, considered as such.* These ends are quite arbitrary . . . It is here as with tastes. They are what they are. They are given facts, which mark off one individual from another.[63]

It is then shown that the consumer will achieve maximum satisfaction in the use of his income when he equalizes the marginal utility of each of the goods and services in each of their uses. More precisely, since goods and services are assigned prices, rational conduct on the part of the consumer will be conduct that equalizes the weighted marginal utilities of these goods and services, that is, their marginal utility divided by their prices. The theory of 'elasticities'[64] then examines the variations in the behaviour of consumers depending on variations in prices.

Here we come upon a difficulty. It seems that the behaviour of the individual is determined by prices and that he is subject to these prices. At the same time it is said that prices are determined by individual preferences. This difficulty reflects the fact that the analysis of consumer

[61] Pareto, *Manuel d'économie politique*, pp. 168–9.
[62] J. R. Hicks, *Value and Capital*, Oxford, 1946, p. 17.
[63] Allais, *Fondements . . .*, op. cit., p. 27.
[64] Developed from Alfred Marshall onward.

behaviour is entirely dominated by the marginal theory of value. According to this theory, consumers' preferences, the order of precedence of consumers' needs, ought to explain the proportions in which each of them is ready to exchange his own resources for those of others. These proportions determine the rates of exchange of goods and services, that is to say, their prices. The exchange-value of consumer goods is thus determined on the basis of the working of supply and (effective) demand by the consumers, and through them the exchange-value of the means necessary for production of these goods is determined. In this way the use-value of goods gives rise to their exchange-value, and the latter, through the prices of intermediate products, reacts back on the production-process.[65] It still needs to be explained, however, why the market price is a single price, whereas individual preferences are many and changing.[66] The solution to this problem is found on the level of the overall functioning of the market, the overall working of supply and demand. Once again, individual behaviour proves to depend on the overall behaviour of the capitalist system.

A certain number of criticisms have been made of this theory of the rational consumer. For Lange the possibility of maximizing satisfactions presupposes that the individual consciously compares the utilities of different goods before he decides to buy. He insists, following W. C. Mitchell,[67] that consumers' demand is more often than not a matter of 'habit, imitation and suggestion – not reflective choice', and bears the imprint of traditional, irrational economy, which survives above all in household economy. This irrationality of tradition is reinforced by the conscious action of the enterprises, which increasingly call on the help of psychologists, psychiatrists and sociologists so as to 'take advantage of the conditioned reflexes or subconscious desires' of the purchasers in order to shape their demand. Lange concludes regarding methods of 'hidden persuasion'[68] and *Werbepsychologie*:[69]

The effect of these new methods of promoting sales is to strengthen the irrational element in household activity.[70]

[65] G. Pirou, *L'Utilité marginale de C. Menger à J. B. Clark*, pp. 164–76.

[66] C. Gide, *Principes d'économie politique*, pp. 60–90.

[67] W. C. Mitchell, *Business Cycles*, 1927, pp. 165–6.

[68] Vance Packard, *The Hidden Persuaders*, 1958.

[69] P. Hofstätter, 'Werbepsychologie', in *Psychologie*, Frankfurt, 1957.

[70] Lange, op. cit., p. 300 (Eng. trans., p. 263).

Without wishing to defend the methods that are used to condition the consumer,[71] it must be said that Lange's objection is not valid theoretically. It is not appeals directed only to conscious thought that make possible consumer behaviour aimed at maximum satisfaction, but the existence of an order of preferences, and this order may be conscious, subconscious or unconscious. Techniques of persuasion are only effective, moreover, because they act upon unconscious desires that are seeking better satisfaction.

It has been more seriously objected[72] that no consumer ever applies the principle of equalizing weighted marginal utilities. This would assume him to be capable of measuring the magnitude of the utility of a class of goods and giving it a number. Since nothing of the sort is to be observed in real life, the principle of maximization is rejected, or at least ascribed to an ideal rational man who is alien to the real world. This objection does not stand up, either, for Pareto's theory[73] of the equalizing of weighted marginal utilities does not assume that the consumer is able to measure quantities but merely that he can arrange the utility of goods in a scale. And that consumers have scales of preference is beyond any doubt.

Another, more solid objection relates to the nature of the scales of preference. Lange[74] does not deny that consumers have these scales, but, in his view, they are unlike those of the entrepreneur and the planner in that they are 'broken' scales which cannot be put together to make a single scale. The individual does not possess a transitive scale of preferences along which he can arrange all his preferences in a single series, and for this reason he cannot maximize his satisfactions. Here, too, the objection seems invalid. On the mathematical plane, Von Neumann and Morgenstern showed in 1947 that it is possible to generalize Pareto's concept of the *extremum* without recourse to transitivity and acyclicity.[75] However, Lange's position is untenable for more decisive reasons than the fact that it is possible for such a calculation to be made. I agree with him that the existence of intransitive preferences on the part of individuals is not to be

[71] Haas, *La Publicité*, Dunod, 1962, p. 169.

[72] Vuaridel, *La Demande des Consommateurs*, ch. 1.

[73] *Manuel d'économie politique*, pp. 574–9. Cf. Volterra's objection to Pareto.

[74] Lange, op. cit., p. 295.

[75] ibid., p. 292: Lange quotes the writings of Von Neumann and Morgenstern, Luce and Raïffa on this subject, but without really discussing them. See the excellent article by Guilbaud, 'La théorie des jeux: contributions critiques à la théorie de la valeur', in *Economie appliquée*, 1949, no. 2, pp. 296–7.

explained merely by eccentricity or differences in taste but is due to the effects of the social structures. But I utterly reject the materialist and historical pseudo-origin of the social structures which he has invented in order to justify socialism. According to him, capitalism brought economic rationality, and with it the rationality principle in general, into a world that was living under the ascendancy of tradition and irrational custom. Following Max Weber, Lange shows capitalism gradually rationalizing social life and attacking the last bastion of tradition, household economy. However – and this is where Lange separates himself from Weber – capitalism necessarily fails because it develops at the same time, and in contradiction with rationality, the irrational practices of advertising, and keeps alive the 'irrational and anti-rational elements' contained in the superstructures of capitalism (religion, the state), which are needed for the exploitation of the workers.[76] Socialism alone, he says, will eliminate these obstacles and bring about the rationalization of social practice.

What value has this interpretation, in the light of modern science? The latter is continually revealing the rationality of the behaviour of individuals belonging to societies of the sort called primitive or traditional, discovering little by little the key to understanding the logic and necessity of the way their structures function. The assumption that traditional societies are irrational merely exposes the ideology of those who accept uncritically the prejudices of Western capitalist societies about themselves and other societies. To give a brief demonstration of this 'rationality' of primitive societies, I will take the example of the forms of money and of circulation of goods that are characteristic of such societies. In our societies money possesses an all-purpose character, the individual can exchange it for almost anything at all – land, labour, material goods, services.[77] This all-purpose use of money assumes the generalization of commodity production on the scale of society as a whole. This overall structure explains the *necessity* the individual is under to maximize his money gains (rationality of the entrepreneur and the worker) and the *possibility* possessed by every consumer of maximizing his satisfactions by relating his income to the price of everything that is for sale.

In contrast to this situation, in primitive societies money of this kind does not exist, and goods are classified in a hierarchy of distinct categories:[78] goods for current consumption, luxury goods, treasures, land.

[76] op. cit.   [77] Dalton, 'Primitive Money', in *American Anthropologist*, 1965, no. 1.
[78] Cf. Bohannan, P. and Dalton, G., introduction to *Markets in Africa*, 1962.

The use of these goods is socially controlled and it is, generally speaking, impossible and unthinkable to exchange goods from one category against goods from any other, regardless. This compartmentalizing and hierarchical ordering of goods results from the role they play in the functioning of distinct social relations – kinship, politics, religion – each of which is invested with a distinct social significance. By entering into these many different functions, goods and money assume many different *utilities and significances*, ordered hierarchically. The compartmentalizing and hierarchical ordering of goods which govern the behaviour and competition of individuals, by giving expression to the special dominant role played in a given society by relationships of kinship and marriage (the Siane) or by political and religious relationships (the Incas), express the *dominant aspect* of the social structure. It is thus the nature and the role played by the various social structures in a particular society that explain the way individuals behave, and not *vice versa*, and it is this nature and role of the social structures that science has to explain. Once again, economic rationality shows through the epistemological rationality of the sciences. Now, the problem that science has to solve, and which is the very kernel of the idea of rationality, is that of the relation between the economic and the non-economic in the evolution of societies. I have tried elsewhere to show,[78a] that the non-existence of an all-purpose currency among a tribe in New Guinea is to be explained, on the one hand, by the absence of commodity production (the negative reason), but also at the same time, by the need to control access to women and maintain equilibrium in the circulation of women between the clans (the positive reason). This second reason, arising from kinship structures and giving expression to the central role of kinship in this society, made it necessary, it seems to me:

(1) to *choose*, among available resources, certain types of goods which had to be made to correspond to women, and these goods had to be limited in quantity, in accordance with the scarcity of women, and to be such as would need more effort to acquire;

(2) to *sever* radically the mode of circulation of these precious goods from that of other goods, which meant setting up a scale of goods consisting of several categories that were heterogeneous and could not be substituted for each other;

(3) to *subject* the circulation of these goods to control by the elders and

[78a] M. Godelier, 'Economie politique et anthropologie économique', in *L'Homme*, IV, 4, pp. 118–32.

the 'important' men, that is, the most representative individuals of the community. This control was at one and the same time an attribute of their functions (their 'role') and also a symbol of their prestige or their merit, that is, of their 'status'.

These assumptions seem to me to illuminate, better than is usually done by economics and sociology, the fact that in primitive societies the significance of an all-purpose currency could not be spontaneously appreciated, since it was neither meaningful nor necessary in social systems of this sort, and also the fact that the introduction, in fairly recent times, of a money economy presents a threat to the working of these systems, and is in fact destroying them little by little without any need for violence.

By this example we can see the rationality of the economic behaviour of individuals as one aspect of a wider, social rationality, based upon the internal relationship between economic and non-economic structures in the different types of society. We can already perceive that there is no such thing as economic rationality *per se*, nor any 'definitive' form of economic rationality. It is now possible to conclude my critique of Lange's views. The intransitive nature of his preference-scales does not stop an individual from maximizing his satisfactions, nor does this intransitivity express any 'irrationality' on the part of this individual or the society in which he lives. On this point I agree with the marginalists. In contrast, however, to the marginalist view, and to any and every formal definition of economics, it is clear that one cannot start from individuals in order to explain the content and hierarchical order of their needs, their values and their purposes. And the fact that everybody uses means to attain ends tells us nothing about the content of anybody's action, but only about the form – something that is general and empty – of all purposive action. It can then be understood that, *without a scientific knowledge of the internal relations* of the social structures, the economist *cannot acquire more than a statistical knowledge* of individual preferences, which necessarily appear to him as matters of taste, in relation to which the question of rationality does not arise. Consequently, this statistical knowledge, useful though it is, has a limited bearing, and, paradoxically, a meaning that largely escapes the economist. This, moreover, can be equally true of an economist in the service of capitalism and of an economist in a socialist country.

I have come to the end of my analysis of theories about the rational behaviour of entrepreneurs and workers, the principal agents in the capitalist system. In appearance, these theories start from the individual and from a formal general theory of economics and of the principle of rationality. In fact, they smuggle back into their explanations the concepts of generalized commodity production, universal currency, and social classes which control functions and factors that are distinct and unequal. In other words, the 'visible' general structures specific to the capitalist system have been brought into the theory, together with the driving force of this system, the maximization of capitalist profit. In appearance, the ultimate criterion of capitalist economic rationality, the principle of maximizing profit, has been deduced from the formal principle of all purposive activity. In practice, while seeming to start from individuals, their preferences and their propensities, these theories start *implicitly* from the general structure of the capitalist system. Accordingly, despite its real and obvious psychologism and formalism, and the pseudo-deductions that are so many theoretical dead-ends, analysis along these lines has succeeded in obtaining some positive results, in so far as the individual has been studied as the personification of definite social functions and social structures: that is, in so far as, through him, the analysts have been examining certain conditions governing the investment of capital. It was on this ground that Marx took his stand, when he wrote in the Preface to *Capital*:

> To prevent possible misunderstanding, a word. I paint the capitalist and landlord in no sense *couleur de rose*. But here individuals are dealt with only in so far as they are the personifications of economic categories, embodiments of particular class-relations and class-interests. My standpoint . . . can less than any other make the individual responsible for relations whose creature he socially remains, however much he may subjectively raise himself above them.[79]

The implications of the positive results that have been attained thus depend, in the last analysis, on the validity of the categories worked out in order to explain the structure and laws of the specific functioning of the capitalist system. We know now that the rationality of entrepreneurs and workers expresses their functions in the activities of production and distribution. We know, too, that the differences and inequalities of these functions arise from differences and inequalities as regards ownership of capital and means of production. This inequality of function and owner-

---

[79] Karl Marx, *Capital*, vol. I, Preface, Allen and Unwin edn, 1938, p. xix. (All quotations from and references to *Capital*, vol. I, relate to this edition.)

ship determines in its turn the inequality of incomes, profits and wages, and restricts in advance the forms and possibilities of individual consumption. Rationality thus means, for the entrepreneurs, managing the system well and getting the maximum profit out of it, whereas, for the workers, rationality means letting themselves be managed and participating to the best of their ability in realizing this same maximum profit. Finally, the inequality of ownership, function and income that exists is not to be taken, it seems, to mean that there is exploitation of the workers by the entrepreneurs; it merely expresses the just remuneration of different functions and factors. The system would be put in jeopardy, however, if some people were to challenge this distribution of resources, functions and income. In order to rebuff these awkward elements it is necessary to prove that the interest of the capitalists coincides with that of the workers and of society as a whole. Even apart from such a fundamental challenge to capitalism, however, an inescapable and decisive problem remains. Nothing actually ensures that the plans and actions of the economic agents will prove to be mutually compatible, even if we suppose that all of them behave rationally in accordance with their functions. This is all the more so because the system is based upon competition between these agents, and because it is this competition that determines, or so it would appear, through the overall working of supply and demand, the levels of prices and rates of interest, and so the conditions governing the activity of each individual and also the growth of the system. The question that inevitably arises is therefore this: 'Given what conditions does a system of competition ensure the maximum satisfaction of all members of society, that is to say, maximization of their incomes, profits and wages, and of their satisfaction as consumers?'

Rationality of the capitalist system

What conditions are needed for the intentional rationalities of the agents to combine so as to bring about an overall rationality in the way the capitalist system functions? We must now proceed from a merely implicit analysis of the system to an explicit one, from studying local rationalities to studying the overall rationality of the system, from examining the rational behaviour of individuals to examining how an entire system behaves.

This means no longer considering individuals, even as embodiments of functions, but instead considering the objective properties of social structures. The answer, as we shall see, lies in the theory of perfect competition. Demonstration of the 'virtues'[80] of perfect competition will, it would seem, dismiss as pointless the threatening question about the historical necessity of inequality in private ownership of the means of production. The 'virtues' of the system will fully justify its existence and this 'justification' will, in the last analysis, take the place of an 'explanation' – as is the case with every ideological demonstration, whether of socialism or of any other system.

The general problem is thus that of determining what the conditions are that can enable the capitalist system to attain efficiency in equilibrium, while realizing the welfare of all members of society. Putting this more simply, we have to determine the conditions under which society's demand-function can best be satisfied while taking account of its production-function.

The problem is an old one. We find it in Adam Smith. Ricardo dealt with it in the more specific form of the theory of comparative costs and the optimum forms of world production and international trade.[81] The general answer to our problem was set out by Walras in his *Elements of Pure Economics*. Equilibrium of the system is obtained, he said, in a situation where there is perfect competition and where supply and demand are equal. Walras undertook to prove mathematically that in such a situation there is an equilibrium solution, and that this solution is the only possible one. He thought he had done this when he carefully showed that his system contained exactly as many equations as unknowns to be determined. However, equality between the number of equations and the number of unknowns is neither necessary nor sufficient for a solution to a system of equations. If the solution is to possess economic sense, the numbers used as prices or quantities must be non-negative, and mere counting of equations is not enough to ensure that, if a solution exists, it will contain only non-negative numbers.[82]

A rigorous proof of the equilibrium solutions in the Walras-Cassel model was carried out by A. Wald in 1935.[83] Wald's model may be compared to the neo-classical model with continuous marginal productivities.

[80] J. Marchal, *Le Mécanisme des prix*, ch. 8, section i.
[81] J. F. Graham, *The Theory of International Values*, Princeton, 1948.
[82] Dorfman, op. cit., p. 350.
[83] Wald, in *Econometrica*, Oct. 1951.

The result is the same in both cases. Competition operates so as to maximize the total value of production and minimize the total cost of the quantities that enter into it, and succeeds in making these two totals equal. Next, it was necessary to prove the existence of a dynamic equilibrium. Von Neumann[84] constructed the first model of balanced growth, and was followed by many others, including Arrow and Debreu.[85] Competition was thus shown to work, in the famous words of Adam Smith, like 'an invisible and rational hand'.

Perfect competition; equilibrium; Pareto optimum; welfare

Proving that a competitive equilibrium exists is not enough, however, to prove that the consumers will be satisfied. In order to proceed from equilibrium to welfare, two additional concepts must be brought in – the concept of efficiency and that of the Pareto optimum. The possibility of making this transition is still based on the 'normative aspects of competitive equilibrium',[86] on the fact that a system of competition is a mechanism that maximizes certain total values. The concept of efficiency is a technological concept that relates to production only, leaving entirely aside everything to do with satisfaction of the consumers. A combination of factors of production is efficient if it is impossible to increase some kinds of production without reducing others, or without increasing the resources invested. Even though the problem as a whole is formulated in physical terms, a certain idea of 'price' inevitably emerges from linear analysis, and this is important for going on to consider the problem of welfare.

A linear programme maximizes a weighted sum of outputs. An economist can hardly resist thinking of the weights as prices and the sum as a value, especially when it turns out that at the maximum the 'prices' are proportional to marginal rates of substitution.[87]

We thus have correspondence between the efficient points, or solutions, and price situations. The prices involved here are 'fictitious' ones, 'efficient numbers', determined by the dual problem, and money serves

---

[84] 'A Model of General Equilibrium', in *Review of Economic Studies*, 13(1).

[85] 'Existence of an Equilibrium for a Competitive Economy', *Econometrica*, 1954, pp. 265–90.

[86] Dorfman, op. cit., p. 390.   [87] ibid., p. 400.

only as the unit of reckoning. Not even the existence of a market is presumed. Nevertheless, the existence of implicit prices enables us to link intertemporal efficiency with the behaviour of a competitive market, since by inverting the problem of the maximum we obtain the dual problem of the minimum that is attached to it, the variables in which can be regarded as implicit competitive prices. We must therefore note, with Dorfman, that:

The efficiency-price concept rises out of the problem itself – it was not put there by institutional assumptions. But we know that any institutional setup that results in the maximization of value sums will achieve efficient (but not necessarily 'good') programmes.[88]

This will be important when we come to examine the equivalence between perfect competition and centralized planning. For the moment, the technological idea of efficiency seems closely bound up with the idea of competitive equilibrium. Competitive equilibria are efficient, and the totality of efficient points is merely the totality of all possible competitive equilibria. Efficiency appears as a necessary condition for optimizing the consumer-utility functions. But it is not a sufficient condition, and the concept of the Pareto optimum needs to be introduced. Pareto defined the optimum situation in these words:

Let us consider any position and let us suppose that a very small movement away from it is made, which is compatible with the relations. If, as a result, the welfare of all members of the community is increased, it is obvious that the new position is better for all of them; and *vice versa*, it is worse if the welfare of all members is diminished. The conclusion holds if the welfare of some of them remains constant. But if, on the contrary, this slight movement results in increasing the welfare of some individuals and diminishing that of others, we can no longer affirm that to make this change benefits the whole of the community.[89]

All Pareto optima present themselves as efficient points, and all efficient points are competitive equilibria with maximization of profits. It is thus possible to prove the fundamental theorem of the welfare economists: 'every competitive equilibrium is a Pareto optimum, and every Pareto optimum is a competitive equilibrium'. In a situation of perfect competition, all the entrepreneurs can maximize their profits, and the con-

[88] ibid., p. 403.
[89] Pareto, 'Economie mathématique' in *Encyclopédie des Sciences Mathématiques*, vol. I, part 4, p. 624 (Eng. trans. in *International Economic Papers*, vol. 5 [1955], p. 87).

sumers their utility-functions, allowing for the way resources and incomes are distributed. There can thus be as many Pareto optima as there are different distributions of real income. The optimum solution thus satisfies, in the last analysis, 'the initial restrictions on resource ownership'.[90] This succession of theorems thus shows that in a situation of perfect competition and perfect forecasting, there is always compatibility between the decisions taken by the economic agents. This compatibility is seen as the expression and consequence of an objective property of a structure, namely, perfect competition, in a definite situation, namely, perfect forecasting, and this property provides the grounds for the 'normative' character of perfect competition. Through this the market is endowed with an automatic and invisible rationality that penalizes those who have shown themselves unable or unwilling to understand the messages sent them by way of prices. In a situation of perfect forecasting in which the prices envisaged *ex ante* correspond exactly to the prices observed *ex post*, each competitor needs to know with precision only the present value of the immediate rate of price-variation:

The truly remarkable thing about the intertemporal invisible hand is that while it results in efficiency over long periods of time, it requires only the most myopic vision on the part of market participants. Just current prices and current rates of change need to be known, and at each moment long-run efficiency is preserved.[91]

From this it is possible to generalize, with Von Neumann, about the possibility of a dynamic equilibrium sustained by an optimum rate of accumulation. The 'strong' hypothesis of perfect forecasting can be abandoned and the future regarded as uncertain. In this case, several different futures are possible, and therefore, several different price-systems. Debreu has sought, with the idea of 'commodities of conditional delivery'[91a] to generalize in relation to situations of uncertainty the classical theorems of equivalence between a price-system and a Pareto optimum. Paradoxes arise from this, which have caused Pierre Massé to reject Debreu's attempt. We have to assume that a consumer can foresee all the possibilities, and that he buys today for all the years to come. Above all, the theory assumes that all future eventualities are:

capable of being listed and defined in advance, . . . thus telescoping the future with the present.[92]

[90] Dorfman, op. cit., p. 414, n. 1.   [91] Dorfman, op. cit. (Eng. edn), p. 321.

[91a] P. Massé, *Le Plan, ou l'Anti-hasard*, p. 170.   [92] ibid., p. 172.

If we assume, however, that a complete listing of future possibilities is impossible, then we have to work out our theory in terms of strategy. This is the path opened before us by the games theory of Von Neumann and Morgenstern, which has been adopted by Massé.

Whatever the conditions of the analysis, the conclusion is the same: the market, in a situation of perfect competition, determines the optimum forms of production, consumption and accumulation within a given national economy.[92a] Perfect competition is thus the rational structure and situation *par excellence*, because it means that, in Adam Smith's words:

'Every individual necessarily labours to render the annual revenue of the society as great as he can . . . He is in this, as in many other cases, led by an invisible hand to promote an end which was no part of his intention' (*The Wealth of Nations*, Everyman edition, vol. I, p. 400).

It is now time to confront this whole approach by the classical and neo-classical economists with capitalist reality, so as to test its intentions and its implications. Did the idea of 'perfect competition' correspond to an ideal state or to a real state of capitalist economy? Both hypotheses have their supporters.

Walras's reply was clear, defining the status of political economy as he saw it:

Pure economics is, in essence, the theory of the determination of prices under a hypothetical regime of perfectly free competition.[93]

And, in our own day, Dorfman echoes him when he declares:

We can't blithely attribute properties of the real world to an abstract model. It is the *model* we are analysing, not the world.[93a]

Ricardo, long before Walras, wrote to Malthus regarding his theory of international trade:

The first point to be considered is, what is the interest of the countries in the case supposed? The second, what is their practice? Now it is obvious that I need not be greatly solicitous about this latter point; it is sufficient for my purpose if I can clearly demonstrate that the interest of the public is as I have stated

---

[92a] Malinvaud, 'Capital, Accumulation and Efficient Allocation of Resources', in *Econometrica*, April 1953, pp. 233–68.

[93] L. Walras, *Eléments d'Economie Politique Pure*, p. XI (Eng. trans., *Elements of Pure Economics*, p. 40); my emphasis, M.G.   [93a] Dorfman, op. cit., p. 351.

it. It would be no answer to me to say that men were ignorant of the best and cheapest mode of conducting their business and paying their debts, because that is a question of fact, not of science, and might be urged against almost every proposition in Political Economy.[94]

For others, free competition is an historical stage in the development of capitalism, a stage that has now passed with the development of monopolies. The capitalism of monopolies is an imperfect world in which a competitive equilibrium cannot be achieved, because monopoly price is not determined by the equalization of marginal cost and marginal revenue.[94a] Without competitive equilibrium there can be no Pareto optimum, and without Pareto optimum there can be no welfare. Ever since Pigou, this reasoning has furnished the chief arguments levelled by welfare economists against monopolies. Looked at in this perspective, competitive capitalism thus appears as a lost reality to which we ought to return so that everything may go better for us. This past reality thus possesses the quality of a 'norm', and functions as an 'idea'. This accounts for the myth of the return to the Paradise Lost of our origins which we find in so many of the welfare theorists. Accordingly, whether it be a reality now behind us or an ideal yet to be realized, free competition is seen as a 'normative' structure, that is, a structure that must be created, or maintained, if society is to achieve an optimum in its economic and social functioning. In all cases, however, this optimum is the same. It is what can be attained within the framework of the capitalist system. It is determined in advance by the structural inequality of the ownership of the means of production and of capital which defines the relations between capitalist and workers.

At the end of the road, the entire theory of the rationality of free competition thus comes up against two kinds of problem which it cannot solve within the limits of economic theory, and it is left hanging over the inner emptiness of this inability to solve them. One of the problems is a problem of fact: how did the capitalist system appear, and how did the stage of free competition disappear, despite the invisible and rational hand that directs the system more or less automatically towards the optimum? The other problem is one of justice: are there 'good grounds' for the inequality in the ownership of capital?

[94] Ricardo, *Letters to Malthus*, ed. Bonar, p. 18: cf. Hutchison, *The Significance and Basic Postulates of Economic Theory*, Kelley, 1960, p. 121.

[94a] Dorfman, op. cit., p. 412.

Political economy since Adam Smith has never found any other way of getting over these awkward questions than that of arbitrarily transforming the question of justice into a factual answer, by assuming that inequality of ownership is a good thing, and even the best possible arrangement. In order to 'verify' this assumption, it was enough to show the virtues of perfect competition (by demonstrating that it could satisfy in the best way possible the entrepreneurs, the workers and the consumers) for the system and its structural inequality to be 'justified'. Questions of fact then lose all point, since one can judge, as history has done, of the right of facts to exist. The capitalist system was thus born because it was the best system, and it is the best system because it was born. By transforming right into fact (question no. 2), this arbitrary procedure has thus simultaneously transformed fact into right, and spared us the need for a scientific explanation. In the last analysis, the theory of free competition is consolidated by an ideological choice which preceded it and organized it in advance. Given this initial bias, it is easy to understand why the epoch, now behind us, of free competition – which historians depict as an epoch of pitiless exploitation of a working class that was without the right to organize itself and had not yet worked out the means of doing this – is presented as an unquestionable 'ideal'.

Actually, things are a great deal more complex than this, for the ideological arbitrariness I have mentioned is unable to put the results of the mathematico-economic theory of the optimum at the service of an exclusive apologia for capitalism. The results are indeed ambivalent, and this is due to the 'innocence' of mathematics in relation to every ideological intention.

The duality theorem and the innocence of mathematics

What does this innocence consist in? It arises from the *duality* of the conditions for solving any mathematical problem of optimum. Through this duality the conditions for optimum are, in an indissoluble way, capable of expression either in terms of perfect planning or in terms of perfect competition.[95] This duality shows, in fact, that it is possible, in connexion with a problem of optimum allocation of resources:

either to solve the problem directly by reasoning about the flow of goods and services, without interpreting the Lagrange multipliers; or to solve it in a de-

[95] Dorfman, op. cit., pp. 213, 286, 413.

centralized way by interpreting the multipliers as a system of prices, price becoming the intermediary between the unit of production (or the consumer) and the rest of the economy.[96]

By showing the formal equivalence between the economic rationality of the capitalism of free competition and that of centralized planning, the mathematical theory of optimum deprives of all technical arguments those who would present the capitalist system as the only rational system, or the most rational of all systems. It thus destroys in its very principle the famous proof by Von Mises,[97] taken up by Hayek and so many others, of the impossibility of rational economic calculation in a socialist economy, and the exclusive possibility of carrying out such calculation on the basis of capitalist structures:

This is precisely what the price system does under competition and which no other system even promises to accomplish. It enables entrepreneurs, by watching the movement of comparatively few prices, as an engineer watches the hands of a few dials, to adjust their activities to those of their fellows.[98]

It destroys the attempts made by Lange and Barone to prove *on this same basis* the superiority of socialism. There would thus seem to be *no positive scientific reason* for preferring one system to another. To make this preference, *additional criteria from outside economics* would have to be brought in, and economics can neither confirm nor disprove these criteria which, though additional, are decisive, because they are no longer economic in character, but *ethical*. Even if the two systems are endowed with equal technical *effectiveness*, and even if the ends they pursue in the sphere of standard of living, leisure, etc., are identical, these two systems exclude each other in radical fashion as regards the *values* they respect. I will take from Pierre Massé a typical example of this theoretical approach.

Two value-systems cannot be reconciled unless they are embraced within a higher system. A violent crisis results from the clash between them . . . .

We cannot choose slavery as an economic organization. We cannot choose torture as a political instrument. In the classical problems of economic ~~~tion, physical constraints which are just as absolute as those delimit th~~

[96] Lesourne, 'Recherche d'un optimum de gestion dans la pensée éco
L'Univers économique, French edn, 1960.

[97] Von Mises, *Bureaucracy*, New Haven, 1944.

[98] Hayek, *The Road to Serfdom*, 1944, p. 36.

acceptable solutions, and only within this field do preferences intervene in order to dictate the final choice. Implicitly, values play the same role as physical possibilities. We do not ask whether a totalitarian regime might be more effective than our own: we want to retain at any cost a certain degree of freedom.[99]

A certain degree of freedom means here the freedom that exists for the capitalist to own capital and for the worker to sell his labour-power.

The structure of capitalism is presented here as an ethical value to be defended. But his 'certain degree of freedom' also means for Pierre Massé a freedom of the capitalists and of the workers which is 'limited' by the state representing the interests of the nation, 'as against the entrepreneur, the individual and the outsider'.

Massé is thus not in favour of the principal contention of those who, from Smith to Walras and from Pareto to Debreu, have put their trust in the laws of the market alone in order to attain economic rationality, on the sole condition that this market be a perfect one. Not because this 'intellectual construct' is false, but because it does not correspond to the real world; whereas Massé starts from the real world, from the existence of monopolies, trade unions and so on, all carrying on 'an *active* policy in so far as they can influence certain prices to their own advantage. The fact that these active policies can be carried on means a fundamental change in the nature of the problem'.[100] In reality, this monopolistic competition is accompanied by imperfect forecasting. The future is uncertain, and profit is subject to risk. Under these conditions, the market, in Massé's view, is found to be incapable of guiding decisions in relation to a distant future and of ensuring the future coherence of investments. The automatic working of the market, far from bringing into action the adjustment-tendencies that were supposed to lead the system of free competition towards optimum and equilibrium, 'tends to worsen the cycles rather than mitigate them'.[101] With the disappearance of free-competition capitalism, there has also disappeared that invisible and rational hand that ensured expansion and confined fluctuations to a mere 'undulation around equilibrium'.

Although Massé starts from a different reality, that of monopolistic competition, he does not start from an economic theory different from the classical one. He has to find theoretical solutions that will once again ensure harmony of interests and balanced expansion, taking account of

[99] Massé, *Le Plan* . . ., pp. 54–5.   [100] ibid., p. 45.   [101] ibid., p. 170.

the uncertainty of the future and without challenging the existence of capitalism. 'The solutions to be envisaged must fit into the framework of a free society.' His solution is the national plan, which does not rule out regulation by the market (useful for short-term decisions) but which opens up 'a future free from automatic effects'. This involves a conscious, willed intervention in real life, needing, if it is to succeed, to be the joint work of the state, the employers and the workers. The state is to be at the service of the nation, and arbiter between the private interests of the partners and between the present and the future. As for the workers, the task in relation to them is 'to associate them with an economic act which concerns them first and foremost, and to develop in them a feeling of participation which is based on facts'. A just incomes policy will reward everyone's efforts and stimulate their readiness to co-operate by ensuring that none of the three factors becomes 'isolated in either privilege or obligation'. The road opened up by the plan is thus a road of dialogue continued by an 'unwritten' contract,[102] combining the will to reform with the spirit of wisdom.[103]

Ensuring internal coherence in development, reducing without eliminating the uncertainty of the future and the conflicts between classes, developing accumulation of capital and increase in the returns needed for technical and social progress, the plan is to restore to monopoly capitalism a rationality equivalent to that of competitive capitalism. However, the rationality will not, for all that, be the same as the rationality of even a largely decentralized *socialist* system, for 'the basis of the problem is not merely the standard of living, it is the way of life'.

This new rationality of capitalism, which respects freedom, is thus fundamentally different from and essentially superior to that which can be attained by a socialist society, because it corresponds profoundly to

[102] Massé's terms are taken from F. Perroux: cf. the latter's *Economie et société*, p. 156. Elsewhere, Perroux writes firmly: 'The big monopolies necessarily take decisions that, by their consequences, exceed the scope of private dealings, and possess extensive and extra-legal means of nominating or promoting those who are to rule. There are few economically effective sanctions against them, they tend to be both arbiters and subjects of arbitration, rulers and ruled, for structural reasons that are not merely "alien" but actually inimical to the sovereignty of the people and of the nation' (p. 151). In the end, though, Perroux, like Galbraith, thinks that the countervailing powers of the trade unions and the state, and the 'vulnerability' of the monopolies can restore equilibrium and optimum. Cf. Perroux, *Théorie générale du progrès*, vol. 2.

[103] Massé, op. cit., p. 77.

the essential values of 'human nature', to ethical values, but this new rationality 'is only one step nearer to the ideal of rationality, which, like all ideals, is an unattainable asymptote'.[104]

And so we find ourselves back at the same result, despite Massé's starting-point being different from that of the economists of free competition and welfare. Established, acknowledged and experienced as an ethical 'value', the *de facto* freedom to be a capitalist or a worker becomes a freedom *de jure*. As a theoretical consequence, the introduction of this 'ethical' criterion finally eliminates the ambivalence and doubt that economics suffered under, owing to the innocence and ideological neutrality of the mathematical proofs of the optimum theory. Thus, by the admission of one of its most eminent practitioners, the 'sociologically neutral' optimum theory (and along with it the general and formal economic theory which called it forth) is found to be fundamentally incapable of defining the essential aspect, which is said to be ethical in character, of the specific rationality of the capitalist system and of economic rationality in general.

In the end, the problem of economic rationality, at its most complex level, appears to escape from the domain of economic science and of science in general, and to be related to a free adhesion to 'ethical values' which are themselves put forward as the 'true' values, those that correspond to 'true human nature'. Knowledge of the true essence of Man provides the decisive 'norm' for revealing the rationality of one system and the irrationality of another. Whether it serves to justify capitalism against the *ancien régime*, as with Adam Smith, or against socialism, as with Pierre Massé, or whether it serves to justify socialism against capitalism, as with the Utopian Socialists or the Marx of the *1844 Manuscripts*, the structure and result of the approach remain the same – economics seems to find its foundation in an ethical and philosophical ideology.

Is there then a method enabling us to analyse the rationality of an economic system without bringing in any *a priori* idea about freedom, values, human nature? This method exists: it was developed in Karl Marx's *Capital*. Before analysing it, however, we must sketch out the overall balance-sheet of the neo-classical and marginalist theories about how capitalism functions. Are they to be seen as deprived of all scientific validity by the ideological 'putsch' which eventually renders them incapable of accounting for the historical necessity of this system?

[104] ibid., p. 84.

Let us at once put a pseudo-problem out of the way. I am not going to hark back to the question of the 'innocence' of mathematics. The defining of optimum and the utilizing of mathematics do not argue in favour of any particular economic theory. By definition, a situation is an optimum situation when no element can be added to or subtracted from it without resulting in a failure to gain. By definition, this is an extreme situation, and this is what justifies the use of the various procedures of marginal calculation.

The problem lies elsewhere, in how to explain *profit*, the decisive criterion of capitalist economic rationality. The scientific validity of the economic theories of capitalism is to be judged by their capacity to explain the origin and essence of profit. But profit itself appears to depend on the prices and the exchange-value of commodities. The ultimate problem is thus that of explaining the origin and essence of this exchange-value and the process of price-formation.

For neo-classical theory, profit is the difference between the selling price and the cost of production of a commodity. It is a value added to the cost of production, and derived from the sale of this commodity. The rate of profit is the ratio between this value-added and the total amount of capital advanced.[105] Price is a rate of exchange of commodities that depends on the supply of and demand for them on a competitive market. These concepts are those used in current business practice, and they express what seems to happen between different variables. Everything seems to happen as though supply and demand ultimately determined the value of commodities, as though labour were a factor like the rest, as though capital returned a profit. Everything seems to happen as though the economic mechanism did not assume any exploitation of man by man. Thus, the current concepts of economics are doubly advantageous: they relate to business practice, and they do not reveal any exploitation of the workers. They are thus *the obligatory starting-point* of an *ideological theory* of how the capitalist system works. But do they correspond to *nothing* real, just because they serve an ideology? No, for profit is 'really' the value added which is a return on capital advanced, and supply and demand do really determine part of the mechanism of price formation.

[105] I am excluding the complications caused by the depreciation and obsolescence of this capital, etc.

The role of supply and demand
in the Marxist theory of value and prices

Accordingly, if there is an alternative theory[105a] to marginalism, this theory must be capable of accounting for the part played by supply and demand without making consumers' preferences the basis of commodity values, and it must explain the action of the different elements of capital on the rate of profit, while excluding the ideological theory of factorial incomes.

This theory is found in *Capital*, but, paradoxically, Marx chose not to develop it:

The actual movement of competition belongs beyond our scope, and we need present only the inner organization of the capitalist mode of production, in its ideal average, as it were.[106]

Though he calls supply and demand 'two driving elements of society', Marx only sketches an analysis of them, because, for him, far from being a mere starting-point, they are a complex end-point of economic analysis:

In further analysis, supply and demand presuppose the existence of different classes and sections of classes which divide the total revenue of a society and consume it among themselves as revenue, and, therefore, make up the demand created by revenue. While on the other hand it requires an insight into the overall structure of the capitalist production process for an understanding of the supply and demand created among themselves by producers as such.[107]

[105a] Let me insist once again that this choice is only apparent. Because supply and demand play a genuine part in the formation of certain prices, the marginalist theory of value seems to supply the general principle of a coherent explanation of value and prices. In face of this sham, Marxist theory *must* show that it can explain how prices are formed without resorting to the utility theory of value. The debate thus assumes the *aspect* of a choice, but it is a choice that is false in two.ways. First, because present-day marginalism (cf. pp. 27, 28, 29 of this book), as a general doctrine, is not a scientific theory but an enormous ideological construction which endeavours, by means of the theory of the marginal income of the factors of production, and the abstract assumption of a state of perfect competition, to prove that an optimum state of welfare can exist that satisfies every consumer, whatever his preferences, and does not call the capitalist system in question. Secondly, because, as we shall see, one can show that in their actual *practice* many marginalists do not stick to the doctrinal assumptions to which they refer, though they ascribe to these assumptions the validity of the results they obtain.

[106] *Capital*, III, FLPH edn, p. 810 [Translator's note: All references to vols. II and III of *Capital* are to this edn.]

[107] ibid., p. 191.

The fundamental reason for Marx's attitude, however, is not this. It arises from the fact that 'everything appears reversed in competition' and the 'inner but concealed essential pattern' of capitalist economic relations is disguised.[108] I am going to bring together the elements of the analysis of competition which is contained in *Capital* and compare them with certain results of the neo-classical theory.

I will begin with Marx's definitions of the concepts of use-value, exchange-value and price.

A commodity is, in the first place, an object outside us, a thing that by its properties satisfies human wants of some sort or another.[109]

For a thing to have exchange-value it must first have social use-value: 'Nothing can have value without being an object of utility. If the thing is useless, so is the labour contained in it; the labour does not count as labour, and therefore creates no value.'[110] Objects with different uses have no common yardstick. In exchange, however, 'one use-value is just as good as another, provided only it be present in sufficient quantity'. What matters to the producer is not the usefulness of his commodity but the proportion in which it can be exchanged for others. In order to be exchanged, however, commodities must have in common something of which each has more or less. This yardstick cannot arise from their utility but only from their common character as products of labour. The substance of value is the labour socially necessary for the production of commodities: 'The labour-time . . . required to produce an article under the normal conditions of production, and with the average degree of skill and intensity prevalent at the time.'[111] And this time 'changes with every variation in the productiveness of labour. This productiveness is determined by various circumstances, amongst others by the average amount of skill of the workmen, the state of science, and the degree of its practical application, the social organization of production, the extent and capabilities of the means of production, and by physical conditions.'[112]

The exchange-value of a commodity is thus the totality of the direct and indirect costs[113] of its production, on the basis of the average productivity of the productive capacities of society. It is easy to understand the usefulness of input-output analyses for measuring the expenditure of social labour needed for production of a definite quantity of goods.

---

[108] ibid., p. 205. [109] *Capital*, I, p. 1.
[110] ibid., p. 8. [111] ibid., p. 6. [112] ibid., p. 7. [113] ibid., pp. 181–2.

When all these commodities appear on the market in order to be sold, they have already cost society part of its resources and its disposable time, and this cost constitutes their exchange-value. They thus have *value*, but not as yet *price*. They must find a buyer if their owner is to recover his expenses and make a profit. Thus, when the commodity-value appears on the market in search of a price, it makes a '*salto mortale*',[114] a death-leap, in transforming itself into a certain sum of money. How large a sum will this be, that is the essence of the matter.

Price is therefore not exchange-value, and the process of price-formation is not the process whereby value is *formed* but that whereby value is *realized*. Here, in the midst of the process of price-formation, the working of supply and demand intervenes. The starting-point must be that 'a want has a limit like every other want'.[115] But there are in fact two yardsticks of want – that of real social want and that of want that is effective in terms of money.

The limits within which the need for commodities in the *market*, the demand, differs quantitatively from the *actual social* need, naturally vary considerably for different commodities.[116]

Here we encounter the fact of the elasticity of wants. 'Quantitatively, the definite social wants are very elastic and changing. Their fixedness is only apparent.'[117]

What connexion is there between the labour-value of the commodities that are offered on a market and the social want of them that is effective in money terms?

There exists an accidental rather than a necessary connexion between the total amount of social labour applied to a social article, i.e., between the aliquot part of society's total labour-power allocated to producing this article, or between the volume which the production of this article occupies in total production, on the one hand, and the volume whereby society seeks to satisfy the want gratified by the article in question, on the other.[118]

The productivity of labour thus has nothing to do with the utility of the products of labour. Here we are faced with a problem typical of those dealt with in calculating the efficiency of combinations of production, that efficiency which, as we have seen, is independent of anything concerned with the satisfaction of consumers. Though the utility of goods has

[114] ibid., p. 79.
[117] ibid., p. 185.
[115] ibid., p. 79.
[118] ibid., p. 183.
[116] *Capital*, III, p. 185.

nothing to do with the value of commodities, it nevertheless influences their price through the volume of the social wants to be satisfied. Indeed, according to Marx, prices coincide with value under the special conditions in which supply corresponds to demand, in which no monopoly affects either sale or purchase, and in which the higher productivity of some enterprises is balanced by the lower productivity of others.[119] Under these conditions 'the market-value is determined by the values of the commodities produced under average conditions'.[120] If the number of enterprises producing under bad conditions is not counter-balanced by the more productive ones, then it is that fraction of the commodities which is produced under bad conditions that fixes the market value. The opposite will be true in an opposite situation. Thus, the make-up of supply influences the relation between price and market-value. But price is equally determined by the structure of demand and its amount. 'If demand is only slightly greater than supply, the individual value of the unfavourably-produced commodities regulates the market-value.'[121] The fluctuations in supply and demand thus regulate the divergences between market price and market value. We accordingly have to envisage all the possible cases: supply variable, demand constant; supply constant, demand variable; supply and demand both variable, either in the same direction or in opposite directions; and supply and demand both constant. In reality they never coincide in the short run – 'or, if they do, it is by mere accident, hence scientifically $=0$, and to be regarded as not having occurred'.[122] In the middle or long run, however, they always do coincide.[123]

How is it to be explained that price changes occur when supply remains equal to demand? In most cases this happens because some producers have succeeded in producing more cheaply and selling in greater quantity, getting control of a substantial slice of the market by offering their goods at less than the market price, so that the others are gradually forced 'to introduce the cheaper mode of production, and one which reduces the socially necessary labour to a new, and lower, level'.

By way of the case in which supply and demand are equal, labour thus shows itself to be the substance of value. When they coincide, supply and demand, by ceasing to affect prices, cease to explain anything at all, and compel political economy to cease being satisfied with appearances.

[119] ibid., p. 178.   [120] ibid., p. 179.   [121] ibid., p. 181.
[122] ibid., p. 186.   [123] ibid., p. 186.

Political economy assumes that supply and demand coincide with one another. Why? To be able to study phenomena in their fundamental relations, in the form corresponding to their conception, that is, to study them independent of the appearances caused by the movement of supply and demand. The other reason is to find the actual tendencies of their movements and to some extent to record them.[124]

To sum up, in Marxist theory supply and demand play a determining role in explaining the divergences between market prices and market values and the tendency through competition and price-fluctuations for these divergences to decrease. The central point of these fluctuations is thus market value. Ultimately, the part played by supply and demand is explained on the basis of the Marxist theory of value.

To this confusion – determining prices through demand and supply, and at the same time determining supply and demand through prices – must be added that demand determines supply, just as supply determines demand, and production determines the market, as well as the market determines production.[125]

Thus, if there is no natural or artificial monopoly enabling super-profits to be made, and if the majority of enterprises are producing under equivalent conditions, then competition sooner or later levels out supply and effective demand, imposing a single market price on buyers and sellers, and this price corresponds roughly to the market value of these commodities, regardless of the costs of production of each separate enterprise. In the case in which supply corresponds in quantity and make-up to effective demand, the allocation of the factors and utilization of resources and incomes are optimum on the scale of society: the profits of the entrepreneurs are maximized, together with the satisfactions of the consumers. We see before us a situation of general equilibrium within the framework of the capitalist system, a situation that has been described from Adam Smith down to Debreu and the welfare theorists.

Furthermore since, in Marx's view, competition leads the market to-wards equilibrium by bringing prices around values, in the more or less long run, by way of their fluctuations, the system of capitalist free competition seems to be endowed with a more or less automatic rationality that makes it tend to equilibrium and optimum. We arrive at a paradoxical situation, with Marx joining Walras on the basis of a completely different theory of value. With Walras, pure competition explains equilibrium.

[124] ibid., p. 186.   [125] ibid., p. 187.

With Marx, the law of value makes itself felt through competition, and accounts for equilibrium.

For marginalism, demand determines prices, and these prices confer exchange-value on the factors of production that do not enter into ultimate consumption. For Marxism, the idea of price is more complex than that of exchange-value, and refers to the transformation of this value into a certain sum of money. This transformation takes place at the point where the exchange-value of commodities meets the effective wants of society, and this confrontation brings into action all the social conditions of production and of the distribution of incomes, etc. However, there is a connexion between the utility of commodities and their exchange-value, for a product does not function as a commodity unless it is socially useful. An enterprise must therefore sound out the wants of the market, or else create new wants through advertising, if it is to ensure that its product will sell and will return a profit. The necessary unity of use-value and exchange-value thus explains the part played by supply and demand in the formation of prices: it explains the link that remains between price and exchange-value, through all their differences, and it takes account of this *apparent origin and re-ascent* of exchange-value on the basis of ultimate demand, the appearance that is systematized by the theory of marginal utility.

With Marx, use-value thus plays a fundamental part, and at the same time exchange-value is not 'value' but the form taken by a product's value when the product becomes a commodity.

The 'value' of the commodity only expresses in a historically developed form something which equally existed in all other historical forms of society, even if *in a different form: namely, the social character of labour* in so far as it exists as the expenditure of 'social' labour power.

At this point the theory of value provides the framework for a comparative theory of economic systems.

It is only where production is under the actual, predetermining control of society that the latter establishes a relation between the volume of social labour-

---

[126] Marx's notes (1881–1882) on Adolf Wagner's *Treatise on Political Economy*. English translation by Angela Clifford in *Karl Marx on Value*, British and Irish Communist Organization, Belfast, 1971, p. 27.

time applied in producing definite articles, and the volume of the social want to be determined by these articles.[127]

But is Marx able, on the basis of his theory of value, to solve the two classical difficulties of the theoreticians of equilibrium and explain why the system of free competition also necessarily experiences disequilibria and periodical crises, and why the capitalism of free competition necessarily evolves towards monopoly capitalism? To solve these difficulties it is necessary to bring in the phenomenon of profit, the driving force and purpose of the capitalist system. By defining profit as the excess of selling price over cost of production one obviously explains nothing about its origin or its effects. What is profit? It is part of the exchange-value of commodities, that is, of the quantity of past and present labour socially necessary to produce them. We know that past labour – machines, raw materials, etc. – conserves its value only if it be really utilized in a new production-process, that is, combined with living labour. It transfers this value bit by bit to the products, and also loses it through the obsolescence of old techniques of production.

Added to this past value is a new value born of the utilization of the living labour-power of the workers. This labour-power has been paid for by wages, and, like any other commodity, its value is determined by the labour-time necessary to produce the means of subsistence the workers need, depending on the level of development of their wants (individual, family, occupational, etc.).[128]

If the production-process lasts only until the point is reached at which the worker has produced the equivalent of the value of the labour-power paid for by the capitalist, there is only production of value, but when the process continues beyond that limit we have production of surplus-value. Surplus-value is thus unpaid labour, labour given free of charge and appropriated by the capitalist. But this unpaid labour is not directly visible in capitalist society, unlike the labour-service imposed on the serf by his lord, because wages remove every trace of the division of the working day into paid and unpaid labour. Wages give unpaid labour 'the appearance of paid labour'.

This phenomenal form [wages], which makes the actual relation invisible, and, indeed, shows the direct opposite of that relation, forms the basis of all the

[127] *Capital*, III, p. 184.   [128] *Capital*, I, op. cit., pp. 150–1.

juridical notions of both labourer and capitalist, of all the mystifications of the capitalistic mode of production . . . .[129]

Since it is not wage-labour that determines value, but the amount of labour at society's disposal, Marxist theory provides us with the tool for analysing a socialist system in which wage-labour continues to exist although capitalist production-relations have disappeared.

When, however, wages appear to be the price of labour, surplus-value appears to be the product of capital, in the form of profit. Profit is surplus-value seen in relation to *all* the capital invested in the production of commodities. In relation to the total capital invested, the value added seems to have arisen equally from all the component parts of this capital – means of production, labour – whereas in reality only that part of the capital devoted to buying the use of labour-power contributes to the creation of this new value. Profit is therefore 'a converted form of surplus-value, a form in which its origin and the secret of its existence are obscured and extinguished'.[130]

Capital then appears as an 'automatic fetish', 'self-expanding value, money generating money'.[131] In everyday reality everything happens *as though* the theory of 'factor income' corresponded to practice and was continually being verified by it. In practice, indeed, every capitalist can observe that he actually influences his rate of profit, so as to increase it, whether he reduces the amount he spends on wages *or* the amount spent on plant, raw materials, etc., *or* the time taken by the processes of producing and circulating his commodities, that is, provided he economizes the labour, whether past or present, necessary for this production and circulation.

The chief means of reducing the time of production is higher labour productivity, which is commonly called industrial progress. . . . The chief means of reducing the time of circulation is improved communications (*Capital*, III, pp. 70-1).

In order to economize on capital expenditure, capitalism has to influence a number of variables. It has to reduce to the minimum the share of its capital tied up unproductively in the form of stocks of raw materials, unsold commodities, and so on. It has to affect its productive expenditure by increasing the productivity of labour. At the same time, the capitalist

---

[129] ibid., p. 550. [130] *Capital*, III, op. cit., p. 47. [131] ibid., p. 384.

benefits from the development of the productivity of other branches, the progress of science, inventions and their technological applications. To these external economies he adds internal ones due to the size of enterprises and the advantages of large-scale production.

Marx's analysis here touches upon the problems of the scientific organization of labour and the rationalization of enterprises that are today the subject-matter of operational research, psycho-sociology and so on. I have outlined these in connexion with the question of the rational behaviour of the entrepreneur and the worker. Ultimately, all capitalist *practice* tends to confirm the Marxist theory of value, since it aims at minimizing the labour-time necessary for the production and circulation of commodities. But this practice does not stop at the 'rational and strictly calculated utilization' of the conditions of labour.

In line with its contradictory and antagonistic nature, the capitalist mode of production proceeds to count the prodigious dissipation of the labourer's life and health, and the lowering of his living conditions, as an economy in the use of constant capital and thereby as a means of raising the rate of profit . . . The capitalist mode of production is generally, despite all its niggardliness, altogether too prodigal with its human material, just as, conversely, thanks to its method of distribution of products through commerce and manner of competition, it is very prodigal with its material means, and loses for society what it gains for the individual capitalist.[132]

In order to maximize his profits, the capitalist thus has to combine his factors of production in the best possible way, and calculate the marginal productivity of each factor when he varies the proportion it occupies in a particular productive combination. But a calculation like this never proves that each factor, taken separately from the rest, possesses a productivity of its own, and yet this is what is presumed proved by the theory of factor incomes and what is referred to as justifying the inequality of these incomes.

According to the theory of marginal productivity it is this *specific* productivity that governs and determines the worker's wages. It must be admitted, however, that the theory defined in this way cannot find either confirmation or the reverse in the facts and statistics, since specific productivity is *an abstraction, not a reality*.[133]

---

[132] ibid., p. 86.
[133] G. Pirou, *Economie libérale et économie dirigée*, S.E.D.E.S., 1946, p. 121: Pirou's own emphasis.

Again we arrive at the same result. The practice of rationalization of production seems to confirm the hypothesis that labour does not create value and profit, and yet at the same time this rationalization can only be explained on the basis of the labour theory of value. And this contradiction between appearance and essence in the functioning of the system finds its highest form in two facts which are also observed in practice – the tendency to the equalizing of the rate of profit in all branches of production, and the distribution of the mass of profit between interest on capital, ground-rent, entrepreneur's profit, commercial profit, taxes, and so on. With the tendency to equalization of the rate of profit, the latter has less and less direct relation to the degree of exploitation of labour-power imposed by each capitalist in his own enterprise. Finally, the forms of profit made by financiers, traders and landowners seem to be completely independent of the exploitation of the workers in the sphere of production.

And so, the closer we get to the concrete and particular forms of profit, the more the internal structure of the capitalist system becomes blurred and the less easy does it become to explain otherwise than by chance or by the ill-will or inadequate information of the economic agents either crises or the appearance of monopolies. When, on the contrary, the real essence of profit is known, a scientific explanation of crises and monopolies becomes possible.

Profit, as we know, is unpaid labour. Under the pressure of competition, each capitalist must, in order to maximize his profit, necessarily minimize his costs by developing the productivity of labour. All capital must therefore increase if it is to be conserved, and this accumulation can be achieved only by transforming profit into new means of production, into capital. Profit must therefore be made in order to increase capital, and capital must be accumulated in order to increase profit.

The rate of profit is the motive power of capitalist production. Things are produced only so long as they can be produced with a profit.[134]

The capitalist system necessarily tends therefore towards unlimited development of the productive forces and accumulation of capital, and this development is governed by the striving for profit and not by satisfaction of society's needs. At the same time, the development of consumption is subjected to the necessities of this accumulation and to the

[134] *Capital*, III, p. 254.

limits imposed on the effective demand of the majority of consumers by the necessity of maximizing the profits of the capitalist class. The functioning of the capitalist system of competition thus tends to develop a contradiction between society's capacity for production and for consumption, between the conditions for the production of surplus-value and those for its realization. This contradiction leads to phenomena of market saturation, to overproduction of capital and commodities, to a fall in the rate of profit in the industrial and commercial branches concerned. Disturbances in economic life make their appearance, stoppages in circulation and production, destruction of products and of capital, and, finally crises, the dimensions of which depend on the nature and number of the sectors in which the process of the realization of value and profit is frustrated.

The cohesion of the aggregate production imposes itself as a blind law upon the agents of production ... In this specific capitalist interrelation the surplus-product assumes a form in which its owner cannot offer it for consumption unless it first reconverts itself into capital for him.[135]

The anarchy of production, between competitors, the intense development of the productive forces, the limits set to consumption on the part of the masses by the maximization of capitalist profit, all inevitably cause imbalance in the working of the economy and destruction of part of society's wealth although society's wants are far from having been satisfied.

Not too much wealth is produced. But at times too much wealth is produced in its capitalistic, self-contradictory forms. ... The crises are always momentary and forcible solutions of the existing contradictions. They are violent eruptions which for a time restore the disturbed equilibrium.[136]

Marx's theory thus explains both the necessity of equilibrium and the necessity of disequilibrium in the working of the capitalist system. Crisis restores equilibrium, but when it ends, the concentration and centralization of capital has advanced further, through the elimination of capitalists who have been ruined. This concentration favours a further development of the productive forces. The crisis thus prepares, 'within

[135] ibid, pp. 251-2.
[136] ibid., pp. 253, 244. In the long run, if we leave aside the fluctuations and crises, we observe a steady increase in the capacity and volume of production.

capitalistic limits, a subsequent expansion of production',[137] and hastens the process of transition from the capitalism of free competition to monopoly capitalism.

Thus, Marx's theory explains both the necessity of the periodical crises of free-competition capitalism and that of the transition to monopoly capitalism.[138] Developing Marx's analysis of the rise of joint-stock companies, Engels wrote:

> The old boasted freedom of competition has reached the end of its tether. . . . And in every country this is taking place through the big industrialists of a certain branch joining in a cartel for the regulation of production. A committee fixes the quantity to be produced by each establishment and is the final authority for distributing the incoming orders. Occasionally even international cartels were established . . . .[139]

Ultimately, our ability to explain the overall rationality of the capitalist system, to discover the inner laws by which it functions and evolves, is based on our ability to discover the limits and contradictions of this system. We must therefore, if we are to accomplish our analysis of the rationality of the capitalist system and define the general concept of economic rationality, explore the idea of contradiction as it appears in Marx's *Capital*.

Before doing this we can evaluate for the last time the overall scientific implications of the neo-classical and marginalist theory. This theory starts from the current concepts that are made use of in practice, corresponding more or less to visible relationships, that is to say, to a certain level of reality. In so far as supply and demand play a real role in the formation of prices, as the many ways of economizing capital really do influence the rate of profit, and as it is possible to deduce certain conditions of equilibrium and growth from the external relations that exist between flows, stocks, prices, wages, value added, and so on, the contemporary theories can achieve a series of positive results, with the effective help of operations research, statistical calculation, etc. And these

[137] ibid., p. 250.

[138] Marx shows that the contradictions of the system dictate a constant expansion of the world market, at the same time 'demanding that countries in which capitalist production is not developed should consume and produce at a rate which suits the countries with capitalist production' (*Capital*, III, p. 252). The modernity of this analysis does not need demonstrating.

[139] ibid., p. 428: cf. *Anti-Dühring*, Lawrence and Wishart edn, 1936, pp. 305-6.

results can serve as 'norms' for 'rationalizing' the management of enter-prises or the direction of the national economy.

In so far, however, as it really adheres to the doctrinal assumptions of marginalism, economic analysis can achieve only limited results, for these assumptions do not take account of the 'internal structure' of the capitalist system, since this structure never shows itself directly on the surface of capitalist society but remains invisible in the course of current practical activity. This essential structure is the mechanism of the production of value and surplus-value. Now, no immediate experience reveals that the value of a commodity is the social labour necessary for its production, and surplus value never manifests itself as such, as unpaid labour, since it appears, in the form of profit, as the product of capital and not of labour. Labour itself appears as an object with a price – that is, wages – like any other commodity.

The visible movement, the apparent relations between the elements of the capitalist system, thus disguise and contradict the internal structure of this system.

The way in which surplus-value is transformed into the form of profit by way of the rate of profit is, however, a further development of the inversion of subject and object that takes place already in the process of production . . . On the one hand, the value, or the past labour, which dominates living labour, is incarnated in the capitalist. On the other hand, the labourer appears as bare material labour-power, as a commodity. Even in the simple relations of pro-duction this inverted relationship necessarily produces certain correspondingly inverted conceptions, a transposed consciousness which is further developed by the metamorphoses and modifications of the actual circulation process.[140]

The process of forming value and surplus-value is the deepest and most important level of the concrete reality of the capitalist system, that of the social relations of production which constitute this system. But this reality can appear only in inverted form, vanishing under the forms that are visible in practice. In practice, everything happens as though a certain object, money, had the power to grow by itself. The social relations of production are thus reified, materialized and inverted. Spontaneous consciousness is deceived by appearances. Unlike, however, what is said in the theses put forward by Marx in the *1844 Manuscripts*, it is no longer the subject or the consciousness that is alienated in the object, it is *reality*

---

[140] *Capital*, III, op. cit., p. 45.

that hides itself from consciousness and deceives the latter, it is the relations of commodity production based on the exploitation of wage-labour that cannot appear in any other way.

Economic science thus cannot start from current impressions, because this would mean that from the beginning it would be the prisoner of appearances and of the pseudo-evidence of experience. In so far as contemporary theories start from visible relations and proceed to systematize these, they rapidly turn into a vast ideological construction which begins with individuals' preferences in order to explain the exchange-value of commodities, and eliminates all reference to labour; which builds thereon a theory of factor income that eliminates any allusion to the exploitation of labour by capital; and which is finally crowned with a theory of general equilibrium and welfare that eliminates every reason for challenging capitalist production-relations.

It is an enchanted, topsy-turvy world, in which Monsieur le Capital and Madame la Terre do their ghost-walking as social characters and at the same time directly as mere things.[141]

By rejecting the chief assumptions of classical political economy, the marginalist theory marks a step backward as compared with the latter.

It is the great merit of classical economy to have destroyed this false appearance and illusion. . . . It did so by reducing interest to a portion of profit, and rent to the surplus above average profit, so that both of them converge in surplus value; and by representing the process of circulation as a mere metamorphosis of forms, and finally reducing value and surplus-value of commodities to labour in the direct production process. Nevertheless, even the best spokesmen of classical economy remain more or less in the grip of the world of illusion which their criticism had dissolved . . . .[142]

By starting from consumers' preferences, from the use-value of goods, in order to explain their exchange-value, the neo-classical and marginalist theory constitutes the most fully worked-out form of vulgar economy.

Vulgar economy actually does no more than interpret, systematize and defend in doctrinaire fashion the conceptions of the agents of bourgeois production who are entrapped in bourgeois production relations. It should not astonish us, then, that vulgar economy feels particularly at home in the estranged outward appearances of economic relations in which these *prima facie* absurd and perfect

[141] ibid., p. 809.   [142] ibid., p. 809.

contradictions appear and that these relations seem the more self-evident the more their internal relationships are concealed from it, although they are understandable to the popular mind.[143]

The intelligibility and coherence introduced by such theories belongs to the mode of thought that produces myths and not to scientific thinking. Myth makes theoretically possible what *seems* to be possible in fact, but *is not*. To talk of 'price of labour' is 'just as irrational as a yellow logarithm',[144] but this absurdity seems an obvious feature of everyday life. To talk, like the theologians of the Middle Ages, about the 'price of time', in order to account for the existence of interest, to build an immense psychological theory of 'the agio in favour of present goods as against future goods', as Böhm-Bawerk does,[145] to invoke 'time preference' and 'human impatience',[146] following Irving Fisher, provides no way of explaining the nature and degree of the rates of interest on capital lent – but it does enable one to justify their existence. These myths succeed, in the minds of their authors, in bringing into relation with each other magnitudes that are incommensurable, such as land, which in itself possesses no value, and rent, which is an exchange-value. Besides, these categories are meaningless in societies in which commodity production is poorly developed and where the land can never be treated as a commodity to be sold.

At the same time, however, if we are to evaluate the results achieved by contemporary non-Marxist economists,[147] we must analyse their *real practice*, which often contradicts the general doctrinal assumptions to which they officially give their allegiance. I will briefly mention a few instances.

Although they start from individuals and their preferences and invoke a formal definition of economics as the form taken by the purposive be-

---

[143] ibid., p. 797. [144] ibid., p. 798.

[145] Böhm-Bawerk, *The Positive Theory of Capital*, London, 1891, p. 280.

[146] I. Fisher, *The Theory of Interest*, 1933. In Fisher's work the psychological explanation by 'human impatience' is reinforced by an objective explanation concerning 'investment opportunity' which has a quite different basis. In Fisher we find the principle of the rate of discounting of the successive returns on a capital, on the basis of the example of ground rent (op. cit., p. 9). Cf. Massé, *Optimal Investment Decisions*, pp. 10–11. Let it be noted that Marx shows that ground rent is a fraction of the value of the harvest and that the price of land is an anticipated, discounted rent (*Capital*, III, p. 788).

[147] Cf. Dorfman, op. cit., p. 414, n. 1.

haviour of these individuals, contemporary theories actually introduce the relations between entrepreneurs and workers, that is, capitalist production-relations. They thus actually start from the system in order to analyse the behaviour of individuals, while appearing to deduce the system from the individuals.

By stating that in a situation of perfect competition the influence of each entrepreneur upon prices and upon his competitors may be considered as nil, they contradict their general assumption that prices are determined by individual behaviour. Similarly, if we assume that supply equals demand, we cannot explain the price-level that is established in a situation of competitive equilibrium on the basis of the subjective theory of value, but only on that of the labour theory of value.

The entire practice of operational research, scientific organization of labour, etc., is aimed at reducing costs of production in order to increase rates of profit. From this standpoint, value and profit thus appear as being determined by the productivity of social labour and its exploitation.

Finally, numerous economists or econometrists, such as Koopmans,[148] hesitate to cross the Rubicon that would make them ideologues and apologists:

A competitive equilibrium, even if it is also a Pareto optimum, may involve a more unequal distribution of income than is regarded as desirable from a social point of view. The concept of a Pareto optimum is insensitive to this consideration, and in that respect the term 'optimum' is a misnomer. A term like 'allocative efficiency' would have been more accurately descriptive of the concept.[149]

Thus, analysis of the results of contemporary non-Marxist research in economics is a much more complicated task than at first appears when we consider the general doctrines to which the researchers in question explicitly affirm their allegiance. These doctrines are, as we have seen, fundamentally incapable of constituting the general economic theory of the functioning of the capitalist economic system, and still less capable of furnishing the basis of a comparative theory of economic systems. When they are put forward as a general theory, they are nothing more than mythologies justifying, in a more or less subtle (even baroque) fashion, on the one hand the apparent functioning relations of the capitalist system and, on the other, the ideological prejudices which

---

[148] Koopmans, *Three Essays on the State of Economic Science*, p. 49.   [149] ibid.

dominate in advance the theoretical approaches adopted by these economists.

Marxism, on the contrary, provides the only complete theoretical basis for embracing all the rational elements in non-Marxist researches and developing these further; but in order to do this, Marxism *must itself develop* beyond the point at which Marx chose to stop in *Capital* – to deal with the forms of competition characteristic of private or state monopolies, the new forms of management of enterprises and of state intervention in the economy, the world market, and so on.

At the same time, Marxism can and must provide the theoretical tools needed to analyse and direct the operation of a socialist economic system:

> After the abolition of the capitalist mode of production, but still retaining social production, the determination of value continues to prevail in the sense that the regulation of labour-time and the distribution of social-labour among the various production groups, ultimately the book-keeping encompassing all this, become more essential than ever.[150]

I do not wish to discuss the specific rationality of the functioning of a socialist system and the theoretical rationality of the researches or the statements of economists in the socialist countries. I will say, though, that the theory of value as socially necessary labour, in the twofold sense of socially required for the production of socially useful goods, is alone capable of making possible the analysis and direction of the working of a socialist system. The practical discussions now going on about how to rationalize management of the national economy and of its branches and enterprises revolve around the most fruitful methods of calculating and minimizing the expenditure of labour socially necessary for producing the articles demanded by the plan.

When Alter, Kantorovich, Nemchinov, Pugachev and Weinstein[151] show that it is necessary to work out a 'cybernetics of retroactive relation-

---

[150] *Capital*, III, p. 830. See also the very important passage in Marx's *Critique of the Gotha and Erfurt Programmes* about the fund that must be formed in a non-capitalist economy in order to ensure expanded reproduction: 'These deductions from the "undiminished proceeds of labour" are an economic necessity and their magnitude is to be determined according to available means and forces, and partly by computations of probabilities. . . .'

[151] See the round-table discussion held in March 1964, extensive extracts from which were published in the special 'planning' number of *Recherches Internationales* (no. 47, pp. 66, 71, 76, 78, 79, 98, 105, 108).

ships' in order to measure the real social cost of production of goods, that these average and differential expenditures depend to a certain extent upon the volume of production predicted, and so upon the wants to be satisfied, that the optimum proportions for utilization of means have to be found, taking account of the structure and size of these wants, and that these proportions can be interpreted as prices or 'objectively determined valuations', we are neither in the world of marginalism nor in that of the three-factors theory, but in that of the Marxist theory of value. We need to appreciate, however, that these 'prices' are here merely instruments for accounting and management, and do not necessarily imply any circulation of money.[152]

In these discussions the contradictions in the development of the socialist countries are being clarified, together with the need to bring into correspondence the new productive forces and the relations of production. This implies a theory of correspondences and contradictions between structures, and brings me to the final stage of my argument, an analysis of the idea of contradiction in Marx's *Capital*.

Two conceptions of contradiction in Capital

Let us first review the occasions in connexion with which Marx talks about contradiction. First we have conflicts of interest between capitalists and between capitalist and workers. Then we have the crises through which are manifested the contradictions between production and consumption, between the conditions under which value and surplus-value are produced and the conditions for their realization, and these contradictions take us back to a fundamental contradiction between production-relations and productive forces. Finally we have the contradictions between capitalism and feudal structures, between capitalism and the petty property of peasants or craftsmen, between capitalism and socialism, etc. The mere listing of these occasions brings out the differences in nature and importance between these various contradictions, which we need to

---

[152] It is hard to understand the attitude of such economists as Boyarsky and Kolganov. Cf. Kolganov's article, 'Political economy and mathematics', in *Voprosy ekonomiki*, no. 12 of 1964, in which he claims to prove that the property of duality leads to absurd results, bringing together the incommensurable magnitudes of labour-value and use-value (the minimum of one being equal to the maximum of the other), whereas what are brought together are the productivity of social labour and all the combinations of products in which *social labour is recovered and realized*.

distinguish theoretically. We have here contradictions within a system and also contradictions between this system and others.

The capitalist mode of production is a combination of two structures: relations of production and productive forces. Capitalist production-relations are relations between the capitalist class and the working class. Each of these classes complements the other, assumes the other's existence. They differ by their specific relation to the means of production and capital. One of them has private ownership of these means of production and capital, while the other one is excluded from this ownership. The profit of the one is the unpaid labour of the other.

What are the characteristic features of this first contradiction?

It is *internal to a structure*. It is specific[153] to the capitalist mode of production. It defines it as such, distinguishing it from the other modes of production – slave-owning, feudal, etc. Being specific, it is characteristic of the system *from its beginning*, and the very working of the system endlessly reproduces it.[154] It is thus original in the sense that it is present from the beginning and goes on being present until the system disappears. It develops as the system develops, becoming transformed with the evolution of the capitalism of free competition into monopoly capitalism and with the trade-union and political organization of the working-class. This contradiction is an antagonistic one: the function of the one class is to exploit the other. It finds expression in the class struggle. It is visible and decipherable to a certain extent by the psychologist, by the sociologist who distinguishes between individuals and groups of differing function and status, by the economist and by the historian: finally, the philosopher can take it as his subject when he reflects upon justice, inequality, and so forth.

Is this fundamental antagonism, which seems to hold the foreground of history's scene, the fundamental contradiction of the capitalist mode of production? No, for Marx this consists in the contradiction between the development and socialization of the productive forces and the private ownership of the means of production.

[153] *Capital*, III, pp. 857–8.

[154] *Capital*, I, pp. 737–8: 'The capitalist system presupposes the complete separation of the labourers from all property in the means by which they can realise their labour. As soon as capitalist production is on its own legs, it not only maintains this separation, but reproduces it on a continually extending scale.' (The French translation of *Capital*, Editions Sociales, vol. 3, p. 155, includes in this passage the phrase: 'As this separation forms the basis of the capitalist system, the latter cannot become established without it.')

The contradiction, to put it in a very general way, consists in that the capitalist mode of production involves a tendency towards absolute development of the productive forces, regardless of the value and surplus-value it contains, and regardless of the social conditions under which capitalist production takes place; while, on the other hand, its aim is to preserve the value of the existing capital and promote its self-expansion to the highest limit . . . .[155]

How does this contradiction show itself?

'This collision appears partly in periodical crises.'[156] In a crisis the fundamental contradiction shows itself through the contradiction between production and consumption, between production and the circulation of commodities. More profoundly, it shows itself in the tendency of the rate of profit to fall.

What are the characteristic features of this contradiction?

It is not a contradiction within a structure but *between two structures*. It is thus not directly a contradiction between individuals or between groups but a contradiction between the structure of the productive forces (their more and more advanced socialization) and the structure of the production-relations (the private ownership of the productive forces).

Now, the paradox is that this contradiction, which is fundamental, since it has to account for the evolution of capitalism and for the necessity of its disappearance, is not *'original'*, in the sense that it did not exist in the system at its beginning. It appears 'at a certain stage',[157] at 'a certain stage of maturity'[158] of the system. And this stage is that of large-scale industry, that is, a certain stage of development of the productive forces. In a letter to Kugelmann Marx explained:

He would have seen that I described *large-scale industry* not only as the mother of the antagonism but also as the producer of the material and spiritual conditions for resolving the antagonism . . . .[159]

In the beginning, on the contrary, far from contradicting the development of the productive forces, capitalist production-relations stimulated them and caused them to progress impetuously, from the organization of the manufactories until the appearance of machine-production and large-scale industry. Mechanized industry, completing the separation between agriculture and the domestic industry of the countryside, which is swept away, 'conquers for industrial capital the entire home market' and gives

---

[155] *Capital*, III, p. 244.   [156] ibid., p. 258.   [157] ibid., p. 237.
[158] ibid., p. 861.   [159] In *Letters to Kugelmann*, 17 March 1868.

it 'that extension and consistence which the capitalist mode of production requires' when it has become 'combined, scientific', with the progress of the industrial division of labour. Before the coming of machinery, manufacturing production 'does not succeed in carrying out this transformation radically and completely'.[160]

So that, far from there having been, right from the start, a contradiction between capitalism and the development of the productive forces, there was originally a correspondence, a functional compatibility that was the source of the dynamism of technical progress and of the capitalist class. However, this very structural correspondence between capitalism and the productive forces meant non-correspondence between these productive forces and feudal production-relations. This non-correspondence was the source of the objective contradiction between feudal relations and capitalist relations, between the seignorial class and the capitalist class – because, for the industrial capitalist to exist, he must find himself facing workers who are masters of their own persons and who are obliged to sell their labour-power, that is, who are deprived of ownership of the means of production.[161]

'The immediate producer, the labourer, could only dispose of his own person after he had ceased to be attached to the soil and ceased to be the slave, serf or bondman of another. . . . The historical movement which changes the producers into wage-workers appears, on the one hand, as their emancipation from serfdom and from the fetters of the guilds . . . In this respect their [the industrial capitalists'] conquest of social power appears as the fruit of a victorious struggle both against feudal lordship and its revolting prerogatives, and against the guilds and the fetters they laid on the free development of production and the free exploitation of man by man.'[162]

Thus, the fundamental contradiction of the capitalist mode of production was born of the development of this mode of production, but it is not a development of a contradiction that was *present from the beginning* of the system. This contradiction appears without anyone having willed its appearance. It is thus unintentional. Though resulting from the actions of all the agents of the system and of the development of the system itself, it has never been anyone's conscious plan or the aim

[160] *Capital*, I, pp. 772, 774 (the words 'combined, scientific', are not in the English translation: see the French edition of *Capital*, I, Editions Sociales, vol. 3, p. 191).

[161] ibid., pp. 146–7.   [162] ibid., pp. 738–9.

pursued by any individual. Marx thus brings out the existence of *aspects of reality that do not relate to any consciousness and are not explicable by consciousness*. It is the mode of production itself, the investment of capital, that produces this result 'unconsciously'.[163]

This contradiction which is fundamental, unintentional and not present from the beginning, is not some opaque unwilled residue, the 'practico-inert'[164] sediment of intersubjective action. It is unintentional and purposeless, but transparent to science because it is 'significant'. It signalizes *the limits* that restrict the capacity of capitalist production-relations, based on private ownership, to correspond to the development of the productive forces to which they have given birth.

These limits are 'immanent' in capitalist production-relations,[165] and cannot be overcome because the investment of capital depends upon the exploitation of the great mass of producers. Thus it is these limits that express the objective *characteristics* of the capitalist mode of production (and so not those of the capitalists as individuals or as economic agents, nor those of the workers).

The entire capitalist mode of production is only a relative one, whose barriers are not absolute. They are absolute only for this mode, i.e., on its basis.[166]

These limits are the limits of invariability of the production-relations, taking into account the gigantic changes that occur in the productive forces. They are thus objective features of the system, and they furnish the basis both for its evolution and for its disappearance. They thus affect the system itself and are *the causality of the structure in relation to itself*.

'The *real barrier* of capitalist production is capital itself.'[167]

This causality of the structure thus operates everywhere without its efficacy being localizable in any particular spot. It always inserts itself between one event and another, so as to give to each of them all the dimensions it can have, conscious or otherwise, that is, its entire field of effect, intentional or not. Between a cause and its effects there is always the totality of the properties of the structure which give human action its objective dimensions. This rules out any simplifying conception of causality.

[163] *Capital*, III, p. 254.
[164] On this point it is necessary to compare Sartre's *Critique de la Raison dialectique* with what Marx says.
[165] *Capital*, III, p. 245.   [166] ibid., p. 252.   [167] ibid., p. 245: Marx's emphasis.

The objective properties of the capitalist mode of production thus provide the basis for the necessity of its evolution and of its abolition by the transformation of capitalist conditions of production based on private ownership into 'general, common, social conditions'.[168] By developing the productive forces, capital 'unconsciously creates the material requirements of a higher mode of production'.[169]

'Necessity and superiority' of socialism : science, ideology, humanism

What criterion defines the superiority of this mode of production? This criterion is the fact that the *structure* of socialist production-relations *corresponds* functionally to the new conditions of development of the gigantic, socialized productive forces created on the basis of capitalist production-relations. This criterion thus expresses the objective properties of a social structure, socialist production-relations, its historically-determined correspondence to conditions of development of specific productive forces. This correspondence is thus entirely independent of any *a priori* idea about happiness, Man's essence, 'true' freedom, and so on.

With Marx, for the first time, a science of man breaks through the ideological ring surrounding every thinker's consciousness and rendering him helpless and shamefaced when confronted with a value-judgment. It was *without starting from* any *a priori* criterion of rationality that Marx showed the necessity and superiority of a new mode of production, and thus provided the basis for a value-judgment.[169a] But this value-judgment was not a judgment on 'persons', and did not point to an advance in 'morality', a victory for 'ethical principles' in socialist society as compared with capitalist society. It was a judgment on the 'properties' of social relations.

Here individuals are dealt with only in so far as they are the personifications of economic categories, embodiments of particular class-relations and class-

---

[168] ibid., p. 259.   [169] ibid., p. 254: my emphasis, M.G.

[169a] In a letter to Lafargue, 11 August 1884, Engels wrote: 'Marx would protest against the economic "political and social ideal" which you attribute to him. When one is a "man of science" one does not have an ideal; one works out scientific results, and when one is a party man to boot, one fights to put them into practice. But when one has an ideal, one cannot be a man of science, for one starts out with preconceptions' (*Engels-Lafargue Correspondence*, vol. I, p. 235).

interests. My standpoint ... can less than any other make the individual responsible for relations whose creature he socially remains, however much he may subjectively raise himself above them.[170]

'Less than any other' does not mean that the individual has *no* responsibility, but that his *real* responsibility has limits that *do not depend* on him. The necessity of the evolution of a mode of production and of its replacement by another is thus not deduced from a norm that transcends history. It expresses the objective properties of a definite social structure, the particular conditions under which it appears and functions. By their structure, social relations are subject to determined laws of functioning, and their evolution establishes *new norms*, imposes necessities and opens up new *possibilities*. Social structures thus have a reality which is both governed by norms and also productive of norms.

The norm for judging the rationality of a mode of production is no longer based on a principle that transcends history, on an absolute definition of eternal justice and reason,[171] on an absolute knowledge that precedes, exceeds and illuminates science. The necessity for the appearance of a new mode of production does not arise from any purpose hidden in the mysteries of man's essence and revealed to the philosopher alone, be he materialist or idealist, for it is no longer possible to behold, in the historically-determined contradiction between capitalist production-relations and a certain level of the productive forces, the philosophical drama of the revolt of the 'true essence' of man against the dehumanized existence imposed upon the workers by the bourgeoisie.

In *Capital*, economic science is thus radically severed from all ideology and Marx once more breaks with 'the young Marx'.

Ultimately, the scientific explanation of the comparative rationality of a particular mode of production, of its relative superiority in comparison with another, is based on the hypothesis of a law of necessary correspondence between the structure of the production-relations and the

---

[170] *Capital*, I, op. cit., p. xix.

[171] For Marx, the content of the rules and principles of justice of a society correspond to the necessities of the functioning of its structures. For example, the forms and rules to which economic transactions must be subject under capitalism, if they are to be 'legal', are not based on the principles of 'natural law'.

'To speak here of natural justice ... is nonsense. ... This content is just whenever it corresponds, is appropriate, to the mode of production. It is unjust whenever it contradicts that mode. Slavery on the basis of capitalist production is unjust; likewise fraud in the quality of commodities' (*Capital*, III, pp. 333–4).

structure of the productive forces. This hypothesis enables Marx to analyse both the historical necessity of the appearance of capitalism and the necessity of its disappearance, and to establish both its relative rationality as compared with feudalism and its relative irrationality at another stage of its development. This historical rationality of capitalism from its origins and down to this stage of its development was the source of the ideology of Adam Smith and Ricardo, who saw in it the only economic system 'in conformity with human nature', and drew arguments from this against the oppressive forms of the *ancien régime*. Their ideology consisted precisely in transforming into a feature of 'human nature' the 'merely historical, transitory' necessity of a certain mode of production.[172] To this 'civilizing aspect' of capitalism during a certain historical period of its development there is added the fact that the development of the system 'unconsciously creates the conditions for a higher mode of production'.

It is one of the civilizing aspects of capital that it enforces this surplus-labour in a manner and under conditions which are more advantageous to the development of the productive forces, social relations, and the creation of the elements for a new and higher form than under the preceding forms of slavery, serfdom, etc. Thus, it gives rise to a stage, on the one hand, in which coercion and monopolization of social development (including its material and intellectual advantages) by one portion of society at the expense of another are eliminated; on the other hand, it creates the material means and embryonic conditions making it possible in a higher form of society to combine this surplus labour with a greater reduction of time devoted to labour in general.[173]

While there is no purposiveness in this process of creating the elements

---

[172] *Capital*, III, op. cit., p. 237. The formulations used by Marx in *Capital*, III, p. 800, and by Engels in *Anti-Dühring*, pp. 311–12, seem open to criticism as ideological, since Marx uses such expressions as 'the true realm of freedom', which he counterposes to 'the realm of necessity'. After the abolition of capitalism, 'socialized man, the associated producers, rationally regulating their interchange with Nature, bringing it under their common control, instead of being ruled by it as by the blind forces of Nature; and achieving this with the least expenditure of energy and under conditions most favourable to, and worthy of, their human nature. But it nonetheless still remains a realm of necessity'. Actually, what Marx is trying to say is that, the more the productive forces increase, the less will labour be *a necessity imposed by nature*, the more the share of necessary labour will diminish, the more will labour be a freely accepted activity directed towards other things than 'the sphere of actual material production'.

[173] *Capital*, III, p. 799.

of a new structure, everything happens *as if* capitalism's existence were 'justified' by its effects.

Development of the productive forces of social labour is the historical task and justification of capital.[174]

Marx's analysis, by showing that the capitalist system creates the conditions for the appearance of a higher mode of production, the superiority of which is independent of any preconceived idea about justice and human happiness, rules out in advance all the 'humanistic justifications' that can be given for this superiority. This does not mean that Marx paid no theoretical attention to the *real* problems that may find expression in the speculative and mystified form of an ideology that is humanistic, even though materialist. But theoretical confrontation of these real problems assumed for Marx no longer the form of ideological reflexion but that of determining the new possibilities of this new system, analysing the real conditions for their creation and operation.[174a] And these possibilities are then grasped as objective properties of the new structure. In the same way the capitalist system, by destroying the former feudal society and its forms of domination, had objectively created new possibilities for social progress. The superiority of a system in comparison with other systems contemporary with it thus expresses the range of objective possibilities offered by this system, in contrast to others, for solving the problems with which these systems are confronted.

The scientific analysis of the internal contradictions of the capitalist system that Marx carried out has thus enabled us, without ideological arbitrariness and keeping within the field of economic science, to discuss the fundamental problem of the *unintentional* rationality of an economic system, its *historical* rationality, the general laws of its *evolution* and of the necessary appearance of a mode of production with a *higher* rationality than its own. Before showing that it is possible to go further, towards a wider conception of social rationality, I shall try to define the specific

[174] ibid., p. 254.

[174a] It is obvious that awareness of the necessity of abolishing capitalism and going forward to socialism, and the slogans that give expression to this awareness and drive the revolutionary struggle forward, are derived from the fact that socialism is regarded as an *advance*, as a social way of life that is *higher in value* than the capitalist way of life. Awareness of new values and struggle to realize them are thus essential elements for a change to be brought about in the social system, but the historical necessity of this change is not based on these values.

structure of the idea of contradiction in Marx's writings, on the basis of my analysis of the two types of contradiction described in *Capital*. This definition will enable us to solve the difficult problem presented since Marx's own time: what is the fundamental difference between Hegel's dialectic and the dialectic of Marx?

The fundamental difference between Hegel's dialectic and Marx's

We know the terms of the problem, which are still obscured by the statements of Marx and Engels themselves.

On the one hand, Marx states that his dialectical method is 'the direct opposite' of Hegel's, and Engels that the dialectical method was 'unusable in the Hegelian form' and that only Marx's dialectic is 'rational'. At the same time Marx adds that 'it suffices to stand it [the Hegelian dialectic] on its feet for it to appear perfectly reasonable', and standing it on its feet means relieving it of the 'mystical aspects' introduced by Hegel's absolute idealism.

It is Louis Althusser's great merit that he has obliged us to see the difficulties entailed by the hypothesis of 'standing Hegel on his feet':

It is inconceivable that the essence of the dialectic in Hegel's work should not be contaminated by Hegelian ideology. . . . that the Hegelian dialectic could cease to be Hegelian and become Marxist by a simple, miraculous 'extraction' (*For Marx*, London, 1969, p. 91).

For Althusser the specific difference of Marx's dialectic lies in the fact that, in it, contradiction is in principle 'over-determined'. Although this reply contributes valid positive elements on a different level, it seems to me that it does not get to the heart of the matter. Let us look afresh at the problem. Marx describes two types of contradiction. One of these, internal to the structure of the production-relations, appears *before* the other, which emerges gradually *between the two structures* of the capitalist mode of production, namely, the production-relations and the productive forces. The first contradiction appears with the system and disappears with it. The second appears with the development of the system, and as an effect of the functioning of the first contradiction; but it is fundamental in character because it creates the material conditions for the possibility of the system's disappearance.

The relation between these two contradictions thus shows that the *first* contradiction, internal to the relations of production, *does not contain within itself all the conditions for its own solution.* The material conditions of this solution can exist only outside it, because the productive forces are a reality completely distinct from the production-relations and *not reducible* to them, a reality that has its own internal conditions of development and its own time-dimension.

The other conditions for the solution of the contradiction of the production-relations are to be found at the level of the political, cultural, etc., superstructures, and these too cannot be reduced to the relations of production, but have their own form of development. Accordingly, for Marx the solution of a contradiction which is internal to the structure of the production-relations is not created by the mere internal development of this contradiction. The bulk of the conditions for this solution lie outside this contradiction and are not reducible to what it contains.

However, the possibility of solving the second contradiction, between the two structures of the economic system, arises from the internal development of this system (and, as we shall see, from the movement of all the social structures). The solution of this second contradiction consists in changing the structure of the production-relations so as to *bring it into correspondence* with that of the productive forces. Now, this change amounts to abolishing private ownership of the means of production, and so doing away with *the very basis of the internal contradiction* of the capitalist production-relations. But this can be done only at a certain stage in the development of the productive forces. Thus, the contradictions between classes within the relations of production may go on 'boiling' indefinitely, but no solution will necessarily emerge if there is no development of the productive forces. (On the contrary, there may be cyclical reproduction of social conflicts, stagnation,[175] etc.)

Ultimately, my analysis rules out the assumption by Marx of an 'identity of opposites'. This assumption was actually invented by Hegel in order to show that there is an *internal solution to the internal contradiction of a structure.* In order that there may be such a solution, each of the contradictory elements within the structure must be at once itself and its opposite. The thesis must be both itself and also its opposite, the antithesis, if the synthesis is to be already contained in their contradictions. For Marx this is basically out of the question, since neither the elements that contradict each other within a structure, nor the structures that

[175] Cf. the problems of the 'Asiatic mode of production'.

contradict each other within a system *can be reduced one to another* – neither is identical with the other.

This shows that the identity of opposites, a fundamental structure of the Hegelian dialectic, is *not necessary* except for the purpose of providing 'proofs' of absolute idealism, *giving a foundation to Hegelianism* as the Absolute Knowledge of the Absolute Spirit, a totality that contradicts itself in itself, both outside in Nature and inside in the Logos, and yet remains identical with itself throughout all its contradictions. The identity of opposites is in fact a magic device that Hegel needs to employ in order to build the 'palace of ideas'[176] of absolute knowledge and to give an appearance of rationality to that ideological 'twist' which serves as the unprovable starting-point for absolute idealism. Hegel's philosophical idealism thus determines the specific internal structure of the idea of contradiction in Hegel; and this structure, based on the principle of the identity of opposites, is the exact contrary of Marx's and makes the dialectic *useless for scientific work*.[177] By means of the assumption of the identity of opposites one can, in fact, prove anything, and so prove nothing.

It is therefore understandable that Marx should have declared so early as the *Contribution to the Critique of Political Economy*:

'Nothing is simpler for a Hegelian than to assume that production and consumption are identical . . .',[178] adding: 'The conclusion which follows [for Marx] . . . is not that production, distribution, exchange and consumption are identical, but that they are links of a single whole, different aspects of one unit.'[179]

---

[176] Kierkegaard uses this, in *The Concept of Angst*, as an argument against Hegel and against rationalism, and opens the way to existentialism.

[177] When Lenin says that the dialectic is 'the theory of the identity of opposites' or 'the study of the contradiction in the very essence of things', it seems to me that he erroneously treats these two definitions as equivalent. Similarly, Mao Tse-tung constantly confuses the *unity* of opposites with the *identity* of opposites: 'How then can we speak of identity or unity [of opposites]? The reason is that the contradictory aspects cannot exist in isolation. Without the other aspect, which is opposed to it, each aspect loses the condition of its existence. . . . Without landlords, there would be no tenant-peasants; without tenant-peasants there would also be no landlords. Without the bourgeoisie, there would be no proletariat; without the proletariat, there would also be no bourgeoisie. . . . All opposite elements are like this; because of certain conditions they are on the one hand opposed to each other and on the other hand they are interconnected, interpenetrated, interpermeated and interdependent; this character is identity' (*On Contradiction*, 1952 pamphlet edn, pp. 54–5).

[178] Marx, *Contribution* . . ., p. 199.   [179] ibid., p. 204.

And Engels, in *Anti-Dühring*, defends Marx's dialectical method by showing that it does not mean 'a state of mental incompetence' wherein, 'as a result of certain mixed and misconceived ideas', it turns out that 'everything is all one in the end',[180] and wherein 'the negation of the negation has to serve as the midwife to deliver the future from the womb of the past', and consists in 'the childish pastime of ... alternately declaring that a rose is a rose and that it is not a rose'.[181]

This is where Althusser's analyses are really telling. The assumption of the identity of opposites guarantees Hegel at any moment an internal, imaginary solution to the internal contradictions he analyses, and this solution is more often than not a magical, ideological operation inside a 'simple' dialectic.

How are we to explain in this case the inability of commentators on Marx to locate the radical difference between Hegel and Marx? The answer is not at all complicated. *The theoretical distinction* between the two types of contradiction, within a structure and between structures, clarifying their mutual articulation, was never explicitly carried out and developed by Marx and Engels. This being so, the contradiction that 'leapt to the eye' was the contradiction between capitalists and workers, and the second contradiction was confused with that one, i.e. with a contradiction that was internal to one of the structures. People were then sucked into the orbit of the mystical and mystifying dialectic of Hegel, the fascinating dialectic of the identity of opposites and the internal solution, and so forth. The ambiguous formulations of Marx and Engels did not help to exorcise this fascination, nor did the anti-scientific habits of dogmatic Marxism. For Marx, 'the capitalist mode of appropriation, the result of the capitalist mode of production, produces capitalist private property. This is the first negation of individual private property, as founded on the labour of the proprietor. But capitalist production begets, with the inexorability of a law of Nature, its own negation. It is the negation of the negation.'[181a]

But what for Marx is merely a metaphor, a way of talking about the movement of capitalism, becomes with Engels 'an extremely general – and for this reason extremely comprehensive and important – law of development of Nature, history and thought'.[182]

[180] Engels, *Anti-Dühring*, p. 139.

[181] ibid., pp. 150, 159.   [181a] *Capital*, I, p. 789.

[182] *Anti-Dühring*, p. 157. Cf. on pp. 154-5, the seventeen-line summary of the

In fact, so long as the specific character of the idea of contradiction in Marx's thought remained unanalysed, the idea of the 'negation of the negation' was the only Hegelian concept that seemed to remain *rational* after the mystification of the identity of opposites had been expelled.[182a]

We must, then, necessarily abandon several fundamental concepts of the Hegelian dialectic and replace them with others if we are to make use of those Hegelian concepts that remain valid to a certain degree, such as those of quantity, quality, transformation of quantity into quality,[183] etc., and if we are to develop further Mao's distinctions between principal contradiction and secondary contradiction, principal and secondary aspects of the contradiction, unequal development of contradictions, and so on.

In this way, Marx's analysis of the fundamental concept of contradiction between structures coincides with the most advanced scientific practice. This concept renders explicit certain objective structures of properties, the objective *limits* of their capacity to reproduce themselves, remaining *essentially unchanging* (allowing for variations in the internal and external conditions in which they function), and, *more profoundly*, to *reproduce* their relations, *their connexion with other structures*. What causes a contradiction to appear is the appearance of a limit, a threshold, to the conditions in which a structure does not change. Beyond this limit a change of structure must occur. From this standpoint the idea of contradiction that I am putting forward would perhaps fit easily into the framework of cybernetics. The latter explores the extreme possibilities and the internal regulators which enable any system whatever – physiological, economic or any other – to maintain itself through the ups and downs caused by variations in the internal and external conditions under which it functions. And this analysis brings closer together the sciences of nature and those of man. To put the point humorously, it could be said, that, if it was an ice-age that caused the dinosaur to vanish from the surface of the globe, then this species did not die out owing to the 'spontaneous development of its internal contradictions' but owing to a

---

dialectical evolution of mankind from primitive communism to ultimate communism, by way of private property.

[182a] I agree with Althusser when he says that Stalin's expulsion of the 'negation of the negation' from the domain of the Marxist dialectic 'might be evidence of the real perspicacity of its author' (*For Marx*, p. 200, note).

[183] *Capital*, I, p. 296: and Engels's commentary in *Anti-Dühring*, pp. 140–1.

contradiction between its internal physiological structure and 'the structure of the external conditions' in which it existed.

The theory of contradiction that I propose would thus restore to the dialectic its scientific character and, for the same reasons, this scientific dialectic cannot but be materialistic. If the objective properties of structures are the causes of their functioning, evolution and transformation, if the contradictions that arise from the functioning of a structure are partly conditioned, as regards their appearance and their solution, *from outside* this structure, then no *inner purposiveness* governs the evolution of nature and history.

The analysis I have made of the contradiction between production-relations and productive forces relates only to the capitalist mode of production. Marx extends it generally to all modes of production:

> Each specific historical form of this process [of production] further develops its material foundations and social forms. Whenever a certain stage of maturity has been reached, the specific historical form is discarded and makes way for a higher one.[184]

At the same time, Marx reminds us that 'this does not prevent the same economic basis – the same from the standpoint of its main conditions – due to innumerable different empirical circumstances, natural environment, racial relations, external historical influences, etc., from showing infinite variations and gradations in appearance, which can be ascertained only by analysis of the empirically given circumstances'.[185]

Finally, he emphasizes that within one and the same society there may co-exist and be interconnected, more or less well, modes of production that were born at different epochs, with, generally speaking, one of these dominant over the others. For example, in a society dominated by capitalism, small-scale individual ownership and vestiges of feudal property may survive in agriculture for a long time. On this theoretical basis it would be possible to undertake a comparative analysis of the multilinear evolution of economic systems. However, accounting for the evolution of economic systems is not the same as accounting for the evolution of societies, since we still have to explain their political structures, their religious and family structures, and so on. Marx generalizes the applicability of the hypothesis that structures must necessarily correspond, by assuming that to the economic infrastructure of a society

[184] *Capital*, III, p. 861.   [185] ibid., p. 772.

there correspond determined political, religious and family super-structures:

> In the social production of their existence, men inevitably enter into ... relations of production appropriate to a given stage in the development of their material forces of production. The totality of these relations of production constitutes the economic structure of society, the real foundation on which arise a legal and political superstructure and to which correspond definite forms of social consciousness.[186]

Just as the relations of production are distinguished from the productive forces, and yet influence and are influenced by them, so the infrastructure influences and is influenced by the superstructures. In the working of this reciprocal causality, however, Marx assumes that the economic structure 'ultimately'[187] plays a determining role.

> The mode of production of material life conditions the general process of social, political and intellectual life .... The changes in the economic foundation lead sooner or later to the transformation of the whole immense superstructure.[188]

The conceptions of correspondence and of hierarchy of structures

How are we to understand this determining role of the economy in a theory which assumes that each structure – social, kinship, political, etc. – has its own content, not reducible to any other, and its own mode and time-scale of evolution? Two kinds of explanation are ruled out by this irreducibility of the structures. On the one hand, the non-economic structures cannot emerge from the economic relations – the causal role played by the economy cannot be presented as the birth of the super-structure out of the womb of the infrastructure. On the other, the non-economic structures are not mere phenomena accompanying economic activity and playing only a passive role in social life, whereas economic relations alone function as active causes, producing more or less 'auto-matic' effects.[188] In both cases it is hard to see by what miraculous

[186] Marx, *Contribution* . . ., p. 20.

[187] Engels, letter to Joseph Bloch, 21 September 1890. 'If somebody twists this into saying that the economic element is the *only* determining one, he transforms this into a meaningless, abstract, senseless phrase' (*Marx-Engels Correspondence*, FLPH edn, p. 499).

[188] *Contribution*, pp. 20–1: see also Engels, letter to Heinz Starkenburg, 25 January 1894.

alchemy the economy could turn into kinship, or for what mysterious reason the economy should need to conceal itself (badly) under the form of kinship. We must therefore look elsewhere.

Let us consider the production-process in our capitalist society. The production-relations between capitalists and workers, the obligation upon the latter to work for the former, who own the means of production, seem to be largely independent of the religious, political and even family ties that may exist between these classes. In an archaic society, however, the situation is not the same. The economist can make out easily enough what the productive forces are in these societies (hunting, fishing, agriculture, cattle-breeding) but he finds it hard to make out the relations of production. At any rate, he usually does not perceive what they are until he turns to examine the functioning of kinship. The kinship relations of individuals and groups seem to be the source of their rights to use land and products, their obligations to work for others, to make gifts and so on. They likewise seem to be the source of the political and religious functions exercised by certain individuals within the group. In a society like this, kinship relations dominate social life. How, then, are we to understand the 'ultimately' determining role of the economy?[188a]

We need, in fact, to analyse more closely these kinship relations, for if they determine the places occupied by individuals in production, their rights to land and goods, their obligations in respect of work and gifts,

---

[188a] Marx himself discussed this type of problem when he replied, in a footnote to the first volume of *Capital* (1867), to the attacks levelled by a German-American paper at his *Contribution to the Critique of Political Economy*, published in 1859:

'In the estimation of that paper, my view that each special mode of production and the social relations corresponding to it, in short, that the economic structure of society is the real basis on which the juridical and political superstructure is raised, and to which definite social forms of thought correspond; that the mode of production determines the character of the social, political and intellectual life generally, all this is very true for our own times, in which material interests preponderate, but not for the Middle Ages, in which Catholicism, or for Athens and Rome, where politics, reigned supreme. In the first place it strikes one as an odd thing for anyone to suppose that these well-worn phrases about the Middle Ages and the ancient world are unknown to anyone else. This much, however, is clear, that the Middle Ages could not live on Catholicism, nor the ancient world on politics. On the contrary, it is the mode in which they gained a livelihood that explains why here politics, and there Catholicism, played the chief part.... On the other hand, Don Quixote long ago paid the penalty for wrongly imagining that knight errantry was compatible with all economical forms of society' (*Capital*, I, 54). Nevertheless, Marx did not provide any theory of this 'explanation'.

etc, then they *function*[189] as production-relations, just as they function as
political, religious, etc., relations.[189a] Kinship is thus here *both* infrastruc-

[189] When Engels says in *The Origin of the Family* that 'the decisive factor in history is,
in the last resort, the production and reproduction of immediate life. But this itself is of
a twofold character. On the one hand, the production of the means of subsistence, of
food, clothing and shelter and the tools requisite thereto; on the other, the production
of human beings themselves, the propagation of the species' (FLPH edn, pp. 13–14),
his formulation is inaccurate, for kinship functions in primitive societies *both* as production-relations and as relations for the propagation of the species. Kinship thus does not
play a determining role *alongside* the economy, since it is itself an element of the economic
infrastructure. Later in his analysis, Engels tries to define the *limits* to the ability of old
forms of social organization to adapt themselves to new circumstances, and describes
the upheavals that result from 'the incompatibility of the two' (p. 14). In principle, this
approach seems to me completely valid.

[189a] Because of the many functions fulfilled by kinship, Beattie and other anthropologists have claimed that kinship has no content of its own but is merely a container,
the symbolic form in which the content of social life – economic, political, religious,
etc., relations – is expressed, in other words, that kinship is only a language, a means of
expression. Without denying that kinship functions as a symbolic language of social life,
Schneider objects that kinship also possesses a content of its own, which emerges if one
subtracts from its functioning the economic, political and religious *aspects* it possesses.
We see then the totality of relations of consanguinity and marriage that serve as means
of expression of social life and constitute the *terms* of the symbolic language of kinship.
The latter is thus here both a particular content of social life and that which serves as
the mode of appearance and expression of every other content.

However, by seeking in this way to identify a specific content of kinship, Schneider
finds it hard not to fall into the biologism that he condemns in Gellner. Everyone knows
that the totality of biological relationships of consanguinity and marriage is not kinship, because a system of kinship is always a particular 'group' of these relationships, within which
descent and marriage-connexions are socially regulated. And it is because these relationships are selected and 'retained' that real kinship is not a biological fact but a *social* one.

The mistake common to Beattie and to Schneider is that of looking *outside of* the
economic, political and religious domains for the content of this type of kinship, since
the latter is neither an external form nor a residual content, but functions *directly*,
internally, as economic, political, etc., relations, and thereby functions as the mode of
expression of social life, the symbolic form of this life.

The scientific problem is thus to determine why this is so in a number of types of
society, and, on the methodological plane, the conclusion seems clear that the pairs of
concepts 'Form/Basis', 'Container/Content', are unsuitable for explaining the way social
structures function. (See Gellner, 'Ideal language and kinship structures', in *Philosophy
of Science*, vol. 24, 1957: Needham 'Descent systems and ideal language', in ibid.,
vol. 27, 1960: Gellner, 'The Concept of kinship', in ibid., vol. 27, 1960; Barnes,
'Physical and social kinship', in ibid., vol. 28, 1961; Gellner, 'Nature and society in
social anthropology', in ibid., vol. 30, 1963; Schneider, 'The Nature of kinship', in
Man, Nov.–Dec., 1964.)

ture and superstructure. Accordingly, the correspondence between productive forces and production-relations is *at the same time* correspondence between economy and kinship. We may thus assume a correspondence between the general structure of the productive forces, their low level of development which necessitates cooperation between individuals, and therefore life in groups, if people are to survive, and the general structure of kinship in archaic societies.[190] What is of interest to us here is not the correspondence between a certain form of economy and a certain form of kinship (unilinear, bilinear, etc.), but the fact that these systems take on, generally speaking, a much larger number of functions than in our own societies, and this may perhaps account for their more complex internal structure. Thus, the determining role of the economy, apparently contradicted by the dominant role of kinship, is rediscovered in this dominant role, since kinship functions as, *inter alia*, production-relations. Here the relationship between economy and kinship appears as an *internal* relationship – *without* the economic relationships of the kinsfolk *merging*, for all that, with their political, sexual, etc., relationships.

Understanding the evolution of archaic societies means explaining the appearance of new functions of the social structures and the disappearance of old ones, and thereby the actual evolution of these structures. Let us take an imaginary example. Let us suppose that new productive forces make their appearance in an archaic society, transform the conditions of production profoundly, and lead to a considerable growth of population. It may be assumed that these new conditions of production, making possible new kinds of work – draining land, irrigation, terrace-cultivation, etc. – require new forms of authority and modify production-relations thus affecting kinship from the angle of its economic and political functions. Beyond a certain limit, the kinship relations will no

[190] See, in this connexion, Claude Lévi-Strauss: 'The situation is altogether different in groups where the satisfaction of economic needs rests wholly on the conjugal society and the division of labour between the sexes. Not only do man and wife have different technical specialisations, one depending on the other for the manufacture of objects necessary for their daily tasks, but they are each employed in producing different food-stuffs. Accordingly, a complete, and above all regular, food supply indeed depends on that "production co-operative", the household. . . . It would be almost impossible for an individual by himself to survive, especially at the most primitive levels, where hunting and gardening as well as collecting and gathering, are made hazardous by the harshness of the geographical environment and the rudimentary nature of techniques' (*Elementary Structures of Kinship*, London, 1969, pp. 38–9).

longer correspond to these new social conditions, these new functions. The latter will go on developing beyond the bounds of kinship, and give rise to social structures distinct from the old kinship-relations – political and religious structures, for example. These new relations (e.g. the Olmec state, the Inca state, the religions of the Sun, etc.) proceed to function as new production-relations. Given this assumption, the necessity for the production-relations to correspond to the productive forces would modify the overall structure of the society, and the nature and importance of each structure. Kinship-relations would slip into a different and secondary role, while the political and religious relations fulfilling new functions would come to hold the centre of the stage. The functions, form, importance and place of each structure would have changed at the same time as the other structures changed. Now, this *relationship* between each separate structure and all the rest constitutes *the actual structure of society*. This relationship, determined by the functions and importance of each structure, gives expression to the intimate correspondence between the various structures. This correspondence provides the basis for the *specific causality* of each structure, and has limits that reveal the objective properties of each structure. With these limits, contradictions between structures make their appearance.

These hypotheses[190a] perhaps make it possible for us to take up again some problems that render difficult the existence of a science of history, that is, a science of the differential evolution of societies which is at the same time a scientific theory of kinship, politics, world-conceptions, and so on.

They enable us to eliminate the myth of a 'stage' of mankind's history when men lived either without an economy, or without kinship-relations, or without any world-conception. As long as mankind has existed, *these functions* have existed, with determined content and form, content and form that have been *transformed* with and by history.

[190a] These hypotheses are not imaginary. They sum up the findings of many anthropologists and ethnologists of our time. As an example, let me quote the big discussion, in the *Journal of the Polynesian Society* in 1957, of Irving Goldman's hypotheses regarding the evolution of Polynesian societies, the appearance of states and monarchies, of new forms of religion in certain islands (Tahiti, etc.). Cf. the articles by W. Mead, W. Goodenough and Sahlins and the criticisms by Hawthorn and C. Belshaw. On the problem of the appearance of the state, see the discussion on the 'Asiatic mode of production' in *La Pensée*, nos 114 and 122, and my article 'La notion de mode de production asiatique', in *Les Temps Modernes*, May 1965.

New political relations – a tribal authority, for example – make their appearance in some societies, seeming to extend kinship, to emerge from it and then to become opposed to it. This is not, however, a case of kinship mysteriously becoming transformed into political relationships. It is the political function that was present in the old kinship-relations, developing and becoming transformed on the basis of new problems. With the formation of classes within a tribe, a fresh transformation of the forms and functions of political authority becomes necessary. The State appears. Thus, scientific study of the evolution of social structures (kinship, politics, religion, economy, etc.) would mean studying the evolution of their functions, the transformations of their internal organization and of their internal correspondence with each other. But the forms of internal correspondence vary with each type of society, since in some cases kinship-relations and in others political relations really function as production-relations, and are both infrastructure and superstructure. For them to be superstructure alone, for kinship to be 'specialized', to be 'only' kinship, that is, a social relationship which ensures the reproduction of the human species and which retains an economic *aspect* without intervening *directly* in the economy, some very special historical conditions are needed.[191] The appearance of class relations, of forms of exploitation of men who are more or less excluded from any bond of kindred or any political relationship with their exploiters (slaves, serfs, etc.), creates some of these conditions. With industrial capitalism the separation of family relationships from both the conditions of production and the circulation of goods as commodities is carried even further, and gradually comes to dominate even agriculture, the sector in which family economy and survivals of village solidarity continue to exist longest. With capitalism, the internal correspondence between the economy and kinship seems to give way more and more to an external, independent relationship, although in fact the new functions of the family stand in a relationship of internal correspondence with the new conditions of production. Moreover, in so far as the capitalist mode of production develops, in societies that vary widely as regards race, culture, etc., the relations between economy, kinship and religion seem to grow more and more external. In the assumptions he makes and the approaches he adopts, the Western economist (and very often the

[191] Cf. Smelser, 'Mechanisms of change and adjustment to change', in *Industrialisation and Society*, 1966, pp. 32–54.

Marxist economist) spontaneously introduces the structures of his own society, or at least the outward functioning of these structures. He thus shows a spontaneous tendency to treat kinship and religion as 'exogenous' variables, and to seek in the other types of society an 'autonomous' economic rationality. Hence the setbacks he meets with in Asia and Africa, and the pejorative judgments he delivers on the irrationality of the 'natives'' behaviour. Only an economic theory that systematically takes account of the structure of the social relations implied in each type of economy can become a comparative theory.

We must go further, though, if we are to analyse the economic rationality of different types of society. We have seen that, depending on the particular type of society, one structure or another holds the foreground of the social scene, as the dominant one. Thus, the correspondence between the structures accounts for the specific role played by one of them in relation to the rest. This dominant role of a certain structure does not mean that it is 'overdetermined'. In order to become a general concept, the concept of 'overdetermination' must lose the precise content it has in linguistics and psychoanalysis and keep only its ambiguous, popular meaning of 'too much determined'. There is never too much determination to explain the role of a structure, but there *is* a specific determination or at least a specific order of determinations affecting it. I do not see any point at present in ascribing to this idea the value of a general and fundamental concept.[192] Actually, the dominant role played by a given structure means that there is a *hierarchy* of structures in a society, and this hierarchy, it seems to me, is the basis of the hierarchy of *'values'* i.e., of norms of prescribed behaviour, and, through this hierarchy of values, the basis of the hierarchy of needs of individuals and groups. In order to explain the rationality of the economic behaviour of individuals it is thus not sufficient to know the hierarchy of their needs and explain the social structures in accordance with this.

On the contrary, one has to start from the structures, the relationship between them and their precise roles, if one is to understand the rationality of individuals' behaviour. When economists see communities devoting a big proportion of their income to non-economic activities, and deplore the absence of a 'true spirit of enterprise' in these communities, their lack of any sense of economic rationality, the explanation is not to

[192] I disagree on this point (of vocabulary) with Althusser ('Sur la dialectique matérialiste', 1963).

be sought in the 'bizarre' psychology of the individuals and peoples concerned, but in the logic of their traditional social relations, in the hierarchy of these relations. It is this hierarchy that provides the basis for the 'social necessity, social utility', of a particular category of goods, a particular form of activity. Ultimately, by way of the hierarchy of 'socially necessary' wants, the hierarchy of structures determines, on the basis of the level of the productive forces of society, the distribution of social labour among the different kinds of production. Marx already pointed out that in a classless society the distribution of labour-time 'maintains the proper proportion between the different kinds of work to be done and the various wants of the community'.[193]

The economic *optimum* is not the *maximum* possible use of the factors of production, but the use of these factors that is best adjusted to the functioning of the society's structure. The time taken for – the pace of – the development of the productive forces thus varies from one type of society to another in consequence not only of its production-relations but of *all* its structures. The intentional rationality of the economic behaviour of a society's members is thus always governed by the fundamental, unintentional rationality of the hierarchical structure of social relations that characterize this society. There is therefore no such thing as economic rationality 'in itself', nor any 'definitive form' or 'model' of economic rationality.

From this standpoint, the abstract contrast between structure and event, between sociology (or anthropology) and history, falls to the ground.[194] For an event, whether it comes from inside or outside, acts upon the entire structure by acting upon one of its elements. Between a cause and its effects there always intervene all of the properties, known and unknown, of one or more structures. It is this causality of the structures that gives an event all its dimensions, whether conscious or not, and explains its effects, whether intentional or not. There is therefore no call to give up the structuralist standpoint, to abandon the structure in order to take account of the event. When men create by their deeds the conditions for the appearance of new structures, they open up, *de facto*, a domain of objective possibilities of which they are largely unaware, which

---

[193] *Capital*, I, p. 50. Cf. *Critique of the Gotha Programme*, p. 20.

[194] Some people are still throwing this in the faces of historians as a sort of challenge, or proclaiming it as an article of faith. Cf. Roland Barthes, 'Les sciences humaines et l'œuvre de Lévi-Strauss', in *Annales*, Nov.–Dec. 1964, p. 1086.

they discover through events, and the limits of which they find themselves subjected to when these structures develop and the conditions of their functioning change.

This brings up the problem of conjuncture, of the (*always specific*) conditions that make a change of structure possible. On this decisive point, Louis Althusser has contributed valuable ideas, eliminating any mechanical explanation, in his thoughts on the conditions of the Russian revolution.

> ... Russia was *the weakest link in the chain of imperialist states*. It had accumulated the largest sum of historical contradictions then possible; for it was at the same time *the most backward and the most advanced* nation, a gigantic contradiction which its divided ruling classes could neither avoid nor solve. In other words, Russia was overdue with its bourgeois revolution on the eve of its proletarian revolution; pregnant with two revolutions, it could not withhold the second even by delaying the first.[195]

The revolution does not necessarily have to break out in the most developed capitalist *country*, but at the weakest point of the world capitalist *system*; and this weakness is caused by the working of all the structures of Russian society, not just its economic contradictions alone. This weakness does not become a propitious conjuncture unless an organized revolutionary force can take advantage of it to lead 'the decisive attack'. But does not the Russian revolution refute Marx's hypothesis of a necessary correspondence between productive forces and production-relations, since on this occasion the socialist production-relations *preceded*[196] the development of the productive forces? In fact there is no contradiction, for the correspondence and the superiority of socialist production relations are shown in their ability to rapidly break through the ring of 'under-development', wiping out industrial backwardness, and to do this without a dominant class being the essential benefactor of the progress made.

By creating the conditions for its own disappearance in a dominated country which can nevertheless continue to develop under socialism, capitalism itself provides proof that the exploitation of labour by capital is not the only historical road whereby to acquire an advanced economy.

[195] Althusser, *For Marx*, p. 97.

[196] Nationalization is, moreover, not the same as 'socialization' of the productive forces. On this, cf. C. Bettelheim, *Problèmes de planification*, no. 5.

When Marx wrote in 1881 to Vera Zasulich, about the Russian village commune:

> The communal ownership of the soil offers it [the Russian village community] a natural basis for collective appropriation, and its historical environment, the contemporaneous existence of capitalist production lends it all the ready-made material conditions of co-operative labour, organized on a vast scale. The community can thus adopt the positive achievements elaborated by the capitalist system without having to undergo its hardships. It can gradually supplant the tilling of the soil by lots, by collective agriculture, with the aid of machines, the use of which the physical configuration of the Russian soil invites . . . . It can become the direct point of origin of the economic system towards which modern society develops . . . .[197]

Here there is no mechanistic picture of the transition to socialism, but an assumption that a mode of production creates new objective possibilities for other modes of production that are contemporary with it.

Once again, the possibility of a science of history that shall be at the same time a theory of the forms and evolution of kinship, of politics, of religion, etc., depends on our knowledge of the functions and laws of correspondence of the social structures.[198] It hardly needs to be stressed that this knowledge is very unevenly developed and that economic science seems to be much more advanced than our knowledge of kinship or religion. Within this uneven development, moreover, the contribution made by Marxism is even more uneven.

It is now possible to answer the question posed at the beginning of this section. The problem of economic rationality is a matter for science and not for ideology. In order to arrive at this answer we have had to build up the concept of economic rationality on the basis of elements scattered among scientific activities or theoretical reflections of the most diverse sorts, often without any direct connexion between them. We then had to note those problems before which science has proved helpless, so that ideology was able to break in. These problems always brought us back to the question of the historical necessity of a system and of the comparative rationality of this system in relation to those which preceded it

---

[197] *Marx-Engels Archiv*, I, p. 338 (Eng. trans. in *Marx and Engels on the Russian Menace to Europe*, ed. P. W. Blackstock and B. F. Hoselitz, pp. 221–2).

[198] The hypothesis of these laws of correspondence and of the ultimately determining role of the economy constitutes the Marxist conception of history.

or were contemporary with it. The question of the rationality of different systems was at the same time that of the rationality of economic science. It was therefore necessary to determine the concepts and methods that would make it possible for this science to compare systems without reasoning in a circle, making an *a priori* value-judgment, an ideological choice. We then had to determine the concepts and methods that would enable us to grasp the economic in its internal relation with the non-economic, in other words to show economic rationality as one aspect of a wider, social rationality.

These concepts and methods converged towards a unifying hypothesis: the existence of laws of necessary correspondence between the different structures of social life, laws that reveal the objective properties of social life and that it is the task of science to discover.

On this theoretical basis it became possible to *construct* the scientific concept of economic rationality. Constructing a concept means *distinguishing* and *defining* the problems it relates to and setting them in an *order* that renders them intelligible and capable of solution. This is what is meant by working out a 'theoretical problematic'. We have distinguished between the rationality of the economic behaviour of individuals and the rationality of the functioning and evolution of the system within which they act. We have distinguished between the intentional and unintentional aspects of the behaviour of individuals and of the local or overall functioning of the system. We have shown that these analyses bring us up against the problem of the conditions for the appearance and the disappearance of this system, its 'historical' rationality, and finally that this historical rationality inevitably requires that we compare the given system with those that preceded it or were contemporary with it.

Finally, we showed that there is no economic rationality 'in itself', nor any definitive form of economic rationality, that economic rationality is only one aspect of a wider rationality, that of social life, that this aspect plays an ultimately determining role, and that it is always provisional and relative – what is rational today becoming irrational tomorrow.

The question of economic rationality will find an answer if the sciences that study man enable us to increase our knowledge of the correspondences and contradictions that develop between the structures of social life. We have found in Marx's work the possibility of analysing economic contradictions scientifically. We have had to rediscover this beneath the ambiguities created by Marx and Engels themselves and beneath the misunderstandings that Marxists had accumulated to the point where the idea of contradiction had become unusable in scientific work.

Thus relieved of its ambiguities or false versions, Marxism can resume its onward march, returning to the frontiers of science in order to hasten their advance. This means that, as I see it, analysing the idea of economic rationality is only a starting point.

THE DISTANCE COVERED

The reader now knows where I have got to in my investigation of the theme of economic rationality. In the sections that follow he will traverse the chief stages of my approach to this point, and will have no difficulty in realizing what a long distance separates me now from my first publications on 'The Method of *Capital*'. He will observe the dead-ends, the setbacks, the theoretical bafflements that I encountered, and will easily understand why this happened. He will also perceive the firm *points d'appui* which later enabled me to realize what had happened, to get out of the hole I was stuck in and to go forward. So as to save him from being ensnared by my own former formulations, I will outline my results here in a rapid general summary.

On the positive side I will put the actual attempt I made to read *Capital* 'the wrong way up', so as to examine it from the angle of its method, hidden from sight in the text, and my effort to show that this method is neither strange nor alien to the most advanced developments in science. I saw the essential reason for this in the fact that Marx was concerned to identify the invisible *real structures* of the capitalist system and that this theory of the structure gave him the key to the origin (primitive accumulation) and evolution of this system (periodical crisis, necessity of socialism).

Economic theory was thus distinguished from economic history, even though providing the latter with an essential tool of analysis. I also laid stress on the idea of the 'functional compatibility' of the structures, and on the possibility of making extensive use of mathematics in Marxist theory. I sketched out an analysis of 'economic' time. Finally, I placed beneath these analyses the theory of value, which I presented as the necessary assumption of any rational economic science. I distinguished strongly between the theory of value and the theory of prices, and reminded the reader that Marx does not give us any really developed theory of competition, crises, etc.

But I failed on the essential point, analysis of the specific character of the idea of contradiction in Marx. I remained content to assume that Marx had stood the dialectic on its feet, and left side by side the idea of the totality differentiated into non-identical elements and that of the identity of opposites. I was therefore unable really to break away from Hegel and connect together the analysis of a structure and the analysis of its contradictions. In what I wrote I declared that there was only one method, but my writing staggered lamely along on two methods.

At the same time my inability to break away from Hegel in analysing the nature of the fundamental, *unintentional* contradiction of the structures of capitalism prevented me from breaking completely with Husserl, too, and rejecting the idea of constituent subjectivity or intersubjectivity, although I was critical of any 'abstract' subject. At the end of this chain of argument I found myself propounding a philosophy of labour as Man's essence, on the brink of a 'humanistic' philosophy that was closer to the young Marx than to Marxism.

My subsequent writings saw some progress made. When I discovered that the Marx of 1844 had rejected Ricardo at the very moment when he was claiming to 'found' political economy, I broke finally with a certain ideological kind of philosophy. With my work on value and prices, on marginalism, I encountered the difficult ideas of optimum and scarcity. But the decisive step was my meeting with anthropology. It was then that I shifted the centre of my thinking in relation to the spontaneous 'evidence' provided by what is called experience, referring to the prejudices of our own society.

I think I have made some progress in economics and in philosophy. The latter was still 'under construction' when I was trying to build up the concept of economic 'rationality'. Through the concepts of correspondence and contradiction between structures, however, philosophy which moves in the same direction as science, and is not a 'science of science', reveals itself as a materialism and a dialectic that needs to be elaborated and liberated, like science itself, from all kinds of ideology.

II

The Rationality of Economic Theory

If a capital, consisting in per cent of 90c + 10v, produced as much surplus-value, or profit, at the same degree of exploitation, as a capital consisting of 10c + 90v, it would be as plain as day that the surplus-value, and thus value in general, must have an entirely different source than labour, and that political economy would then be deprived of every rational basis.

Karl Marx, *Capital*, III, p. 147

ACKNOWLEDGMENT

The Table on pages 212 and 213 is from Lenin's 'On the So-called Market Question', in *Collected Works*, vol. 1, and is reproduced by kind permission of Lawrence and Wishart. The Figures on pages 240 and 241 were drawn for this edition by Paul White.

1. Political Economy and Philosophy

A fortunate coincidence has made available to us in one and the same year Marx's *Economic and Philosophic Manuscripts (1844)*, translated and introduced by E. Bottigelli,[1] and Volume III of Auguste Cornu's great book on Marx and Engels, which discusses the work done by Marx in Paris, that is to say, the *Manuscripts* and *The Holy Family*.

A scientific analysis of this crucial period in the formation of Marxism has thus become possible for a wider public. At the moment when a fundamental discussion on the transition from the Hegelian dialectic to the materialist dialectic has begun in France,[2] we have at our disposal two irreplaceable tools of great worth.

It is hard to say what is most admirable in the work of Auguste Cornu – the confident learning, the rigorous analysis, the structure of a biography that gives so little attention to its subject's private life but patiently reconstitutes the distinctive historical origins of a universal mode of thought, or the delicate undertaking of applying Marxism to Marx, applying to the origins of a mode of thought the theoretical results of that mode of thought.

It is not at all easy, however, to introduce to readers a book that does not lend itself to being summarized, dealing as it does with works from Marx's pen that are less than any others definable in a few formulae.

In October, 1843, Marx settled in Paris, ready to take up, alongside Ruge, the editing of a new periodical, the *Deutsch-Französische Jahrbücher*. The *Rheinische Zeitung*, the great newspaper of the liberal opposition on which he had been working in Cologne, had just been suppressed by the German censorship.

---

[1] Discussed with profundity and firmness by Louis Althusser in *La Pensée*, no. 107, February 1963 (English translation in Louis Althusser, *For Marx*, London, 1969).

[2] See Althusser's article, 'Contradiction et surdétermination', in *La Pensée*, no. 107, and the discussion that followed: G. Besse, 'Deux questions à propos de contradiction et surdétermination', also in no. 107; G. Mury, 'Matérialisme et Hyperempirisme', in no. 108; and R. Garaudy, 'Les Manuscrits de 1844', in *Cahiers du Communisme*, March 1963.

Where had Marx got to in 1843?

At what stage was Marx at that time, as regards theory?[3]

In his *Critique of Hegel's Philosophy of Right* he had developed the idea of the necessity of 'true' democracy and turned towards communism. How had he arrived at this result? Basing himself on Feuerbach's materialist conception of alienation,[4] generalizing Feuerbach's criticism of speculative philosophy[5] so as to apply it to the spheres of politics and law, Marx showed that, just as Hegel had made of the Absolute Idea the Creative Subject of the world, and Man, the real subject, a mere determination of the concept, so also he had made the state the subject and society the attribute. This idealist dialectic presented relations the wrong way round and made a mystery of them. In order to understand the state one must turn this dialectic the right way up and start from social reality.

When he contrasted state and society, Hegel had transposed the contradiction between the sphere of public interest, inhabited by the citizen, and that of private interest, where the bourgeois lived. This contradiction was based on the existence of private property. Hegel had thus, in his philosophy, justified bourgeois property and made the Prussian monarchist state the realization of Reason and Liberty.

Marx showed that the opposition between state and society would be overcome by 'true' democracy, in which the state would have for its content the life of the people, realizing in itself the unity of public and private interest. How was this rational state to be realized? Through the coming of the Republic, through universal suffrage. This identified Marx with the attitude of bourgeois radicalism. But he went further, for his critique of private property opened a path for him towards communism, although he did not see clearly the role to be played by the class struggle and the proletarian revolution in the realization of 'true' democracy. A radical transformation of bourgeois society would enable Man to live in accordance with his 'true' nature.

Marx's transition to communism was made with *On the Jewish Question* and the *Contribution to the Critique of Hegel's Philosophy of Right: Introduction.*

Carrying further the idea that society explains the state and not the other way round, Marx concluded that political emancipation leaves

[3] Cornu, op. cit., vol. II.   [4] Feuerbach, *The Essence of Christianity*, 1842.
[5] Feuerbach, *Provisional Theses for the Reform of Philosophy*, 1843.

intact the social alienation resulting from the régime of private property, and that the abolition of this régime, through the proletarian revolution, would bring about communism and the emancipation of mankind. The proletariat, which had fallen to the lowest level of de-humanization, incarnated mankind and, in fighting for itself, would re-establish an existence that would really conform to Man's essence.

The transition from 'true' democracy to communism was thus accomplished. To help grasp the real content of this transition I will present it schematically by saying[6] that:

(1) Marx wages against Hegel a struggle that is both philosophical and political. The starting-point of his offensive is Feuerbach's materialist critique of speculative philosophy. The finishing point is his exposure of the mystifying role played by Hegel's idealism and his political conservatism.

(2) In this struggle, the concept of alienation holds the central place, as with Feuerbach. Unlike the latter, however, Marx does not simply 'thrust Hegel aside', he retains his method of analysing contradictions, necessity, etc. – the dialectic.

(3) This philosophical approach, this battle of ideas, enables Marx to find his way to communism, to become politically committed. He questions and criticizes the world as a philosopher, in the name of the 'true' essence of Man. This approach is speculative in structure, and this speculation on Man's true essence accounts for the special operative role assigned to the concept of alienation and its content.

For Marx, however, at this moment of his life and in this historical context, this still speculative philosophy and this special concept of alienation provide him with the real possibility of starting and carrying through the *critique* of bourgeois society, of understanding in a certain way the *necessity* of proletarian revolution and adhering to this cause.

Thus, on this new theoretical basis which combines (a) criticism of Hegelian idealism and appreciation of the need to turn it upside down, (b) the dialectical method in the service of a theory of alienation that is at once materialist and speculative, and (c) a political adherence to communism justified on philosophical, not historical grounds, Marx will go

---

[6] I am offering here an interpretation of the *Manuscripts* which is presented rather differently from Cornu's but which I think is nevertheless in accordance with his work. By doing this I am not merely summarizing but also continuing a discussion I began long ago with this writer.

forward to continue his critique of bourgeois society, and, in doing this, will refashion the elements of this theoretical basis. He will increasingly seek reasons for the necessity of communism that are not speculative but historical, in the very logic of the development of capitalism. In doing this he will become aware of the still speculative nature of his thinking and therewith of the ineffectiveness of *all* reflexion that tries to give a *philosophical* basis to reality. At the same time the special importance of the concept of alienation will be swept away, so that henceforth it is restricted to particular and localized use.[7] The problem of the foundations of reality and of its alienated aspects will be referred henceforth no longer to thought but to reality itself, conceived as a totality of practical, historical relationships between men, and between men and nature, as *praxis*. Before Marx turned to reality itself, without any addition of speculative ideas about its content, the concept of *praxis* was to take over the special status of his old concept of alienation. Had he given up speculating with one concept in order to renew speculation with another?

This supreme temptation, this ultimate dizziness of philosophical consciousness, the desire to base the practical world upon a concept – even if, paradoxically, this was the concept of *praxis* – was to lie in wait for Marx when he encountered political economy. But the concept of *praxis* did not yet possess its *subsequent* meaning, which was to enable Marx to eradicate all speculativeness from his theoretical thinking. And yet it was already making possible this meaning which it did not yet possess. For the moment the *name* of *praxis* was a cover for the concept of *alienated labour*, labour in which Man's essence is alienated in order to be found again, labour that receives from Man's essence its conceptual meaning and role. By having this content, it could and had to serve as ultimate, paradoxical refuge for the last victories of the philosophical consciousness. But the paradox is only apparent, is only such through its subsequent meaning free of all speculation, for, if philosophical consciousness had been able to install itself triumphantly in this concept of labour, this was only because the latter *had previously installed itself* in philosophical consciousness. It is the presence behind the *same* word of these *two* meanings – that which it will soon cease to possess and that which it does not yet quite possess – which gives to the concept of *praxis* and the content of the *Manuscripts* their elusive ambiguity, to which I shall return.

This essential step taken by Marx, in which he first loses his footing

[7] Cf. in *Capital*, the analysis of commodity fetishism.

and then finds it in the concept of *praxis*, to emerge on the threshold of Marxism, is revealed to us by Auguste Cornu with patience and mastery.

What Paris gave Marx

He points out straightaway the three elements that his period in Paris contributed to Marx's thought: (a) a degree of economic development that was much more advanced than in Germany, (b) a proletariat that was already numerous and which had a strong revolutionary tradition and was aware of its class interests, and (c) the experience of a great social revolution, the revolution of 1789, completed by that of 1830. This was the basis on which there had multiplied those socialist and communist doctrines that Marx would seek to analyse. He was to go deeply into a study of the French revolution, to come upon political economy at last, and to analyse, through political economy, the material foundation of bourgeois society.

The socialists – Saint-Simonians like Bazard, Fourierists like Victor Considérant, Christians like Lamennais – criticized bourgeois society without challenging its basis in private property. They wanted democratic reforms, not a social revolution. They rose up against big capital and the proletariat, supported Ledru-Rollin's party, and advocated the conquest of political power.

The Communists – Cabet, Dezami, Blanqui – wanted to destroy, not to reform, bourgeois society, and advocated social revolution, but in order to build an ideal, utopian society. Some of them, like some of the socialists, even rejected atheism.

Marx, as a supporter of social revolution, was obliged to repudiate the socialists' ideas and draw closer to the communists, but he blamed the latter for their Utopianism. Socialists and Communists had great influence on the many former members of the secret organization of the German workers and craftsmen in Paris, the League of the Just. Marx mixed with them but never joined them. Already, as Cornu brings out very well, two of Marx's characteristics call for emphasis:

(1) Marx's action and thought are always strictly in accord with each other. The succession and character of his conflicts and breaks with Bauer, Ruge and Feuerbach result from the logic of the development of his thinking, his radical criticism of bourgeois society, and his adherence to communism. The best proof of this is furnished by the history of his relations with Engels, whom he looked upon in 1843 as a 'free spirit', a

representative of the Hegelian Right, and therefore received with coolness. In 1844 he was to discover, through Engels's *Outlines of a Critique of Political Economy*, both the need to study political economy and the close similarity of their two lines of development, which until then had been independent of each other. On this basis an alliance was effected between them that was to last throughout their lives and which resulted straightaway in the composition of *The Holy Family*.

(2) Marx does not develop through mechanically compiling ideas he finds around him, but actively and critically makes them his own, so as to change them into something new. The use he makes of the concept of alienation, borrowed from Hegel and Feuerbach, is the best proof of this.[8]

Marx was to break with the 'Young Hegelians', the 'free spirits' of Berlin, Bruno and Edgar Bauer. Increasingly, the latter were withdrawing from the political and social struggle, contrasting the pure, universal and free consciousness to the 'mass' of the people, indifferent to manifestations of the Spirit and hostile to progress, and, while directing all their criticism against this 'mass', sparing and justifying the reactionary Prussian state, with which they united to fight against liberalism and communism. Anarchism, soon afterwards put into theoretical form in Max Stirner's *The Ego and His Own*,[9] was to crown this impotent individualism.

The divergence between Marx and Ruge was to become complete, despite their common adherence to humanism. For Ruge, humanism meant the freedom of every man, the abolition of egoism. Communism seemed to him to symbolize the egoism, enviousness and greed of the propertyless. He broke with Marx, and his opposition to him grew into hatred.[10] He moved close to Stirner, the defender of individual freedom. As for Fröbel, so for Ruge the break had to made as soon as communism appeared as the revolutionary doctrine of the proletariat. The clash between Marx and Proudhon was to occur on the same basis as this.

On the other hand, Marx was to draw closer to Heine, and to encourage him to give expression to his revolutionary attitude in *Germany, A Winter's*

---

[8] Scientific study of Marx forbids acceptance of mechanical explanations, simplistically functional in character, of philosophical systems. Sève's book *La Philosophie contemporaine* provides some striking examples, especially in connexion with Husserl and phenomenology.   [9] November, 1844.

[10] Cf. Ruge's correspondence with his mother, November–December 1844, in Cornu, pp. 24–5.

Tale, his greatest political and satirical work. After Marx's expulsion, Heine was again attracted, and then repelled by communism.

Marx drew away from Feuerbach. The latter had not agreed to work for the *Deutsch-Französische Jahrbücher*, preferring to pursue his criticism of religion and putting his trust in education rather than in social and political struggles for the emancipation of mankind. This idealistic view of development was what lay enshrined in his materialist conception of the world, and this was the content of his humanism. There were some, however, such as Moses Hess and Karl Grün, who were able, while quoting Feuerbach, to differ with him on the means whereby the contrast between Man's inhuman reality and his true essence might be abolished. Understood in this way, Feuerbach opened the road to socialist interpretations, and we shall see that Marx was to take the road thus opened.

Hess had attempted, in his famous article, 'The Essence of Money', a generalization of Feuerbach's theory of alienation. By its domination of everyone's life, money reflects the de-humanizing of man in bourgeois society, the universal exploitation of man by man. In 1844, taking a step backward as compared with this view, he was to stress the Utopian nature of his socialism, which he called 'true socialism', sketching, in the manner of Fourier, a new, harmonious society in which labour would be a free activity.

The same Utopian tendency was steadily growing stronger in the Communist Weitling, who, since writing *Guarantees of Harmony and Freedom*, which Marx greatly admired, had increasingly indulged in mysticism, with his *Gospel of the Poor Sinners*. Bakunin cultivated his anarchistic dilettantism, remaining on the sidelines of the working-class movement, though at the same time drawing closer to Proudhon, whom Marx regarded as the greatest of the French socialists. In 1843 Proudhon published his work *On the Creation of Order in Mankind*, in which he criticized private property and the state, without seeking to destroy bourgeois society. Proudhon denounced the absolute right to property which results in the appropriation of other people's labour and the expropriation of the middle classes, and also denounced common ownership of goods, which makes slavery and degradation universal. He upheld the principle of private property, but with its dangers tempered, in the form of a 'right to possess' the income that everyone derives from his own work. In this way he adapted the opposites and neutralized them.

Marx appreciated Proudhon's atheism, though he did not share his desire to replace the old religion with the religion of science. What he saw as a contribution of decisive importance, though, was Proudhon's criticism of bourgeois political economy.

Proudhon blamed political economy for treating private property as a *premise*, as the *fundamental principle* of economic science without subjecting this principle to a critical analysis. Economic science thus remained based on a faulty principle, lacking a firm foundation and in need of such a foundation. Proudhon claimed to supply this missing foundation, in his work of speculative philosophy, *On the Creation of Order in Mankind*, by way of criticism of the abuses of private property.

True, Marx reproaches Proudhon for not carrying through this criticism to the end, and for using an adapted and adjusted form of private property as the principle of construction of his system. But he does not yet see, as he was to do later, in *The Poverty of Philosophy*, the origin of this compromising attitude in Proudhon's reformism. Nevertheless, Proudhon's approach, bringing to economic science the basis that it lacked, filling up *by philosophical means* a deficiency in principle, was not structurally distinct from Marx's when the latter set about studying political economy. Proudhon carried out speculatively and in the interest of reformism an analysis that Marx was to undertake for the cause of the proletarian revolution. Marx, reinforced by Engels's article,[11] settled down to a thorough study of political economy, in the writings of Quesnay, Ricardo, Say and Schultz.[12] After these numerous encounters and fresh studies, he wrote, between March and August, 1844, the well-known *Economic and Philosophical Manuscripts*.

The 1844 Manuscripts : is Marx already a Marxist?

In this connexion, let me sum up Auguste Cornu's central argument.

Marx criticizes political economy in the name of Man's alienation caused by the 'reification' of social relations, by labour that produces commodities and has itself become a commodity, a thing. He thus generalizes, in analysing political economy, his theory of alienation, and elaborates the critique of bourgeois society and private property which it had enabled him to begin.

[11] Engels, *Outlines of a Critique of Political Economy*.

[12] Cornu has brought out the importance of Schultz as author of the book *Die Bewegung der Produktion*, 'an historical and statistical study destined to provide the basis for a new science of the state and of society' (1843), from which Marx derived the primary elements of historical materialism.

Since, however, he saw economic science as the non-critical theory of alienated labour, what it showed him was that what Man alienates is his labour, and that labour is his essence. The movement of self-creation of the self, presented in upside-down form by Hegel as the development of the Absolute Idea, re-presented by Marx as the development of the real subject, of generic man, was now to appear as the self-creation and objectification of Man by himself, through labour. Having begun with alienation as his special concept he now moved the concept of *praxis* into the forefront.

Cornu shows very clearly this replacement effected by Marx by withdrawing the concept of alienation in favour of the concept of *praxis*. For him, it is here that historical materialism emerges, with the essential role of labour, of *praxis*, in Marx's conception of the world. This is true, but only, it seems to me, if we see in this concept of *praxis* both the last triumph of speculative consciousness and that which brings near its moment of death, only if we realize why this historical materialism is no sooner born but it needs a further (and final) thorough re-working in order to do away with the speculative character that *it* bears and to become the *scientific* consciousness of nature and history.[13]

The *development* of historical materialism was to make this modification of materialism both *possible* and *necessary*. Marx took up this task, on his own in the *Theses on Feuerbach* (especially theses 2, 8, 9) (1845), and with Engels in *The German Ideology* (1845–6), and the task consisted precisely in 'settling accounts' with his 'former philosophical conscience'.[14] In my

[13] Roger Garaudy, in his article on the *1844 Manuscripts* (in *Cahiers du Communisme*, 1963, no. 3), has not grasped Marx's need, after writing the *Manuscripts*, to destroy for the last time (that is, for the first time) his speculative consciousness, and this warps his interpretation. The *Manuscripts* are not Marx's 'decisive step' (p. 112), they are not the scientific theory of the class struggle and of socialism, 'the outline of *Capital*' (p. 113). The transition from the concept of alienation to the concept of *praxis* does not signify the end of speculation but only that this end has become possible.

[14] Marx wrote in 1859, regarding *The German Ideology*, in his preface to the *Contribution to the Critique of Political Economy* (p. 5): 'We decided to set forth together our conception as opposed to the ideological one of German philosophy, in fact to settle accounts with our former philosophical conscience' (*Contribution*, p. 22).

Once this account was settled, scientific materialism began: 'Where speculation ends – in real life – there real, positive science begins: the representation of the practical activity, of the practical process of the development of men . . . when reality is depicted, philosophy as an independent branch of activity loses its medium of existence' (*The German Ideology*, p. 15). It was to the scientific representation of this reality that Marx and Engels were to devote their whole lives.

view, the ultimate stage, the moment of birth of Marxism for Marx and Engels, occurred not in 1844 in Paris but in 1845 in Brussels.[15]

Let us, however, return to the encounter between Marx the philosopher and political economy, so as to explain more precisely how it was that the transition from the concept of alienation to that of *praxis* did not yet do away with the speculative mode of thought, and what consequences followed from this.

If, I said, the philosophical consciousness was able to install itself triumphantly in this concept, it was because the latter had previously installed itself in the philosophical consciousness: but how?

Economic science showed Marx that the basis of all wealth and all property was labour; yet it took labour not in its 'true' but in its alienated form, as labour alienated by and in the régime of private property. Labour appeared – and this is the tremendous and irreversible contribution made by political economy to philosophy – as the essence of Man and of human history. For Marx, now, Man's essence is alienated, and Man is dehumanized, when his labour is alienated through the very functioning of the régime of private property. The alienation of labour appears as the matrix of all other forms of alienation – political and religious. Atheism is more than ever justified, and also the social revolution, which by destroying will give back his humanity to Man, through restoring to labour its universal and creative character, the basis for 'true human society'.

But Marx's view of the necessity of the social revolution, if we look at it closely, is no less ambiguous than the concept of *praxis*, because it conceals two meanings behind a single word. On the one hand, the necessity of social revolution arises from the very development of private property, appearing as a concrete, historical necessity, but, on the other, it arises from the *contradiction between historical reality and 'Man's true essence'*, and this contradiction – between reality and essence – provides the *basis* for the other contradiction, the first-mentioned necessity, internal to private property. Now, this second necessity, or, more precisely, this second aspect of the same necessity, is abstract and speculative. The whole

---

[15] Proof of this birth, specific evidence for it, appears, in my view, with the formulation of the idea of a 'law of correspondence' between the productive forces and the relations of production. Marx, in his *Contribution* (1859), saw this as the 'general conclusion' of his work, and referred explicitly to *The German Ideology* and his stay in Brussels (*Contribution*, p. 20).

ambiguity of the *concept* of *praxis*, lies there in these two meanings hidden behind the same word.

Presented in this double way – one meaning, the concrete one, being based on the other, abstract meaning – the necessity of the revolution *is no longer wholly internal to the concrete, determined elements* of the historical reality of capitalism, it no longer emerges entirely (that is, truly) from the opposition between classes, from a real process with determined conditions and 'empirically verifiable',[16] but from the conflict between reality and 'Man's true essence', invisible to everyone but the philosopher. For it is only the philosopher who is traditionally dedicated to knowledge of the essence, only he has access to the concept of truth, and so to the truth of concepts, whether the concept of 'true' democracy or that of Man's 'true' essence.

Thus, the way in which Marx recognizes the necessity of the revolution and of communism presumes that philosophy is an independent and privileged activity which explores the domain of the *fundamental reasons* of reality and existence. Its task is seen as the discovering and explaining of these fundamental reasons: in other words, providing a basis for reality.[17] Providing a basis, in the philosophical sense, means working out and demonstrating the connexion between all theoretical representation and all practical activity, on the one hand, and, on the other, that domain of fundamental reasons to which the philosopher has access through his approach to and his way of presenting the truth.

I think my analysis has partly explained why, in the *Manuscripts*, the transition from the concept of alienation to the concept of *praxis* did not yet eliminate Marx's speculative way of thinking but, on the contrary, offered Marx the philosopher the opportunity to win his last victory, to enjoy his last dizzy spell before finally becoming 'Marxist' and acquiring a 'scientific depiction of reality' that destroys all philosophy's independent role by depriving it of its 'medium of existence' – before 'settling accounts with his former philosophical conscience'.

[16] Marx, *The German Ideology*, p. 14.

[17] This claim by the philosophers to contribute to science and practice the basis that they allegedly lack has not ceased since Marx's day. A few years back, the philosopher (even the Marxist philosopher) sought to be king and give direction to politics. The paradox – which made it so hard to criticize this claim – was that this ancient Platonic dream was justified in the name of knowledge of the primacy of *praxis*. The 'Marxist' philosopher thought he had emerged from the cave, but the sun that he gazed upon belonged

This 'independence' of philosophy is assumed only by the philosophical mode of thought itself, by the form of this consciousness, which causes it to imagine its own activity as possessing a specially privileged character, giving access to the foundations of reality. Yet this form of self-awareness, this image that the philosopher makes of himself and of reality is merely the *speculative alienation* of the consciousness of former times, and causing it to lose its 'medium of existence' merely signifies *sacrificing* this claim,[18] eradicating the *imaginary* independence of the philosopher, this alienated form of self-awareness in which and by which, inevitably, reality finds itself and loses itself, because it no longer possesses *all* its meaning within itself, in its concrete content, but receives this in part from an abstract 'other world', the world of 'its true essence', accessible to the philosopher alone. Marx made this supreme sacrifice when he explored afresh the theoretical possibilities that had been opened for him by the (still speculative) demonstration of the primacy of practice in history. As he plunged deeper and deeper into the concrete, determined content of the practice of his time, he would be compelled, *en route* to *destroy the image of himself that he constructed in order to reach this content*. And this image was not just part of the content of his consciousness, but the actual, long-established form of his consciousness.[19]

---

to the faded heaven of the ancient philosophical consciousness, the one that Marx had abolished in order to become Marxist.

[18] I refer the reader to the excellent analysis by J. T. Desanti, 'Histoire et vérité', in *Revue Internationale de Philosophie*, 1958, no. 45–46. My interpretation of the relationship between the two concepts which dominate Marx's philosophy in its first stages – alienation and *praxis* – differs from his on one point. Desanti takes the *1844 Manuscripts* and the *Theses on Feuerbach* together (p. 5) as showing the abolition of Marx's speculative philosophical consciousness. In my view, it was not in the *Manuscripts* that this abolition was accomplished *completely, and so really*, but in the *Theses on Feuerbach* and in *The German Ideology*, and this is why the concept of *praxis* is ambiguous in the *Manuscripts*. Leaving aside this argument about the chronology of Marx's elimination of his speculative consciousness, Desanti's theoretical interpretation of this abolition seems to be the same as mine.

[19] This abolition, which establishes scientific consciousness of practice, does not consist in a *mere subtraction* of a certain content from consciousness, but the *radical recasting of the very form* of this consciousness. This is why the materialist dialectic is not the *same* dialectic as Hegel's, turned round and cleansed of its mystical (mystified and mystifying) aspect, but a different dialectic, different in structure, that is, in its *operational rules*, since it has to explain *without deducing* reality from the concept and *without*

It is in the light of this 'old' form of Marx's consciousness that we can properly understand, it seems to me, the way in which, in 1844, he encountered political economy and criticized bourgeois society.

For Marx, political economy seemed to give exact expression on the theoretical plane to the practical contradiction between bourgeois society and Man's true essence, the self-creation of self through labour. True, political economy takes as its fundamental principle not labour in its true form, but alienated labour. But it *thinks, wrongly*, of this alienated labour, the real principle of bourgeois society, as the true natural, necessary form of labour, and thereby presents bourgeois society as the normal and natural form of society, justifying its maintenance for ever and ever.[20] By conceiving its own basis mistakenly, however, political economy deprives itself of all real basis, and is left hanging over this inner void, which calls out to be filled. It is to this appeal that the philosopher replies when he is conscious of *contributing* to economics the critical foundation that it lacks, and he is thus able to accomplish *the task* to which he imagines himself devoted.

Actually, what Marx takes to be a shortcoming in principle of this science is the way in which the laws of bourgeois economy *appear and justify themselves* in the mind of the economist: it is the ideological

---

reducing reality to the concept. Not reducing and not deducing means taking reality as it is, in all its concrete determinations, in their *specific* order. This is why I agree with Althusser's analysis, in 'Contradiction and Over-determination' – though I must say that the term '*over*-determination' has the disadvantage of bringing with it an ambiguous problematic, since whereas, for Hegel, there are never enough determinations to explain history, for Marx there are never too many. Another disadvantage it has is that it conceals the fact that the *specific order* of all the determinations is what makes them effective. Nevertheless, this term has the advantage that it rules out any reduction of the 'superstructures' and the conjuncture to the infrastructures. And analysing *all* the determinations in their own *order* does not mean dialectical pluralism or hyperempiricism. I shall come back to this confrontation shortly, when examining the dialectic employed by Marx in *Capital*, but it must be said that, thanks to Cornu, we have a little more light on Marx and also a little more on Hegel, and that this was needed (cf. my articles on 'Les structures de la méthode du *Capital*', in *Economie et Politique*, nos 70, 71, 80; pp. 130ff. below).

[20] Cf. Marx, in *Economic Studies from Marx's Notebooks (1844–1845)*, in MEGA I/3, p. 537 (Eng. trans. in Bottomore and Rubel, eds., *Karl Marx: Selected Writings in Sociology and Social Philosophy*, p. 171): 'According to Adam Smith, *society* is a *commercial enterprise*. Every one of its members is a *salesman*. It is evident how political economy established an *alienated* form of social intercourse, as the *true and original* form, and that which corresponds to human nature' (Marx's own emphasis).

depiction of this economy, ideology being mixed up with valid elements of scientific consciousness, rather than knowledge of these elements.

Marx thus takes political economy as it is *given*, that is, as it appears, or, to employ Bottigelli's exact formulation,[21] 'as a phenomenology'. And what Marx destroys is an ideology, is what the bourgeois economist thinks of the mechanisms he is theorizing about, but he does not *alter the state* of these theories. He does not yet take this science, separated from its ideology, in order *to develop it in itself*, as he was later to do in the *Contribution* and in *Capital*.

In my view, it is precisely because, in 1844, Marx took this content just as it was given, that he was led to reject, like some bourgeois economists, Ricardo's theory of value, which he was later to appreciate as the fundamental *scientific* contribution of bourgeois political economy. And he rejected it, as Cornu shows plainly, because, for him, value was determined by competition, and profit and rent were included in price, in addition to wages,[22] and, above all, because Ricardo's thesis would, he thought, justify the capitalist régime.[23]

Thus, the same theoretical basis – the theory of the alienation of Man's true essence – both *enables* Marx to criticize bourgeois ideology and society and *prevents* him from changing the state of economic science, from developing the scientific conception of capitalist economy. This criticism of bourgeois ideology would make scientific knowledge *possible* without, however, *replacing* that ideology. Accordingly, the critique of bourgeois economy and society is based on the way in which Marx *imagines* the 'true' manner of being human, namely, creating oneself, asserting oneself as human by one's all-round, free activity in unison with that of other human beings, acting upon nature so as to reproduce it in a human way, and recognizing oneself in it.[24] By living in accordance with his essence,

[21] The *1844 Manuscripts* (French edition, Editions Sociales, p. xli, Bottigelli's introduction).

[22] We are at the antipodes of *Capital*, Cf. vol. III, chapter 10, where Marx was to show that competition determines the market price, but not the value of a commodity, and that surplus-value is the common source of profit, interest and rent.

[23] 'Ricardo explains that labour embraces all the elements making up price, since capital is also labour. Say points out that Ricardo has forgotten that profit of capital and land are not supplied free of charge. Proudhon concludes, rightly, that where private property exists, an object *costs* more than it is *worth*, this excess constituting a tribute paid to the private owner' (*Economic Studies from Marx's Notebooks, 1844–1845*, in MEGA I/3, p. 494. Apparently no published English translation).

[24] Cornu, op. cit., p. 122.

Man inaugurates the 'true 'society, which is at the same time 'the true resurrection of nature'.[25-26]

This ideal image functions as a normative model that provides the philosopher with the norm both for criticizing bourgeois society and for deducing the content of the rational society of the future, of socialism. Possession of this normative image *provides the basis and justification* for the jurisdiction that the philosopher wields over practical reality and its theoretical expressions, such as political economy. It enables him first and foremost to develop his critique of bourgeois society and political economy by deducing from the alienation of labour the entire *logic of the process* of social alienation and arranging parallel with each other all the categories of bourgeois economy.[27]

What is the logic of this process by which man deprives himself of his own humanity and gradually destroys his substance?[28] In the first place, man alienates himself by transforming his product into commodities. He thus loses control of his own product and transforms his activity into a means of acquiring wealth, by exchanging for the surplus of other people's production a part of his own labour. Thenceforth, production loses its human quality, being no longer a personal relationship between the producer and his product, the expression of his 'true' needs. Human relations become depersonalized, become relations between things, commodities become 'reified'. The extension of commodity production makes the alienation of the producers a universal phenomenon. Private interest and profit are the sole universal bond between men, and not their humanity. Antagonism and struggle prevail, their finished form being the opposition between bourgeois and proletarians. Finally, in connexion with these

[25] 'Thus society is the accomplished union of man with nature, the veritable resurrection of nature, the realized naturalism of man and the realized humanism of nature' (*1844 Manuscripts*: Eng. trans. from *Karl Marx: Early Writings*, ed. Bottomore, p. 157).

[26] 'Let us assume *man* to be *man*, and his relation to the world to be a human one. Then love can only be exchanged for love, trust for trust, etc.' (*1844 Manuscripts*: Eng. trans, from *Karl Marx: Early Writings*, ed. Bottomore, p. 193).

[27] In *Capital* Marx was to start from the commodity in order to understand money and surplus-value, and only then would the alienation of labour appear on the scene.

[28] 'He creates his own production as a vitiation, a punishment, and his own product as a loss . . .' (*1844 Manuscripts*: Eng. trans. from *Karl Marx: Early Writings*, ed. Bottomore, p. 131. [The passage reads in the original: '*Wie er seine eigne Produktion zu einer Entwirklichung, zu einer Strafe, wie er sein eignes Produkt zu dem Verlust . . .*' (MEGA, I/3, p. 91).]

struggles, and in order to consolidate private ownership, religion, morality and bourgeois law carry further the practical alienation of labour, the matrix of all alienations. In this way the class struggle is 'deduced' from the alienation of Man's essence.

But why did mankind hurl itself to destruction? Through the progress of production and the division of labour, through the abolition of 'natural' economy, that is, for historical reasons. And here the ambiguity of Marx's thinking becomes quite plain, for this historical necessity falsifies real human activity, that is, it contradicts the necessity of Man's essence. Man confined to his speciality (historical necessity) becomes a physical and intellectual 'monster' (in contradiction with the necessity of his essence). *Two* necessities illuminate the same reality, seeming to give support to each other, but, in fact, one of them is always sustained by what it *takes away from* the other, and assumes density and concrete existence only by transforming the other into an abstraction, deprived of any possibility of accounting for itself.

From that point onwards what task does Marx consider is necessarily imposed upon mankind? The task of abolishing the contradiction between reality and Man's essence by 'realizing humanism' as communism. Thus, knowledge of Man's essence enables us to provide a basis for criticism of bourgeois society, and *contrariwise, to deduce* the necessity of the revolution and the content of the 'real' society that it will establish.

More than ever, Marx's political adherence to Communism is seen to be justified philosophically and ideologically. We need, however, like Auguste Cornu, to pay attention to what Marx meant by communism at that time:

Communism is the phase of negation of the negation and is, consequently, for the next stage of historical development, a real and necessary factor in the emancipation and rehabilitation of man. Communism is the necessary form and the dynamic principle of the immediate future, but communism is not itself the goal of human development – the form of human society.[29]

Communism is thus grasped as the political tool, the practical means for establishing the definitive form of human society, the realization of '*positive* humanism which contains its own *raison d'être*'. Communism is not yet thought of as a stage in the development of mankind corresponding to certain productive forces. It is a tool in the service of history, and

[29] *Manuscripts*, p. 99 (Bottomore trans., p. 167). See Cornu, p. 172.

history is in the service of the true essence of Man, at once the driving force and the end of its development. It is this teleology of self-recovery (*Wiedergewinnung*) that the philosopher anticipates and illuminates when he reveals its basis in the contradiction between reality and essence. Through this teleology based on the necessity for Man to submit himself to his true essence, all history is endowed with a meaning, an order, a rationality – that of a lost essence that has to be recovered. This ambiguous image of reality will have to be smashed if the latter is to be given back its meaning, which is not given in advance, and its necessity, which does not correspond to any ideal essence. For this to be done, however, Marx will have to abolish his reassuring image of *himself*, as a philosopher devoted to the fundamental domain of primordial reasons and definitive ends.

Nevertheless, communism defined in this way justifies and consolidates Marx's old criticisms of utopian communism, reformist socialism and egalitarian communism.[30] Of the first, because it makes communism a merely ideal necessity and not an historical one, of the second because it refuses to abolish private property, and of the third because it seeks not to destroy this property but to generalize it, to divide it up among everybody.

Beyond these political positions, however, Marx's philosophical positions are about to be developed further and contrasted with those of Feuerbach and Hegel.

(1) He is extending the application of Feuerbach's materialist theory of religious alienation to the spheres of material and social life. He praises Feuerbach for having opened the way for a real science of man conceived in his relations with nature and society.

(2) He is criticizing Feuerbach and starting to break with him for having thought of the relation between subject and object not as a dialectical unity but as a contemplative relationship. By merely setting Hegel aside, Feuerbach had allowed dialectics to vanish, and remained an idealist in his understanding of history.

Through dialectics Marx comes closer to Hegel, drawing away from Feuerbach, but in the end he abandons both of them by conceiving dialectics as the dialectics of man defined as *praxis* and not as Spirit. Hegelian idealism appears to him in all its grandeur and speculative alienation.

The outstanding achievement of Hegel's *Phenomenology* – the dialectic of negativity as the moving and creating principle – is, first, that Hegel grasps the

[30] Cornu, pp. 128–9.

self-creation of man as a process, objectification as loss of the object, as alienation and transcendence of this alienation, and that he, therefore, grasps the nature of labour, and conceives objective man (true, because real man) as the result of his own labour.[31]

Here we see Marx dissociating the elements of Hegelianism, either taking them up or rejecting them – in other words, not accepting them as given. He is thus doing with philosophy what he is not yet able to do with political economy. He is showing that Hegel reduces Man to mind, the self-creation of self to thought-activity, and the opposition of Man to the world to the opposition of consciousness to its object. History is reduced to the dialectic of this opposition, its order to the sequence of thought-categories, and its purpose to the necessity for recovery of the Self in the Object and of the Object in the Self.[32] Analysing Hegelian dialectics, Marx considers it a 'false positivism', an 'apparent' criticism, since it results in justifying the established order and confirming man within his alienation.

At the end of this confrontation we find maintained and developed the elements of the theoretical basis of Marx's thought: philosophical and political criticism of Hegelian idealism, revival of the dialectical method in the service of a theory of alienation. In developing, however, this basis has changed, bringing forward and putting in the forefront the concept of *praxis*. But this concept would offer Marx the occasion for his dizziest philosophical speculation. Reflecting itself in the speculative image of Man's true essence, the concept of *praxis*, was to be diffracted into two contrasted concepts, true Labour and alienated Labour, and this contrast was nothing but the contradiction that Marx conceived to exist between essence and reality. This splitting of the concept of *praxis* into two antagonistic contents was only the effect and mirror of the struggle between the real and the rational, through which, in Marx's view, history acquired meaning and necessity, and both political economy and philosophy acquired critique and foundation. But this 'mirror-essence' was only the

---

[31] *Manuscripts*, p. 132 (Bottomore trans., p. 202). See Cornu, p. 146.

[32] See Cornu's discussion of this, pp. 144–53. I am inclined to reproach the author a little for not illustrating what he calls Hegel's reduction of reality to 'some concrete concepts' (p. 143). This remains obscure unless one has read the *Zusätze* of the *Logic* and the *Encyclopaedia*, because it is *on principle* that Hegel presents reality as the concept 'in itself' and at the same time 'other than itself', and this principle is the speculative 'act of violence' that inaugurates *Absolute* Idealism.

reverse side of the 'philosophical consciousness' of an earlier period. By smashing the speculative image of himself, the form in which his reflexive operations appeared to him, Marx was going to smash at the same time the speculative image of the world, the form in which the latter appeared to him. But Marx was not there yet. Communism had just struck him as philosophy triumphant, and thereby (the ultimate paradox) as the suppression of all philosophy.

Communism as a fully-developed naturalism is humanism, and as a fully developed humanism is naturalism. It is the *definitive* resolution of the antagonism between man and nature, and between man and man. It is the true solution of the conflict between existence and essence, between objectification and self-affirmation, between freedom and necessity, between individual and species (Bottomore trans., p. 155).

Appearing as the practical solution to all the debates of ancient philosophy, communism takes them up and unravels them. But by losing its problems philosophy loses its subject-matter and *raison d'être*; by realizing itself it suppresses itself and abolishes its own medium of existence.

Has Marx now finally broken through the invisible thread of speculative consciousness, has he at last deprived speculative philosophy of any future, any existence? And is it the concept of *praxis* that has enabled him to break down these inner walls?

The resolution of the theoretical contradictions is possible *only* through practical means, only through the *practical* energy of man. Their resolution is not by any means, therefore, only a problem of knowledge, but is a *real* problem of life which philosophy was unable to solve precisely because it saw there a purely theoretical problem (Bottomore trans., p. 162).

If my interpretation does not collapse like a house of cards, the reason is that Marx is here both very close to Marxism and very far away from it. Very close because here we have the themes of the suppression of philosophy and of practice as the truth of truth; but the meaning he gives them is that which Marx will go on to abolish. Here philosophy is transcended because it has triumphed in practice. With the coming of communism, human existence is subjected to Man's true essence and no longer stands in contrast to this. Man's true essence leaves the sphere of philosophy, where it had carried on its ideal existence, to start existing in practice. By starting to exist in practice it puts an end to its ideal existence in the consciousness of the philosopher who had recognized it, and recognizes itself in the world that is henceforth under its jurisdiction. Philosophy is abolished at the very moment of its victory, and by its victory philosophy destroys itself because it finds itself anew as the 'world' of practice. Practice is from now on the truth of its truth, its verification. Victorious philosophy can therefore only be ¡in one movement, essence becomes existence, and philosophy resolved, that is to say, ended.

Philosophy at an end because it has invaded existence – this is the real meaning of the *Manuscripts*, a meaning unclear only to those who let themselves be misled by the associations of words, and hear already Marx's future discourse, in which the same words will mean something different.[33]

The other suppression of philosophy is that which will entirely get rid of the *problematic* of the true essence and alienated existence of Man, which will grasp the necessity of the revolution in history itself, in its *real* contradiction, as the inner contradiction between the productive forces and the relations of production. The resolving of this contradiction will no longer be the victory of the essence, but the *bringing into correspondence* of the productive forces and the relations of production. Analysis will lose its speculative character and be based henceforth on scientific knowledge of the *law* of necessary correspondence between productive forces and relations of production, a law set up as a general hypothesis needing to be verified theoretically and practically. From now on, the rationality of history will have lost all overall purposiveness, all meaning that precedes and transcends it. Philosophy will no longer be able to develop for its own sake and substitute itself for the real science of the practical process of development of men.[34]

---

[33] The problem before scientific method when analysing Marx or any other body of thought is precisely that of not mixing up different meanings, not merely explaining what comes before by what comes after, or *vice versa*. Cornu's historical method triumphs admirably over these difficulties.

[34] I shall come back later to the status of Marxist philosophy and the notion of historical rationality. Let us, however, recall what Marx himself said:

'At the best its place can only be taken by a summing-up of the most general results, abstractions which arise from the observation of the historical development of men. Viewed apart from real history, these abstractions have in themselves no value whatsoever. They can only serve to facilitate the arrangement of historical material, to indicate the sequence of its separate strata. But they by no means afford a recipe or schema, as does philosophy, for neatly trimming the epochs of history. On the contrary, our difficulties begin only when we set about the observation and the arrangement – *the real*

The alliance with Engels : The Holy Family

Before reaching this final stage Marx was to seal his alliance with Engels. England had enabled Engels to see the importance of production in the development of mankind. Bourgeois society appeared to him, as it did, independently, to Marx, as the inversion of 'true' human relations, the supreme alienation of de-humanized humanity. A social revolution was needed that would establish a rational and human social order.[35]

Engels's theoretical basis was thus the same as Marx's. The concept of alienation and the concept of *praxis* maintained the same relations, through a philosophical problematic of Man's true essence. This community of ideas independently attained was to cement the alliance between the two men; but Engels had not *developed* his new conception of the world, and it is this difference that explains the leading role played by Marx from the start of their alliance. Together they decided to fight the Right Hegelians. *The Holy Family* was born of this project, and in this work they were to achieve new results.

Marx showed that Hegelian idealism, which made a subject-object of the Idea and bound the world and the idea together in a single development, had become with the Young Hegelians the meagre and bloodless counterposing of consciousness of self to the 'mass'. The illusions of speculative philosophy now appeared in more grotesque fashion, resulting in a helpless individualism subordinated to the reactionary enterprises of the Prussian state. Marx defends the French Revolution against Bruno Bauer: if the Terror failed, this was because it contradicted the class interests of the bourgeoisie. He defends Proudhon for having opened the way for a fundamental critique of private property; but he emphasizes how far Proudhon is from carrying through this radical criticism, since he wants to make private property universal in the form of possession. He develops the idea of the necessity of socialism, 'the union of materialism and humanism'. Finally, he criticizes Bauer's refusal to accord political emancipation to the Jews on the excuse that they are not emancipated as regards religion. He shows that bourgeois society allows religion to be a

---

depiction – of our historical material, whether of a past epoch or of the present' (*The German Ideology*, p. 15. My emphasis, M.G.).

This lesson should be learnt by those who turn the concept of *praxis* into a recipe and make philosophy a substitute for real knowledge.

[35] Cornu, pp. 184–5.

'private matter'. The political emancipation of the Jews is thus possible, but it is not the radical, social emancipation that all men will accomplish with the suppression of capitalism. Finally, he devotes much space to denouncing the pseudo-*Mysteries of Paris* of Eugène Sue, who preaches class-collaboration and the morality of redemption – in other words, hypocritically sustains bourgeois society while claiming to reform it.

It was in this book, then, that the analysis of materialist philosophy was developed, the idea of class struggle and class interest defined, the break with Hegelianism publicly carried out. Ruge and others would now finally break with Marx – a logical, irreversible, break. But these results had not yet smashed the speculative form of Marx's problematic. This last and first step was to be taken in Brussels, after Marx had been expelled from Paris for his participation in *Vorwärts* and his communistic humanism.

Soon, continuing with his great work, Auguste Cornu will throw light upon this decisive moment. I hope he will forgive me for having anticipated him. If I have been able to analyse the speculative nature of the concept of *praxis* and its consequences, this has been possible only on the basis of the results of his efforts.

His book gives rise to too many questions, and contributes too many confident replies, for me not to wish to relate it to our own discussions, for its practical topicality not to be apparent, linking it with all the questions in suspense among Marxists and non-Marxists. The best homage I can render to Auguste Cornu's work is to add to it a little of my own, so as to increase the scientific understanding of Marx to which he has devoted his life.

(*La Pensée*, no. 111, Oct.–Nov., 1963)

APPENDIX

Here is a table outlining a point-by-point comparison between the *Manuscripts* and *Capital*. This task needs to be carried further in a systematic way.

The Manuscripts	*Capital*
1. Central place given to the theory of alienated labour.	1. Central place given to the law of correspondence between production-relations and productive forces.
2. Rejection of Ricardo's theory of value – importance accorded to competition.	2. Central place given to the theory of value. Competition explains market price but not value.
3. The class struggle deduced from alienation.	3. The class struggle depends on the level of the productive forces and the production-relations.
4. Communism as the political instrument of victorious humanism.	4. Communism as a mode of production.

2. *The Structures of the Method of* Capital

It is not possible to separate the method of *Capital* from its content. From the start one has to grasp the roots of this method that lie within the content. What is this content? It can be first defined in a formal way as a certain 'subject-matter' analysed in a certain 'order'. *What is this order' and why has it been chosen?* Here is the problem of method grasped immediately in its connexion with the content, the subject-matter, of *Capital*.

In a still very external way we can say more precisely that this subject-matter is the *theory* of the capitalist system of production and circulation, that is, an organized totality of historically determined economic structures. This system is analysed by way of a conceptual procedure that explores this content, gaining access to it with the aid of those special concepts which are economic categories, such as the category 'commodity'.

In order to reveal the content of the capitalist system, Marx employs these economic categories, developing them in a certain order that expresses the content of the system and its mode of internal organization, in other words, its laws. The order of the categories 'reproduces' the actual order of the economic system being analysed. The economic categories are thus the 'ideal subject-matter' of the theory of *Capital*, and it is the actual way in which they are handled and put in relation to each other that makes a theory out of this subject-matter: the method transforms reflexion into theory and ensures that it is both rational and true.

Since the method consists in a certain way of handling categories, the question arises: *what is an economic category?* I would define it as the concept of an economic structure. It is something ideal, an 'ideal object', a product of the reflective consciousness that engenders it so as to be able to look through it at a reality that is external to consciousness but which the latter wishes to know. This definition seems to me to clarify a phrase of Marx's:

The categories of bourgeois economy . . . are forms of thought expressing with social validity the conditions and relations of a definite, historically determined mode of production . . . (*Capital*, I, 1938 edn, p. 47).

It is this ideal subject-matter that the method organizes into a theory. If this is so, then we can now define the nature of Marx's procedure by contrasting it with Hegel's. We thus refute a comparison between Marx and Hegel which is as common as it is confused.

Marx's procedure works *with* concepts, analyses categories, but it is not a theory of the concepts which it elaborates, nor a 'logic of the concept'. It is a logic of *reality*, in other words, of what is not the concept but what the concept looks at. Though, as we shall see, Marx's theory involves a dialectical movement, this is not the movement of the concept (*Begriff*) opposing itself to itself and identifying itself in what is other than itself. This dialectic is not Marx's and has only formal resemblances to Marx's. It resembles it in being, like Marx's, a certain handling of concepts, of ideal objects. But the logic of reality is not the ideal logic of concepts. The latter, for Marx, has its basis and source only in the former, which it 'reproduces'.[1] The dialectic, as a tool of analysis, is transformed when it has ceased to be the tool of a speculative procedure, in order to become a mode of access to the content of economic reality.

For economic science to be able to make use of this re-worked tool, however, a preliminary philosophical elaboration was needed, in order to smash the speculative use of it, by carrying out a critique of philosophical idealism. This is what essentially distinguishes Hegelianism from dialectical materialism. This is what Marx meant when he wrote: 'My dialectic method is not only different from the Hegelian, but is its direct opposite'.[2]

I have shown that the problem of the method of *Capital* lay in the extent to which the work is organized in accordance with a certain order. We have seen that what is 'arranged' in this way is an ideal domain, a set of categories. I have made clear the nature of these categories and the function they fulfil. I have been able straightaway to prevent a misunderstanding about Marx's method and get rid of the confusion between Hegel and Marx. But the latter's method then appears as the outcome of a twofold procedure, philosophical and scientific, which it presupposes and

[1] This fundamental point is analysed by Marx in his *Introduction to the Critique of Political Economy*. The idea of 'reproduction' is to be distinguished from that of 'reflexion', which, however, it presupposes. It is *this* idea, and not that of reflexion, that lies at the heart of the theory of cognition implicit in Marx's work.

[2] Afterword to the second German edition of *Capital* (*Capital*, I, p. xxx).

which underlies it. The complexity of this method is thus the price to be paid for its richness.

We must now show fully the difficulties involved in analysing Marx's method, so as to complete our preliminary reconnaissance of the nature of the problem that it presents. Marx's method, we can now say, is a method that organizes the categories of political economy in a certain order, which makes the work an exposition of the theory of capitalism. *What is this order?*[3]

Starting with the category 'commodities', Marx proceeds to analyse the conditions for exchanging commodities, the existence of money, and then shows that money is transformed into capital. In order to explain this transformation, he reveals that its secret lies in the buying and selling of a particular commodity, namely, labour-power. We are thus present, so to speak, at the production of surplus-value (Volume I).

After this analysis of the immediate production-process of capital, Volume II goes on to analyse the process of the reproduction of capital, a process that embraces the process of production, and that of circulation. Here we have the theory of the accumulation of capital.

Possessing now the theory of surplus-value and the theory of expanded reproduction, Marx can undertake to expound the process of capitalist production as a whole (Volume III). We observe the mechanism whereby surplus-value is transformed into profit, and then into average profit, this latter being the basis of the division of profit into profit of enterprise, interest on capital and ground-rent. Expanded reproduction is now seen as being determined by the law of the tendency of the rate of profit to fall, a law that expresses the relation between the increase in the productivity of labour and the fundamental structures of the capitalist system of production and circulation.

This, then, is, in outline, the 'order' of *Capital*, the structure that makes it a theory of capitalism. When we examine this outline we perceive at once that profit, the actual result of the process of capital, and the tendency of the rate of profit to fall, are not studied directly. It is necessary

[3] I am analysing *Capital* in its definitive form, that is, the three volumes that were published under that title. Volume IV, which Marx wanted to distinguish from the others under the title of *Theories of Surplus-Value*, a fundamental work that completes *Capital*, is the result of a theoretical approach that I shall briefly analyse below, and which throws much light on the methods of *Capital*. See on this, *Briefe über das Kapital*, Berlin (Dietz), 1954, p. 127.

first of all to study surplus-value. The latter is thus seen as the origin of profit, as what 'reappears' later on, in concrete but derivative forms, as interest, profit of enterprise and rent. In order to arrive at the essence of profit and define its nature, the thinker has to go back to its origin and then move forward from this origin to the concrete category of profit. On his return from this journey, the category of profit becomes 'intelligible'.

The order of *Capital* is thus:

(1) Expressive of the structure of the thinker's mode of access to the content aimed at (for example: theory cannot grasp the essence of profit before it has grasped that of surplus-value).[4]

(2) This mode of access is itself expressive of the content being thought (for example: profit is a derived, 'developed' form of surplus-value).

The method of *Capital*, the order of the thought embodied in it, is dictated by the objective content of what is being thought about. At the same time, the objective truth of this content is to be discovered only through a certain mode of access, through a certain type of advance from theoretical thinking to objective reality.

This circularity of the method of *Capital* is actually an example of the circularity characteristic of all rational cognition, all theory. Whatever is known has been discovered only through a certain procedure that revealed it, and this procedure succeeded in revealing what it revealed only because it submitted itself to the content it was illuminating, and struck root in this content.[5] In this way we see made very clear the difficulty of analysing

---

[4] Which is not the case with thought that is immersed in practice, with empirical consciousness.

[5] This general structure of rational cognition seems to me to provide the foundation of the philosophical theories of cognition. The first factor, the procedural work, provides the root of those philosophies which seek in the ideal activity of the rational subject the source of the objectivity of rational cognition. This aspect is given a privileged position, especially by the transcendental philosophies.

The second factor is the gnoseological root of those ontological philosophies which, more often than not, simply sweep aside the activity of rational subjectivity. These philosophies are traditionally opposed to each other, and their opposition 'reproduces' the circularity of the movement of rational cognition. It is through their one-sidedness that these philosophies fail in their effort to constitute a complete theory of cognition. They think out and develop only one aspect of the knowing process. Marxist philosophy can and must avoid this dead-end, while assimilating the positive results achieved by these two types of philosophy. For this circular structure is the unity of two opposite

the method of *Capital*, and at the same time we see better how this method was determined.

The difficulty lies, then, in the fact that the method simultaneously expresses the subjective approach of the thinker and the objective content of what he is thinking about. In the last analysis, though, it is the content that provides the 'grounds' for the method, since, while the method expresses the procedure adopted by the thought-process, the latter expresses the nature of what is being thought about.[6]

This becomes perfectly clear when we try to define the nature of the thinker's subjective procedure, the outcome of which we see in the method of *Capital*. We come to the last difficulty to which Marx's method gives rise. When we have analysed this, Marx's method will have been determined, in its abstract structure and in its problematic.

*

At the time when he wrote *Capital*, Marx was, in fact, in possession of the essential results of his theoretical reflexion. Since 1844 he had pursued his project, which culminated in 1859 in the *Contribution to the Critique of Political Economy*, written several years before the first volume of *Capital*. The method of *Capital* is thus not the *mode of discovery* of the results, but the *mode of presenting* them. This is fundamental, because it is the mode of presentation that *makes* the work a theory, giving it unity, ensuring its rationality and development, and enabling the reader to

---

movements. In order to think out this unity and this contradiction we need to use the dialectic, but the dialectic re-fashioned so as to be free of all dogmatic speculation.

On this basis a critical confrontation could be developed between Marxism, Husserl's transcendental philosophy and the new ontologies. It should be noted that Hegel had already 'recognized' this circularity of cognition, and elaborated the dialectic to account for it; this is the problem of the relationship of the *Phenomenology of the Spirit* to the *Science of Logic*.

[6] This assumes that the criterion of truth is not merely 'formal' but, in the last analysis, always 'material'; in other words, is always provided by proof of the adequacy of thought to its subject-matter. 'Proof' that a theory is true will never, in the last analysis, be founded on these formal characteristics alone, but they make it a theory and furnish the conditions for its truth to be possible. (On this point see the first part of Husserl's *Formal Logic, Transcendental Logic*). Where then is the 'true' proof of a truth to be found? In its practical verification. A more subtle analysis would have to be made of proof in mathematics, since there the truth of a theory and its formal possibility seem to merge. But the subject-matter of mathematics is something special, something ideal, like a concept.

'comprehend' it. The proof of the truth of Marx's theory is to be found
on the one hand in the process of discovery, and on the other in the practical verification that men have been able to subject it to subsequently.
Marx was perfectly aware of the nature of his method when he wrote:

> Of course the method of presentation must differ in *form* from that of inquiry.
> The latter has to appropriate the matter in detail, to analyse its different forms
> of development, to trace out their inner connexion. *Only after* this work is done
> can the actual movement be adequately described.[7]

Through the method of exposition a 'systematic' theory becomes possible.[8] The latter is possible, however, only when the truth has already
been attained, possessed, the content clarified; yet it is also by this method
that the truth of the theory will be demonstrated. There is thus a formal
distinction and an essential identity between the method of investigation
and the method of exposition.[9]

The method of *Capital* thus makes possible both the ideal origination
of the capitalist system, its 'deduction', and the rationality of this deduction. Consequently, clarification of Marx's method is merely the reverse
side of a clarification of the content of the capitalist system. Within the
limits of an article I obviously cannot undertake a complete explanation
of the theory. At the same time I cannot really leave its content out of
account. I will therefore place this on the horizon of my analysis, assuming
it to be broadly familiar.

This marks the end of the first stage of my approach, which has enabled
us to 'recognize' the abstract structures of the method of *Capital* and to
clarify the nature of the problems that analysis of this method involves.
*We know that the method is inseparable from the content, that this content
is the ideal subject-matter of the economic categories, that this subject-matter
is arranged in a certain order, that this order depends on the method and the
method on the content, that this circularity is the major difficulty in the study*

[7] Afterword to second German edition (*Capital*, I, p. xxix). My emphasis, M.G.

[8] On this subject see M. Rosenthal, *Les Problèmes de la dialectique dans le 'Capital' de
Marx*, chapter 10, section 2. This work contains some interesting analyses. It is, however, muddled in construction, since it lacks a rigorous preliminary problematic.

[9] The problem of the difference and the identity of the two methods is an epistemological and historical problem of great difficulty. It is that of the real origins of Marx's
theory, and has hardly been studied at all. See, however, Rosenthal, op. cit.; Cornu,
Karl Marx et Friedrich Engels, vols. I and II; and Lenin, *The Three Sources and Three
Component Parts of Marxism* (1913), and *Karl Marx* (1914).

of Marx's method, but that this difficulty is cleared up when we grasp the distinctive function of the method, which is, here, to expound.

We can now set about analysing the concrete structures of Marx's method: but we know now that they must ensure the unity, rationality and development of the theory. We shall see how, concretely, they accomplish this task.[10]

i. *The hypothetico-deductive method*

'Exposition' of the laws of the capitalist system of production is carried out by way of two different procedures, or at least, as my conclusion will show, *by way of a procedure* that is the synthetical unity of two different methods. In order to *facilitate* our analysis, we will for the moment consider the two methods as they differ. We will call the first of them the 'hypothetico-deductive method' and the second the 'dialectical method'.

The use of assumptions

The analysis of *Capital* proceeds by way of ideal hypotheses, three types of which can be distinguished:

(a) *Capital* is entirely based on a simplifying assumption which *limits a priori* the field of analysis, while at the same time enabling the latter to 'organize itself'.

The content that Marx is studying is the 'pure' structure of capitalist relations of production. It is not a study of capitalism in any particular country or in any particular epoch, but a study of the *essence* of the economic relations that make capitalism a definite economic 'system', possessing a typical unity and homogeneity. This production-relation contains only the relation between capital and labour, and, in its social aspect, the relation between the capitalist class and the working class.

For there are here only two classes: the working class, disposing only of its labour-power, and the capitalist class, which has a monopoly of the social means of production and money.[11]

When this simplifying assumption has been made, rigorous deductions

[10] My procedure may give the impression that I am 'deducing' Marx's method, just as Marx seemed to be 'deducing' the laws of capitalism. This is merely the *appearance* of the presentation of the *logic* of Marx's procedures (just as Marx's procedures presented the logic of the capitalist system).

[11] *Capital*, vol. II, p. 421.

become possible. The relations that are established in theory between the economic structures therefore do not correspond exactly to economic reality:

In theory it is assumed that the laws of capitalist production operate in their pure form. In reality there exists only approximation;[12] but this approximation is the greater, the more developed the capitalist mode of production and the less it is adulterated and amalgamated with survivals of former economic conditions.[13]

This overall assumption enables the subject-matter being studied to *show itself* in its real essence, for in concrete reality, which is never totally governed by capitalist production-relations, this real essence shows itself only via phenomena that conceal it and even contradict it.

By using assumptions, thought can work out the pure theory of economic structures, grasp their essence: that is, it can work out their concept. We now realize why theory organizes the concepts that are the categories of political economy.

In a general analysis of this kind it is usually always *assumed that the actual conditions correspond to their conception*, or, what is the same, that actual conditions are represented only to the extent that they are typical of their own *general case*.[14]

This can already show us the root of the apparent deduction of reality given in *Capital*. It is, in fact, as we shall see, only the *appearance* of the synthetical approach of rational cognition.

(b) I have given an example of a general procedure of Marx's method: this procedure is repeated in every phase of the work. Other assumptions are made which, though general, are not overall in character, as the first one is, which I have already explained. Here are two examples.

In Volumes I and II and at the beginning of Volume III, an assumption

---

[12] These passages provide important materials for the construction of a theory of economic cognition. Marx was not unaware that concrete investigation in economic matters requires the tool of statistics and that rational cognition is always 'approximate'. 'Pure' analysis furnishes the concepts, the definitions, for an inquiry that will be neither empirical nor blind. But cognition of concrete economic reality can never be other than approximate. The mathematical device of the calculation of probabilities is thus one of the tools needed for this cognition. This should serve to establish the idea of economic law (see Granger, *Economic Methodology*).

[13] *Capital*, vol. III, p. 172.

[14] *Capital*, vol. III, p. 141. My emphasis, M.G.

is formulated in order to facilitate use of the theory of value and application of it to the theory of production:

It is furthermore assumed that products are exchanged at their values and also that there is no revolution in the values of the component parts of productive capital.[15]

In Volume II Marx makes the assumption of simple reproduction, and develops this over about a hundred pages; yet this 'premise of simple reproduction, that I(v + s) is equal to II c, is . . . incompatible with capitalist production . . .'[16] He had warned us at the beginning of this analysis: 'simple reproduction . . . appears as an abstraction . . . a strange assumption. . . .'[17] But this assumption is needed for the purpose of analysing the mode of reproduction that is compatible with the capitalist system: expanded reproduction.

Thus, the making of simplifying assumptions is *operationally* necessary, and makes other processes of reasoning possible. This method ensures the rigour and coherence of the theory and constitutes one of the essential aspects of the apparatus of proof. The thinker can, at each stage of his thinking, either give or refuse himself the right to make certain 'deductions'. Here is an example from among hundreds. 'Here . . . we presume . . . We thus leave aside for the present that . . .'[18]

(c) A third type of assumption is the type most frequently met with in the book. These assumptions are similar to the two other types, but differ in the relative narrowness of their field of application. They concern the study of certain *functional relations* between economic structures that may vary and thus modify their mutual relations. Each assumption relates to the variation of one or more variables, and these variations are imagined as being either successive or simultaneous.

An example of this use of assumption is the study of 'the relation of the rate of profit to the rate of surplus-value'.[19]

$$p' = \frac{s'}{C} = s' \frac{v}{c + v}$$

---

[15] ibid., vol. II, p. 393.   [16] ibid., vol. II, p. 520.   [17] ibid., vol. II, pp. 394–5.

[18] ibid., vol. III, p. 49. There is a logical 'time', an ideal time in reflexion, which is not that of concrete time-relations. On this subject see the studies by Victor Goldschmidt on logical time and the structures of philosophical systems.

[19] ibid., vol. III, chapter 3.

where p′ = rate of profit; s′ = rate of surplus-value; v = variable capital; C = total capital = c + v; c = constant capital.

Marx proceeds to imagine the variation of one or several terms of the equation:

(1) s′ constant, v/C variable (four cases possible);

(2) s′ variable (two cases possible);

(3) s′, v and C variable (five cases possible).

This use of assumption makes possible a mathematical *calculation*. Marx's economic theory *leads necessarily*[20] to the setting up of mathematical models that substitute mathematical analysis, calculation, for qualitative conceptual analysis. Conceptual analysis provides the definition of the structures. In so far as these structures are magnitudes, quantities, mathematical analysis must necessarily be employed in economic theory. Marx planned to work out a mathematical theory of economics. It is noteworthy that analysis of the relations between two variables led him to develop his theory of the mean of a series of simple equations and inequations. In the chapter in which he studies the relation between the rate of surplus-value and the rate of profit, he states: 'The analysis . . . first is carried on purely in the mathematical field.'[21]

This type of assumption thus provides an initial formal possibility of using calculations – obviously only in so far as the structures being analysed are quantifiable. Through this aspect, Marx's thought makes possible the constitution of a 'model' and use of the mathematical instruments worked out since *Capital* was published. Some attempts at doing this have already been made.

Klein, for example, has constructed a mathematical model of the Marxist theory and contrasted this with the 'classical' and 'Keynesian' models.[22] Hehas shown that the Marxist model is more complete than the simplified Ke ynesian model (in which the quantity of money and the rate of interest do not figure as variables). However, his model of Marxism is not a dynamic one and is to some extent unfaithful to Marx's theory.

Charles Bettelheim presented, in the *Revue d'Economie Appliquée* (1959), a model intended to define the relation between variations in the

---

[20] Marxist economists have not always perceived this. They did not analyse all the possibilities present in Marx's theory. They criticized the use made of mathematics by certain non-Marxist economists, but from this position went on to reject the use of mathematics as such.   [21] ibid., vol. III, p. 49.

[22] See Charles Bettelheim, *Nouveaux Aspects de la théorie de l'emploi*, C.D.U., p. 11.

rate of profit and increase in the productivity of labour. This model utilizes concepts similar to those worked out by Marx, and in this way completes the investigations in *Capital*.[23]

By setting up a mathematical model we arrive at a *symbolic* representation of the economic movement, in the form of curves. For example, in the manuscript of *Capital* there are some very detailed calculations on the difference between rate of surplus-value and rate of profit (s' — p'), a difference that has some interesting peculiarities, and the movement of which points to cases where the two rates move away from each other or come closer together.[24] Curves of these movements can be constructed, and their intersections or distances studied.

The use of assumptions thus enables us to calculate and thereby to grasp certain laws of the functioning of an economic system.

It is to be observed: (1) that the relations may be stochastic if to a determined variable A there corresponds a probable value B. A 'probabilist' model will then be constructed: A is a function of an aggregate of values of B; this model fits reality more closely, since it leaves room for the probable;[25] (2) that the making of assumptions regarding the variations of variables presupposes that assumptions have been made regarding the time in which these variations take place. Analysis of these variations will be substantially modified if the assumptions regarding time are different.

To take up again my example from *Capital*, the study of the relation between s' and p' is carried out within the framework of an assumption regarding the influence of the time of turnover of capital on s'. Marx says, explicitly: 'We shall leave this factor entirely out of consideration for the present.'[26] Engels observes in a note that this simplifying assumption made by Marx renders the formula

$$p' = s' \frac{v}{C}$$

[23] See, also by Bettelheim. 'Modèle du rapport du taux de croissance économique du long terme et des choix technologiques', *Revue économique*, no. 1, and his *Studies in the Theory of Economic-Planning*, Bombay, 1959: also *Tiers Monde*, no. 1, 1960.

[24] Though Engels did not publish these materials, they should not be overlooked.

[25] What are called 'determinist' or 'probabilist' models are used in operational research: linear programming, games theory, simulation methods, all of which make up an important contribution to economic knowledge. See G. Guilbaud, 'Rapport au Congrès des économistes de langue française', *Revue d'Economie Politique*, 1954. See also Blackwell and Girschich, *Theory of Games and Statistical Economics*.

[26] *Capital*, vol. III, p. 50.

'strictly correct only for one period of turnover of the variable capital'.

We see that the introduction of other hypotheses regarding economic time would have led Marx to set up a dynamic mathematical model,[27] or at least to make use of such mathematical devices as differential and integral calculus.

Our analysis has thus enabled us to demonstrate a certain number of important aspects of the methodological apparatus of the theory of *Capital*.

Simplifying assumptions are necessary in order (1) to constitute ideally the field of scientific analysis; (2) to make it possible, within this field, to determine the concept of the economic structures and their laws, to work out the economic *categories*; and (3) to make it possible, within this field and within these conceptual determinations, to carry out mathematical *calculation*, and to employ an operational formalism and symbolism.

Simplifying assumptions make a rigorous procedure possible, give economic theory much of its rationality, its unity and extent, and realize concretely the task that I have ascribed abstractly to method. The overall result of the operational use of simplifying assumptions is to facilitate the coherent development of reflexion, in other words, the development of a theory, and to *deduce* certain laws of the functioning of the system.

We thus arrive at the deductive operations that the method enables us to undertake. The task of analysis is now more delicate, however, for we are at the heart of the structure of the argument of *Capital*.

The deductive operation

These are of several types:

(1) the first is made up of a group of partial and local deductions which depend upon assumptions of the third type, assumptions that are equally local in character. If we take once more our example of Marx's study of the relation between the rate of profit and the rate of surplus-value, we see that it leads to the determination of a number of structural possibilities. Given the assumption that s', v and C are variables, it is deduced that:

It follows from all of these five cases, therefore, that a rising rate of profit may correspond to a falling or rising rate of surplus value, a falling rate of profit to a rising or falling rate of surplus value, and a constant rate of profit to a

[27] On this point, Marx was not able to rise above his epoch. Besides, what was essential for him was less the working out of a mathematical theory than that of a theory of the *categories* of political economy.

rising or falling rate of surplus value. . . . A rising, falling or constant rate of profit may also accord with a constant rate of surplus value (*Capital*, III, p. 68).

This result is a striking example of deduction of the laws of an economic system, the modes of connexion between variable structures. What is deduced here is the *possibilities* of functioning that depend on the *structural necessities* of a system. Reality will always 'realize' a particular case of functioning that will 'appear' as the realization of one of the possibilities of the system.[28] But these possibilities are the result of variable combinations of essential economic structures which are themselves defined in their necessity.

This necessity is analysed not through calculation but through the elaboration of concepts. The variables are *defined* before they become objects of calculation and symbolic construction. They are defined through the elaboration of the categories that relate to them. This elaboration is made possible, as has been shown, by the making of overall assumptions of types 1 and 2. Thus, the structural 'possibilities' are dependent on the structural 'necessities', just as the local assumptions are embraced by the overall assumptions. The possible is linked to the necessary.

The theory forms a complex structure of ideas, a mixture of the necessary and possible which enables us to picture reality in its necessary and contingent aspects. From the epistemological standpoint it is important to note that abstract, theoretical thought transforms reality, as met with in experience, into a 'realized possible'.[29] It thus enables us to grasp, behind the confused and fleeting appearances, the structures that constitute both the origin and the meaning of these appearances.

The theory is thus an ideal field in which the possible finds a meaning, even if this possible is never 'realized'. Marx's thought does not proceed empirically, or, contrariwise, by way of obscure deductions. It operates, like all rational thought, with simplifying assumptions, and builds an ideal 'model' of reality. See, for instance, this significant passage:

[28] This is partly responsible for the speculative illusion of theoretical thinking that it 'deduces' reality, 'establishes' it. I shall come back to this point in another article, looking at the idea of 'reproduction' as it appears in Marx, and the epistemological conception that lies behind this.

[29] In so far as theory has to make deductions from possibilities, it cannot do without the tool of mathematics.

This is possible only if the working day is reduced by one-third ... It need hardly be said that this reduction of the working time, in the case of a fall in wages, *would not occur in practice*. But that is *immaterial*. The rate of profit is a function of several variable magnitudes, and if we *wish to know* how these variables influence the rate of profit, we *must* analyse the individual effect of each in turn, regardless of whether such an isolated effect is economically practicable with one and the same capital.[30]

We have therefore seen that special assumptions make possible partial deductions, the revelation of possibilities. The latter are linked dependently to necessities that are determined by more general assumptions. Mathematical thinking is linked dependently to conceptual thinking. Local assumptions are embraced by overall assumptions. We must now analyse the nature of the deductions that these overall assumptions make possible.

*

(2) My task is now to try to explain the secret of the overall architecture of *Capital*, to make clear the overall order of Marx's theory. Here we reach the plane of the fundamental definitions of the economic categories of the capitalist system, the work of conceptual thought which seeks to elaborate the concept of an economic structure.

Let us take up again our outline of the order of *Capital*. If we analyse this closely, we see that this order is based upon the 'deduction' of certain categories from the category of surplus-value. The latter appears as the *invisible origin of the visible categories* – profit of enterprise, interest, rent. The theory develops the relationship of these categories with each other, starting from an 'originating' category that *provides the basis* for the existence and the essence of the others. It is therefore necessary to proceed by way of surplus value in order to perceive the essence of profit, and thereby to rediscover the concrete by starting from the abstract.

The method is thus highly expressive of the approach by theoretical thought to that which is being thought about, and this approach reproduces the internal links of the structures being analysed, their mutual relationship to their common basis.

The method is thus a method of exposition, and this consists in deducing structures that are derived from an originating structure, basing these derived structures upon this initial structure, and showing how the whole

[30] *Capital*, Vol. III, p. 58. My emphasis, M.G.

edifice is compatible, in other words, showing the structural unity and homogeneity of the capitalist system.

This threefold operation causes the theory to construct a sort of 'ideal genesis' of the capitalist process. In thought we are able to be present at this engendering of some structures by others.

The method thus establishes *a way of referring back* from one structure to another which enables us to grasp how these structures are linked to their origin. This reference 'back' does not reproduce a movement of real, historical formation of structures; actually, as soon as the capitalist system is historically present, these structures are contemporary with each other. This movement cannot therefore be confused with the historical origin of capitalism, with its real origins (see, below, the analysis of primitive accumulation); but this movement is the *revelation of the internal relationship* and content of the general structures of capitalism as a specific system of production. Already we can perceive the relationship between economic theory and the science of history, each of them referring to the other but not merged one with the other. A real science of history must be a synthetical unity of these two scientific approaches. This clarifies the following phrase of Marx's:

The transformation of surplus-value into profit must be deduced from the transformation of the rate of surplus value into the rate of profit, not vice-versa. And in fact it was the rate of profit that was the historical point of departure.[31]

Let us pursue our analysis further by trying to describe the nature of this way of referring back in the realm of ideas from a group of structures to an originating structure. How is this 'ideal' genesis of the capitalist system established?[32]

This genesis can be presented by recalling that the different forms

[31] Ibid., Vol. III, pp. 42–3.

[32] This ideal origination, this relation of the basis to what is based upon it, are not Hegelian procedures, but a procedure akin to what Husserl was to follow when he tried to establish a 'genealogy of logic', or to grasp the ideal structure of the birth of modern physics, with Galileo. Cf. his *Krisis der Europäischen Wissenschaften*. Phenomenology as a science of 'essences', an eidetic analysis, is distinguished from phenomenological philosophy as a system of transcendental philosophy. Phenomenology as a technique of eidetic analysis is not subject to the destructive blows of the critique of transcendental phenomenology. Marx's thinking here carries out a phenomenological approach that is not that of Hegelian phenomenology. However, Marx's dialectical method adopts certain aspects of the Hegelian dialectic. This indicates the basis on which a contrast between Hegel, Marx and Husserl should be undertaken.

assumed by profit are forms of distribution of the mass of profit. The latter has to be produced before it can be shared out. We must therefore analyse how profit is produced before we study how it is shared.

When we try to find out how profit has been produced, in other words both the origin and the structure of the mechanism whereby it is produced, we find that profit presents itself, as regards its origin, in the form of surplus-value. Profit is thus both distinct from surplus-value and identical with it. The distinction is due to the fact that profit is a structure that arises from the collective, overall functioning of the macro-economic mechanism, that is, from the real system of capitalism, a system that functions as a whole. Surplus-value, however, is a structure that arises at micro-economic level, at the level at which the capitalist enterprise functions (being imagined as independent of the effects of its relationship to the system as a whole).[33]

Thus we are brought back from the product, the effect, to the cause, to the mechanism that produces surplus-value. The theory causes the structures to emerge ideally, so to speak, from one another, and our thinking seems to be present at this birth. We have arrived at an important point.

This 'genesis' actually enables us to define the fundamental economic categories, giving each its place, that is, in logical relationship with the others. *A logical relationship is established between the concepts.* We see in a category the essence of an economic structure, and the relation between one category and another shows the 'origin' and foundation of this structure.

This relationship is a 'logical' one, that is, it shows the *necessary* relationship between the structures. Thus, the essence of each economic structure can be defined, by means of this method, in the form of a concept, and the clarification of its ideal origin makes plain the logical relationship between the concepts.

We appreciate why economic theory can and must be a form of logic, the logic of the economic system being studied. Our analysis has thus partly explained the origin of the economic thinking that proceeds by way

[33] This shows us how Marx effects the transition from micro-economics to macro-economics. The former does not directly offer the means of picturing the actual economy. Only macro-economic analysis (volumes II and III) enables us, taking up the results of micro-economic analysis, to rejoin the real economic movement, which is always all-inclusive. An interesting comparison could be made, as regards this transition from the micro-economic to the macro-economic, between Marx, Keynes and the post-Keynesians. See, e.g. Kurihara: *Post-Keynesian Economics.*

of concepts, and the nature of the domain it explores – namely, the necessary relations which it defines, in such a way as at the same time to open the field of mathematical analysis, of thought that proceeds by way of calculation and determines the functional potentialities of a system.

This 'logic' here implies no 'dialectic'. It moves, so to speak, from the simple (surplus value) to the complex (average profit). We shall see how the inner contradictions of the mechanism of surplus value 'engender' a whole series of contradictions and a contradictory development of the capitalist system. All this will relate to a logic that is now dialectical in character, and of which we shall indicate the nature and purpose.

While, however, the relation between the categories is a logical one, it is also chronological, but the *time* of this chronology is wholly *determined by the logic of the relations between one structure and another.* The procedure followed by *Capital* puts at the start of the analysis the study of the production of surplus-value, that is, study of the production-sphere. What is produced is then sold and the income from this is shared out. But the circulation, exchange and distribution of this income presuppose this production of what is to circulate and to be exchanged and shared. Logical relations are therefore at the same time chronological ones, in so far as the logical moments correspond to the different moments of time in the economic process.

Chronological time is thus altogether structured by the logic of the functional relations between economic structures. This time is logicized – which means that this logicized chronology both is, and, at the same time, is not concrete historical time.[34] In the latter, what is successive in logicized time, is also simultaneous, and this is fundamental to understanding the relationship between abstract economic theory and concrete history.

Marx carries out this transition from the concrete to the very heart of abstract economic theory. In order to rejoin concrete reality he makes a transition from micro-economics to macro-economics, that is, to a theory that comes increasingly closer to the concrete. This is the movement we see in Volumes II and III of *Capital*: compare, for example, this passage:

What we previously regarded as changes occurring successively with one and the same capital is now to be regarded as simultaneous differences among capital investments existing side by side in different spheres of production.[35]

[34] Concrete historical time is not merely time structured by concrete economic relations but time structured by all the rest of Man's relations with himself and with the world.   [35] *Capital*, III, p. 142.

In this way the logical connexion between categories also reveals the structure of the development of the economic process in time. The pace of the process depends on the functional relations between economic structures forming a unified whole; in concrete historical reality, however, time has two directions, two vectors at once, a successive order and a simultaneous order. A capitalist enterprise functions in accordance with a successive order, but this is modified because:

(a) a capitalist enterprise always effects several simultaneous rotations of capital. Micro-economic analysis becomes much more complex and requires a more developed model (cf. Volume II, chapter 15, of *Capital*, on the effect of the time of turnover on the magnitude of advanced capital);

(b) a capitalist enterprise always exists in relation to the total functioning of social capital. Now at the overall social level, all the phases of a particular process are realized simultaneously. At any given moment, production, circulation, exchange, etc., are all taking place. On the macro-economic plane the method needs to be modified. Besides, since, at any given moment, production, circulation, etc., set in motion total quantities of products or of money, the macro-economic method can be developed on the plane of calculation. At the same time, however, as we shall see, analysis is led more and more towards employing the dialectical approach that grasps reality as a totality. We see again the conceptual approach interlinked with mathematical calculation, all within a macro-economic method that aims at approximating to reality.

We see also that economic theory, in order to picture reality, has to utilize the two methods, micro-economic and macro-economic, at the same time, but not in the same place; when the model needs to rejoin reality, the macro-economic methods has to take the place of the micro-economic. This replacement is dictated by the actual content of reality, for in the capitalist system a 'single' capitalist enterprise does not exist as such – it exists only as one element in a larger whole.

We see, then, why the categories were presented in *Capital* in a certain order. But we have not yet explained the actual starting-point of the theory, namely, the analysis of the category, 'commodity'. We began with the 'logical' starting-point, that is, the moment at which surplus-value is born, in order to understand the reference back of the other structures to this one: but this moment is not the starting-point of the theory.

Whereas the moment of birth of surplus-value leads us to move from production to what is produced, which seems logical, we now notice that the moment of production was itself analysed after what is produced, namely, the commodity. Why this order? Is this a fault in construction that contradicts the rigour we have hitherto observed in Marx's theory? If we can establish the *necessity of this starting-point*, we shall have explained the entire process of construction of the theory and defined the last aspect of this 'ideal genesis' of capitalism.

In fact, it is analysis of the category 'commodity' that alone makes possible an understanding of the *unity and sense* of the capitalist system of production. Far from compromising the rigour of the theoretical construction, it ensures its complete coherence. Why is this?

The capitalist system of production becomes fully clear when the intimate nature of the commodity is revealed, for the capitalist system constitutes the most developed form of commodity production. The essence of the 'commodity' bears the 'sense' of the entire capitalist system: hence the words at the beginning of *Capital*:

The wealth of those societies in which the capitalist mode of production prevails presents itself as 'an immense accumulation of commodities'. . . . Our investigation must therefore begin with the analysis of a commodity.[36]

The method will consist in analysing ideally the essence of the object known to mankind under the name of 'commodity', and discovering in this product the nature of the process whereby it was produced, allowing oneself to be carried back by the characteristics of the object to the characteristics of the production-process that gave rise to it; in other words, to the structures of productive human labour.

The method proceeds from what is formed to that which forms it. Here could be found one of the most precise foundations for comparison between Marx and Husserl. But the forming activity to which Marx refers is human labour, in other words, an historically determined social relation, and not the transcendent activity of an absolute consciousness. Comparison between Marx and Husserl relates to an identical way of analysing the essence of an object, so that this essence bears the *intelligibility* of the system of social actions that has produced it. The difference between Marx and Husserl is revealed when the nature of the forming activity is analysed. The philosophical assumption of an ideal absolute subject is rejected because of the experience that it cannot explain (the material and historical *praxis* of societies). The philosophical assumption of an histori-

[36] ibid., I, p. 1.

cal subject that is both product and producer of its own practical activity, the assumption of dialectical materialism, was developed by Marx to account for this forming activity.[37] This is the general relationship between philosophy, economic theory and history in Marx's work.

But how is this reference back, from what is formed to that which has formed it, carried out concretely, how is this particular analysis linked to that which is developed on the basis of the theory of surplus-value?

When he analyses the 'commodity object', Marx isolates two outward structures of this object: its use-value and its exchange-value.

Use-values relate to 'human wants of some sort or another'. On this basis, it is not possible to grasp the distinctive features of the process that produces commodities. Use-values relate merely to men's natural or artificial wants, to a qualitative relationship: 'Use-values . . . constitute the substance of all wealth, whatever may be the social form of that wealth.'[38]

Exchange-value 'at first sight presents itself as a quantitative relation, as the proportion in which values in use of one sort are exchanged for those of another sort'. If they are to be exchanged in a definite proportion, commodities must have something in common, whatever may be the differences in their qualitative aspect. This something-in-common, once the use-value of commodities is set aside, can only be the quality they all possess 'of being products of labour'. Labour thus forms the substance of the value of a commodity. In this way a structural analysis makes possible a demonstration of the origin of the structures being analysed.

How can labour account not only for the substance of value but for its magnitude, that is, for what makes it possible to relate one commodity, in quantitative terms, with another? It can do this because the labour that forms this substance is social labour, that is, 'the time socially necessary for the production of commodities'. On this basis, a quantity of commodities can be exchanged for another because what is exchanged is the relation between one quantity of labour and another. Value appears as 'congealed' labour.

This analysis of the origin of exchange-value and its nature makes it possible to grasp the money form of the commodity, the money form of

[37] See J. T. Desanti's remarkable article on the relation between Marxism and phenomenology, and on the notion of the historical subject, in *Revue Internationale de Philosophie*, 1959, special issue on Marx.

[38] *Capital*, I, pp. 2–3.

exchange-value. On the basis of the results achieved, Marx presents the ideal genesis of the money form:

> Here . . . a task is set us, the performance of which has never yet even been attempted by bourgeois economy, the task of tracing the genesis of this money form, of developing the expression of value implied in the value relation of commodities, from its simplest, almost imperceptible outline to the dazzling money form. By doing this we shall, at the same time, solve the riddle presented by money.[39]

Money is to be revealed in its essence as a special commodity whose 'specific social function, and consequently whose social monopoly, is to serve as universal equivalent in the world of commodities', and so to make possible the exchange of products of labour among men. Economic theory provides the concept of money, in its logical relationship with the original structure that serves as its basis – the exchange value of the commodity.

Marx's method is always the same and just as rigorous. The category 'money' presupposes the category 'commodity', since money is a special form of commodity. This special form is meaningless except through the exchange of commodities. Theory is therefore able to provide an analysis of money only after the commodity has been analysed. This logical relationship throws light at the same time on a chronological and historical relationship, and serves as an ideal guide to understanding the nature of historical development. The theory, being a work of rational thought, rules out any empiricism.

> Money is a crystal formed of necessity in the course of the exchanges whereby different products of labour are practically equated to one another and thus by practice converted into commodities . . . At the same rate, then, as the conversion of products into commodities is being accomplished, so also is the conversion of one special commodity into money.[40]

At this level of analysis Marx can at one and the same time define the essence of a commodity and show why appearances conceal and contradict this essence.[41] Theoretical thought thus challenges the naïve, practical

---

[39] ibid., I, p. 15.   [40] ibid., I, p. 59.

[41] The theoretical thinking that employs this procedure may seem close to that of Hegel, who bases phenomenology, meaning the figures of consciousness, upon Logic, that is, the moments of the concept. The resemblance is due to the fact that (a) at the moment when the thinker sets forth the theory, he already knows the truth and is 'ex-

understanding of the commodity effected spontaneously by each individual. The human, social character of labour *appears* as a characteristic of things. The producer is dominated by his product and no longer recognizes himself in his product. Man alienates himself in the thing and no longer grasps either commodity or money as a social, human object. Scientific thought challenges appearances and at the same time accounts for them. Thus, the categories of political economy, forms of the intellect, can define the essence of real social relations while challenging appearances and 'common sense'. But scientific thought needs as a pre-condition for its own existence the full development of commodity production.

It requires a fully developed production of commodities before, from accumulated experience alone, the scientific conviction springs up that all the different kinds of labour which are carried on independently of each other . . . are continually being reduced to the quantitative proportions in which society requires them . . . . Man's reflexions on the forms of social life, and consequently also his scientific analysis of those forms, take a course directly opposite to that of their actual historical development (*Capital*, I, 1938 edn, pp. 46–7).

Accordingly, scientific analysis of the commodity category, of its exchange-value and of the money-form of this exchange-value, requires that the modes of everyday practical consciousness be challenged, and demands that the source of the concealment of reality be revealed. It is certain practical, social relations between men that hide reality. It is the things they produce and the way in which they produce them that hide from the individual both their distinctive essence and the relationship of man to himself through the products of his labour.

The deductions that lead from what is formed to that which forms it thus present very great complexity, for the following reasons.

(1) They are carried out by requiring that we become aware, in the midst of economic theory, of the nature of the relationship of man to himself and his objects – that we both reject and at the same time account for the images of everyday consciousness, *which are adequate for practice*

---

pounding' it in the form of a theory, and (b) the moments of the theory are arranged by the relations between the categories, but this relationship between categories is never present, in its real content, for everyday consciousness. So far as the latter is concerned, the categories are reflected by forms of consciousness which at once express them and conceal them. But the essential difference lies in the fact that the thinker knows he cannot create his theory until a certain moment has been reached in men's practical history.

but do not constitute scientific knowledge. Thus, in requiring us to account for the relationship between rational knowledge and reality, these deductions still include a series of philosophical assumptions. Philosophical reflexion necessarily manifests itself in the midst of economic theory, and this in the contradictory form of a reflexion that is prior to economics and at the same time demanded by it. Theoretical reflexion in economics tends towards philosophy, while at the same time it presupposes philosophy.

(2) These deductions are increasingly endued with the dialectical approach. They reveal the essence of a given economic structure, but this essence contradicts the appearance. The hypothetico-deductive method cannot avoid a dialectical analysis of these contradictions, and already we perceive coming together again the two methods that we distinguish in order to clarify them better but which are inseparable in the work itself.

*

We still have to explain the essential link that joins the deduction which proceeds from commodity to surplus-value to that which proceeds from surplus-value to ground-rent. It is this link that ensures the unity of the theory.

The link is provided by the analysis of the transformation of money into capital (part 2 of Volume I). We know that money makes possible the simple circulation of commodities in accordance with the movement $C - M - C$ (C = commodity, M = money). Contrariwise to simple commodity circulation the circulation of money as capital takes the form $M - C - M$.

In the circulation $C - M - C$, the money is in the end converted into a commodity that serves as a use-value; it is spent once for all. In the inverted form, $M - C - M$, on the contrary, the buyer lays out money in order that as a seller, he may recover money. . . . The money, therefore, is not spent, it is merely advanced (*Capital*, I, pp. 125-6).

Between these two forms there is therefore a formal difference behind which lies a real difference. The movement $M - C - M$ takes place only because of the quantitative, and not qualitative, difference between the end-terms, for: 'More money is withdrawn from circulation at the finish than was thrown into it at the start.'

The exact form of this process is therefore $M - C - M'$, where $M' = M +$

$\triangle$M = the original sum advanced, plus an increment. This increment or excess over the original value I call 'surplus-value'. The value originally advanced, therefore, not only remains intact while in circulation, but adds to itself a surplus-value, or expands itself. It is this movement that converts it into capital (*Capital*, I, 1938 edn, p. 128).

The formula $M - C - M'$ has thus enabled us to perceive surplus-value as a certain quantity of value, which possesses this *qualitative* difference from the money initially put into circulation, that it results from this circulation. We see that Marx's deduction is established with full rigour. In order to understand the structure of capital, its specific essence, we must have grasped that it is a specific form of money, and realized that the latter is a developed form of the exchange-value of the commodity. Only from Part 2 of Volume I onward, then, is the theory of capital, of the capitalist system of production and circulation, worked out.

A capitalist is an individual who is the 'conscious bearer of this movement'. The formula $M - M'$ is the general formula of all capital. At this point in the work the theory of value thus dominates the analysis of all the forms of capital – productive capital (Volumes I and II), commercial capital, financial capital (Volume III) – and yet these three forms are not contemporary with each other in history, the two last-mentioned preceding the first-mentioned historically.

The commodity category, a product of the capitalist system, the most highly-developed system of commodity production, thus bears the *intelligibility* of the entire system, and provides the basis for the order of the theory. The theory of value has revealed the essence of value, human labour; in this way we are enabled to understand the order that puts the mechanism of the production of capital, that is, the mechanism of the *production* of surplus-value, before the mechanism of the *realization* and *distribution* of this surplus-value. In this way the basis is laid for the structure of the movement that led from surplus-value to ground-rent. It is thus analysis of the commodity that provides thought with the means of referring back from one structure to another.

*

I have shown (1) that analysis of surplus-value depends on analysis of the commodity, and (2) that analysis of the commodity forms the nucleus of 'meaning' upon which the entire movement of reference back from one structure to another is developed.

I have not yet explained, however, the reversal of method that takes place at the moment when surplus-value is analysed, and when there is substituted, for the movement that leads from what is formed to that which forms it, a movement in the opposite direction. I have thus not finished accounting for the architecture of *Capital*.

We have deduced the general formula of capital, M — M', and seen that capital is money that 'multiplies'. M produces M + $\triangle$ M, and $\triangle$ M is surplus-value. The question that arises is, therefore, this: since 'surplus-value cannot be created by circulation, ... in its formation something must take place in the background which is not apparent in the circulation itself' (*Capital*, I, p. 143).

Unless we are to suppose that money itself engenders money, we have to find a special sort of commodity 'whose use-value possesses the peculiar property of being a source of value, whose actual consumption, therefore, is itself an embodiment of labour and consequently, a creation of value' (*Capital*, I, p. 145).

This commodity, which has to exist if capital is to exist, is labour-power.

The whole capitalist system is now revealed, in its structural unity and homogeneity. The relation M — M', which seems to be a relation of thing to thing, is in fact an historical, social relation between persons, a relation that is effected through the medium of things.[42]

Capital is the relation of those who possess means of production to those who do not, but who do possess a specific commodity, their labour-power. In this way we find deduced and grounded in necessity that structure of the capitalist system which constitutes its significant and essential nucleus. But we see why the commodity category is what bears the intelligibility of the system. In fact, labour-power, the producer of commodities, itself belongs to this category and is bought and sold on the market. The product dominates the producer.

The speculative alienation that takes the relation M — M' for a relation between things is rooted in the practical relation, which is both economic and social, of production: 'The characteristic thing is not that the commodity labour-power is purchasable but that labour-power appears as a commodity' (*Capital*, II, p. 28).

This economic relation is also a social relation. Economic theory is thus immediately linked with sociology, but both are illuminated by history,

[42] Cf. in *Wage-Labour and Capital*: 'Capital, also, is a social production-relation. It is a bourgeois production-relation, a production-relation of bourgeois society.'

in so far as this economic and social structure is a product of historical development: 'This relation has no natural basis, neither is its social basis one that is common to all historical periods ... Capital ... announces from its first appearance a new epoch in the process of social production' (*Capital*, I, pp. 147, 149).

Marx's economic theory thus takes shape in a way that makes clear its relations with sociology and history, appreciating that it is neither of these but that it both illuminates and is illuminated by them.[43] This explanation is not always mastered by Marxists, who in that case remain below the level of theoretical analyses *already* carried out by Marx.

Thus we see that analysis of the commodity, traced back to its origin, human labour, enables us to understand the essence of money and how money becomes capital. Analysis of the origin of surplus-value repeats in a specific way the reference back from the commodity to human labour, by showing wage-labour as the origin of this surplus-value. From this point onward the process of capital can develop before our eyes: and so we find linked together the two movements of *Capital*, and find determined the exact starting-point of what is in the strict sense the theory of capital.

The theory of value is thus the fundamental assumption on which is based not merely the theory of capitalism but all rational economic science. The theory of value makes it possible for economic theory to become a science. It frees the field of analysis from all ideal premises, from any and every transcendence, whether God or Nature, that might be supposed the source of the value of the products of human labour.

At the origin of value it places man. The theory of value thus presupposes the philosophical criticism of those conceptions that explain human activity by reference to ideal worlds-beyond-the-world, or to Nature.

The theory of value – which did not, of course, begin with Marx – makes of the economic field a *domain open to science*, to rational thought. This is why it is of crucial importance on the epistemological plane. It rules out all kinds of speculative alienation and explains what man

---

[43] I have already shown sufficiently the scope of the synthesis carried out by Marx to be able to leave it to the reader to meditate upon this dazzling proof of intelligence by one of Marx's 'critics', Jules Monnerot: 'A key that opens all doors is a bad key.' Unfortunately, this 'thought' serves as the conclusion to the chapter refuting Marx that is put into the hands of students of economics: see *Economie et Politique*, vol. I, Collection Thémis, p. 23, by M. Barre.

produces by man alone, so that it possesses a directly human and humanistic significance.

The theory of value makes it possible to treat economics as a domain open to science, but it also makes possible another operation, inside this domain – grasping *the functional unity and balance of the structures* of capitalism, taken as a *system*. The theory of value makes it possible to form the theory of capital in the form of a deduction in which the structures reveal the balance and homogeneity that lies behind their differences. This theory enables economic science to appreciate the rationality and the irrationality of reality, to reduce the heterogeneous to the homogeneous, and to link effects with causes.[44]

*

One final point will enable us to see how, through the theory of value, Marx's theory can serve as a general theory of the economy and realize that 'generalized' economic theory of which some economists talk.

We have shown that the theory of capital does not really begin until the formation of surplus-value is explained. The latter, however, does not determine the capitalist production-relation directly and by itself. What is specific to capitalism is the appropriation of this surplus-value by the individual who possesses the means of production, in other words, private appropriation of the surplus product: surplus-value is unpaid surplus labour. Now, given the setting of an industrial economy, surplus labour is a consequence of the development of the productive forces. If this surplus labour is appropriated by society as a whole, which implies the socialization of the means of production, we have not the theory of capital but the theory of socialism:

This appropriation of surplus value, or this separation of the production of value into a reproduction of advanced value and a production of new value (surplus-value) which does not replace any equivalent, does not alter in any way the substance of value itself or the nature of the production of value (*Capital*, II, p. 385).

If the capitalist system is based on a particular structure of appropriation of the surplus product, then it is possible to construct ideally, by means of a different assumption regarding the structure of appropriation,

[44] Bettelheim puts this very well in the foreword to his *Problèmes théoriques et pratiques de la planification*: 'It is the sole [objective conception] that gives us at once a homogeneous unit of reckoning and a unit of reckoning that has human significance.'

the way a socialist economy would function. We arrive at a model that is different but which is also based on the theory of value. The latter thus enables us to build a model of socialist development no less well than one of capitalist development, and it also enables us to work out the theory of pre-capitalist production-processes. From this standpoint, the different systems of production appear as realized possibilities, as particular cases of that general relation between man and himself and between man and the world which is called labour. This has fundamental consequences.

(1) We understand why and how it was that Marx's theory could anticipate ideally a socialist system of production that did not yet exist historically. Many have accused Marx of prophecy in the illuminist style. In fact, however, this 'prophecy' of his was a rational prediction. No other economist has been able to anticipate reality in this way.[45] (We recall that, in Keynes's opinion, the Soviet economy had no future. This clearsightedness of his was obviously not 'prophetic'.) How was he able to achieve this ideal anticipation? The analysis of the process of circulation of capital, in Volume II, elaborates the concepts of Department I and Department II, and studies the effects of the 'material' form of the product upon the process of production and reproduction. This material basis of the social division of labour is likewise that of a socialist system. We thus appreciate why the socialist system has planned its production using models with two departments (which can, moreover, be made highly complex). We appreciate also why macro-economic methods of studying the circulation of goods are perfectly compatible with Marx's theory.

If production were socialized instead of capitalistic, these productions of Department I would evidently just as regularly be redistributed as means of production to the various branches of this department, for purposes of reproduction, one portion remaining directly in that sphere of production from which it emerged as a product, another passing over to other places of production, thereby giving rise to a constant to-and-fro movement between the various places of production in this department (*Capital*, II, pp. 424–5).

Marx's ideal anticipation of socialist economy was also rendered possible by this dialectical approach and his analysis of the dynamic laws of the capitalist system. This brings us back again to the second method employed in *Capital*.

[45] See M. Domarchi's article in *Les Temps Modernes*, 1947, on 'L'Economie politique marxiste et l'économie politique bourgeoise'.

(2) It is possible to build a mathematical model that presents capitalism and socialism as two particular cases of economic development, and to bring out the functional potentialities of each system. The particularity of each of the two assumptions is the abstract equivalent of their historical relativity. This model thus 'corresponds' to concrete reality, without, however, containing the latter's richness in events. The simplifying assumptions enable us both to obliterate the concrete and to reinstate it.

We have now come to the end of our analysis of the first aspect of the method of *Capital*, and will bring together the results we have obtained.

The method makes it possible to create a scientific 'theory' of the capitalist system of production and circulation. It consists in making simplifying assumptions that mark out *a priori* the field of analysis and open it up to rational thought. These assumptions make it possible, within the field thus defined, to work out the concepts of the economic structures – in other words, the economic categories – and to link them together in theoretical deductions. These assumptions also make it possible to create a mathematical economic theory and to utilize formalism and symbolism.

The method thus permits the construction of a deductive system the ultimate nature of which consists in reference back from one structure to another, starting from an originating structure. The theory consequently consists in an 'ideal genesis' of the capitalist system. These deductive operations are based on the logical necessary relations between the categories, and this ideal logic 'reproduces' the actual logic of the concrete capitalist system. These logical relations are also chronological, that is they structure economic time. In order to proceed from this abstract time into the vicinity of concrete time, it is necessary to link together micro-economic and macro-economic methods.

In the end, the basis of all these methodological structures, their necessary unity, lies in the theory of value. This complex architecture of methodological structures presupposed an explicit awareness of the relations between economic theory, history as a science, and sociological science, and of the relations between these sciences and concrete reality. This therefore presupposed a many-sided epistemological elaboration, implying the use of a philosophical approach. At the heart of the latter lies the analysis of the relation between essence and appearance upon which the relation between the rational concept and the everyday practical image is based. At the heart of this method we therefore find a dialectical analysis of the contradictory relationship between thinking and being. We are led now to perceive the dialectical method. The hypothetico-deductive method integrates Marx's theory perfectly well into the body of most up-to-date economic theories, using the most elaborate formal tools. There is nothing to stop Marxists using these tools – quite the contrary. The formal possibility of using them has been shown in Marx's own work. The hypothetico-deductive method makes *Capital* a very complex 'model' that explains some of the essential structures of the capitalist system, and of some of the laws of its functioning. We shall now see that the dialectical method completes this structural analysis and provides what is essential for a dynamic theory of capitalism.

ii. *The dialectical method*

In analysing the dialectical method we shall show how the two methods of *Capital* are linked together, their synthetical unity. The analysis will be deliberately simplified, for the subject-matter calls for handling a great deal more delicate than the hypothetico-deductive method, and is also much more fundamental.

The object of the dialectic

In order to grasp the function of dialectical thinking we must first describe the objective content that it enables us to analyse. This content appears from outside as the organic solidarity of the structures of an economic system. This solidarity expresses the reciprocal interdependence of the structures of a system that is always an organic whole. For example, production is the pre-condition of consumption, and consumption reproduces the conditions for production.

Analysis of this relationship implies the use of dialectical thinking. In *Capital* this relationship appears at several moments of the theory:

(1) in the analysis of the process of human labour, the heart of the theory of value;

(2) throughout Volume II, which analyses the cyclical process of capital;

(3) in Volume III, in the analysis of the contradictory relations between the different forms of profit.

In all these passages we are faced with the same content – explanation of the general relation of interdependence between production and distribution, exchange and consumption. This general relationship is established by an abstract approach that aims at isolating certain determinations of productive activity that are common to all epochs of production.

Production in general is an abstraction, but a sensible abstraction in so far as it actually emphasizes and defines the common aspects and thus avoids repetition (*Contribution to the Critique of Political Economy*, 1971 edn, p. 190).

A similar approach had already been followed in the *Grundrisse der Politischen Okonomie*. These results are used in abridged fashion in *Capital*, with a less obvious dialectical development. To study the content of these results, I will use the text of the *Contribution*.

In order to produce, the individual consumes his own faculties and also the means of production he uses: 'The act of production itself is thus in all its phases also an act of consumption' (*Contribution*, p. 195).

Consumption is also directly production. By consuming, man produces and reproduces his labour-power. There is thus productive consumption and consumptive production, and the latter presupposes the former, the product of which it destroys by consuming it. Thus, in each case, there is a direct unity of production and consumption. However, 'the direct unity, in which production is concurrent with consumption and consumption with production, does not affect their simultaneous duality' (ibid., p. 196).

Each, moreover, appears as the means of the other, mediated by and at the same time mediating the other: 'Each appears as a means of the other, as being induced by it; this is called their mutual dependence; they are thus brought into mutual relation and appear to be indispensable to each other, but nevertheless remain extrinsic to each other (ibid., p. 196).

Finally, and more fundamentally, each of them, in realizing itself, creates itself 'in the other's form'. In political economy this last-mentioned identity is commented on in many different forms, in connexion with the relations between supply and demand, objects and wants, wants created by society and natural wants. The identity of production and consumption thus appears a threefold aspect.

Dialectical thinking seeks, through this abstract approach, to recognize the identical in the different and the different as identical. Each structure is the other, presupposes the other, and creates it in a certain way. Abstract thought has to grasp the unity of a process in its very contradictions. Consumption 'realizes' production by destroying the product, but thereby it 'reproduces' the need for production and its pre-conditions.

The categories of dialectical thinking that are employed here are thus the categories of opposite, identity, mediation, opposition and reciprocal relations. Thus, Marx observes ironically: 'After this, nothing is simpler for a Hegelian than to assume that production and consumption are identical' (*Contribution*, p. 199). The Hegelian's mistake would in fact lie in assuming an abstract subject as the bearer of this organic solidarity; society, *homo economicus*, etc. Indeed, it is always possible, 'however dissimilar the mode of distribution at the various stages of society may be, . . . just as in the case of production, to emphasize the common aspects, and it must be likewise possible to confuse and efface all historical differences in laws that are *common to all mankind*' (ibid., p. 192). By imagining an abstract ideal subject that does not exist (man in general), we substantiate an approach and a concept that are operational, in other words, strictly intended to bring out the common relations within different determinations. The philosopher or the speculative thinker embodies his approach in the abstract concept he invests in order to unify the field of his analysis, but 'man in general' does not exist. There 'exist' only men in real, historically-determined relations. The abstract rational approach contains the possibility of speculative alienation. Marx was quite well aware of this danger:

To recapitulate: there are categories which are common to all stages of production and are established by reasoning as general categories; the so-called *general conditions* of all and any production, however, are nothing but abstract conceptions which do not define any of the actual historical stages of production (ibid., p. 193).

This shows us how Marx uses the dialectic, without making it into a tool of speculation:

'The conclusion which follows . . . is . . . that production, distribution, exchange and consumption . . . are links of a single whole, different aspects of one unit . . . there is an interaction between the various aspects. Such interaction takes place in any organic entity (ibid., pp. 204–5).

The identity of the different structures is thus due to their being inside the *same* economic system. The dialectic is the operational tool for analysing this overall unity; but the thinker cannot be satisfied with developing the analysis of the general relations between economic structures. He must always use this abstract analysis to study concrete historical forms of production and consumption, *make it serve* this study. Otherwise, dialectical analysis remains an empty generality. The real task of the scientist is to explain concrete reality. We thus understand what Marx writes, early on in Volume III, when he recalls that, in part 3 of Volume II, 'it developed that the capitalist process of production taken as a whole represents a synthesis of the processes of production and circulation. Considering what this third book treats, it cannot confine itself to general reflexion relative to this synthesis. On the contrary, it must locate and describe the concrete forms which grow out of the movements of capital as a whole' (*Capital*, III, p. 25).

The need to confine the dialectic to its operational role thus results from the very nature of the object. There is no man 'in general', no object 'in general'.

The object is not simply an object in general, but a particular object which must be consumed in a particular way, a way determined by production. Hunger is hunger; but the hunger that is satisfied by cooked meat eaten with knife and fork differs from hunger that devours raw meat with the help of hands, nails and teeth (*Contribution*, p. 197).

We have thus brought out the operational character of the dialectical method and the field in which it is applied. We have grasped the dialectical method in its connexion with a certain content of thought. The passages from the *Contribution* and from *Capital* are not passages on the dialectic in general, but on the relation between a series of real structures, production, etc. However, this relation is analysed in a rather general and formal way. What is being analysed is the formal structure of the general relation of the general economic structures. Thereby, the analysis opens out an ideal, general and abstract field of operations, thanks to which thought can set out to find the concrete relations of the concrete structures of a particular economic system (for example, analysis of the contradictory unity of capital and labour).

iii. *The dialectic as an operational field*

So we see that the abstract analysis of the relation between production in general and consumption in general does not constitute, strictly speaking, an economic theory, but is a fragment of the methodology of economic science. Dialectics becomes internal to the content of the theory only when it enables us to conceive some particular determined, historical relation. This abstract analysis accordingly forms an ideal moment in the formation of a rational knowledge of the economy, the moment when this knowledge explicitly opens out the abstract field of operations in which certain concrete acts of cognition are possible. This operational field of dialectics is linked, as we shall see, with that which is opened out by the first method, and the two together make up the total field of operations in which and through which theoretical knowledge of the capitalist system is achieved.

This moment of the abstract deployment of an aspect of the methodology of economic science enables us to grasp the general relation of the economic structures, and at the same time justifies for the theoretician his right and his need to use the dialectical method in his investigation and exposition. It is in so far as the field he is investigating presents the structure of an organic whole that the thinker is obliged to use the dialectical method.[46]

The dialectical method thus shows that circularity which we observe in the formal aspect of any rational approach. The dialectical method makes it possible for the content being analysed to appear as a whole, but it is because this content is a whole that the method is required in order to make it appear.

This method was not created by Marx. He was able to enrich it,[47] but

[46] We find a proof of the operational character of the dialectical method in the fact that it seemed to Marx unnecessary to begin the *Contribution* with the passage on methodology the structures of which we have analysed. Cf. what he writes in the preface to the *Contribution*: 'A general introduction, which I have drafted, is omitted, since on further consideration it seems to me confusing to anticipate results which still have to be substantiated, and the reader who really wishes to follow me will have to decide to advance from the particular to the general' (*Contribution*, p. 19).

Marx suppressed this methodological introduction so not to make his book look like a 'deduction' of results from *a priori* generalities. His method does not exist apart from these results, or at least it is operational only as it makes these results possible. It is at one and the same time the procedure that constitutes these results, that precedes them, and that is included within them. It is both external and internal to the results; and this clarifies Marx's phrase about the merely formal difference between the method of investigation and the method of exposition. This difference does not rule out their essential identity. This twofold aspect is based on the twofold nature of the relation between the method and the content, a relation that is both external and internal to the latter.

Since our concern is to 'make explicit' Marx's method hidden in the content of his theory, we can put the method back 'before' the content.

[47] There are in Marx's writings a number of passages about the dialectic which ought to be brought together. See the *Economic and Philosophical Manuscripts* and *The Poverty of Philosophy*, also Engels's *Ludwig Feuerbach and the Outcome of Classical German Philosophy*.

in the first place he inherited it from philosophical tradition, above all from Hegel. The latter had worked out the dialectical tool to serve his system, and had formed his system by means of this tool. Thereby, the categories of the dialectical method, the concepts of opposite and of synthesis, were at once worked out in an abstract and universal way but also devoted to the task of developing absolute idealism.

The elaboration of this method had enabled Hegel to enrich his analysis of the logical relation between positive and negative, identity and non-identity, essence and appearance, that is, to unfold the logical relations of a group of abstract categories of thought. But Hegel had invested this logical analysis in the entire field of human experience and knowledge, so as to 'recognize' in it the movement of the 'Absolute Spirit'. Consequently, the dialectic was employed in science only in order to recapture therein the truth of the Hegelian system, the presence of the Absolute Spirit in all its forms. But it was first of all necessary to have established that the unity and meaning of human experience were capable of being grasped mentally by means of the philosophical assumption of an Absolute Spirit, if one was to be able, so to speak, to 'rediscover' them in each structure of thought and reality.[48]

Marx, then, inherited the dialectical tool, but declined to use it in order to show, in a particular science or field of experience, that some speculative assumption was 'true'. We see by this both that the scientific method was becoming a tool of scientific cognition and also that it was serving, as part of this cognition process, to open out a certain field of operations.

Philosophy may elaborate the dialectic, that is, it may clarify the logical relations between abstract concepts that made it possible to think in terms of the negative and the contradictory, and generalize the results of each separate science. It no longer analyses the dialectical relation of one concrete structure, rendered formal and general, such as 'production in general', but the relation of 'same' in general and 'other' in general, of 'identity' in general and of 'difference'. The history of philosophy is the most abstract field in which the movement of the elaboration of rational thought has developed.

Philosophy constitutes, then, a general field of operations of rational

[48] This difficulty is that of the link between Hegel's *Phenomenology of the Spirit* and his *Science of Logic*.

thinking, but must not take substance, giving itself the form of a system by means of which one might be able to 'deduce' some concrete structure, some particular science or even some particular reality.[49]

We have thus shown the nature of the dialectical method by grasping it as the tool for analysing a certain type of object, 'organic wholes', and the inter-structural relations that these involve.

Use of the dialectical method in Capital

The method is used by Marx to lay bare the internal and contradictory relations of the capitalist economic system, that is, of an historically-determined concrete whole which the thinker analyses in its 'pure' essence.

In an initial phase, the dialectical method thus serves to bring out the dialectical structures of that which in the capitalist system, is *not specific* to it but is common to other economic systems too. The result of this approach does not amount, strictly speaking, to an economic theory, but is the deployment of a set of operational structures that serve economic theory. Economic theory begins only at the moment when these structures are used to analyse a particular economic system, being employed in an actual, historically circumscribed domain of analysis.

This phase, when the thinker is both setting out his tools of analysis and determining the relations that are common to all economic systems, that is, a set of concepts and relations that do not constitute the essence of any definite economic system, has been eliminated by Marx in the presentation of his theory because he refuses to put the method before the work, preferring to put it after the latter – something that his death

[49] Historically, philosophy has developed in the form of 'systems', a pattern of development corresponding to the philosopher's claim to be an absolute thinker. It is both this absolute thinker and his product, the system, that have been 'dead' for some little time now. His death-throes constitute what is called the 'crisis' of philosophy, which means merely the crisis of the absolute systems and not the end of philosophy, as some, both non-Marxists and Marxists, suppose, interpreting wrongly Marx's eleventh thesis on Feuerbach. It seems that modern philosophy cannot be merely a general methodology and at the same time *ought not* to congeal into a system. Hence the tension and the difficulties of philosophical reflexion that form the problematic of the nature of this dual impossibility. This tension is to be found in Sartre's work. How can one form a philosophy that is not a whole, that is not solidified into a system? Or at least a philosophy that is an 'open system'? This is one of the structures of the problematic of present-day philosophy.

prevented him from completing.[50] His refusal to put the method at the beginning was due to the fact that it is both external and internal to the theory, in other words it exists at the heart of the theory, upholds it and is embraced by it, while at the same time having served as the instrument originating it.

Marx was content to offer his work without defining the methods he had used, because these methods had *become* internal to the theory, *had been enveloped in their turn by the content that they had developed*. For Marx the primary task of theory was to allow this content to develop, now containing as it did, enveloped in itself, the operational procedures which had formed it. Consequently, his thought effected the ideal reproduction of the concrete, while at the same time effacing, as it were, operations that were 'retained' in the result.

We have here brought out the fundamental difficulty in studying the method of *Capital*, the difficulty we described earlier as that of the *circularity* of this method. Our task was, indeed, to 'develop' the method that the content enveloped – in other words, that it at once manifested and concealed. Our aim was to look at *Capital* from behind, that is, to discern in its content the structure of the methods that had produced it, right side out.

The dialectical tools of Marx's operational field are thus in *Capital* enveloped in the content and not made explicit as in the *Contribution*. Nevertheless, they are the same tools, but this time invested in the working out of a specific theory, the theory of the capitalist system of production and circulation. They are present in every phase of the work, but they now have the task of explaining the specific character of the system being studied, and at this stage, as we shall see, they directly encounter the hypothetic-deductive method and become interlaced with it to form the synthetical unity of the two methods, that is, the real method of *Capital*, the nucleus that unites all the structures of the theory.

(1) *The study of the process of the circulation of capital*

We shall make do with a brief analysis of this process. The formal analysis contained in the *Contribution* of the dialectical relation between production in general and circulation in general has become the tool of the theory of

[50] We know the pledge he made in the last years of his life to synthesize in a few pages his ideas on the dialectic. This pledge was never fulfilled, for lack of time and opportunity.

the circulation process of capital. The theory studies the *forms* assumed by capital during its process of circulation. The latter is the reproduction of itself by itself, that is, the cyclical movement of a whole. But in this movement capital is 'metamorphosed'. The first part of Volume II is devoted to studying these metamorphoses and the 'circuit' they follow.

If, then, we pay attention to the concepts here employed by Marx (metamorphosis, circuit, circulation, etc.), we see that he undertakes to study the process of capital as the process of a particular system, that is, a whole in movement circulating around itself. Marx distinguishes three figures in this cyclical process: the circuit of money-capital, the circuit of productive capital and the circuit of commodity capital.

(a) *The circuit of money capital*

$$M - C \begin{cases} L \\ MP \end{cases} - P - C' - M'$$

M = money advanced as capital, C = money converted into elements of production, L = labour-power, MP = means of production, P = productive capital, C' = commodities produced = C + c, or the ratio, expressed in commodities, of capital-value to surplus-value, M' = product converted back into money = M + m, or the same ratio as above, but expressed in money terms.

(b) *The circuit of productive capital*

$$P - C' - M' - C - P$$
$$(C' - M' - C = \text{process of total circulation})$$

We can transform this formula, getting:

$$P - C' \begin{cases} C \\ c \end{cases} - M' - \begin{cases} M \\ m \end{cases} \begin{matrix} c \\ C \end{matrix} - MP \begin{cases} L \ -P \\ MP \end{cases}$$

From this circuit, P' = P + c. We see here the formal structure of expanded reproduction.

(c) *The circuit of commodity capital*

$$C' - \begin{cases} C \\ c \end{cases} - M' - \begin{cases} M - C \\ m - c \end{cases} \begin{cases} L \ -P-C' \\ MP \end{cases}$$

Here the capitalist relation C' is the starting point. Here we see that consumption as a whole, that is, both individual and productive, constitutes a permanent condition of the reproduction process, and at the same time C' reappears as a result of the production-process and no longer of the circulation process.

These three formulas are the three forms of the total circulation process. The dialectical structure of this process is at once apparent, since C' presupposes P, which presupposes M, which itself presupposes C, and so on. Marx concludes:

If we combine all three forms, all premises of the process appear as its result, as a premise produced by it itself. Every element *appears* as a point of departure, of transit, and of return. The total process *presents itself* as the unity of the processes of production and circulation. The process of production becomes the mediator of the process of circulation and vice versa (*Capital*, II, p. 100. My emphasis, M.G.).

We thus see the analysis being carried out by means of the dialectical method. Each structure is the condition of the other and also its effect, and at the same time the movement of capital demands that the circuit be passed through in all its forms. The movement of capital is thus a single movement, and this unity is based on the identity of the different structures – the identity in their difference. This identity that makes the unity of the total process consists in the fact that 'all three circuits have the following in common: the self-expression of value as the determining purpose, as the compelling motive' (*Capital*, II, p. 100). What is at the heart of this movement is the very structure of capital, the movement of M which becomes M', $M + \triangle M$, that is to say, the very 'concept' of capital. We see the perfect rigour of Marx's theory, and we are present at the interweaving of the results of the dialectical method and the first method.

The operational nature of the dialectical method is stressed by Marx himself when he states that the difference between these three circuits 'appears to be a merely formal one, or as a merely subjective distinction existing solely for the observer' (*Capital*, II, p. 101).

The method makes it possible to isolate the structures of the cyclical movement of a process that exists only through their simultaneity and not merely through their succession. 'In reality every individual industrial capital is present simultaneously in all three circuits' (ibid., p. 101). But this simultaneity both excludes and includes succession. The cyclical process of capital is a constant interruption, 'the leaving of one stage and the entering into the next, the discarding of one form and the assuming of another. Each one of these stages not only presupposes the next but also excludes it' (ibid., p. 102). In fact, this succession of phases presupposes their juxtaposition, that is, the functional divisions of capital.

In this way each phase has a functional existence, and the latter has been defined by the fundamental categories of economic theory. The dialectical method is thus linked with the hypothetico-deductive method. Both presuppose and at the same time make possible the working out of the categories of economic science.

But we shall carry further the analysis of the circular movement of the capital process, and see the dialectical method both enveloping the first method and also becoming still further interwoven with it. It is indeed 'considered as a whole' that capital simultaneously occupies its different phases, but at the same time each phase succeeds another. This is how the web of economic time is formed; the economic structures are at each moment in a relation of co-presence and of succession, and this ensures the *continuity* of the economic process. The latter is the synthetical unity of discontinuity and continuity. It is a synthesis in time, accomplished with time. But this synthesis in time can be interrupted in the process of an individual capital, whereas 'the aggregate social capital always has this continuity and its process always exhibits the unity of the three circuits' (ibid., p. 104).

We now appreciate that capital is not a 'thing' at rest but a movement, the movement of value which simultaneously is conserved and expanded. Here we have rejoined the first method, and we see the two methods strike root in the very nature of capital as value that is expanded. We shall now draw some initial conclusions from the foregoing analysis.

(2) *Capital is not a 'thing' at rest but a reality in movement*

(a) Dialectical analysis of the capital process shows that capital is not a 'thing' at rest but a reality in movement. By this very fact, economic theory has to be *essentially dynamic*. Consequently Marx's thought can find expression only in a dynamic model, and dialectical analysis appears as the most fundamental operational method. Thus the categories of economic science possess reality only through their reciprocal relations, and point to a content that exists wholly in time, synthetically, historically.

(b) Dialectical analysis enables us to imagine the circular relations of structures that are organically solid with each other. It is of service on both the micro-economic and the macro-economic planes, but it makes possible the transition from one to the other. For instance, Marx shows that the formula $C - C'$ is the form of movement of an individual capital, but also:

a form of movement of the sum of individual capitals, consequently of the aggregate capital of the capitalist class, a movement in which that of each individual industrial capital appears as only a partial movement which intermingles with the other movements and is necessitated by them (ibid., pp. 96–7).

It is therefore the whole that conditions the part which, however, in no way precludes the possibility that the movement of the latter, of an isolated individual capital, may present

other phenomena than the same movement does when considered from the point of view of a part of the aggregate movement of social capital, hence in its interconnection with the movements of its other parts, and that the movement simultaneously solves problems the solution of which must be assumed when studying the circuits of a separate, individual capital, instead of being the result of such study (ibid., p. 97).

Thus, Marx develops his analysis on both the micro-economic and macro-economic planes, shows the transition from one to the other in the functional identity of the structures, and yet shows the distinction between them in their functional differences, while stressing that the latter become apparent only after a macro-economic analysis of capitalism as a system. In fact, a 'single' capitalist enterprise does not exist, it exists only as an element in a totality, in other words, in a system of elements that are compatible and homogeneous and yet distinct.

This dialectical analysis makes possible the transition from Volume I to Volume III. It interweaves with the first method and so facilitates bringing out the existence of an average profit born of the overall functioning of collective capital. Dialectical analysis thus provides the basis upon which the order of the categories can be developed.

(c) Dialectical analysis handles operational concepts (unity of opposites, identity and difference, etc.) which serve in the elaboration of economic categories but which also lead us towards calculation, the making of dynamic models, etc. We shall see better how this happens when we analyse the essential laws of motion of the capitalist system.

Analysis of the circulation process has revealed the particular forms of movement of the capital process. These are the formal structures of the movement of a whole that reproduces itself, 'circulates' around itself.

Theoretical analysis will seek to identify the effects of time on each of the elements of capital. Let it be repeated, the capital process requires time. And the turnover time is the period during which the processes of production and circulation are carried out. Taking note of turnover time results in distinguishing between fixed capital and circulating capital. Fixed capital is made up of all the means of production that gradually yield up their own exchange-value along with their use-value. This delivery of value 'is determined by a calculation of averages' (*Capital*, II, p. 157). Economic theory thus brings us to mathematical calculation. The latter has been practised spontaneously by capitalism on the plane of accountancy. It can be made the subject of special mathematical treatment on the theoretical plane.[51] In calculating the profitability of a capital, the effects of turnover time on the amount of capital advanced possess a great importance that Marx emphasized, and which deserves to be given complex mathematical study. This is valid on the micro-economic no less than on the overall social plane, and raises the problem of the choice of an economic period as one's basis when making a theoretical analysis. We thus arrive at the distinction between 'short-term' and 'long-term', and so on.

Within this time there takes place the movement of that capital the formal structures of which have been revealed by analysis but of which the specific content and specific law have not yet been defined. This cyclical structure has hitherto appeared as 'simple' reproduction of one and the same movement – but simple reproduction is *not* the characteristic movement of the capitalist system. The assumption of simple reproduction: 'is . . . *incompatible* with capitalist production' (*Capital*, II, p. 520: my emphasis, M.G.).

This incompatibility stands out when we analyse the circuit of productive capital, that is, one of the three formulas of the total process of capital. This circuit has a specific character, that of producing surplus-value, engendering the accumulation of capital, that is, of 'characterizing' the movement of capital as 'expanded' reproduction. It is in the circuit of productive capital that the process of expansion of value takes place – in other words, that the capitalist system of production is effective. Exchange-value is born in this process, but it is realized in the process of circulation (marketing of commodities, sales, price-systems),[52] which is in

[51] Keynes and the post-Keynesians have made studies of this problem within the framework of the theory of 'marginal utility of capital'.

[52] It must never be lost sight of that it is generally exceptional for prices of goods to

turn the condition for repetition of the circuit of productive capital. Production expands the market, the market expands production, the unity of the two also shows itself in a negative way when inadequacy of demand paralyses production, and so on. It is this specific role of the circuit of productive capital that dialectical analysis brings out.

(3) *The specific role of the circuit of productive capital*

The structure of this circuit is P — P'. The formula

$$P - C' - M' - C' \left\{ \begin{array}{l} L \\ MP \end{array} \right. - P'$$

expresses a productive capital that reproduces itself on a larger scale and with a greater value, and, thus augmented, 'begins its second circuit, or, what amounts to the same, renews its first circuit' (ibid., p. 79). Whence comes this greater value? From the production of surplus-value, that is, because P (the transformation of C into P) produces C'. In P — P', P' expresses not the production of surplus-value but the capitalization of the surplus-value produced, and so the accumulation of capital that has been affected; it expresses the fact that P', in relation to P, is made up of the original capital-value *plus* the value of a capital that has been accumulated by its movement.

In this process, part of surplus-value is converted into capital, and this accumulation appears as the means of constantly extending the production of surplus-value, and so increasing the wealth of capitalism. In order to conserve a capital it has to be expanded. This general tendency of capitalist production, this objective law of its movement, is a necessity for each individual capitalist which at the same time appears as his aim. The capitalist system is thus a totality that expands itself, swelling as a result of its own movement, maintaining itself by growing.

The capitalist system is a dynamic reality the movement of which has as its specific structure the expanded reproduction of productive capital, a dynamic structure that is derived from the very essence of capital, namely, the essence of a value that develops and expands.

---

correspond to their value. They are either higher or lower than the latter, which is an ideal axis of reference. The whole beginning of volume III, part 1, would have to be analysed in order to determine the role of the theory of value in explaining the relationship of supply and demand.

(4) *The basis of the system's dynamic*

The whole dynamic of the system, its growth, is based on that originating structure constituted by an historical, social production-relation between, 'on the one side, the possessor of the means of production and subsistence, on the other the possessor of nothing but labour-power' (*Capital*, I pp. 582–3), a relation of separation between the product and the producer, the means of production and the worker, the capitalist class and the working class.

The dynamic of capitalism is thus based on the existence of an industrial capital, that is, on the fact that the selling of individual labour-power is no mere isolated phenomenon but the decisive social condition of commodity production, the generalization of a particular, historical way of combining the factors of production, namely, workers and means of production (*Capital*, II, p. 55).

The dynamic of the system is based on the sphere of productive capital, industrial capital, which shows the historically relative nature of the capitalist system, corresponding to a certain stage of development of the productive forces of human labour, a degree of development that makes possible the creation on a mass scale of a surplus-product that is appropriated by the capitalist, as owner of the means of production. The dynamic of the system is thus based on the existence of a surplus-product and on the private appropriation of this in the form of surplus value.[53]

---

[53] The dynamic of the capitalist system depends on the existence of industrial means of production; but it is the dynamic of a particular sort of industrial society. If the structure of appropriation is changed, the capitalist relation disappears but the production of surplus labour continues. We then have an industrial society of the socialist type, marked by socialist ownership of the means of production. The dynamic of the socialist system cannot be the same as that of the capitalist system. This can be observed from the statistical conclusions drawn from growth-rates, etc., but it can equally well be deduced from mathematical theoretical models. We should therefore not confuse the two systems on the pretext that they are two forms of industrial society with the same material and technical production basis. Inadmissible also is the 'merging' prophesied for these two systems, in a distant phase 'beyond capitalism and socialism'. On the theoretical plane it is possible to construct a dynamic model of industrial society which allows of the structure of private appropriation of social surplus labour being introduced as a particular case. It should also be noted that the dynamic of the capitalist system is not merely that of the industrial capitalist countries but that of all the countries dominated by the capitalist world market and forming elements of this market. This includes the 'under-developed' countries. A dynamic model of capitalism ought to integrate the dynamic of the under-developed countries. A specific model of the development of the under-developed countries could also be constructed. All these studies are still largely waiting to be undertaken.

In order to grasp, in the actual structure of the capitalist production-relation, the structure of its movement, the dialectical method needs to be employed. The dialectical method reveals in the mechanism of the formation of surplus value the basis of the dynamic of the system.

The two methods we distinguished in *Capital* turn out in the end to have the same structure as their object. They are thus linked together in so far as they relate to the same object.

Some consequences of this analysis of expanded reproduction must be shown. Among the different structures of the capitalist system, and in the context of their reciprocal solidarity, the group of structures of production and their particular movement occupy an exceptional position. The sphere of production within the capitalist system taken as a whole is the essentially *propulsive* sphere of the system: on it the development and maintenance of the system depend.

Marx, in the Introduction to the *Contribution* which he did not publish, showed the fundamental, originating character of production in any economic system. He did this in the form of an abstract analysis of the general relation of production in general to the other structures – of a relation common to several distinct systems, that is, in the form of a general methodological analysis:

A distinct mode of production thus determines the specific mode of consumption, distribution, exchange and the *specific relations of these different phases to one another*. Production *in the narrow sense*, however, is in its turn also determined by the other aspects (*Contribution*, p. 205: Marx's own emphasis).

In *Capital*, this abstract dialectical analysis becomes 'operational' and is not to be found any longer in its general form. It confirms its general laws, the latter, at least, are the truth of what is common to several different systems. In *Capital*, the method is thus applied to a particular field of analysis, and is enveloped by the results that it has made possible to develop.

It is in the sphere of capitalist production that the production of surplus value occurs. Capitalist production regulates individual as well as productive consumption, and governs the distribution of income and products. It is basically commodity production and production on an indefinitely expanding scale. It thus stimulates trade, causes a world market to be formed, develops the credit system. The very structure of capitalist production thus implies the transformation of the structures of consumption, distribution and exchange into an aggregate that is compatible with the nature of this production and forms a unified system functioning as a whole.

Thus, it is the totality of the relations of production that becomes the basis of the unity of the economic system – the part of a whole that makes of this whole a specific system. This special structure will influence the other economic structures in order to make them compatible with itself. This result is at once necessary and possible at a certain level of development of the new production-relations. When the movement of re-working of certain structures that are *anterior and external* to the production-relation (structures of trade, banking, etc.) has broadly been completed these structures make up, together with the structures of production, a new *economic system* within which they are placed again, to play a *new role*. This movement has been completed historically in all the capitalist countries that are now 'developed'. When the fundamental economic structures have become capable of co-existence, the capitalist system is imposed as the economic structure dominating the economic development of these countries and determining their growth. Thus, dialectical analysis will serve to explain the way in which an economic system is formed, and to bring out the origin and structure of this process of generation in the specific, moving creative role played by the production structures.

And so we see that:

(1) The practical, material and social relations in which men are caught up are not inert structures but dynamic realities which *set* problems, and *demand* the transformation of realities co-existing with them and functionally united to them. The field of human practice throws up groups of problems that men will solve through their subsequent practice.

(2) Men's practical activity is the instrument of this transformation of practical relations. Individual and subjective activity is thus provoked and absorbed by the objective practical field in which it is exercised. At the same time, however, it opens a new field of problems at the very moment in which it solves another. For example, in proportion as the industrial capitalists developed their production, they created a group of problems (transformation of the market, training of the labour-force, etc.) that would again call for solution. Men's practical activity re-encounters itself through the intermediary of the field in which it is carried on. The field of practice is developed only through the practical activity of the men engaged in it. The dialectical method enables us to grasp this circularity

which refers back from the pole of men's practical activity, the subjective pole, to the pole of the field in which this activity is carried on. Each of these poles develops only through the other, and they make up a total and dynamic reality in which the unity of the subjective and the objective is both accomplished and yet still to be accomplished.

(5) *Relations between economic theory and historical reality*

The dialectical method thus enables us to grasp the relations between economic theory and history (here, in the sense not of the science but of the actual movement). In so far as it reveals the specific relation between production and the other structures of the system, and shows that capitalism is an economic system only when widely-differing economic structures have become mutually compatible, it clarifies historical events as a whole and discovers in them common overall structures, an historical 'significance'. To take an example, interest-producing capital is a developed and transformed variety of the usurers' capital of Antiquity, which was associated above all with the development of trade in money. The development of the credit system destroyed usurers' capital, but that meant that, in the form of the credit system, interest-producing capital, the most ancient form of capital, had adapted itself to the conditions of capitalist production. Whereas the rate of interest was often very high in pre-capitalist economies, capitalist economy required for its development the development of a system of credit and an average rate of interest that would be 'native' to it, so to speak, compatible with capitalism. We know that Keynes, in his *General Theory of Employment, Interest and Money,* advocated bringing down the rate of interest to the lowest possible level, so as to eliminate certain faults in the working of the system, especially in connexion with crises. Keynes was here raising a problem of the compatibility of structures within a given system.

Marx was able to define the real meaning of the historical struggle waged against usury:

The credit system develops as a reaction against usury. But this should not be misunderstood, nor by any means interpreted in the manner of the ancient writers, the church fathers, Luther or the early socialists. It *signifies* no more and no less than the subordination of interest-bearing capital *to the conditions and requirements of* the capitalist mode of production (*Capital*, III, p. 586: my emphasis, M.G.).

Economic theory thus becomes increasingly capable of explaining the significance of the historical transformations of different societies, and so becomes the tool of historical science. In his *Notes on the pre-capitalist period* (*Capital*, III, chapter 36), Marx himself uses theoretical conclusions to illuminate such facts as the birth of credit associations in Venice and Genoa in the 12th and 14th centuries, and the development of banking in Holland in the 17th century and then, in the 18th century, in England and France.[54]

(6) *Relations between economic theory and historical science*

Economic history as a science is blind (1) if it is ignorant of the content of economic categories, that is, the content of economic science, and (2) if it is ignorant of the essential properties of each of these categories and is unable to grasp the particular relation of the production-structures and the demands of reciprocal balance between the economic structures. These demands may or may not be realized historically.

Economic theory is thus the body of ideas that must guide the historian if he does not wish, proceeding empirically and blindly, to lose himself in the mass of facts and if he wants to discover the historical structures that give meaning to events. Reciprocally, however, the diversity of historical data leads to the re-working of economic categories, their theoretical re-examination. This circularity makes up the process of rational cognition, but within the context of this twofold, mutual reference, it is economic theory, as an ideal group of economic concepts, that provides the operational field that is essential for entering into the mass of facts and grasping their internal order, for doing the work of a historian of the economy. Economic theory enables us to construct models of the functioning of an economic system, and these models must serve as working hypotheses for the historian. When the latter finds a body of facts that is incompatible with the content of the categories, he will have to work over them afresh and himself become a creator of economic knowledge. Historical science develops through this synthetical movement, which overcomes the division of intellectual labour that was the condition and the result of its own development. This synthetical movement results in better knowledge of the object being studied and in making more thorough the conditions of

[54] It will be seen how the reproach made against Marx that he was guilty of 'confusion' in 'mixing up' history and political economy constitutes one of the most serious errors made in connexion with *Capital*.

this knowledge, in other words, in enriching the methodology of the scholar's abstract operational field.[55]

Furthermore, in the light of our subsequent developments, we see that the historian cannot neglect the use of mathematical calculation and other formal instruments in working out his own scientific procedure. It is not mathematics that is incompatible with the social sciences,[56] but certain philosophies of mathematics, certain conceptual constructions, certain assumptions about the nature of human phenomena that seek root and justification in the use of mathematics.

At the end of this stage of our study of dialectical analysis of expanded reproduction and the specific dynamic role of production, we have found opening before us the methodological problem of the relation between economic theory and history, as reality and as science. The dialectical method not only enables us to study the dynamic of a set of structures but also enables us to tackle the problems that are presented by the progress of scientific knowledge, that is, the epistemological problems of the relations of the humane sciences among themselves and with reality. It thus enables us to enter into the field of the philosophical problems of the theory of knowledge, and can provide the scholar with means of clarifying the nature of the procedure he follows.

We are now in a position to resume our study of expanded reproduction and of the dynamics of the capitalist system. The epistemological conclusions we have reached will be of assistance to us, it will be seen, in this last stage, and they will themselves be carried further.

We have seen that the capitalist system has a general, overall tendency

[55] The *Faculté des Sciences Humaines* aims at carrying forward this movement, by bringing about links between different scientific disciplines. In this context it is understandable that problems of methodology have occupied much attention. (See, for example, the periodical *Annales: Economies, Sociétés, Civilisations*).

[56] For example, Lévi-Strauss has shown the structural unity of certain kinships. He has carried out an investigation into the mutual compatibility of a certain type of kinship structure with a certain group of myths, and so on. He has even tried to reduce this investigation and its outcome to formulae, by using certain mathematical devices. His anthropological research has shown how the individual always lives in the midst of a set of structures that are interlinked to form a significant totality. Cf. his *Structural Anthropology*, passim. Nevertheless, Lévi-Strauss often leaves in shadow the problem of the origin of these structured institutional aggregates. He has been led to construct certain concepts in order to justify his approach, and this is where the discussion begins. But the work he has done to reveal structural isomorphisms is rigorously scientific and deserves to be carried further.

to expand its material base uninterruptedly, to extend its own production-relations over the whole of society. The theory of accumulation enables us to understand that the capitalist production-process, considered in its continuity, produces not only commodities and surplus-value but also

produces and reproduces the capitalist relation; on the one side the capitalist, on the other the wage-labourer (*Capital*, I, p. 591).

The development of capitalist production develops simultaneously the capitalist class and the working class, for each is the condition of the other, presupposes the other and creates the other (cf. *Wage-Labour and Capital*). At each moment, accumulation of capital means also increase in the proletariat, but at the same time, the more accumulation takes place, the more does capital become concentrated. This concentration means 'the ruin of many small capitalists, whose capitals partly pass into the hand of their conquerors, partly vanish' (*Capital*, I, 1938 edn, p. 641). The dynamic of the system consequently develops a dual contradiction:

(1) the external contradiction between the capitalist system of production and the other economic structures which lack the same dynamic and are destroyed by competition in proportion as commodity production becomes general; and

(2) the internal contradiction of the capitalist system, in that the dynamic of the system presupposes competition and yet tends towards the formation of monopolies, that is, towards its opposite. At the same time, however, the concentration of capital and its growing accumulation cause the proportion of workers needed for industrial production to decline. Relative overpopulation is caused by the same process that makes wage-labour universal.

iv. *The external contradiction of capitalism*

If we clarify this contradiction we see that it was presented historically by the dynamic power of the capitalist structures of production, and resolved to their advantage. When it was resolved – and it was history that acted as midwife to this solution – capitalism was the dominant structure of social production and became a specific system that worked over and changed the formerly-existing structures and invented new ones in order to be able to function as a whole developing by its own spontaneity:

To the extent that it [industrial capital] seizes control of social production, the technique and social organization of the labour-process are revolutionized, and with them the economico-historical type of society. The other kinds of capital, which appeared before industrial capital amid conditions of social production that have receded into the past or are now succumbing, are not only *subordinated* to it and *the mechanism of their functions altered in conformity with it*, but move solely with it as their basis, hence live and die, stand and fall with this basis. Money-capital and commodity-capital, so far as they function as vehicles of particular branches of business, side by side, with industrial capital, are nothing but modes of existence of the different functional forms now assumed, now discarded by industrial capital in the sphere of circulation – modes which, due to social division of labour, have attained independent existence and been developed one-sidedly (*Capital*, II, p. 55. My emphasis, M.G.).

Economic theory enables us to conceive in its necessity the mode of origin of the modern capitalist nations, and the necessity of the disappearance in these nations of non-capitalist economic forms (the village community, craft-guild organization, etc.).

The capitalist system imposes itself because at every moment it reproduces and develops its originating structure, in other words, the capital-labour relations. The capitalist system is an historical totality that re-engenders its own origin at every moment and expands its field of application by causing whatever was opposing it to fall within it. The small independent producers were expropriated through the development of capitalist production-relations, and, once deprived of ownership of their means of production, found themselves owners only of their labour-power, 'free' to work as wage-earners.

There are, then, two concepts of 'origin' that emerge from a dialectical analysis of the mode of development of the capitalist system.

(1) The first is that which the historian habitually uses when he studies 'the origins of . . . etc'. This concept relates to a succession in time and a chronologically dated origin. It is central to investigations into the 'genesis' of capitalism, the formation of capitalism (or of any other system).[57]

(2) The second looks at the fact that every system includes within itself its own originating structure, on which it is based, and which it reproduces at any moment, so that this originating structure is *co-present* at every moment of the system's development. This is what Marx meant when he showed that the capitalist production-process continuously

---

[57] See M. H. Dobb, *Studies in the Development of Capitalism*. Also P. Vilar, 'Problems of the Formation of Capitalism', in *Past and Present*, no. 10, November 1956.

renews capitalists at one pole and wage-earners at the other. Once capitalism has become a system, it seems to possess its origin within itself and to depend only upon itself.[58] This originating structure which is co-present at every moment of the reproduction of the system by itself is clarified by economic theory. This is possible only because the capitalist system has attained a degree of development such that it is essentially self-dependent, having eliminated the other economic structures that contradict it. We see again how economic theory and economic history are linked together.

Furthermore, we have here the key to the celebrated distinction between what is called primitive accumulation and accumulation on an expanded scale, and at the same time the reason why historical chapters appear in the midst of the theory. In fact, accumulation on an expanded scale is due to the permanent presence of the originating structure of the system at every moment of its development – including at its birth. This structure is the actual basis of the system's dynamic; but this structure itself has an origin, an historical genesis.

It is the product of an historical process that caused the overall structure of the capital-labour relation to appear – in other words, the historically determined economic structure of the separation of the worker from his instruments of labour.

How the fundamental, originating relation of capitalism was born within a non-capitalist economic system is the problem analysed by the theory of 'primitive' accumulation, with the aid of the concept of 'origin' in the sense of 'origin of . . .'. What 'primitive accumulation' describes is the movement that is the origin of what was to become 'originating' – fundamental for the development and generalization of capitalist production-relations.

The capitalist system presupposes the complete separation of the labourers from all property in the means by which they can realize their labour. As soon as capitalist production is once on its own legs, it not only maintains this separation, but *reproduces* it on a *continually extending* scale. The process, therefore *that clears the way for* the capitalist system, can be *none other than* the process which takes away from the labourer the possession of his means of production. . . . The so-called primitive accumulation, therefore, is nothing else than the *historical process* of divorcing the producer from the means of production. It appears as primitive because it forms the prehistoric stage of capital and of the mode of production corresponding with it. The economic *structure* of capitalist society

---

[58] I shall develop elsewhere the philosophical aspect of these two concepts of 'origin'.

has grown out of the economic structure of feudal society. The dissolution of the latter set free the *elements* of the former (*Capital*, I, p. 738. My emphasis, M.G.).

What the history of the origins of capitalism shows is the genesis of the originating relation that is the basis of capitalism. This history thus presupposes the results of economic science, but the latter must in turn presuppose that the structure it interprets has had a genesis, and so must refer to history. Knowledge of history works through this dual reference-back, but it can at any moment become congealed at one of the poles. The social division of scientific labour makes it possible for this circularity to break down, so producing mutilated, unilateral reflexions, false quarrels and false solutions. Marx's own procedure was already far in advance of this numbing sort of reflexion.

Nevertheless, in this dual reference-back, economic theory has a specific and primordial role to play. It constitutes the abstract elaboration of the concepts that serve the historian as tools and illuminate history. It does not, however, constitute the theory of any particular, historically-determined economico-social formation (e.g. French economy in the 16th century). Such a theory is the work of the historian, whose very difficult task it is to account for the specific realities, in other words to explore realities that are at once unique and universal. *Capital* is fundamentally a work of economic theory which nevertheless refers constantly to historical science and is continued in historical investigations to which it serves as guide, but which are either the premises for concrete studies or else overall syntheses. (Cf. the studies of the genesis of the capitalist farmer, and of the expropriations from the end of the 15th century onward, in *Capital*, I, chapters 28 and 29).

In the last analysis, *Capital* constitutes a synthesis similar to that which the most self-aware historical science *ought to be*, a synthesis that needs to be constantly developed in accordance with the development of economic and historical knowledge.

The conclusion that seems inevitable is that the capitalist system forms a totality that reproduces itself and either eliminates whatever contradicts it or else re-works what it destroys so as to adapt this to its own needs. This being so, the dynamic of the system should be that of a process of continuous growth which perpetually reproduces the conditions for its own further expansion and offers itself an unlimited future. In fact, the dynamic of the capitalist system is that of a system which, as it develops, also develops its own contradictions, and necessarily knows internal disequilibria, or at least ensures its equilibrium through disequilibrium and realizes its harmony through crises.

We here come both to the heart of the theoretical analysis of the dynamic of the system and to the moment of maximum operational effectiveness of the dialectical method. This will be the explanation of the second contradiction mentioned above, a contradiction no longer external to capitalism but internal to it. Upon this contradiction are based the fundamental laws of the dynamic of the system. These laws complete the theory of expanded reproduction, the dynamic theory of the growth of capitalism.

v. *The internal contradiction of capitalism and the fundamental laws of the dynamic of the system*

The dialectical method will enable us to understand the essential aspect of the dynamic of capitalism. Not only does expanded reproduction bring about the victory of the capitalist mode of production over other modes, and result in the constitution of a complete economic system, but this system, just because it constantly reproduces itself, also changes itself in itself through its own immanent laws.

Dialectical analysis has already revealed to us the overall working of capitalism as a differentiated totality each structure of which is the condition and result of the functioning of the others. Within this overall unity the different structures are all unified despite their differences. This concrete identity arises from a particular structure, the structure of production, and it is on this basis that a group of mutually compatible structures is formed. However, this basis is, in the setting of capitalism, endowed with a particular form of movement that animates the entire system, the process of expanded reproduction.

As a result of this, the system reproduces itself as it was before and yet already different from what it was. The difference develops within this identity, and is manifested when we take into consideration the reciprocal action of the other structures upon production. Production develops the market, but, when the market increases, production has to carry out a deeper division within itself. Moreover, a transformation of distribution entails a transformation of production (e.g. when there is a change in the distribution of population between town and country).

Dialectical analysis enables us to grasp the identity of the system through its differences, but this identity is in a sense grasped on the spot when we analyse the reciprocal relation between the structures of the system, or else it is grasped in time, and then there seems to be merely a quantitative difference between two growing magnitudes of accumulated capital. This dynamic is here a dynamic of equilibrium.

What we are going to try to grasp is the origin and structure of the constant disequilibria that the system develops and which are based on the contradictory character of the originating capitalist relation. So far, we have left aside this contradictory character that is enveloped by the reciprocal unity of capital and labour. Now, the process of reproduction of capital *also reproduces this contradiction and at the same time develops it.* The more the capitalist class expands, the more the working class expands, the more capital is accumulated, the more does production become concentrated, and this concentration and accumulation of capital cause the proportion of living labour necessary to production to undergo a relative decline. There is thus at once development of the capitalist class and concentration of this class, development of the working class and unemployment of part of this class. At the same time, the more capital becomes concentrated, the more does the contradiction develop between the social character of production and the private character of appropriation. These contrasts and disequilibria endow the process of expanded reproduction with particular structures that we will recall to memory.[59]

(1) *The short run.* In the short run, numerous fluctuations and cyclical crises occur, being repeated periodically at varying intervals of time. The antagonistic tendencies

may at one time operate predominantly side by side in space, and at another succeed each other in time. *From time to time the conflict of antagonistic tendencies finds vent in crises.* The crises are always but momentary and forcible *solutions* of the existing contradictions. They are violent eruptions which for a time *restore* the disturbed equilibrium. The contradiction, to put it in a very general way, consists in that the capitalist mode of production involves a tendency towards

[59] Let us recall that Marx has no 'theory' of crises. There are theoretical elements of an analysis of crises in his work, but they were not worked up into a special 'theory'. Duret has attempted to bring these elements together in his book *La Théorie marxiste des crises.* Let us also recall that volume III, chapters 27 to 32, could be compared with the Keynesian theory of the cycle. See, for example, Marx's notes on the irrationality of a high rate of interest at the moment of crises, etc.

absolute development of the productive forces, regardless of the value and surplus-value it contains, and regardless of the social conditions under which capitalist production takes place; while on the other hand, its aim is to preserve the value of the existing capital and promote its self-expansion to the highest limit . . . (*Capital*, III, p. 244. My emphasis, M.G.).

In fact, the contradiction exists *in nuce* in the capitalist mode of production, because the latter produces for profit and cannot realize profit without selling commodities. Now, the absolute necessity of converting real wealth into wealth in money,[60] in money capital, comes into conflict with the possibilities of carrying out this conversion, which depend on the structures of distribution, and the latter depends on the nature of the social production-relation. Accordingly, the real barrier of capitalist production is capital itself. The accumulation of capital and its constant growth are realized through periodical disequilibria the cost of which, ultimately and essentially, is borne by the workers. But this constant accumulation of capital has this contradictory aspect, that it develops in the long run a tendency for the average general rate of profit to fall, 'an expression peculiar to the capitalist mode of production of the progressive development of the social productivity of labour' (ibid., p. 209).

(2) *The long run.* It is to be observed that the relative decline in the *rate* of profit goes along with a simultaneous increase in the *mass* of profit, and that the cause of this is the increase in the productive power of social labour. At the same time, the same causes that give rise to the fall in the general rate of profit bring about contrary effects that check, slow down and counter the effects of the law of the fall in the rate of profit.[61]

Consequently, in the long run,[62] the rate of profit, the stimulus of capitalist production and the condition and driving force of accumulation, is threatened by the very development of production. We perceive here the relativity of the capitalist system.

It comes to the surface here . . . that it is not an absolute, but only a historical mode of production corresponding to a definite limited epoch in the development of the material requirements of production (ibid., p. 254).

---

[60] 'A mad demand which, however, grows necessarily out of the system itself' (*Capital*, III, p. 560).

[61] I am leaving discussion of this problem entirely aside, as my purpose is merely to show the nature of dialectical analysis and its field of application.

[62] Cf. Güsten, *Die langfristige Tendenz der Profitrate bei Karl Marx und Joan Robinson*, Munich, 1960.

(3) *General evolution*. The relative nature of capitalist production brings out at the same time the 'transitory' nature of this system of production. The most general dynamic of the system, that of its 'general evolution', is based upon the development of the contradiction between the ever increasing socialization of production and the structures of the appropriation of social surplus labour.

The necessity of abolishing private appropriation is dictated by and for the general development of the productive forces. Men have already partly accomplished this abolition, and will have to put an end to the capitalist system in order to replace it by a socialist system of production based on social ownership of the means of production. Then will begin the conscious reorganization by society as a whole of its mode of economic development.

vi. *Conclusion : The method of* Capital *as a synthetic unity of the two methods*

The dialectical method

So ends the analysis of the economic domain that the dialectical method enables us to explore. It has not been possible to describe this method apart from its field of application. Instead, the method has been grasped in the midst of this field, emphasizing once again the extent to which the study of a method is inseparable from the content with which it deals. The dialectical method, too, is a certain way of approaching a certain content.

In *Capital*, on the strictly economic plane, this content is twofold:

(1) the dialectic serves to analyse the mutual relations of the economic structures and the overall functioning of the capitalist system. It is thus the tool used in a study of structures.

(2) it serves to analyse the ways in which the capitalist system moves. It is thus the tool used to form a dynamic theory.

These two fields of analysis are, moreover, linked together. In so far as the essential relation that the dialectic brings out is that of identity in difference and difference in identity, it makes possible both study of the compatibility of the structures of a system and study of their contradictions and of the particular ways of movement that result from this. Concretely, the unity of the two fields of analysis is based on the special role that is generally played by the production-structures in human economic activity, and on the specific content of these structures in the capitalist system. The production-relations require for their development the formation of an economic system that is homogeneous and compatible with them, but at the same time they impose upon the development of this system the necessity of coming into contradiction with the other economic structures that co-exist with it, and with itself.

The dialectical method enables us to reveal the contradictions in reality and to analyse them: for example, to understand why the capitalist system has to ensure its equilibrium through disequilibrium. On this basis a certain amount of rational prediction can be developed. Economic time appears as marked by the rhythm of these overall equilibria and dis-equilibria, but the latter depend on a content that changes and that also changes them. This rhythm, these equilibria and disequilibria, these changes in structure, with their direct and indirect consequences, can be analysed with the appropriate mathematical tools, through the building of dynamic models. Thus one can make a mathematical study (over a long period) of the decline in the rate of profit resulting from the accumulation of capital.

The dialectical method can enable us to study the contradictions of the world-wide capitalist system, the unity of the development of the industrial capitalist countries and the under-developed countries, and the contradiction that this unity envelops and develops. Within the under-developed countries, study of the cumulative contradictions that characterize the growth of these countries, of what is called the 'vicious circle' of under-development, can be carried out by means of dialectical analysis leading to the construction of a model of under-development.

Finally, dialectical analysis of the capitalist system, of its origin, its growth, etc., brings out the relative nature of this system. On this relativity is based the rational prediction of the necessity for the capitalist system to disappear, but this prediction is of an overall character and supplies no particular date.

The hypothetico-deductive method

(1) serves to analyse the essence of the fundamental economic structures of the system, of their 'logical' relations, and places them in dependence on these relations, in an 'ideal genesis' that explains the order in which they appear:

(2) serves to deduce the possible combinations that such structures can form, and so indicates certain ways in which these structures move.

This method largely ensures the transition from thinking in terms of categories to thinking in terms of calculation. The ultimate problem of the method of *Capital* now can at last be considered and solved.

The linking and synthesis of the two methods

(1) The hypothetico-deductive method defines the essential structures of the economic system, and it is these essential structures that illuminate the genesis of the capitalist system analysed by the dialectical method. The latter thus presupposes the first method.

(2) These essential structures are analysed in their mutual compatibility by the hypothetico-deductive method. Now, this compatibility is engendered by and for the development of the production-relations. Consequently, the hypothetico-deductive method presupposes what is explained by the other method.

There is thus a circularity of the two methods, a reciprocal implication between them, and not an exclusion. This is why, in *Capital*, each stage assumes both methods, and each theoretical conclusion drawn is their joint achievement. For example, average profit is explained by reference to profit and surplus-value (the hypothetico-deductive method), but it assumes the overall functioning of the system and the theory of accumulation (the dialectical method). The rate of profit is analysed mainly by the first method and the law of the tendency of the rate of profit to fall is analysed mainly by the second method.

In the last analysis, the synthetical unity of the two methods is rooted in the following situation: what is at the heart of the procedure that refers back to surplus-value is the same thing as is at the basis of the dynamic of the system, namely, analysis of capitalist production-relations.

Accordingly, the two methods are necessarily internal to each other, complementary to each other, because they both study the same essentially dynamic reality. While the first method mainly illuminates the structures of the system and works out its categories, the second mainly illuminates the way the system grows, but they are inseparable from each other in the process of rational cognition.

The two methods are united because they are two ways of approaching *one and the same* object. This object can be analysed in its parts or as a whole. The two methods are thus both micro- and macro-economic. Finally, in so far as this object is quantifiable in its aspects and as a whole, and is in movement, thought in terms of calculation can carry further both of the two approaches.

Thus, the methods of *Capital* are the reverse side of the content that they develop but in which they are themselves enveloped. We have re-developed for their own sake these differing operational fields that were buried in their object. This made our task difficult and gave it an abstract character.

If, however, the method of *Capital* is the synthesis of two complementary procedures, are the latter on the same plane? Is there not a disequilibrium between them that determines their mutual relation and shows at which pole the source of the synthesis lies?

There is indeed a dissymmetry between the two methods. Both of them analyse the same 'object', but not the same aspect of the object:

(1) The specific economic system called capitalism is not an inert thing but essentially a practical reality in movement, existing in time. Its internal structures are thus time-governed throughout, enveloped by time and enveloping it in their turn. The hypothetico-deductive method assumes the mutual compatibility of these structures and illuminates it, but this compatibility did not emerge readymade from history. It is the product of history, is changed in the course of history, and eventually is threatened by history. At the same time it structures history, enveloping men's deeds, causing them to be linked together in significant behaviour that expresses this content that is felt and lived, accepted or challenged.

Now, all these time-determinations are analysed by the dialectical method (cf., for example, the theory of primitive accumulation, the theory of expanded reproduction, etc.).

(2) The capitalist system, a specific set of practical relations, a reality that essentially exists in time and is dynamic, organizes the way of life of millions of human beings, 'involves' them in a certain set of problems, threatening them or delighting them, and constitutes, for each of them, *a practical a priori that is both material and social*. At the same time, this human reality, through its very contradictions, its dynamic, gives rise to antagonisms, becomes the object of reciprocal challenges between men who are tending, within this reality, towards different forms of relationship, other modes of existence. This negativity inscribed at the heart of the capitalist system bears on the most burdensome problems of practical life and theoretical understanding, the problems of the everyday existence of millions of human beings. It is this negativity that dialectical reflexion is explicitly concerned with.

For these reasons, primarily, the dialectical method is the essential pole of the operational field worked out by Marx. This is why Marx set out this method for himself in the unpublished Introduction to the *Contribution*, developing it ideally so as to define production in general, that is, in order to give himself the means of grasping in its fundamental content the movement of the capitalist system of production. Towards the end of his life, moreover, he intended to write a special study of this method, though it eventually proved impossible for him to accomplish this. Here we have an additional proof of the importance he attributed to it.

This brings us to the final reason why the dialectical method is the richest and most complex of procedures.

The two methods, as we have shown, imply each other, and make possible, through their unity, a synthetic theory of capitalist economy. Now, this reciprocal unity, this circularity, itself needs to be thought out and established. Every economic theory thus assumes a reflexive awareness of the ideal operations that constitute this theory, and of their grounds.[63] Every economic theory includes a certain number of epistemological problems that are the object of the theory of scientific cognition. This set of highly abstract problems is itself too the object of dialectical reflexion and assumes a dialectical analysis of the relations between economic theory and economic reality, between thought and being.

We have seen that the two methods arrive at the same conclusion. Rational cognition challenges appearances *and* accounts for them, grasps the unseen behind what is seen, but also explains the latter. The theory of the capitalist system cannot but come upon the reality of man's alienation in the thing he produces, and therefore cannot develop without revealing the root of this. Without method, economic theory remains poor, abstract, fleshless.

Accordingly, the relation between ideal, theoretical thought and practical reality is based upon a dialectic of essence and appearance that can be explained only by an analysis that is itself dialectical:

'It is a work of science,' said Marx 'to resolve the visible, merely external movement into the true intrinsic movement' (*Capital*, III, p. 307).

[63] Volume IV of *Capital, Theories of Surplus Value*, develops a fundamental aspect of this reflexive awareness. Here Marx gives the ideal genesis and critique of the categories that he has himself drawn upon in order to work out a theory. Few authors have been so careful to query the concepts they handled, to grasp the ambiguities of their origins, the burden of false problems they bear, their actual validity. This is the critical approach that is an integral part of Marx's method of investigation and belongs to the dialectical method. Volume IV calls for a special study, which I shall undertake later.

Grasping the essence means working out the scientific concept of economic structures, grasping their movement; it means reproducing the reciprocal order of these structures and rising from the abstract to the concrete, which is always 'a synthesis of many definitions'. 'The latter is obviously the correct scientific method,' said Marx in the *Contribution* (p. 206), and the phrase quoted above from the manuscript of *Capital* echoed this twenty-five years later. The dialectical method thus provides thought with the most advanced tool of rational consciousness, that of the synthetical-ideal reconstruction of the concrete 'by way of thought'.

The many-sided fecundity of the dialectical method is the reason why it cannot find on the plane of calculation and formal symbolism the means of developing its whole content. Mathematics is too poor to be the sole instrument of cognition. Reality is not quantity alone. True, it is possible to show how production is consumption by constructing a table of the consumption of products required in one form or another of production, but mathematical thought cannot replace the concept in all fields, and will never be able to explain how man alienates himself in his own products.

We find these many functions of dialectical analysis and its relation to the hypothetico-deductive method in the theory of value which serves as foundation and premise to the theory of capital.[64] Now, the value of a thing refers us to human labour, that is, to the practical relation between man and nature, a relation that responds to the negativity of wants, overcoming and developing it at the same time. Fundamentally, the dialectic is the instrument for analysing man's essence, which is labour. Man is the only natural being that produces himself in reproducing himself, and who finds himself involved in this dialectical relation through the negativity of his wants. The dialectical unity of each of the moments of this process is co-present at every moment of the development of the different modes of man's existence. But this development, which diversifies this unity into an infinity of structures that seem isolated from each other, at the same time hides this concrete unity that is co-present at every stage of this development. As it develops, human labour becomes divided, and its concrete unity is masked and hidden by its own development. We see how the capitalist economic structures are a particular form of the history of human labour, and why the economist always has to keep this idea on the horizon as he works if he is not himself to become alienated.

[64] The two methods thus find their common basis in the theory of value, which finally demonstrates the rigorousness of the synthesis effected by Marx.

At the heart of the method of *Capital* lies the assumption of dialectical materialism, the philosophical assumption that man is a natural being in so far as he always finds in himself the practical *a priori* of need, but that he is thereby involved in history, in so far as he responds to this need with a number of practical deeds that are at once a way of access to himself and to the world, that is, they are deeds of birth of history and truth. Here we conclude our attempt to determine the operational fields that accomplished the transformation of Marx's reflexion into a theory.

We have isolated two methods, grasped the specific role each of them plays, and seen their unity delineated in the content that they enable us to picture. We have sought to define what it was that made possible and necessary use of the concept and use of calculation for establishing knowledge of an economic system. We have shown the paths that are opened in *Capital* for use of the formal tools that have been developed since Marx's day.

Mobilization of these tools is a concrete task that is incumbent upon Marxist economists. Perhaps we have already helped to define better the basis for a serious confrontation between the Marxist economic theory and non-Marxist theories – those of Keynes and the post-Keynesians, for instance.

But my article shows sufficiently, I think, that the actuality of *Capital* is bound up first and foremost with its method. Marx was able to link together a structural analysis and a dynamic theory, to combine the analysis of structures with the analysis of origins, to grasp the connexion between history, economic theory and economic sociology, and to realize this model of 'reasoned history'[65] which has found hardly any imitators. At the heart of this reasoned history lies the philosophical assumption that there is no world-beyond-the-world, except in the sense of ideas, and that man explains himself, through his real life-process.

But the actuality of *Capital* is not confined to its method – it attaches also to the book's content and to its subsequent developments, theoretical and practical. This is the crucial problem of the actuality of *Capital*. I hope that my analysis of the method alone will not have been useless in helping readers to appreciate this content.

[65] To use Schumpeter's excellent expression.

*

Notes on the simplifying assumptions

Note 1 : Non-Marxist writers often accuse Marx of having developed some incoherent thinking on the nature of classes, and contrast *Capital*, which basically shows two classes confronting each other, with *The Civil War in France*, where six or seven classes appear.

Let it be pointed out at once that Marx gives us no 'theory' of classes developed in its own right, so to speak. Nevertheless, it does not seem to me that there is any contradiction between the many theoretical 'elements' he analysed in his writings.

Capital is a work of economic theory. Marx undertakes in it to analyse the nature of the capitalist production-relation. As has been said, this production-relation contains *only* the relation between capital and labour, and in its social aspect, the relation between the capitalist class and the working-class.

For there are here only two classes: the working class disposing only of its labour-power, and the capitalist class which has a monopoly of the social means of production and money (*Capital*, II, p. 421. My emphasis, M.G.).

Capital thus constructs the theory of an economic relation and develops the content of this relation (conditions of existence of the worker, structure and degree of exploitation of his labour-power: Volume I, part 2, for example). An economic relation is at the same time a social structure, a structure of social existence (cf. Volume III, last chapter). *Capital* then makes a differentiated analysis of the different categories of capitalists connected with different economic functions in the economic system (commercial capitalists, financial capitalists). All these categories together, make up the capitalist class and enter into a conflict of interest with the working class.

The Civil War in France is a work not of economic theory, but of history, and of history as a series of events. Now, this series of events occurs as the outcome of a number of economic and social contradictions. The latter are not solely those of the capitalist production-relation, but of that and of the other, pre-capitalist structures. I refer the reader to my analysis of the internal and external contradictions of the dynamic of the capitalist system.

Marx's theoretical intentions are thus not the same in the two works mentioned, and there are no grounds for saying that Marx wanted to reduce the number of social classes to two only. I shall carry this analysis further on a later occasion. Meanwhile, the point brings us to a second, correlative observation, on the subject not of the theory of classes but of the national income.

Note 2 : Capital contains the elements of a theory of the national income – but, strictly speaking, it is not a 'theory' of the national income. For that to be so it would be necessary to assume that all the non-capitalist sectors of production (craftsmen, independent agricultural proprietors, etc.) had vanished.

Some excellent analyses have been devoted to this subject by J. Marchal and J. Lecaillon, in Vol. 3 of *La Répartition du Revenu National* ('Classical and Marxist Models', see, for example, p. 374). Several points call for discussion and I shall shortly attempt to do this. For example, though there is no theory of the national income in *Capital* that coincides with the historical structures of the capitalist nations (which included in Marx's day, and still include, substantial non-capitalist structures), I cannot agree with this criticism of Marx:

It would have been normal to recognize the existence, alongside the workers and the capitalists, of other types of agent, and, consequently, other participants in the distribution of the national income (Marchal, p. 377).

Marx was quite explicitly aware of the simplifying character of his working hypotheses, his 'model'. For example: '. . . we placed all money and commodities from the very start exclusively into the hands of capitalists I and II *when we drew up our scheme* and . . . neither merchants, nor money-changers, nor bankers, nor merely consuming and not directly producing classes exist here . . .' (*Capital*, p. 504. My emphasis, M.G.).

Furthermore, the existence of agents other than the capitalists and the workers is explicitly mentioned in order to explain the structure and rhythm of one of the specific mechanisms of a competitive capitalist economy – the equalization of the rate of profit:

Capital succeeds in this equalization to a greater or lesser degree, depending on the extent of capitalist development in the given nation: i.e. on the extent the conditions in the country in question are adapted for the capitalist mode of production. With the progress of capitalist production, it also develops its own conditions and subordinates to its specific character and its immanent laws all the social prerequisites on which the production process is based. . . . But this equilibration itself runs into greater obstacles whenever numerous and large spheres of production not operated on a capitalist basis . . . filter in between the capitalist enterprises and become linked with them (*Capital*, III, p. 190).

We see once more how essentially dynamic Marx's model is, and how it envelops its abstract analyses in the density of historical time.

This model employs two methods, each of which grasps essential aspects of the time and motion of the economic structures. I can therefore not agree with Marchal's criticism (op. cit., Vol. 3, p. 384) regarding the inadequacy of Marx's conception of time.

(*Economie et Politique*, May and June 1960, nos 70 and 71)

I should like to go back to and say more about some aspects of my analysis of the method of *Capital*.[1] Let me make clear once more that my standpoint is that of epistemology, in other words, analysis of the procedures and abstract tools employed by scientific, rational cognition in political economy.

What conclusions do I regard as being already established?

The method of *Capital* is both *one* and multiple. Its unity is the *synthetical* unity of different approaches. A structural analysis is fused with a dynamic theory of these structures. This dynamic is itself twofold. It illuminates, on the one hand the historical genesis of these structures and on the other, the mode of motion of this particular group of structures.

An example will illustrate these different poles of the theory. In *Capital* we find the structural analysis of capitalist production-relations (relations between capital and wage-labour) and we find this structure illuminated as regards its origins (theory of primitive accumulation, of the genesis of the capitalist farmer, etc.) and also its mode of motion: cyclical fluctuations and crises in the short run, law of the declining rate of profit in the long run, and law of the necessity of the transition to socialism in the ultimate prospect of general evolution.

A theory like this, uniting structural analysis with dynamic analysis, implies the use of two methodical procedures:

(a) the total analysis presupposes, therefore, simultaneous use of economic theory (economic concepts, e.g. surplus-value, wage-labour, etc.), sociological analysis (relations between social classes, social groups, etc.) and historical facts (birth and evolution of commodity production-relations, exchange, capitalist production-relations, etc.);

(b) this simultaneous use of these scientific tools corresponds, looked at from another angle, to the combined use of a qualitative analysis and a quantitative analysis.

Qualitative analysis is the approach by way of categories, which works

---

[1] See the previous chapter.

out definitions of economic facts and utilizes these definitions – for example, the concepts of surplus-value, relative surplus-value, absolute surplus-value, and so on.

In so far as the realities to which these concepts relate are quantities (mass of profit, amount of productive capital, volume of exchanges, etc.) *measurement* of these realities is possible and necessary, and brings into play mathematical calculation. This calculation is also a tool of investigation and discovery: an example in *Capital* is the mathematical study of the relation between the rate of surplus-value and the rate of profit; another example is provided by the studies in Volume II of 'the effect of the time of turnover on the magnitude of advanced capital' and on 'simple reproduction and reproduction on an extended scale'.

The simultaneous use of these different tools of analysis is demanded by the very nature of the object being studied: the system of capitalist economy, which is the dynamic unity of a number of aspects. In the actual course of these different methodical procedures, and forming the nucleus that requires them, combining and unifying them, we find the fact that capitalist economy is an historically determined system of production and that it involves, being a system, or 'organic totality', a necessary internal compatibility and a necessary incompatibility of its structures, and that it is the unity in motion of this compatibility and this incompatibility.

The methodological tool that enables us to grasp this system in its unity and its diversity is therefore the dialectic, the instrument that makes it possible to picture at once the contradiction and the non-contradiction of a real system, and the unity of these two.

The dialectic is not sufficient on its own to make a theory rational and scientific. Another root of this scientific rationality is the philosophical assumption of historical materialism. This defines man as a practical subject to be explained by his process of real life, and not by his belonging to some transcendent and ideal world-beyond-the-world (critique of idealism and religion). The consistent use of scientific tools, economic theory, sociology, history, etc., can be undertaken only on the basis of historical materialism, which explains man rationally, by the necessity in which he is practically placed, to produce and reproduce his material conditions of existence in order to satisfy his needs. The rational basis of the work of the historian, the economist, the sociologist, is the assumption of historical materialism, according to which 'what men are coincides with their production, both with *what* they produce and with how they produce'.[2]

Historical materialism is the very basis of the dialectical method, for man is grasped as the practical subject who is involved in history by nature and opposed to nature by his history.

Consequently, the method of *Capital* is formed on the basis of the philosophical assumption of materialism. This philosophy is enveloped in the heart of the theory which it has itself made it possible to develop. *Capital* therefore presupposes the critical movement that led Marx to dialectical idealism and then to materialism through the *1844 Manuscripts, The German Ideology*, etc.

In my first article I emphasized the genesis of the method of *Capital* in the works that preceded it. I think that I have, in the end, succeeded in identifying the function and nature of the abstract procedures used by Marx in *Capital*, and I hope especially that I have shown the levels and aspects of reality for which he worked them out and employed them in action. The distinguishing of these levels of intervention of structural analysis and dynamic analysis, qualitative analysis and quantitative analysis, of political economy, historical science and philosophy, was a delicate business, for it was imperative never to lose sight of their necessary unity.

Thus, the method of *Capital*, a synthesis of several procedures, is thoroughly dialectical.

On this point, my last article, while describing Marx's overall procedure as 'synthetical', did not adequately stress that it is 'dialectical'. This inexactitude, easy enough in itself to correct, was made worse by my using the expression 'dialectical method' in relation to certain aspects of the method of *Capital*. Consequently, the dialectical method might appear as alien to the use of operational hypotheses, and so on: moreover, it did not explicitly describe *the* method of *Capital*, that is the total movement of the theory in its complex synthetical unity. Therefore, after the summary of the structures of the method of *Capital* that I have just given, I am going to criticize and eliminate this ambiguity, and abandon the terms I have used, because the formulations made in this ambiguous setting seem now to me inexact and due to be retracted.[3]

[2] *The German Ideology*, p. 7.
[3] See previous chapter: 'The hypothetico-deductive method cannot avoid a dialectical analysis of these contradictions'; 'The dialectical tools . . . will directly encounter the hypothetico-deductive method and become interlinked with it.'

On the other hand, the actual basis of the dialectical method, historical materialism, was explicitly shown as such in my article: for example, I showed how it subtends the theory of reproduction[4] and, above all, the theory of value,[5] the foundation of the whole of Marxist economic science.

*

After this general résumé, let me develop some particular points.

Several levels need to be distinguished in the use of the dialectical method.

(1) There is first the dialectical movement, in a sense unconscious of itself, that is carried out by the overall movement of rational cognition. The latter develops and elaborates concepts, tools of analysis that involve contradictions expressing both the contradiction of the reality seen through these concepts and the historical contradictions of the practice by which this reality has been attained. Thus, scientific cognition uses the inductive method and the deductive method, which seem to be opposed to each other, but the unity of which is the actual movement, circular and dialectical, of scientific cognition: going from the particular to the general, and from the general to the particular. Other operational procedures, like the analytical approach and the synthetical approach, enable us to break up the whole into its parts and also to put the whole together again from its parts, ideally or experimentally.[6]

The categories, the scientific concepts, which emerge from this movement of rational cognition, are the end-point of a dialectical movement and the starting-point of a new stage. They are therefore always definitions that are proposed for phenomena, hypotheses needing to be verified.

I have rapidly described the dialectical approach of cognition in its formal structure, common to all rational cognition, whatever its object. But this abstract structure is always present in a particular approach of cognition aimed at a particular field of objects. This field may be the feudal system of production, the evolution of the child's personality, the relations between health and illness in the lives of individuals. The dialectic is used to give knowledge of definite sectors of the world, and is then effectively operational.

(2) Even, however, at the level of the study of definite systems of objects, dialectic may remain unconscious, reflected upon, so far as the

---

[4] Previous chapter, p. 175. [5] Previous chapter, p. 155.
[6] Depending on the science and the sphere of reality concerned.

person who uses it is concerned. By being reflected upon, conscious of itself, the dialectic becomes richer and achieves greater effectiveness: the tool, the procedure of cognition, is now taken as an object of cognition. At this level it is the formal structure of the dialectic that is unfolded and elaborated. At the end of this movement, the dialectic is 'handed over' to particular, concrete knowledge, re-deployed in the field in which it is valid, but it is now endowed with greater effectiveness because it has been worked out and reflected upon by the scientist.

This has enabled us to define the relation between the method of *Capital* and the methodological reflexions of the *Contribution to the Critique of Political Economy*. This also shows how Marx breaks away from Hegel's thinking, while keeping the tool that Hegel had enriched in his work – especially the *Logic* and the *Encyclopedia of the Philosophical Sciences*. At the same time I have shown that the philosophical assumption of historical materialism saved Marx from engaging in purely speculative 'deductions' of the concrete on the basis of abstract concepts.[7]

We realize why the method of *Capital* has become internal to the theory in being enveloped by what it has itself made it possible to develop, by the content that it had caused to become manifest. This is why analysis of the method of *Capital* implies showing how in practice this method works in *Capital*, and not just showing all that it implies and requires theoretically. For this reason I have tried to bring out the nature of the method, step by step, in some of the analyses in *Capital*. For example, the study of the process of circulation of capital and the analysis of expanded reproduction.[8]

The implicit methodological procedures need to be shown for the *whole* of *Capital*. Let me take as an example of the investigations that remain to be undertaken the analyses devoted to the metamorphoses of the commodity into money and of money into the commodity.

Marx uses a formal schema:

a sells to b, and so C becomes M;

a buys from c, and so M becomes C.

The metamorphoses of the object are thus based upon changes in relations between persons, and, reciprocally, relations between persons bring about changes in things. Marx shows that the transformation of commodity into money is simultaneously the transformation of money into commodity. Buying is selling: 'The apparently single process is a

[7] Previous chapter, p. 186.   [8] Previous chapter, pp. 159–60.

double one.'⁹ 'The sale and the purchase constitute one identical act, an exchange between a commodity-owner and an owner of money, between two persons as opposed to each other as the two poles of a magnet.'¹⁰

Here we have a dialectical analysis of a particular type, since it brings out the relations between the abstract subjects a, b and c. However, these subjects are abstract because the buying-selling relationship is a simple and abstract social relation between individuals, and all that is involved so far as the object is concerned is 'merely a matter of changes of form which commodities undergo in their transformation into money and their reconversion from money into commodities'.¹¹ Marx is thus carrying out an abstract, formal analysis, because he is studying a social relation which is itself abstract, and the formal metamorphoses of commodities. Once again, the method expresses the content.

In Volume III, however, Marx aims at studying the concrete reality of value, which is the market *price*. At this level it is no longer 'immaterial whether the price of the commodity lies above or below its value'. The task is to explain the quantitative divergences between the prices and the value of commodities, and to define, for example, the part played by supply and demand. Marx says, briefly:

In simple purchase and sale it suffices to have the producers of commodities as such counterposed to one another. In further analysis supply and demand presuppose the existence of different classes and sections of classes which divide the total revenue of a society and consume it among themselves as revenue, and, therefore, make up the demand created by revenue. While on the other hand *it requires an insight into the overall structure of the capitalist production process* for an understanding of the supply and demand created among themselves by producers as such (*Capital*, III, p. 191. My emphasis, M.G.).

A number of conclusions can be drawn from an analysis of this new example:

(1) The relation of supply and demand presupposes the relation of buying and selling. The latter, analysed in Volume I, is thus simpler, more abstract than the other relation, and was analysed first. The approach of *Capital* is thus here, once again, from the abstract to the concrete, and the abstract reappears as an element of the concrete:

The proportion of supply and demand *recapitulates*, first, the relation of use-value to exchange-value, of commodity to money, and of buyer to seller; and

---

⁹ *Capital*, I, p. 82.　　　¹⁰ Ibid., p. 87.　　　¹¹ *Capital*, III, p. 189.

second, that of producer to consumer . . . (*Capital*, III, p. 189. My emphasis
M.G.).

(2) This passage testifies to the *order* of *Capital*, as between concepts
and as between analyses, and its general advance towards the concrete.
And this order makes it possible to understand concrete reality on the
basis of the abstract. This order reproduces the concrete ideally, by revealing to us its inner logic.

(3) The individual who, at the level of simple purchase of a commodity,
was any kind of commodity–producer, is defined at the level of the working of supply and demand as belonging to the capitalist production
system and explained by this social nature of production and consumption.

The formal dialectical analysis of Volume I is now developed as a
dialectical analysis of overall and historically determined relations.

(4) This example shows us how rigorous Marx's procedure is. It is not
empiricism, since it does not start from an unintelligible mass of facts,
but *makes* them intelligible. It is not the Hegelian dialectic, which deduces
reality from a concept. It is not the movement of a concept that develops
itself and produces phenomenal reality. It is a logic of reality that reproduces itself through concepts, advancing from the most abstract to the
most concrete.

This further example illustrates once more the statements made in my
previous articles. It shows how interesting it would be to account for the
diversity of the methodological procedures implied *at each stage* of
Capital, the unity between them, and so on. It would be a prolonged and
delicate task, but a fruitful one.

*

I want to stress another point that brings us to a difficult controversy. I
showed that the starting-point of *Capital* was the study of the category
'commodity'. Why this starting-point? Because the capitalist system of
production is the most highly developed form of commodity production.
Furthermore, in the capitalist system the producer has himself become a
commodity. The commodity category, I said, enables us to understand
the *unity* and *meaning* of the capitalist system of production. It makes all
the subsequent analyses intelligible. As it carries the entire theory of
value, it is the very foundation of rational and economic cognition.

'The characteristic thing is not that the commodity labour-power is purchasable but that labour-power appears as a commodity' (*Capital*, II, p. 28).

[If surplus-value, 'and thus value in general', had a 'different source than labour'], '*political economy would then be deprived of every rational basis*' (*Capital*, III, p. 147. My emphasis, M.G.).

My analysis brings me to two aspects of Marx's scientific approach, each of which would require very extensive discussion.

(1) It is striking to observe that Marx carries out, in economic investigation, a procedure that is used in other sciences and has been subjected to precise epistemological analyses. When a psychiatrist allows his patient to talk, he lets him go on setting out the elements of what he has to say until a moment comes when, for the psychiatrist, one of these elements illuminates the rest and unifies around itself that which has up to then been described in apparently disorderly fashion. What is revealed at this moment is the 'characteristic thing' on the basis of which the analysis of the patient and his illness can be undertaken, organized, effected in a scientific way.

What has happened is the re-structuring of a totality around one of its elements, which reveals the structure, the organization of this totality. This moment when the rational re-structuring of a mass of data becomes possible is, however, the fruit not of a mysterious intuition but of the previous movement of the expert's cognition. He must have learnt to observe facts, to classify them, to explain them by means of theoretical schemas, to form hypotheses. The moment of re-structuring emerges from this preliminary activity, and pre-supposes it.

This dialectic of investigation and proof was developed by Marx in the way we have traced, in *The German Ideology*, the *Contribution*, and, above all, in *Theories of Surplus Value*. There we see Marx taking up the concepts of economic science worked out from Aristotle to Ricardo, and re-working them critically by confronting them with reality, with history, and so on. The moment of re-structuring – end-point and starting-point at the same time – is that which causes hypotheses to arise in the sciences. This clarifies some of the arguments in my previous articles, by placing them in the perspective of the total dialectical movement that made possible the birth of *Capital*.

I have compared this movement with that which some phenomenologists aim to carry out. It seems to me that the analysis attempted by the latter gives excessive attention to the study of structures without being able to explain their origin, or at least, as will be seen later, by failing to consider the contradictions in them and developing their investigation of origins on a basis that is not materialistic but idealistic. The origin is sought not in the activities of an historically determined practical subject but in the constituting activity of an imaginary subject, the transcendental absolute subject. On this point, already outlined in no. 70 (p. 13), I should be glad to have an opportunity to discuss and reflect along with specialists in modern idealist thought.[12]

(2) The second aspect of the analysis of the commodity category that calls for a thoroughgoing methodological commentary is the procedure by which Marx moves from the characteristics of the object, a commodity, towards the origin and characteristics of the activity that has produced this object. Let me recall the structure of this procedure.[13]

Marx *describes* the 'appearances' of any commodity – a pipe, for instance. This object has a use-value (it is used for smoking) and an exchange-value (it costs a certain price). Marx then investigates the origin and conditions of the possibility of exchanging commodities with qualitatively different use-values. They must have something in common despite their qualitative diversity. The analysis advances towards the origin of the property that commodities possess of being exchangeable. This common property that makes them exchangeable is 'the fact that they are products of labour'. The process of cognition thus consists in letting oneself be carried by the analysis of the object's structures towards the origin of these structures. Once this origin has been revealed, the actual nature of the object is intelligible. Synthetical knowledge has been achieved. The exchange-value of an object is 'congealed labour'.

This bringing out of the origin and movement of a reality, this climb back from what has been formed to the genesis that formed it, is a dialectical procedure essential to rational cognition.[14] It is what Hegel meant in

[12] Here I concur with some recent analyses by R. Garaudy, in *Perspectives de l'homme*, on Husserl: see, e.g. p. 33.

[13] Cf. my analysis of this above. The analysis of the commodity in Volume I, Part I, of *Capital* deserves to be studied in detail, in all the stages of the demonstration.

[14] On the philosophical plane, it is to be noted that this schema of a procedure that moves back from what is formed to the activity that has formed it is found in the Hegelian dialectic, in Husserl's transcendental genesis, and in Marx's dialectic. However, the approach is not effected on the same philosophical basis in each case, but either on the basis of an idealist assumption or on that of a materialist one (so far as Husserl is con-

his famous formulation: 'The result is nothing without its becoming.' The intelligibility of a reality is attained only when the cause illuminates the effect, the origin illuminates the result, the production illuminates the product.

It is to be noted that what Marx does in Volume I of *Capital* is not to set forth the concrete genesis of the many historical processes that made man into a commodity-producer. On the contrary, what he gives us is an ideal genesis that illuminates an abstract and universal relation. But this ideal genesis is itself dialectical. In my previous article, because of the ambiguous distinction I made between two methods, only one of which was styled dialectical, the analysis of this climb back towards the origin that is carried out by rational cognition may have seemed non-dialectical. In fact, the entire analysis of the commodity, of money on the basis of the commodity, and of capital on the basis of money, was described as a 'genesis'.[15]

This ideal genesis is to serve as the tool for analysing the concrete genesis of the historical processes that transform man into a commodity-producer. Theoretical knowledge of the essence of the commodity thus serves as ideal guide to the understanding of historical development. Marx's method is thus the opposite of empiricism, without, however, falling into abstract speculation.

The analysis of the commodity, the starting-point of *Capital*, thus illuminates Marx's method for us, and appears as the most complex dialectical nucleus of *Capital*, all the more so because it begins the succession of categories and *provides the basis* for them. The schema that follows shows clearly how the characteristics of the object 'commodity' become those of the producer himself in the capitalist system of production (hence alienation, commodity fetishism, etc.) [see figure 1].

When the dialectical development of the commodity has been completed, capital has been defined in its essential nature, and man himself is shown as a commodity of a certain type, producing surplus-value. The foundations of the scientific analysis of the capitalist system have been

---

cerned, moreover, this approach is not explicitly based on the idea of contradiction). *And it is this difference that is essential.* The fruitfulness of dialectical analysis and its scientific rationality are *radically* effective, 'only on the basis of materialism'. Cf. Engels, *Ludwig Feuerbach*; Marx, *The German Ideology*, etc.

[15] Previous chapter, p. 150, Cf. *Capital*, I, p. 15.

Figure 1

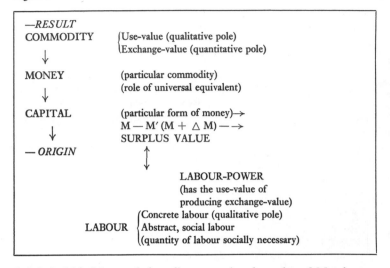

definitely laid. I have tried to diagrammatize the order of Marx's procedure [see figure 2].

What I call 'dynamic' is the analysis of the forms of motion of the capitalist system in their genesis (primitive accumulation) and in their modes of motion, both general (expanded reproduction) and more particular and concrete (crisis, tendency of the rate of profit to fall). At the same time, however, that this dynamic becomes clear, analysis of the increasingly concrete structures of the system (profit, rent, etc.) is carried out, the two procedures conditioning each other dialectically.

This diagram enables me to answer Professor Stefan Heretik, of the Institute of Economics in the Slovak Academy of Sciences, who commented on my last study of this subject:

It is said that Volumes II and III of *Capital* are concerned with macro-economics whereas Volume I proceeds on a micro-economic plane. I find this view expressed in your article. A few days ago I read a similar view in *Voprosy Filosofii*, no. 11 of 1960, in a critique of James's book which was recently translated into Russian. I must say frankly that I cannot accept this view. At most, I can agree that the method of exposition in Volume I resembles micro-economic analysis. The content itself, however, the results of the analysis, their meaning and bearing, are not micro-economic. For example, the explanation given of the essence

Figure 2

THEORY OF VALUE	THEORY OF CAPITAL			
Commodity	Dynamic			
→ money	absolute	Accumulation (simple primitive)	Circulation. Expanded reproduction	
→ capital				→ *Profit* (transformed form of surplus value)
→ *surplus-value* (element of capital)	→ Relative surplus value			Entrepreneur's profit. Rate of interest. Ground rent
Vol. I, part 1	Vol. I, part 2	Vol. I, part 3	Vol. II, parts 1 and 2	Vol. III, parts 1, 2, 3
Vol. I Production of surplus value on the micro-economic scale (the enterprise) Abstract ―――――――→ Concrete		Vol. III Distribution of surplus-value as effect of overall macro-economic process		

of the commodity, of value, money, the working of the law of value, capitalist accumulation, etc. . . .

I fully agree with this opinion. I did not say that Volume I is *entirely* developed on the micro-economic plane, and the other two volumes on the macro-economic plane. My diagram shows clearly that Volume I includes elements that elude this distinction: the essence of the commodity, of money, the theory of value, and other things that are directly macro-economic: reproduction, primitive accumulation.

The micro-economic element in Volume I consists, to my mind, in the description of the mechanism of surplus-value within a *single* firm, and also in the fact that this surplus-value is an *abstract* reality as compared with profit, the real form of the surplus-value, which comes back to the firm through the working of the relation between it and the whole of social capital. Marx himself points to the difference between the planes when he mentions that the movement of an isolated individual capital presents

> other phenomena than the *same* movement does when considered from the point of view of a *part* of the aggregate movement of social capital, hence its inter-connexion with movements of its other parts, and that the movement simultaneously solves problems the solution of which must be assumed when studying, the circuit of a separate, individual capital instead of being the result of such, study (*Capital*, II, p. 97. My emphasis, M.G.).

It is on precisely this point that I pointed to a transition between Volume I and Volumes II and III.[16] I did not include in this transition either the analysis of value or the analysis of accumulation. The point of transition is analysed dialectically by Marx. Profit both is and is not identical with surplus-value. Surplus-value is the unpaid labour *actually produced* in the firm, but profit is the surplus-value *actually realized* and appropriated by the capitalist of this firm. Marx thus maintains the distinction between the planes, shows the transition from one to the other, the dialectical unity, and does not fall into the impotent 'no bridge' theory[17] of the bourgeois economists. Furthermore, as the production of surplus-value is characteristic of every capitalist productive enterprise, the theory of surplus-value defines a general structure of the *entire* capitalist system of production. The analysis of a micro-economic mechanism thus does not forbid transition to the macro-economic plane.

*

These few elaborations, to which I shall return in other articles, enable me to make another point more precise: the operational role played by assumptions in *Capital*. I have shown above that the assumption is a moment in the dialectical development of scientific cognition, that it is a point of arrival and a point of departure at one and the same time. For

---

[16] Previous chapter, p. 162.

[17] Meaning the theory that no transition is possible from the micro-economic to the macro-economic.

materialism, scientific truth is not an ideal, closed essence, accessible once for all to an illuminating intuition, but an assumption to be checked, to be tested. Truth is for the materialist essentially experimental, and must provide practical proofs.[18] Marxism itself appears as an assumption to be checked, and which has already been largely verified by practice. This is why materialism is the philosophical basis on which the modern sciences can be developed in a consistent and thorough way. This is why there are grounds for using, at all levels, hypotheses and the deductive operations that they demand and make possible. Historical and dialectical materialism is itself included in this perspective. Auguste Cornu,[19] Professor at the Humboldt University in Berlin, has taken this idea, which he completely agrees with, and has written to me:

This clearly appears in the *1844 Manuscripts* in which he [Marx] starts from the Hegelian assumption of man's creation of himself through an activity, a self-creation and activities to which he at first gives a concrete meaning, and he establishes this assumption by putting '*praxis*' at the centre of his conceptions and by drawing from this a dialectical and historical materialist conception of the world, and thereby of man's creation of himself. It seems to me that this method of conceiving and dealing with a subject, by way of an hypothesis, checked and supported by historical and dialectical materialism . . . is a regular process with Marx. . . .

Once it is solidly rooted in this materialist and dialectical perspective, the use of hypotheses seems to me trebly necessary and fruitful. I showed in my previous article (cf. previous chapter) that an hypothesis serves:

(1) to define abstractly the field of scientific analysis:

(2) to develop and test the concepts of economic realities, for example, and their laws;

(3) to make possible within this field, and through these conceptual determinations, the setting-up of a mathematical calculation and the use of an operational symbolism and formalism, in so far as these qualitatively distinct realities are quantitatively measurable.

By this procedure the rigorousness of the theory is ensured, as also its logical sequence. Furthermore, the economic theory can be developed in the form of a 'model', a device for exposition and analysis at the same time,

---

[18] This is the nucleus that materialism derives from empiricism. Cf. Marx, *The Holy Family*.

[19] Author of remarkable studies on the formation of the thought of Marx and Engels (Auguste Cornu, *Karl Marx et Friedrich Engels*, P.U.F.).

which is much favoured and widely employed by the natural and social sciences in their present phase of development. I analysed the most explicit example of this procedure in *Capital*; the study of the relation between the rate of profit and the rate of surplus-value.[20]

Marx establishes the relation

$$p' = s' \frac{V}{c + v}$$

and studies the consequences that follow from this, assuming successive or simultaneous variation of each of the variables of the equation.[21]

It should be noted that this assumption is a dialectical *moment* of *Capital* – also that the terms p', s', v, c, have already been defined and refer us back to other 'moments' of the theoretical elaboration. The use of assumption and of deductive reasoning is thus (something that my articles failed to make clear enough) internal to the dialectical method of economic science. Thus, in the use of hypotheses of this type, conceptual thinking and mathematical quantitative analysis are combined dialectically. Marx's economic thought can and must lead to the formation of dynamic 'models'.[22]

*

A striking proof is provided by Lenin's work entitled *On the So-Called Market Question* (1893). Lenin was 23 years old. He had just read and digested *Capital*. He was contributing to discussion of a theoretical question that was fundamental for the revolutionary struggle in Russia: could capitalism develop in Russia despite the predominance of the very poor agricultural economy? From his analyses were to emerge *The Development of Capitalism in Russia*[23] and the revolutionary strategy of the Bolshevik Party aimed at the weak point of the capitalist system, the Russian economy. Lenin showed, in opposition to the Narodniks, and in 1893 to Krassin, that the peasantry were disintegrating and capitalist production-relations becoming the characteristic and dynamic feature of Russia's economy.

[20] *Capital*, III, p. 49.   [21] Cf. pp. 140–1 above.

[22] L. Althusser has pointed out to me that Marx wrote towards the end of his life a *Manual of Differential and Integral Calculus*, which Lafargue mentions several times. This completes my reference (in the previous chapter, p. 140) to the possibility that existed already in Marx's time of using differential and integral calculus in economics.

[23] Cf. chapters 1, 2 and 8. This book has another actuality if we compare pre-revolutionary Russia with the India of today.

Lenin builds a 'model' of the historical development of capitalism. He wants us to watch the transformation of the natural economy of the direct producers into commodity economy, and the transformation of the latter into capitalist economy. He wants to check and to show that the division of labour makes the first transformation possible and that competition accounts for the second. He wants also to prove that these transformations develop the market, without necessarily increasing production.

I will confine myself to a few remarks about this 'schema', which calls for a detailed commentary:

(a) Lenin first indicates the method he uses: 'We must *begin by ascertaining the content* of the concepts dealt with.'

(b) He puts forward two definitions that summarize Marx's thinking: 'By commodity production is meant . . .,'[24] 'By capitalism is meant that state of the development of commodity production at which not only the products of human labour, but human labour-power itself becomes a commodity.'[25]

(c) He points out the simplifications he has made in order to carry out the analysis: 'All extraneous circumstances have been *abstracted*, i.e. *taken as constants* (for example, size of population, productivity of labour, and much else), *in order to analyse* the influence on the market of *only those* features of the development of capitalism that are mentioned above.' (Ibid., p. 94. My emphasis, M.G.)

(d) These simplifying assumptions are completed, moreover, by the extremely abstract assumption of a society made up of only six producers, producing three kinds of goods necessary for their existence. Far from hindering analysis, however, this assumption makes it possible. This community is, furthermore, not historically defined as such and such a one, at such and such a period, but is the abstract, simplified expression of a structure common to all the communities of isolated individual producers known to history. Here we have an eloquent example of my analyses of the operational character of a model, of the use of mathematical formalism and symbolism, etc.

(e) Again, this model contains a dialectical moment, a qualitative leap: the transition from the third to the fourth period, of non-capitalist commodity production to capitalist commodity production. In the fourth period, the ruined independent producers, II, III, V and VI, have lost their economic independence and are 'engaging themselves as wage-

[24] Lenin, *Collected Works*, 4th edn, vol. I, Eng. trans., p. 93.   [25] ibid.

EXPLANATION OF THE TABLE

I–II . . . –VI are producers.

a, b, c are branches of industry (for example, agriculture, manufacturing and extractive industries).

a = b = c = 3. The magnitude of value of the products a = b = c equals 3 (three units of value) of which 1 is surplus-value.*

The market column shows the magnitude of value of the products sold (and bought); the figures in parentheses show the magnitude of value of the labour-power (= 1.p.) sold (and bought).

The arrows proceeding from one producer to another show that the first is a wage-worker for the second.

Simple reproduction is assumed: the capitalists consume the entire surplus-value unproductively.

*The part of value which replaces constant capital is taken as unchanging, and is therefore ignored.

	Producers	Production			Total	Natural consumption
		Branch of industry				
		a	b	c		
1.	I	a	b	c	9	9
	II	a	b	c	9	9
	III	a	b	c	9	9
	IV	a	b	c	9	9
	V	a	b	c	9	9
	VI	a	b	c	9	9
	Total	6a	6b	6c	54	54
3.	I	a	—	2c	9	6
	II	a	2b	—	9	6
	III	a	—	2c	9	6
	IV	a	2b	—	9	6
	V	a	—	2c	9	6
	VI	a	2b	—	9	6
	Total	6a	6b	6c	54	36
5.	I	2a	—	6c	24	11
	II	½a ➤—⌐—¬—		—	1½	1½
	III	½a ➤—⌐—¬—		—	1½	1½
	IV	2a	6b	—	24	11
	V	½a ➤—¬	—		1½	1½
	VI	½a ➤—⌐	—		1½	1½
	Total	6a	6b	6c	54	28

| Market | | Producers | Production | | | | Natural consumption | Market | | |
| Sells | Buys | | Branch of industry | | | Total | | Sells | Buys | |
			a	b	c					
—	—	I	a	—	2c	9	6	3	3	**2.**
—	—	II	a	$\frac{6}{5}$b	$\frac{4}{5}$c	9	$8\frac{2}{5}$	$\frac{3}{5}$	$\frac{3}{5}$	
—	—	III	a	$\frac{6}{5}$b	$\frac{4}{5}$c	9	$8\frac{2}{5}$	$\frac{3}{5}$	$\frac{3}{5}$	
—	—	IV	a	$\frac{6}{5}$b	$\frac{4}{5}$c	9	$8\frac{2}{5}$	$\frac{3}{5}$	$\frac{3}{5}$	
—	—	V	a	$\frac{6}{5}$b	$\frac{4}{5}$c	9	$8\frac{2}{5}$	$\frac{3}{5}$	$\frac{3}{5}$	
—	—	VI	a	$\frac{6}{5}$b	$\frac{4}{5}$c	9	$8\frac{2}{5}$	$\frac{3}{5}$	$\frac{3}{5}$	
—	—	Total	6a	6b	6c	54	48	6	6	
3	3	I	a		6c	21	10	11	3 (+8 l.p.)	**4.**
3	3	II	a ➡ —⌐ —	—		3	3	(4 l.p.)	4	
3	3	III	a ➡ —⌐ —	—		3	3	(4 l.p.)	4	
3	3	IV	a	6b	—	21	10	11	3 (+8 l.p.)	
3	3	V	a ➡ —	—		3	3	(4 l.p.)	4	
3	3	VI	a ➡ —⌐	—		3	3	(4 l.p.)	4	
18	18	Total	6a	6b	6c	54	32	22 (+16 l.p.)	22 (+16 l.p.)	
1	(+10 3 l.p.)	I	6a	—	—	18	6	12	6 (+6 l.p.)	**6.**
(5 l.p.)	5	II	➡	—	—	—	—	(6 l.p.)	6	
(5 l.p.)	5	III	—	6b	—	18	6	12	6 (+6 l.p.)	
13	(+10 3 l.p.)	IV	— ➡ —	—	—	—	—	(6 l.p.)	6	
(5 l.p.)	5	V	—	—	6c	18	6	12	6 (+6 l.p.)	
(5 l.p.)	5	VI	— ➡ —⌐	—	—	—	—	(6 l.p.)	6	
26 (+20 l.p.)	26 (+20 l.p.)	Total	6a	6b	6c	54	18	36 (+18 l.p.)	36 (+18 l.p.)	

workers in the enlarged establishment of their fortunate rival'.[26] Parallel with this, the branches of industry, b and c, are concentrated in the hands of two producers, I and IV. Finally, the wage-earners do not receive the entire product of their labour. One part is appropriated by the employer – this is surplus-value. This results in an intensified division of labour and extension of the market, because the wage-earners will have to buy in the market what they formerly produced for themselves.

(f) Lenin himself notes that the simplifying assumption of simple reproduction which he has made prevents him from building an exact model of the concordance between division of labour and volume of the market in capitalist society, since the latter develops according to the law of expanded reproduction.

(g) Finally, in chapter 6, he deduces five essential conclusions from his model, which I shall not analyse.

Here we have, dealing with a problem of exceptional scope, an example that confirms the epistemological arguments of my previous articles. The use of assumption is here shown to be absolutely dialectical and undertaken on the basis of historical materialism. Let me make clear that while the use of 'models' does not in the least contradict Marxist economic science, it is no guarantee of the 'validity' of non-Marxist theories that they do use models. Far from finding in this an argument in favour of bourgeois theories, I would remind the reader that the value of a model depends on its fundamental concepts and that it is at this level alone that Marxism and the other theories are opposed to each other.

I have now finished the additions I wanted to make to my first series of articles. I should be glad if a scientific discussion were to take us further on these delicate points of methodology. In particular, I should like to discuss the problems of economic time and of the difference – which I have deliberately ignored for the time being – in the way the law of value works in capitalist and socialist economies.

(*Economie et Politique*, no. 80, March 1961)

[26] ibid., p. 95.

4. The Measurement of Value: a Problem of Optimum Management in a Socialist Economy

These brief remarks and suggestions have as their sole purpose to engage in a dialogue with the economists of the socialist countries, to inaugurate an exchange of reflexions for the greatest advantage of everyone, in order to cleanse the theoretical schemas of their obscurities and to mark off precisely the contours of the real practical problems.

The discussion on value and prices is as old as the political economy of which it constitutes the fundamental element. It already has a long history in the USSR and in the Peoples' Democracies. It is enough to recall the names of Strumilin, Ostrovityanov, Mstislasky, Miszewski, among the numerous participants in a public controversy.[1] Recently this discussion has been renewed with fresh vigour and with some new features that Professor Csikos-Nagy's[2] articles enable us to appreciate.

What is the new element in the discussion? Not a doctrinal contribution on the idea of value, but the affirmation that it is now possible, or almost possible, to measure, to *calculate* the social expenditure of labour realized in the production of the goods and services of a socialist economy, and to construct a system of prices which translate the reciprocal proportions of the social costs of these goods and services.

These two objectives are dictated by the need to improve the management of the national economy and to define the optimum conditions of its working. This practical orientation means that the theoretical elaboration of the most complex economic categories – value, price – is not primarily intended as a critique of general conceptions of value but rather as a way to improve the institutions and mechanisms of the conscious management of the economy.

Consequently the discussions have arisen from a concern for effectiveness similar to that which the founders of economics, Smith and Ricardo,

[1] Cf. the discussions in the USSR Academy of Sciences in 1956 and in Lomonosov (Moscow) University in 1958. See also the writings of Kantorovich and the polemics launched by Boyarsky, etc. (cf. *Etudes Economiques*, no. 134).

[2] Béla Csikos-Nagy, 'Le rapport prix-valeur dans l'économie socialiste': 'The real first cost and the Smith dogma' (*Figyelö*, 9 September 1962).

felt in relation to the problems of their own day. More profoundly, the discussions hinge directly upon the concepts of classical political economy, and it was not by chance that analysis of Smith's 'real first cost' was undertaken by Professor Csikos-Nagy.

What, then, are the practical problems that have made it necessary to analyse the ideas, both connected and separate, of price and value?

Briefly, they are the problems created by the great rigidity of the price-systems at present in use in the socialist economies. Production is consciously planned, in other words, quantities and prices are fixed before the products are put into circulation. The decisions are taken on the basis of calculation of the cost of production, but as to express costs is not the only function of prices, the price system does not necessarily coincide with the system of costs. In fact, prices have a threefold function:

(1) They serve as an accounting device to measure the social costs of production.

(2) They operate as an instrument of distribution of the net social income.

(3) They play the part of economic stimulus by giving producers an incentive to innovation.

Through their functions (2) and (3), the prices of products may diverge from costs of production. Csikos-Nagy shows clearly how, for example, planning of the prices of agricultural products is indirectly planning of peasant incomes and constitutes an essential element in social relations between the working class and the peasantry. The structure of agricultural prices thus depends very much upon decisions concerning the structure of the distribution of the national income.

The separation of prices from costs through the effect of decisions relating to the distribution of the national income is accentuated by the simultaneous development of two types of distribution – according to needs and according to work done. The relative importance of each of these forms is based on the relative scarcity of the means of production at society's disposal.

Several other factors contribute to displace the centre of gravity of the price-system as compared with the centre of the system of costs; the existence of bottlenecks, the desire to allow substitution of some products for others, the desire to stimulate the export industries that bring in foreign exchange, and, in general, innovations.

In practice, therefore, for many reasons, the price-system functions in a way that is at once rigid and thrown off centre by divergences that are more or less intentional. This means that in reality the price-system, through its very stability, remains intact, or alters very little, while the conditions of production change. Thereby it diverges farther and farther from the structure of real costs, while making more delicate and more indistinct the evaluation and distribution of the national income.

Consequently we can appreciate that it has become necessary to change the price structure in order to improve the conscious management of the economy and minimize the social costs of realizing the objectives of the plan.

The foregoing makes it easy to perceive the essential difference between a capitalist market economy and a socialist economy. In the former, price changes take place through a process that is suffered rather than willed by society. The conscious organization and management of the various aspects of economic activity – production, consumption, investment – are bound up with blind processes that remain largely uncontrollable. In a socialist economy, because production is not based on autonomous and competing production-units, the changes in the price-system can be decided with overall social benefit in mind.

In practice, how can this price system be modified otherwise than by the free formation and automatic regulation of prices in a market economy?

Csikos-Nagy puts the problem perfectly:

What are the most flexible administrative means, best adapted to each sector and branch of the economy ... to avoid sclerosis of the price-structure and en-sure the possibility of re-structuring prices whenever important changes in value-relations occur?

Thus, the basic answer to the problem of price-management seems dependent on the solution of the problem of the closest approximate measurement of the relative value of products, the basis for any subsequent reform. One road is blocked from the start so far as the construction of a new price-system is concerned – that which begins with consumer prices, on the grounds that these broadly coincide with value. This coincidence actually takes place through consumer prices each of which, in fact, is often considerably divergent from value. Whether, therefore, one proposes to adopt a single level or two levels of prices, it is necessary first of all to know what the value is.

What problems are presented by knowledge of value? Practical problems, and not a theoretical problem of definition, since the formula for the value of a product is known. The value of product x is $c_n + v_n + m_n$, where c = constant capital, v = variable capital, m = value added, and n means that we are at the nth stage of the production-process of x.

These practical problems arise from the fact that determination of $c + v$, of cost of production, comes up against three obstacles. Analysis of them forms the richest part of Csikos-Nagy's survey.

(a) First obstacle: the vicious circle, price/value of labour-power. In practice, $c + v$, cost of production, is calculated on the basis of a given price-system. In a given system, it is of little significance that $c + v$ contains a fraction of the net income of society. Calculation of social income on the basis of a given price-system thus proceeds in a vicious circle.

(b) Second obstacle: the regression of costs to infinity. In the formula, C_n, congealed labour, refers back to past living labour, and so to a process

$$c_{(n-1)} + v_{(n-1)} + m_{(n-1)}$$

and $c_{(n-1)}$ refers back also to

$$c_{(n-2)} + v_{(n-2)} + m_{(n-2)}, \text{ and so on.}$$

The calculation of c_n becomes lost immediately in a *regressus ad infinitum*, in an infinite convergent series.

(c) Third obstacle: the opacity of reality as seen via the enterprise.

The accounting practice of the enterprises calculates a cost of production that is controllable but does not correspond to the real cost of production. The division of productive labour in successive stages in many enterprises leads to a contradictory result.

At the level of the enterprise, the nature of the total production-process is concealed, hidden by the enterprise's own accounting. The latter can give information only about the effective cost of the phase of the total production-process that is carried out within the enterprise. Now, what is put down to expenditure on raw materials by one enterprise is put down as $c + v + m$ of the enterprises that produce these raw materials.

The order of the division of labour thus forms the line followed by the chain of the *regressus ad infinitum* which appeared as the second obstacle to knowledge of value.

The organic isolation of the enterprise within the social division of labour thus explains why the cost of production as a practical concept is an effective tool for the management of the enterprise without, for all that, corresponding to the real social cost of production. The cost of production revealed by accounting at enterprise level is thus both capable of expressing the practice of the enterprise, and deriving its effectiveness from this, and at the same time incapable of bringing out the real total cost of production. The latter, as a theoretically exact economic category, can be determined only by leaving the micro-economic scale of the enterprise and moving to the macro-economic level of the national economy. Csikos-Nagy's analysis naturally led him to the classical economic discussions in which the micro-economic and macro-economic points of view were set forth.[3] With Keynes, and especially with the need to establish the problematic of the development of the national economies, Western thought is also involved in a return to the classical economists.

For practical reasons, the economic process cannot be grasped completely and exactly at enterprise level. Economic science finds the answers to its essential questions by taking as its standpoint the whole, and not a part, of the economic machine.

We are clearly aware that any production can be analysed by way of two divergent approaches. One of these starts from the individual enterprises and adds up their accounts. This approach is mistaken. National accounting must subtract a part of the data before adding up what remains.

The price-structure thus obtained directly combines expenditure on wages with net national income, after progressively eliminating the whole of the entry 'material', in order to rediscover this in the form of living labour.

The formula $c_n + v_n + m_n$ becomes $(V + v) + (M + m)$. V and M are the values (wages plus incomes) of the products accumulated during the stages preceding the nth and last phase of the production-process. The problem thus becomes: is it possible to reduce all the formulas to this one?

Csikos-Nagy gives two reasons for believing that it is possible.

(a) The socialist economy is able, through its distinctive production-relations, to gather information about itself and acquire a transparency that exceeds the possibilities of capitalism, functioning as the latter does through the entrepreneur's striving for private profit, and safeguarding as it does the freedom to conceal information.

(b) Recent developments in mathematics and electronic techniques make it possible to calculate the amount of wages accumulated per product and per branch, for any initial price-system. By assuming that the ratio

[3] Hence the article: 'The real first cost and the Smith dogma.'

v/m is the same for each product it is possible to work out the social cost of production.

Through the convergence and combination of these two positive conditions, the threefold obstacle of the *regressus ad infinitum*, the vicious circle of wages and prices, and the opacity of the production-process can be overcome and the way opened for calculation of the real value of products. A crucial stage in the management of the national economy can be passed, making possible the optimum allocation of resources, speeding up the rate of growth and bringing nearer the moment of wider generalization of rules of distribution *based no longer on the law of value* but on the law of social needs.

The determination of value would thus seem to be a necessary stage towards better management of production and distribution and the creation of conditions for abolishing the regulatory role of value in man's material activities. Csikos-Nagy thus places current Hungarian scientific work in the perspective of a long-term transition of his society towards a situation in which the relative scarcity of means of production will have been greatly reduced. He even visualizes the order of succession in which price functions will gradually disappear in the course of this evolution in which commodity and money relations *wither away*. The functions of redistribution of the national income and economic stimulation will be, he considers, the first to go.

Accordingly, the disappearance of prices presupposes first that prices be perfected. On this the writer's attitude is partly the same as that of Kantorovich and Novogirov, who have built a mathematical model of a price system that ensures optimum allocation of national resources, taking account of the purposes of the distribution of the social income.[4] Csikos-Nagy's analysis makes a substantial contribution on these points, by its clarity and precision, and makes me regret not possessing more information about the theoretical work going on in Hungary. This analysis also raises several questions, the principal ones being the following:

(1) In order to analyse one of the reasons for the gap between the actual price-system and the social cost of production, one needs to be able to measure the growth of the productivity of labour, which constantly puts prices off centre as compared with costs. How is this productivity measured in Hungary?

[4] See Lange, *Introduction to Econometrics*, ch. 3: also in Poland, Kalecki, Brus, Laski and Minc.

(2) Determining the value in labour of a country's output also presupposes that it is possible to distinguish between, and to combine, simple and complex labour. In East Germany work has been done on this problem, without, apparently, any positive result being achieved. How is this problem dealt with in Hungary?

(3) Calculating output in labour terms presupposes that tables of interindustrial exchanges have been constructed; at present, however, this work comes up against difficulties in aggregating and disaggregating the sectors of the economy. The more they are disaggregated, the more does their economic content disappear, and the less stable do the coefficients remain. The more they are aggregated, the more do substitution-factors appear and the less rich does the information obtained become.[5] Before thinking of direct planning in terms of labour, therefore, many improvements in economic technique will be needed.

(4) In getting to know the value of the products that are used in a socialist economy one must come up against an obstacle that, in this case, is due not to forms of awareness or analysis of the problem, but to the mechanisms of reality itself.

Actually – and the writer mentions this without developing the difficulties that arise, with external prices differing from internal ones, agricultural from industrial prices, and so on – it is impossible to construct a homogeneous price system, and precise knowledge of the value of products is hard to obtain. These differences are based both on distinct forms of production and on distinct forms of ownership. Improvement in management thus presupposes the transformation of economic structures on the national and international scale no less than the transformation of ways of defining and calculating. To take merely the problem of comparing costs internationally can one determine the relation between prices on the world market and international value-relations as Csikos-Nagy claims one can? Again, if the world price is taken as basis of reference in socialist exchanges, will this not tend to consolidate this price, and thereby certain negative effects of the present structure of world exchanges? Countries like Hungary, where foreign trade is of vital importance, can contribute a great deal to the analysis of these problems of the world market and to the working out of complex planning methods from which other developing countries can benefit.

[5] Cf. Malinvaud, *Aggregation Problems in Input–Output and Models*, New York, 1954: Cukor, *L'établissement et l'utilisation des tableaux interindustriels en Hongrie*, Paris, 1962.

We see, then, that the problem of our knowledge of value is one that constantly requires to be dealt with afresh, as national economies and their international relations evolve. The problem of value is therefore wholly immersed in the ebb and flow of life, and, developing along with this, sheds its academic character.

(5) Finally, an entire section of the problems of economic optimum has remained in the shadow. It seems to me that economic optimum means the solving of a dual problem – that of the choice of objectives and that of the choice of means for realizing these objectives. As a rule, only the second of these two aspects is dealt with. Knowledge of value seems above all to be needed in order to secure a better allocation of means, but what criteria and what sort of calculation must be employed to determine the objectives and the necessary proportions between them? Depending on the objectives that are decided upon, means will vary in their utility and scarcity, and the price-system will no longer possess the same structure. This field of analysis needs to be linked with that dealt with by Csikos-Nagy. It is the field of the rationality of ends, and no longer that of the rationality of means.

(6) It especially seems to me that a certain confusion prevails at the beginning of Csikos-Nagy's analysis. He defines the law of value as the law that lays down that socially-necessary labour-time is the origin of the value of products, and he makes this value the regulating centre of price-formation. This law governs all forms of commodity production – pre-capitalist, capitalist and socialist alike. But the writer has in mind the particular way this law operates in a competitive capitalist economy in which the product dominates the producer, and the spontaneous functioning of which remains partly opaque, escaping the conscious intentions or analyses of the economic agents.

Now it is clear that this type of functioning does not continue to prevail in a socialist economy, except where a private sector of production survives. Consumers' freedom of purchase does not constitute a reason for this type of functioning to persist, since the law of value governs the prices of products exchanged, and these are planned.

Csikos-Nagy's ambiguous distinction between (1) the law of value in general and (2) the working of this law in capitalist economy – what is commonly and loosely meant by the law of value – leads him to a contradictory conclusion:

He does not speak of the law of value in sense (2) when he should do this, in relation to the private sector. And he speaks unsatisfactorily about the law of value in sense (1), which has to explain the relation between value and price, because he is still thinking of sense (1) in the perspective of sense (2).

Hence we get these ambiguous formulations:

The value-price relationship cannot be determined exclusively by the fact that commodity production survives and the law of value continues to function.

This means that the law of value does not govern production but, within certain limits, does govern the circulation of commodities.

The law of value cannot, therefore, overstep the bounds laid down by state regulation. It is consciousness that decides everything ... (?!)

Now, it is necessary to be clear about this. Commodity production survives, but this is no longer capitalist commodity production. It does not operate in accordance with the law of value that is specific to capitalism. The latter can therefore no more govern circulation than it can govern production, and the desire to fix bounds to its operation is pointless, for these bounds are not those of circulation, even when connected with a sector of spontaneous demand. By not clearly distinguishing sense (1) from sense (2), Csikos-Nagy proves unable to describe adequately the way the law of value works in a socialist society, and lumbers himself with false problems. This does not prevent his analysis of value from being very useful, because, when he makes this analysis, he no longer confuses the two meanings.

These reservations and criticisms in no way detract from Csikos-Nagy's work. Thanks to him, we can view in a living way the problems that are presented by the evolution and progress of a socialist economy. He has helped us to clarify some delicate points of scientific theory, to take a differentiated view of the problems and methods of the socialist and Western economies, and renew our links with the common trunk of the classical economic theories. It is to be hoped that the dialogue thus begun will be continued for the benefit of all.

(*Problèmes de planification*, no. 3 May 1964)

5. The Marginalist and the Marxist Theories of Value and Prices: Some Hypotheses

> There exists an accidental rather than a necessary connexion between the total amount of social labour applied to a social article ... and the volume whereby society seeks to satisfy the want gratified by the article in question – (*Capital*, III, p. 183).

One of the most surprising and most interesting aspects of the discussions that have been going on in recent years between the economists of the socialist countries is the appearance of a controversy about the 'scarcity'[1] of capital goods, their 'rental value', and so on.

With the concept of 'scarcity' the whole question of the relations between the marginalist and Marxist theories could not but arise once more.[2] Now – and this seems to me the interesting feature of this resurrection – the controversy has so far remained unaffected by the shadows cast over these questions by the immense, confused polemic that took place at the beginning of the century. The reason for this is to be sought in the practical character of the investigations that have led to the controversy, and which were concentrated upon the problems of optimum management of resources. I should like to contribute a few hypotheses to the discussion on the major point of the relations between the marginalist and Marxist theories of value and prices.

*

It seems to me necessary to emphasize at once that the use of 'marginal calculation' confers no guarantee of theoretical validity upon any economic doctrine, whatever it may be. Marginal calculation is a mathematical tool for analysing the effects of the extreme variations of a variable upon the variables that are associated with it. Use of this technique, as of any other mathematical or statistical procedure, is indifferent to the nature of the

---

[1] Y. Kantorovich, *The Best Use of Economic Resources*, pp. 75 et seq.

[2] See Guy Caire, 'Planification soviétique et recherche de la rationalité', in *Revue économique*, May, 1963, pp. 384–440: Alec Nove, *The Soviet Economy*, pp. 278–9: Zauberman, 'New Winds in Soviet Planning', in *Soviet Studies*, 1960, pp. 1–13; Montias, 'Rational Prices and Marginal Cost in Soviet-Type Economics', in *Soviet Studies*, 1957, pp. 369–79.

realities that it measures and the validity of the economic categories that define these realities. Marginal calculation is employed, moreover, both by marginalism and in Ricardo's theory of market prices, which Marx took over,[3] and does not constitute an argument in favour of either of these theories. The problem of the relation between the Marxist and marginalist theories of value is thus a problem not of finding which of these theories provides a basis for using this calculation, but of finding which of them really accounts for the value and the price of commodities.

*

Historically, the two theories confronted each other as two opposed and exclusive solutions of one and the same problem: why are goods with different uses exchanged in a certain proportion, which is expressed in the relation between their prices? In the thinking and writing of the supporters of marginal utility, marginalism was explicitly put forward as a theoretical structure that would completely reconstruct economic science – which would, indeed, really inaugurate this science, by sweeping away the classical or Marxist assumptions.[4] Faced with this militant determination to clear the slate, the Marxists reacted mainly by rejecting the marginalist analyses altogether.[5]

My hypothesis is that these two theories are not one hundred per cent mutually exclusive, and that they can therefore be combined, *on the plane where they are not mutually exclusive*, and provide an extension of the Marxist theory of value and prices. This would mean both that marginalism was neither an exclusive theoretical alternative to Marxism, as its authors supposed, nor a set of analyses to be rejected completely, as many Marxists considered. To prove this, we must carefully distinguish between what the marginalists *thought* they were explaining and what they really were explaining: in other words, we must separate their actual theoretical practice from the idea that they themselves had about it. This

[3] Ricardo, *Principles*, MacCulloch's edition, pp. 37–9, and Marx, *Capital*, III, p. 176.

[4] Rudolf Hilferding, *Böhm-Bawerk als Marx Kritiker*, 1904, passim: V. Pareto, *Les systèmes socialistes*, 1902, Vol. II, ch. 13.

[5] Cf. Stollberg's recent article: 'Zum vulgären Character der Methodologie der Grenznutzentheorie', in *Wirtschaftswissenschaft*, Berlin, Jan. 1964: J. Domarchi, 'Economie politique marxiste et économie politique bourgeoise', in *Temps Modernes*, October 1946: A. Colombat, *Misère de l'Economie Politique*, Paris, 1958, chapters 1 and 2.

method, consisting in isolating from among a group of theoretical proposi-
tions those that really belong to the sphere of science, as against those that
belong to the sphere of ideology, is the essential method of any science.
Thus, Newton's physics is nowadays entirely detached from the idea that
its inventor had of it; it no longer appears as conclusive knowledge of the
material universe but as knowledge of that universe at one of its levels.[6]

From this standpoint it seems to me that the marginalists thought they
were building a theory of value but were in fact developing elements of a
theory of prices. Over against them, the Marxists replied with a theory of
value while supposing that they were also developing a theory of prices.
To get rid of any misunderstanding, let me make clear that I do not consider that marginalism explains all aspects of a theory of prices and
Marxism none. My hypothesis is that Marxism constitutes the only
possible theory of value, and thereby provides the basis of the theory of
prices, but that the latter requires, if it is to develop on this basis, the
integration of several marginalist analyses relating to price-formation.
The marginalist theory appears as a partial theory of price-formation –
partially correct, but lacking a foundation.

The basis of my argument is the distinction made by Marx between the
process of *formation of value* and the process of *realization* of value. The
realization of value is the selling of commodities. The conditions of this
selling explain the process of *price-formation*. It is in this sphere of the
formation of prices, bound up with the conditions of the selling of commodities, that marginalism seems to me to contribute some theoretically
valid explanations, whereas the marginalists think it also explains the
process of the formation of value. Let me develop this point.

For Marx, a commodity is an object characterized by two properties:
(a) It is useful; and so, a commodity has a use-value.

A commodity is, in the first place, an object outside us, a thing that by its properties satisfies human wants of some sort or another. The nature of such wants,
whether, for instance, they spring from the stomach or from fancy, makes no
difference.[7]

[6] Similarly, it was when Marx was really able to distinguish in Smith and Ricardo
what belonged to the realm of science from the ideas that these economists held about
the economy that he ceased to be merely the critical philosopher of the *Economic and
Philosophical Manuscripts* (1844) and became an economist capable of changing the
theoretical state of his science. Cf. my article 'Economie politique et philosophie', in *La
Pensée*, no. 111, Oct.-Nov. 1963 [pp. 107-27 above].

[7] *Capital*, I, 1.

(b) It is exchanged in a certain proportion for goods of a different utility. It has an exchange-value, and has this only because it first of all has a use-value for someone else.

On the other hand, they [commodities] must show that they are use-values before they can be realized as values. For the labour spent upon them counts effectively only in so far as it is spent in a form that is useful for others. Whether that labour is useful for others, and its product consequently capable of satisfying the wants of others, can be proved only by the act of exchange.[8–9]

The exchange-value of a commodity is for Marx the amount of social labour expended on producing it. Marx calls 'constant capital' (c) all the means of production and raw materials needed for the making of any useful product, and calls 'variable capital' (v) the sum of the workers' wages. The latter, by expending their labour-power, produce the equivalent of their wages and an unpaid surplus. The latter is called 'surplus-value' (s).

The value of a commodity when it leaves the enterprise is: $V = c + v + s$,[10] with $(c + v)$ being the capital advanced by the owner of capital

---

[8] ibid., p. 57.

[9] Marx stresses early on in *Capital* the following distinctions: 'A thing can be a use-value without having (exchange) value. This is the case whenever its utility to man is not due to labour. Such are air, virgin soil, natural meadows, etc. A thing can be useful, and the product of human labour, without being a commodity. Whoever directly satisfies his wants with the produce of his own labour creates, indeed, use-values, but not commodities. In order to produce the latter he must not only produce use-values but use-values for others, social use-values. Lastly, nothing can have value, without being an object of utility. If the thing is useless, so is the labour contained in it; the labour does not count as labour, and therefore creates no value' (*Capital*, I, p. 8). Engels added a note, after 'social use-values', in the 4th German edition (*Capital*, I, p. 804), as follows: 'I am inserting this bracketed passage because its omission has very frequently led to the mistaken idea that every product consumed by someone other than the producer is treated by Marx as a commodity – F.E. '(And not simply for others. The medieval peasant produced his corn-dues for the feudal lord, his tithe-corn for the parson. But the fact that the corn-dues and tithe-corn were produced for other people did not make either of them a commodity. To become a commodity a product must be transferred by an act of exchange to the individual for whom it serves as use-value.)' Marx adds elsewhere that conscience, honour, etc., may have their price without possessing exchange-value. It should be mentioned that Auguste Walras criticized J. B. Say on this point, showing, with the aid of the example of air, that something can have use-value without exchange-value (*Elements of Pure Economics*, p. 203).

[10] It is here assumed, abstractly, that the production of a single commodity implies consumption of all the constant capital.

and (s) the development of this capital. The process of forming value and surplus-value (development of capital) thus takes place within the enterprises and appears as a process that is at once micro-economic and macro-economic.

The Marxist theory of value thus brings out the fact that when the totality of commodities appears on the market, to be sold, these commodities *have already cost society* a part of its available resources and time. They have *already been paid for* by society *without having been sold*, and this constitutes their exchange-*value*. They must then be sold in order that their owner may recover the capital advanced to produce them ($c + v$) and realize some profit, that is, may derive from the sale of his commodities a surplus of capital over the amount of capital advanced ($C^2 \rightarrow C^1 + \triangle C$).

Recovery of this capital advanced and realization of a profit therefore depend on the price at which the commodity will be sold. The process of price-formation is thus not the process of value-formation but that of the possible realization of value, if the price of a commodity corresponds to the sum of the social cost of producing it, to its value. Accordingly, when the commodity-value appears on the market in search of a price, it makes a '*salto mortale*',[11] in which it transforms itself into a certain amount of money.

Now, if the supply of commodities exceeds the effective demand, some of these commodities will not be sold, or will be sold at less than their real cost of production, and thereby a part of social labour will have been superfluous and 'consequently useless'.[12] Society's resources will have been partly wasted. If, however, supply proves lower than demand, all the commodities will be sold, whatever their cost, until the point is reached when the effective demand for these products has been exhausted. The working of supply and demand thus results in the formation of a market price which is an equilibrium price without thereby actually corresponding to the value of the commodity, to its social cost of production. It is this aspect of the mechanism of price-formation, through the relation between supply and demand, that is usually analysed by the marginalist theory of value, and for which it provides a certain number of valid explanations. At this level, which to a marginalist is not distinct from that of value-formation, price-formation *seems* to depend *entirely* on the extent of the 'social want' of the goods produced, the nature of consumer-

[11] *Capital*, I, p. 79.   [12] ibid., p. 80.

preferences. The value of goods seems to be *born* of these preferences and to 'refer back'[13] from consumption towards production, and this apparent movement is put forward by the marginalists as the real movement of value-formation, whereas it is nothing but a real aspect of the movement of price-formation, of the more or less adequate realization of value.

This brief analysis reveals how much more complex, as Marx showed, the idea of price is than the idea of value, and how greatly they differ. Nevertheless, the difference between price and value does not break the bond linking value and price. Marx, following Ricardo, assumes that, depending on the relation between supply and demand, the price of a commodity will be formed around the market value of the commodities produced at the lowest cost, if supply exceeds demand, or around that of those produced at the highest cost, if supply is less than demand. These two extreme cases are the cost-limits of the production of commodities.[14] The process of price-formation, far from being entirely separate from the process of value-formation and connected only with the intensity of social want, remains bound up with the process of value-formation. The bond is especially apparent when one considers the evolution of prices over a long period. Marx, following Ricardo, put forward the hypothesis that prices in a market economy *tend*, in the very long run, to coincide with value, evolving in the same direction as the costs of production. It is significant, in this connexion, that Marshall, in his *Principles of Economics*, after approaching as a marginalist the problem of price-formation in the short and middle runs, turns to Ricardo's explanation when it comes to accounting for prices over a long period.[15] In the long run fluctuations are

[13] Cf. G. Pirou, *L'utilité marginale de C. Menger à J. B. Clark*, pp. 164–176, 240–7. See the well-known exposé of marginal utility, with the example of the pails of water, in C. Gide, *Principles of Political Economy*, 1903 (Eng. trans. by Veditz, pp. 55–6), and Pirou's account of 'modern theories' of value and price in *Economie libérale et economie dirigée*, SEDES, 1946, ch. 2, pp. 63–8.

For a more modern, mathematical formulation, see Dorfman, Samuelson and Solow: *Linear Programming and Economic Analysis*, ch. 13, on general equilibrium, and the critique of Pareto's implicit assumptions in Koopmans, *Three Essays on the State of Economic Science*, p. 53.

[14] *Capital*, III, p. 184.

[15] *Principles*, 1890, Book V, chapter 3, para. 7: Macmillan edition, 1961, p. 291.

'Thus we may conclude that, *as a general rule*, the shorter the period which we are considering, the greater must be the share of our attention which is given to the influence of demand on value; and the longer the period, the more important will be the influence of cost of production on value' (Edition of 1946, p. 349).

eliminated and so 'in the long run persistent causes dominate value completely'.[16]

The marginalist analysis appears, when looked at in this way, as a partial explanation of the role played by supply and demand in the formation of prices over a short or medium period. Through the fluctuations of these prices, the tendency of evolution over a long period is explained by the evolution of the conditions of production. By combining these results, a general theory of prices in a market economy becomes possible. It would have to take account also of the different degrees of competition between producers and consumers on the market. Depending on the producers' power to control supply,[17] the divergences between price and value will be bigger or smaller, effecting transfers of surplus-value towards the monopoly sectors at the expense of the non-monopoly sectors. The theory of value must thus lead to a theory of prices developed in relation to the evolution of conditions of production, to supply and demand, and to the competitive or monopolistic nature of production and distribution. Marx was pointing to this task, I think, when he wrote:[18]

For prices at which commodities are exchanged to approximately correspond to their values, nothing more is *necessary* than (1) for the exchange of the various commodities to cease being purely accidental or only occasional; (2) so far as direct exchange is concerned, for these commodities to be produced on both sides *in approximately sufficient quantities to meet mutual requirements* . . .; and (3) so far as selling is concerned, for *no natural or artificial monopoly* to enable either of the contracting sides to sell commodities above their value or to compel them to undersell.

My first figure shows the processes of value-formation (social cost of production) and of value-realization (prices and profits). I have sought to bring out the fact that the price-system takes shape at the meeting-point of the value of commodities and of effective social demand. The Marxist theory of value thus provides the theoretical basis of the analysis of the relation between value and price, and is able to integrate elements of the marginalist analysis of the formation of prices as dependent on the rela-

[16] ibid.

[17] J. Marchal, *Le mécanisme des prix*, pp. 266–282: E. H. Chamberlin, *Monopoly and Competition*, chapters 5 and 7.

[18] *Capital*, III, pp. 174–5. My emphasis, M.G.

tive scarcity of goods.[19] At the same time it can illuminate the nature of this scarcity, which is expressed in the working of supply and demand, with greater thoroughness and precision than the marginalist doctrine itself, and this for two reasons:

(1) In the capitalist production-process itself, the Marxist theory, following that of the classical economists, brings to the forefront the social relation between the capitalist class, which has the monopoly of means of production and money, and the working class, which is obliged constantly to sell its labour-power on the labour-market. This relation, based on unequal access to the means of production, determines the inequality between the two classes in their access to the social product. The theory of production thus provides the basis for the theory of distribution of the social product through the mechanism of wages and profits. It brings out the principle that organizes effective demand and determines the limits, and in part, the composition of this demand (necessities, luxuries, etc.). It opens the way for a unified theory[20] of production and distribution.

[19] I had written this passage when Leif Johansen, Professor at the Oslo Institute of Economics, sent me his article of August, 1963: 'Some Observations on Labour Theory of Value and Marginal Utilities' (published in *Economics of Planning*, Sept. 1963). The writer constructs a simple mathematical model showing the effects of the preference-functions of capitalists on the quantities of commodities produced and their prices, and comes to conclusions similar to my own. See, by the same author; 'A note on aggregation in Leontief matrices and the labour theory of value', in *Econometrica*, 1961, no. 2, and 'Marxism and mathematical economics', in *Monthly Review*, January, 1963. In the same direction are: R. Cameron, 'The labour theory of value in Leontief models', in *Economic Journal*, March 1952; M. Morishima and F. Seton, 'Aggregation in Leontief matrices and the labour theory of value', in *Econometrica*, 1961, no. 2; R. Meek, *Studies in the Labour Theory of Value*, London, 1956; O. Lange, *Introduction to Econometrics*, 1959, ch. 2, 'Market Analysis', pp. 95 and 185.

[20] From this follows the possibility of a rigorous theory of the national income. It must be pointed out that *Capital* contains the elements of a theory of the national income without strictly providing an actual theory. Marx describes the working of an economy based on capitalist production-relations alone. The model of this economy is thus a simplified one, and does not correspond to the actual economy of any capitalist country: 'For there are here only two classes: the working class disposing only of its labour-power, and the capitalist class, which has a monopoly of the social means of production and money' (*Capital*, II, p. 421).

Because of this, the criticism of Marx made by J. Marchal and J. Lecaillon in their book *La Répartition du revenu national* (Vol. 3, 'Modèles classiques et marxistes') collapses. ('It would have been normal', they write, 'to recognize the presence, alongside the workers and the capitalists, of other types of agent, and thereby of other participants

The 'social demand', i.e. the factor which regulates the principle of demand, is essentially subject to the mutual relationship of the different classes and their respective economic position, notably therefore to, firstly, the ratio of total surplus-value to wages, and, secondly, to the relation of the various parts into which surplus-value is split up (profit, interest, ground-rent, taxes, etc). And this again shows how absolutely nothing can be explained by the relation of supply to demand before ascertaining the basis on which this relation rests.[21]

Looked at like this, the limit of social demand no longer appears as merely the subjective limitation of the utility of a commodity for some individual, but as the objective limit to the possibilities of satisfying their wants that are open to social categories (classes, groups, etc), as a result of their place in the structure of production.

(2) The Marxist theory, by throwing a bridge between production and distribution, therefore attempts to analyse the relation between supply and demand in a macro-economic way, and deals with individuals' preferences in the context of the overall social relations to which they belong.[22] Marxist theory thus possesses the theoretical possibility[23] of grasping the consumer as he really is – not, in other words, as an abstract and universal subject torn from any social relations and regulating demand in accordance with the 'natural' principle of the equalization of weighted marginal utilities,[24] nor as a subject with unique demand unrelated to those of any other individual.[25] Demand no longer appears as an abstract

---

in the distribution of the national income' – p. 377.) See my article, 'Les structures de la méthode du *Capital* de K. Marx', in *Economie et Politique*, June 1960 [pp. 130–93 above].

[21] *Capital*, III, p. 178.

[22] In this connexion, compare the analysis of Marxism by P. L. Reynaud, in *La Psychologie économique*, 1954, p. 96, in which the writer contrasts marginalism and Marxism, saying that the latter is a theory that is more 'sociological' than psychological.

[23] Which does not mean that the Marxists always put this possibility into practice and provide a scientific analysis of the evolution of social needs and demand.

[24] Cf. the critique of marginalism in Vuaridel, *La Demande des consommateurs*, chapter 1, on the basis of statistical inquiries carried out among consumers.

[25] So far back as 1903 Charles Gide wrote in his *Principes d'Economie Politique* (p. 60): 'This theory [marginalism], which explains facts very well when we have to do with isolated man (like Robinson Crusoe), does not explain them when we enter the real world of exchange, except by means of complicated abstractions. Indeed, as values are entirely subjective, a given object has as many values as there are buyers and sellers in the market. We must therefore still ask: How is a uniform market price evolved from this great variety of values' (*Principles of Political Economy*, 8th edition, trans. Veditz, 1904, p. 58).

reality either wholly determined or wholly indeterminate, but as a concrete contradictory reality both determined in an overall way and yet locally indeterminate.[26] Marxist theory enables us to analyse demand without confining ourselves to the abstract arbitrariness or helplessness of marginalism – meaning here a speculative conception of the economic subject and of the basis of his activities.[27] Far from being the simple starting-point of political economy, the theory of supply and demand is its complex end-result.[28]

In further analysis, supply and demand *presuppose* the existence of different classes and sections of classes which divide the total revenue of a society and consume it among themselves as revenue and, *therefore, make up the demand created by revenue.* While on the other hand it requires *an insight into the overall structure of the capitalist production-process* for an understanding of the supply and demand created among themselves by producers as such.

In offering the possibility of a scientific analysis of *real* economic subjects and their behaviour in a field of historically determined social relations, Marxism brings out the speculative character of the marginalist philosophy of the economic subject, while *taking seriously* as facts the social wants that were the object of the ideal constructions of this philosophy and the starting point of the ideas that the marginalists formed of economic relations and of themselves as theoreticians of these relations. In the context of the hypotheses I am putting forward, Marxism is able, it seems to me, both to expose the 'ideological' nature of marginalism conceived as an economic philosophy (and this has been done), and also to take over for its own use, providing a basis for them, the objective results of marginalism conceived as a practical method of analysing the formation of prices (and this has hardly been begun).

Here ends my analysis of the relations between the Marxist and marginalist theories of value and prices in relation to the problems of analysing a capitalist commodity economy. The possibility of combining these two theories on the plane where they are not mutually exclusive (price theory) seems to me to be based, in the last analysis, on the fact that the category of prices is more complex than that of value. I shall now start from this

[26] This provides the basis for the use of statistical calculation.

[27] From a certain standpoint, Keynesianism and post-Keynesianism have dropped some of the marginalist assumptions in so far as they have developed a macro-economic theory that seems like a return to the classical doctrine.

[28] *Capital*, III, p. 191. My emphasis, M.G.

fact in putting forward some hypotheses regarding the role of the price system in achieving optimum economic development in the framework of a socialist planned economy.

*

The possibility of optimum economic development in general seems to be based on three conditions:

(1) The possibility of knowing social demand, its composition and evolution, with sufficient approximation to accuracy;

(2) The possibility of combining the means of production in the best way to satisfy this demand;

(3) The possibility for the whole of society really to exercise control over the utilizing of available resources.

When these three possibilities are brought together in the setting of an economic system, the latter is theoretically capable of establishing an optimum allocation of its resources. In the present historical situation, these conditions appear to be present in the socialist economic systems.

It is only where production is under the actual, predetermining control of society that the latter establishes a relation between the volume of social labour-time applied in producting definite articles, and the volume of social want to be satisfied by these articles.[29]

Optimum management of an economy therefore means the best technical combination of resources (means), given the best possible knowledge of the structure of social priorities (social needs, objectives). I leave aside the question of how to discover scientifically the future structure of social priorities, the basis for laying down an objective programme of production. If we assume this problem solved, another arises which I shall try to formulate logically in as clear a manner as possible: given a programme of objectives for production and for ultimate consumption for the end-year of a plan, will the choice of this programme have effects on the prices existing at the moment when this decision is made? If the decision does have effects on the price-system,[30] how will the latter register these future choices in such a way as to facilitate their realization by providing the economic agents with a system of references enabling them to carry out

[29] ibid., p. 184.

[30] In particular on the partial price-system constituted by the prices, taken together, of the means of production.

effective economic calculation and so making possible optimum management of resources in accordance with the objectives of the plan at both
the micro-economic and macro-economic levels?[31]

Marxist theory assumes that the value of a product is the amount of
social (dead plus living) labour expended in producing it. It assumes that
the price of this product is established by bringing together a past labour
(value) and the amount of a present want (social demand). Through this
confrontation products and means of production appear more or less
'scarce'. In my view, price ought, in an advanced Marxist theory, to be
seen as a category more complex than value because it reflects not merely
social cost (exchange value) but also social utility and scarcity (use-value).
In the context of a planned economy a general confrontation is consciously
arranged between the means of production available in the present and
the future objectives of production and consumption. This confrontation
thus takes place, on a social scale, between the productive forces and the
present and future needs of society, that is, the present or deferred
consumption of goods.

Now, the production-capacities available in the first year of the plan

---

[31] This formula does not mean that I assume that it would be possible to construct a
single price-system such that all the decisions taken, in a decentralized way, on the basis
of these prices, would combine so as to produce optimum general development. The
problem is to determine in rigorous fashion the nature of the decisions to be taken at the
central and at the decentralized levels. Depending on the nature of the decisions and the
level at which they have to be taken, several price-systems are conceivable, which would
have to be linked together in order to make possible the best combination of economic
decisions, whatever the level at which these are taken. On this point Malinvaud writes,
regarding the article by Koopmans and Heckmann, 'Assignment Problems and the
Location of Economic Activities', in *Econometrica*, January, 1957, pp. 53–76: 'If it is
recognized that each factory uses the products manufactured by other factories, and if
transport costs are taken into account . . . it does not seem that systems of prices or rents
can be imagined that would enable an equilibrium to be maintained by the mere working
of decentralized decisions' (*Documentation Economique*, 57/1320).

Similarly, Pierre Massé declared at the congress held in Paris in June, 1963, on the
possibilities of operational research in developing countries: 'One is *obliged to exceed
the marginal*, that is, an optimization based on prices that reflect the differential characteristics of the economic environment. An accumulation of marginally advantageous
operations may, indeed, lead to an overall unfavourable situation, as is shown by certain
excesses of industrial and urban concentration.'

Marxist analysis must note well these critical reflexions by marginalists on their own
principles, at the moment when Marxist analysis itself needs to integrate the rational
aspects of marginalist analysis.

will seem more or less scarce depending on the nature of the objectives decided on by the planners. It if is decided to satisfy the need to use a particular kind of vehicle, by opting either for production of more of these vehicles, or for the establishment of a national park of them from which they can be hired out to users, the future demand for steel will be modified accordingly, and also the ratio between this future demand and the present capacities for production of steel, rubber, and so on.

This ratio reflects the constraint exercised upon the present by the kind of future that has been chosen, and this constraint determines the relative 'scarcity' of present production-capacities in relation to this future. It does not, however, determine all on its own the 'scarcity' of production-capacities, for this scarcity also depends on the techniques that will be chosen in order to secure the ultimate consumer-goods, the choices made as regards location, and so on. The determining of scarcity can only be the outcome of an analysis that proceeds by successive repetitions. There is thus no scarcity of resources 'in itself', but only a scarcity relative to needs and means. In the practice of planning, the present is no longer wholly determined by the past, and the future is not a mere prolongation of the past, an extrapolation of it. The present is the place where two constraints meet and struggle – the constraint represented by the means inherited from the past, and that represented by the needs that the future dictates. In this practical context, the problem arises of how to express in the price-system of the means of production not merely their value (social costs of production) but also their scarcity in relation to future requirements. If the price-system does not reflect these future choices, it will guide economic calculation towards investments that do not correspond to the optimum programme for realizing the plan. For a rational utilization of resources it is therefore necessary that the price-system shall not merely express more accurately the actual costs of production,[32] but shall also reflect fairly exactly the relative scarcity of goods.

[32] This is the line taken in the writings of Csikos-Nagy in Hungary and of other economists in the USSR and East Germany. Cf. previous chapter. See Samsonov: 'Correspondence between the sum of prices and the sum of values in the economy of the USSR', in *Ekonomicheskie Nauki*, 1960, I, pp. 26–31; and Kondrashev, 'Problems of prices, costs and profitability', in *Den'gi i Kredit*, 1961, IX, pp. 15–23.

Even if we assume the three problems of calculating value to have been solved (transformation of complex into simple labour, and of dead labour into living labour, and transition from micro-economic to macro-economic accounting), the problem of the best utilization of resources is still not solved unless account is taken of the relation between the resources available for production and the objectives laid down for it.

This formulation coincides with that of Kantorovich and his attempt to define 'objectively determined valuations' and 'hire valuations' of plant and machinery[33] within a price-system. The latter appears as a system of indices of costs, weighted by a system of indices of scarcity in relation to the objectives of the plan. Such a system then provides the basis for calculating the effectiveness of investments.

When efficiency is computed (in calculating the cost of investment and also the cost of the completed production), the valuations of production, objectively determined by the situation, and the optimal plan, are taken as a basis rather than current prices and costs.[34]

A price-system like this would therefore make it possible to take decisions at local level in accordance with the overall objectives of the plan, and would facilitate the establishing of a flexible relation between centralized and decentralized decisions, that is, an exact relation between the economic subjects that really control the productive forces at their level, whatever may be the legal framework in which they possess or do not possess a corresponding status.

However, the real problem raised by the forming of a price-system such as this is not that of its existence but that of its evolution, as the plan's objectives are achieved. The coefficients of scarcity introduced into the price-system will have to be modified as the fulfilment of the plan draws nearer, and the price-system will have to reflect this modification if optimum management of the economy is to be maintained. This is an initial difficulty to be overcome. Besides, as the production-capacities of the economy change, so the price-system will have to register the increases in productivity secured by the fulfilment of the plan and the variation in the costs of production of goods, and consequently of their value.

[33] Kantorovich, *The Best Use of Economic Resources*, Pergamon, 1965, pp. 75 et seq. See C. Sarthou: 'Méthodes mathématiques et gestion économique en URSS', in *Gestion*, Nov. 1961, pp. 410–18. The writer considers that Kantorovich's theory of prices entirely abandons the standpoint of Marxist theory and proceeds on the basis of the marginal theory of value. I do not agree; it seems to me that Kantorovich works out his price-theory on the basis of the labour theory of value and not outside this theory or in opposition to it. See also Minc, 'Economic effectiveness of investments in socialist economy', in *Ekonomista*, 1961, pp. 515–26, and Bilek: 'The influence of the time factor on calculation of the effectiveness of investments', in *Statisticky Obzor*, 1961, I, pp. 11–14.

[34] Kantorovich, op. cit., p. 238. It is to be observed that the effectiveness of investments plays the role in Kantorovich's theory of a rate of discounting.

Finally, the last difficulty, as the plan draws near its fulfilment so the next plan starts to take shape and, in a sense, starts growing underneath the current plan. In so far as the initial scarcity of the means of production disappears with the fulfilment of the current plan, new coefficients of scarcity need to be estimated, reflecting the ratio between the new production-capacities and the new objectives for consumption, in other words the ultimate demand aimed at by the next plan.[35] The dynamic of the price-system is based on this need to reflect in contradictory fashion the changes in scarcity of goods, in relation to the past and to the future. In this way the contradiction that is dominated by the practice of economic management is continually renewed, but never at the same level. It thus forms one of the historical contradictions that a socialist society must dominate, and the economic practice of this society is optimal when the best way of dominating this contradiction has been found.

I have confined myself to formulating conceptually and logically the problem of the relation between the nature of the price-system and the optimal realization of the objectives of a plan in a socialist economy. The question arises – and I offer it to the mathematicians – of determining the mathematical procedures that would make it possible to construct this dynamic price-system and make it operational.[36] But the problem is not merely mathematical, it is social, and it begins with the problem of determining social priorities, the needs to be decided on by policy as the objectives of production. Underlying the search for the optimum is the problem of knowing the conditions needed for policy to be able objectively to interpret the evolution of social needs. And the solution is to be found not only in more mathematics but also in better democracy. A socialist system contains the possibility of an improvement in democracy because it is not based on private ownership of the means of production, and has excluded on principle the possibility of the exploitation of one class by another.

*

To conclude, it seems to me necessary to emphasize that the existence of a difference between value and price means something different in the setting of a capitalist system from what it means under a socialist system.

---

[35] I have tried to express these different variables in my second figure.

[36] To determine the price-system at the start of the period, the solution may be found through the method of solving the dual problem in linear programming. The problem remains that of rendering the system dynamic.

In the former case it reflects the impossibility of consciously adjusting production to demand under a regime of private property and competition. In the second case it reflects in reverse fashion the possibility of controlling economic development and consciously adjusting production to the objectives of social consumption decided on by the planner. Once again, the same element, the difference between value and price, has a different meaning, depending on whether it functions within a capitalist structure or a socialist one. Beneath the formal identity we find a functional, structural difference. And the same would be true of other categories of political economy – wages, capital, etc.

If the socialist system consciously aims to eliminate the scarcity of a large number of goods and to replace the formula 'to each according to work done' by the distribution principle 'to each according to his need', this prospect presupposes the eventual disappearance of the categories of value and price alike. And yet (and this is not a paradox), this struggle against scarcity presupposes improvement in the means of measuring scarcity, and along with this the perfecting of the theory of value and prices.

In this context, the Marxist criticism of the early years of this century, which was content to reject the marginalist philosophy of value without troubling to sort out the real significance of certain practical results of the marginalist analysis of prices, appears now both justified and out-of-date: justified because it exposed the inability of marginalism to explain the social cost of production and the relations between classes in production, relations that were obliterated in the abstract picture of a crowd of individuals maximizing their utilities; and out-of-date because the very practice of socialist development now calls for measurement of the scarcity of production-capacities, so as to be able to overcome them and increase the possibilities of collective and individual satisfaction.

Far from needing to fear confrontation with marginalism, Marxist economic theory can enrich itself thereby, and provide for concepts that lack theoretical foundation the basis that they need and that many of the marginalists themselves would be glad to have.[37]

(This paper was the material of two lectures given in April 1964 in Prague and Bratislava at the Institutes of Economics of the Czech and

---

[37] Cf. I. M. D. Little, *A Critique of Welfare Economics*, chapter 1, 'Utilitarian economics', and his discussion of Arrow's book, *Social Choice and Individual Value*, in *Journal of Political Economy*, Oct. 1952.

Slovak Academies of Sciences, and was one of the reports presented at the world congress of Marxist economists held in Sofia in May 1964. It was published in *Problèmes de Planification*, no. 3 of May 1964, and in *La Pensée*, no. 120, March–April 1965, with an introduction by Charles Bettelheim.)

Figure 3

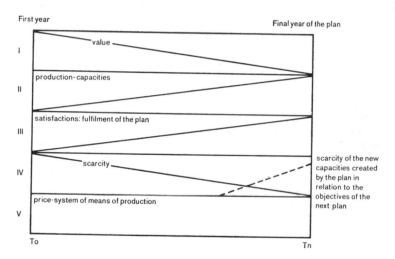

Scarcity (IV) diminishes with the fulfilment of the plan (III). It thus varies inversely with production-capacities (II) and directly with the diminution in the value of the goods (I) that are available in To.

Constructing the price-system thus means applying (IV) to (I) scarcity to costs, and weighting the indicators of value with indicators of scarcity. In proportion, however, as the plan is fulfilled, production-capacities evolve (II) and their scarcity depends on the objectives decided upon for the next plan.

On this condition, space (V) can be filled.

To construct the price-system as a function of these variables and variations, a mathematical tool is needed that will make effective calculation possible. With this model it would be possible, instead of drawing illustrative diagrams, to construct graphs of functions.

Figure 4

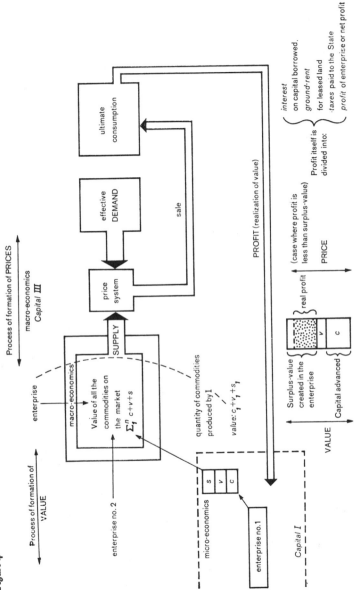

III
The Rationality of Economic Systems

*Political economy . . . as the science of the conditions and forms
under which the various human societies have produced
and exchanged and on this basis have distributed their products –
political economy in this wider sense has still to be brought into
being. Such economic science as we have up to the present is almost
exclusively limited to the genesis and development of the capitalist
mode of production.*

Friedrich Engels, *Anti-Dühring* (1877), Lawrence and
Wishart edn., 1936, pp. 168–9

Note

This article, written in 1964 and published in 1965, brought into confrontation with each other, from a certain angle, both anthropology and history and also anthropology and Marxism. The problems involved are still being widely discussed, as they deserve to be. Nevertheless, in view of some positions I took up which reveal at least a lack of information, if not of rigour, I will add a brief commentary to what I wrote then.

The reader will find without difficulty that the anthropology I discuss has nothing in common with the vague and naïve philosophy of 'human nature' and 'men's tastes and needs', that ideology which permeates the functionalism of Malinowski and the culturalism of Linton and Margaret Mead.

Anthropology appears here first of all in a restricted sense, but one that is close to its actual practice as a theoretical discipline that seeks both to describe (ethnology) and to explain scientifically (anthropological theory) the mechanisms of functioning of concrete societies, known as 'primitive' and 'traditional' societies – negative terms that moreover fail to coincide, and refer to a group that is defined very vaguely. In the last analysis, a society seems to provide subject-matter for the anthropologist if *it has not been* studied by the historian, the sociologist or the economist, or *does not possess* the characteristics of Western societies, whether pre-industrial or industrial. Sometimes, even, certain fragments of an industrial society are abandoned to the anthropologist: those sectors, generally agricultural, that are regarded as survivals from earlier phases of the society's development.

But, whatever the precise nature of its subject-matter, anthropology deals with historical realities, and that is enough for us to rule out two mistaken ways of confronting and contrasting anthropology and history. These are sometimes presented as disciplines that contrast with each other because they deal with realities of different *kinds*, in the one case historical and in the other non-historical. Sartre has given a sort of philosophical consecration to this idea by declaring, in his *Critique de la Raison Dialectique*, that 'man *can* be historical . . . [but] man ought not to be defined by historicity, because *there are* societies that have *no* history. . . . History itself turns back to act upon these societies, first transforming them from the outside and then by and through the internalisation of what was external' (pp. 103–4, note 2).

Yet all the materials studied by the ethnologist testify indisputably that the societies he examines are *inside* history and *have* a history – but this is a history of specific structures evolving at different speeds.

Although these differences of structure and rhythm make it necessary to use different methods in studying them, such differences of method do not signify, as some would have it, a contrast between anthropology, concentrating on the study of structures, disdaining concrete events, and history, accumulating avidly but ingloriously ever more documents on ever more numerous events. Actually, the anthropologist and the historian work in a really scientific way when they see the event as occurring within a structure and perceive structures through events. It is enough to refer to the work of R. Firth, who has followed for thirty years the evolution of the Tikopia society, or P. Labrousse's classical study of the economic evolution of France in the 18th century. There is therefore no justification for making a psuedo-dilemma of principle out of what is merely factual incompetence or negligence.

Moreover, while history seems to be getting closer to anthropology by becoming increasingly the study of structures, anthropology is getting closer to history by ceasing to dodge, as did structuralism at a certain stage, the formidable problems of the origin and evolution of social structures. For some time now, linguistics has been trying to find its way in diachrony, and Lévi-Strauss has recognized the need to do this.

The anthropology of which I speak here, and in the development of which I am taking part, is therefore not a philosophical ideology of human nature but a social science that has been rid of psychologism, hasty functionalism, and a-historical culturalism, a science that aims to account for structures without forgetting their origin or their evolution, and which seeks eventually to explain structures and concrete events by clearing its path to the point where it can make the comparisons needed in order that laws may be discovered.

But if anthropology is both description of particular societies and analysis of their structures and theory of kinship, religion, authority, and so on, this body of knowledge cannot exist as such unless it links together several levels of knowledge, and discovers the rigorous problematic of this linkage. Economic anthropology, for example, collects and analyses information about the functioning and evolution of the economy of primitive or traditional societies, and tries to construct a theory of this functioning and this evolution. It thus combines two types of approach, corresponding to those that economic history and political economy employ in order to know our own societies.

History, for its part, as it becomes the study of structures, calls in the aid of theories of religion, politics, and so on, and depends on their development, so that it becomes linked more and more closely to political economy, the sociology of religion, and so on, and requires that its problematic and methods be remodelled in order to make a success of this linkage. Thereby it becomes plain that scientific knowledge of the societies that the historians study is not based exclusively on the practice of the latter, but just as much on that of the economists, sociologists, etc. History and anthropology therefore tend to base themselves on the same problematics, and these coincide with that of Marx.

Everyone knows that *Capital* is not an historical work and that, despite many allusions to the history of European countries, especially England, Marx did not write a history of English, or Dutch, or any other capitalism. *Capital* undertakes to set forth the theory of the invisible logic of the functioning of the capitalist mode of production. For Marx, real knowledge of the history of capitalist societies is not to be reduced to this theory, though without this theory such knowledge is impossible.

Through this common problematic we perceive the relations between anthropology and history, taken, in the way that I understand them, as theoretical wholes with several different levels, and historical materialism defined as scientific knowledge of the evolution of mankind.

This anthropology and this history then appear as two fragments of historical materialism, 'regional' bodies of theoretical knowledge concerned with distinct types of society. When, however, history seeks to be fully itself, that is, universal history, and when anthropology seeks to become a general theory of the structural differences between societies, each of them needs to cease being a regional discipline, in order to penetrate into the other's domain and take account of it. Thus, projects for 'universal history' and 'general anthropology' overlap and come to coincide with the actual subject-matter of historical materialism.

Looked at from this angle, my investigation of economic anthropology therefore forms part of the current development of historical materialism by virtue of its subject-matter, of its formal problematic and of the assumptions that it puts to the test: a realistic definition of economics, a definition of an economic system as a combination of the structures of production, distribution and consumption of material goods, the idea of the reproduction of a system, the problematic of surplus and scarcity, the idea of correspondence between social structures, the idea of objective properties and causality of structures as the content of the intentional and unintentional dimensions of social practice, the assumption of multilinear evolution. For example, it will easily be observed that what I call the technical structure of production corresponds to what Marx calls the technical division of labour, that what I call the structure of the distribution (the actual control) of the factors of production is equivalent to the idea of production-relations, and so on.

These hypotheses, however, are not solutions so far as I am concerned, but problems. The existence of 'artificial scarcities', the fact that kinship in primitive societies is both infrastructure and superstructure and dominates social life, the fact that the different social structures do not have the same object or the same rate of evolution, and so on – all this demands the re-examination of proofs that have seemed established in the eyes of many Marxists or non-Marxists, and this is of interest not only as regards the understanding of primitive societies. In this way, anthropological research is already providing knowledge that is irreplaceable and of wide general significance. For anthropology possesses a heuristic quality through the rigorous forms demanded by the scientific study of societies the structures of which seem at first sight, in the behaviour of their individual members, not only strange but even absurd. Thereby the anthropologist seeks to discover a *hidden logic* that explains the meaning of this behaviour and the functioning of these structures. Moreover, the latter are such that it is usually impossible to deal with one aspect of social life – the economy, for instance – without trying to find its *inner bond* or its relation of correspondence with others. Finally, these structures appear in such a way that, through their inner bonds, one of them *dominates* social life – kinship in societies without classes, the politico-religious aspect in stratified societies with a state, like those of the Mayas, the Incas, and so on.

By the characteristics of its field of investigation and its method, which collects and discusses information by way of a variety of interlinked theoretical procedures, anthropology is developing and will continue to develop a type of rigorousness that historians, economists and even those involved in politics will soon be unable to afford to neglect.

The Object and Method of Economic Anthropology

Economic anthropology[1] has as its object the comparative theoretical analysis of different economic systems, actual and possible. In order to work out this theory, economic anthropology derives its material from the concrete information provided by the historian and the ethnologist on the functioning and evolution of the societies they study. Alongside 'political economy', which appears to be devoted to the study of modern industrial societies, both commodity-producing and planned, economic anthropology sees itself as a sort of 'extension' of political economy to the societies that the economist neglects. Or at any rate, by its very conception, economic anthropology paradoxically causes political economy, both old and new, to appear as one of its own special spheres, illuminating the particular mechanisms of modern industrial societies. In this way economic anthropology takes upon itself the task of constructing a general theory of the various social forms of man's economic activity, for comparative analysis must necessarily result one day in anthropological knowledge of a general character.

Today, however, the comparative study of economic systems is something more than and something different from a theoretical necessity imposed by abstract concern to widen the field of political economy and unify it under the body of principles of a hypothetical general theory.

The concrete and imperative urgency of the transformation of that part of the world which has remained 'under-developed' gives a practical character to the need to understand the economic systems of other societies. It should be remembered that this twofold need, theoretical and practical, to compare different economic systems was manifested at the very birth of political economy and even constituted the reason why it was born.

For the Physiocrats, seeking the principles of an economy that would be 'rational' because 'natural',[2] the economic structures and rules of the

---

[1] The expression first appeared, according to Herskovits, in 1927, with the article by Gras on 'Anthropology and Economics' (Ogburn, *The Social Sciences and their Interrelation*, pp. 10–23).

[2] Cf. Mercier de la Rivière: 'Personal interest drives every individual, vigorously and

ancien régime, inherited from feudalism, seemed so many obstacles to the progress of trade and production, and therefore to the welfare and harmony of society. It became necessary to change or destroy the old 'irrational' economic edifice, in order to bring the world into line with the principles of natural reason. From the beginning, economic reflexion was thus engaged in the twofold task of explaining 'scientifically' the different functioning of two historical economic systems, one of which was still in process of being born from the womb of the other, and of justifying 'ideologically' the superiority of one of them over the other – proving its 'rationality'. Adam Smith and Ricardo followed along this dual path. Consequently, political economy was both science and ideology, and so placed in an ambiguous situation which it has constantly to overcome by ridding itself of its ideological element in order to reconquer itself as a scientific domain that grows greater each time this is done. In this way the socialist critique of liberalism and its apologia for a society that the principles of *laissez-faire* and competition were to maintain mechanically in a state of social harmony, resulted in exposing some of the ideological content of classical political economy, demanding from the latter a new, scientific answer to problems which, in the absence of ideological criticism, it was unable to see or appreciate properly: the problems of under-employment, economic inequality, cyclical crises, etc.

Consequently it is understandable why the idea of 'rationality', situated at the heart of all economic reflexion, should be the most necessary and yet the most challenged of all the categories of political economy. If economic anthropology is an enlargement of political economy, it must lead the latter to a renovation of the idea of economic rationality. This, however, will happen only as the outcome of its replies to a series of questions that are as formidable as they are inevitable.

What domain of human activities forms the distinctive object of econo-

---

continuously, to improve and increase the things that he can sell, so enlarging the mass of satisfactions he can procure for others, in order to enlarge thereby the mass of satis-factions that others can procure for him in exchange. *The world thus goes by itself* ' (*L'Ordre naturel et essentiel des sociétés politiques*, 1767, chapter xliv: Daire's edition, p. 617). In 1904 Rist was still affirming: 'Free competition brings about justice in the distribution of wealth as well as maximum well-being in exchange and production' ('Economie optimiste et économie scientifique', *Revue de Métaphysique et de Morale*, July, 1904). See A. Shatz, *L'Individualisme économique et social*, Paris, A. Colin, 1907, ch. iv.

mic science? What is an economic 'system'? What is meant by an economic 'law'? Are there laws that are 'common' to all systems? And, finally, what is meant by economic 'rationality'?

It goes without saying that I shall be able to do no more than make a first approach, in these few pages, to these very large topics, and that I wish–only to offer my reflexions as mere hypotheses submitted for challenge and criticism.

1. THE IDEA OF AN ECONOMIC SYSTEM
AND ANALYSIS OF ITS WORKING

The domain of the 'economic'

The object of economic anthropology, the study of economic systems, seems at first sight to be a domain with clear-cut limits that one ought to be able to define without difficulty. Before considering, however, what is meant by a 'system', what social activities does the term 'economic' enable us to mark off from other social relations, bound up with politics, kinship, or religion? Have we to do with a domain of specific activities or with a specific aspect of every human activity?

The production of capital goods in the USA, the collective clearing away of scrub from a field by the men of a village in New Guinea, the conduct of the Fugger bank in the 16th century, the storing of agricultural and craft products in state storehouses and the distribution of these products under the Inca Empire, the nationalization of the subsoil in the USSR, household consumption in Abidjan – all these seem to be specifically economic activities. But the presenting of gifts between clans that give, and clans that receive, wives among the Siane of New Guinea, the struggle for prestige and the competition in gifts and counter-gifts in the potlatch of the Kwakiutl Indians, the daily offering of consecrated meals to the Egyptian gods – these seem to be social realities with many-sided significance, the essential purpose of which is not economic and in which the economic is only one facet of a complex fact. Is there then a common element that can bring together in the same domain, under the same definition, a particular *field of activities* and also a particular *aspect of all human activities* that do not fall within this field?

To answer this question means to become involved in the dark maze of definitions of what is economic, and to desire to put an end to the ceaseless, vain clashes between these definitions. The economic was first defined, from Plato[3] to Adam Smith, as the material wealth of societies. This definition relates to the structures of the real world, and for this reason Karl Polanyi calls it 'substantive'.[4] To reduce economic activity to the production, distribution and consumption of goods means, however, to cut off from it the huge field constituted by the production and exchange of services. When a musician receives fees for a concert, he has produced not any material article but an ideal 'object' for consumption – a service. The old definition of what is economic, while not wholly mistaken, is nevertheless inadequate to bring together in a single domain the two groups of facts which it has to account for.

On the other hand, some have wished to see in the economic an aspect of *all* human activity. Every action that combines scarce means so as the better to attain an objective is said to be economic. The formal property of all purposive activity, namely, possession of a logic that ensures its effectiveness in face of a series of constraints, becomes the criterion of the economic aspect of every act. This criterion has been adopted by Von Mises,[5] Robbins[6] and, nearer to the present time, Samuelson,[7] among the economists, and by Herskovits,[8] Firth,[9] Leclair[10] and Burling[11] among the

[3] Plato, *The Republic*, ed. Budé, 369 b–73 d; Aristotle, *Politics*, Book I, chapters 2, 3 and 4, and *Economics*, Book II, chapter 1; Xenophon, *De l'économie* [*Oeconomicus*], ed. Hachette, 1859, pp. 137–96; Marshall, *Principles of Economics*, 8th edn, Macmillan, chapter I, p. 1: 'Political economy or economics is a study of mankind in the ordinary business of life; it examines that part of individual and social action which is most closely connected with the attainment and with the use of the material requisites of well-being.' See, on the history of economic thought: Schumpeter, *History of Economic Analysis*, 1955, Part II, chapters 1, 2, pp. 51–142.

[4] K. Polanyi, 'The Economy as Instituted Process', in *Trade and Market in the Early Empires*, Free Press, 1957. The definition of the economic as 'substantive' refers to 'an instituted process of interaction between man and his environment, which results in a continuous supply of want-satisfying material means' (p. 248).

[5] Von Mises, *Human Action*, Yale, 1949.

[6] Robbins, *The Subject-Matter of Economics*, 1932.

[7] Samuelson, *Economics, an Introductory Analysis*, New York, 1958, ch. 2.

[8] Herskovits, *Economic Anthropology*, New York, 1952, ch. 3.

[9] Firth, *Primitive Polynesian Economy*, 1939.

[10] Leclair, 'Economic Theory and Economic Anthropology', *American Anthropologist*, 1962, no. 64.

[11] Burling, 'Maximisation Theories and the Study of Economic Anthropology', *American Authropologist*, 1962, no. 64.

economic anthropologists – followed, to some extent, by Polanyi and Dalton.

Certainly, the behaviour of an entrepreneur or of a firm that strives to maximize its profits, and organizes accordingly the strategy of its production and selling, is relevant to this criterion and seems to testify unanswerably in its support. But if we take Robbins' definition of economics as 'the science that studies human behaviour as a relation between ends and scarce means that have alternative uses', we see that it does not grasp the economic as such, but dissolves it in a formal theory of purposive action in which it is no longer possible to distinguish between economic activity and activity directed towards obtaining pleasure, power or salvation. At this rate, while all purposive action comes to be called economic in principle, no action actually remains economic in fact.

The absurdity of this thesis has been shown by one of its most subtle advocates, R. Burling, who says:

If all behaviour involving allocation is economic, then the relationship of a mother to her baby is just as much an economic one, or rather has just as much of an economic aspect, as the relationship of an employer to his hired laborer. . . . There are no specifically economic techniques or economic goals. It is only the relationship *between* ends and means, the way in which a man manipulates his technical resources to achieve his goals, that is economic (Burling, op. cit., p. 811).[12]

This attitude leads him logically to see in the Freudian theory of the personality ruled by the pleasure principle, in Leach's[13] analysis of Burmese political systems, in Lasswell's[14] theory of power, and in Zipf's[15] essay on 'least effort', so many expressions of the 'economic' principle of

[12] Firth was moving in the same direction when he said in *Elements of Social Organisation*, Watts, 1951, p. 130:

'The exercise of choice in social situations involves economy of resources in time and energy. In this sense a marriage has an economic aspect . . . quite apart from the exchanges of goods and services that may go on. But by a convention the science of economics concerns itself with those fields of choice which involve goods and services.' By virtue of the obvious fact that man, like every other living creature, needs time to do anything at all, anything at all 'naturally' has an economic aspect.

[13] Leach, *Political Systems of Highland Burma*, Cambridge (Mass.), 1954.

[14] Lasswell, *Power and Personality*, New York, 1948.

[15] Zipf, *Human Behaviour and the Principle of Least Effort*, Cambridge (Mass.), 1949.

the optimum use of scarce means.[16] The road indicated by this abstract criterion leads him, as happens with Hegel's 'bad' formalism, to mix up what needs to be distinguished, in a twilight in which 'all cats are grey'.

It is no paradox to claim that the proof of the radical helplessness of the formal theory of action to define the economic as such lies in the very fruitfulness of that operations research which has so perfected in recent years the practical tools of economic management. The formal theory certainly sees in this an apodictic proof of its correctness: but operations research is not a branch of economics, it is a set of mathematical calculation procedures that enable one to minimize or maximize the value of an objective function. Whether the objective be the maximum destruction of the strategic points of an enemy's military system, the optimum circulation of the Paris bus services, the transmission of a flow of information, the 'rational' management of the stock of a department store, or a game of chess, the mathematical procedures remain 'indifferent' to the 'objects' they manipulate, and the logic of the calculation remains the same throughout. Thus, operations research defines the economic no better than it defines the art of war or the theory of information. On the contrary, in order to find employment it has to presuppose that these 'objects' already exist and have been defined, and that manipulating them presents the type of problem that it can solve.[17] Now, the principle governing the practices of operations research, that of achieving the best combination of limited means in order to attain a quantifiable objective, is precisely the formal principle invoked by Robbins, Samuelson and Burling to define specifically what is economic. If operational research cannot define the objects it manipulates, the principle that is its norm and basis cannot do this either.

And so here we are, after these two analyses, faced with a 'real' definition

[16] In *Capitalism, Socialism and Democracy*, Schumpeter even claims that the 'logic' of economic activity is the basis of the principles of 'all' logic. This feat of reducing the non-economic to, or deducing it from, the economic is the usual outcome of 'economism', the naïve imperialism of one science in relation to the rest.

[17] See F. N. Trefethen, 'Historique de la Recherche opérationnelle', in *Introduction à la Recherche opérationnelle*, by McCloskey and Trefethen, Dunod, 1959, pp. 7–20. More precisely, Pierre Massé wrote in his article 'Economie et Stratégie': 'Koopmans has defined the activity of production as the "best utilisation of limited means in order to achieve desired ends". However *different* our respective ends may be, it seems to me that this *definition* could apply *just as well* to the art of war' (in *Operational Research in Practice*, NATO, Pergamon, 1958, pp. 114–31. My emphasis, M.G.).

which is inadequate because it is incomplete and onesided, and a general 'formal' definition that fails directly to come to grips with its object.[18]

The way to make progress seems plain – to get away completely from the dead end of formalism and push along the path of realism, already half-opened. Since the 'realistic' definition was inadequate because it removed from the economic sphere the reality of services, can we construct a unifying definition by saying that economics is the theory of the production, distribution and consumption of goods and services?

It is not hard to see that now we fall, for the opposite reason, into the same helplessness as the formal theory suffers from. If the production of services is economic, then economics absorbs and explains the whole of social life, religion, kinship, politics, science. Again, everything becomes economic in principle while nothing remains economic in fact.

Are we condemned, as Burling ironically suggests, to say that what is economic is the production, distribution and consumption of 'economic' services, and shut ourselves up for good in this splendid tautology? No: the realistic definition is wrong when it assigns the *whole* of the production of services, all the aspects of a service, to the economic sphere, whereas only *one aspect* of any service belongs to this sphere.[19] Let us again take the example of a musician, or a singer. What is there that is 'economic' in his recital – the work by Mozart that he interprets, the beauty of his voice, the pleasure it gives, the prestige he derives from it? What is economic is the fact that we pay to hear the singing, and that the singer receives some of this money that we pay. This is what gives an economic aspect to the social relation between the singer and his public, between the producer and the consumers of that ideal object, the opera *Don Giovanni*.

With this fee the singer will perhaps be able to live, to maintain his family, to improve his skill, to obtain some or all of the goods and services that he wants or needs. This money is therefore, for him, the virtual

[18] For this reason, the position taken up by Polanyi and Dalton, who claim to bring side by side under the same term the two definitions of the economic, one 'formal' and the other 'substantive', seems to me a theoretical failure (*Trade and Market*, pp. 245–50). The writers themselves admit that these two definitions bear no relation to each other, and that the formal definition expresses the logic of all 'rational' action. Their compromise position leaves them awkwardly placed in relation to the problem of 'scarcity'. Cf. Neil J. Smelser, 'A Comparative View of Exchange Systems', in *Economic Development and Cultural Change*, 1959, Vol. 7, no. 2, pp. 176–7.

[19] See in this connexion, Walter C. Neale, 'On defining "labour" and "services" for comparative studies', in *American Anthropologist*, December 1964, Vol. 66, p. 1305.

equivalent of the practical conditions for the satisfaction of his needs and desires. The size of the fee also serves him as an indicator of his success with the public. But it is hard to claim that the first objective of a performer is to maximize his gains. Rather is it the striving to achieve greater perfection in his art, and acknowledgement of this perfection through the favour and the aesthetic emotion of the public. For the listener, the price of his seat constitutes the economic aspect of his taste for music. This assumes that he has a choice in the use he makes of his income, and that he distributes it, in accordance with a personal scale of preference, over a series of objects of consumption. As for the owner of the concert-hall and organizer of the performance, his aim is certainly to get the biggest possible return from the sale of a service to a body of customers, and this determines his choice of performer, the price he charges for seats, the frequency of performances, and so on. But it is also possible to assume that the concert is free, the opera-house a state enterprise, and the cost of the performance covered by the state without its getting any profit therefrom in money terms.

Instead of the opera-singer we could take as our example a Malian 'griot' who sings before a Keita prince of the exploits of Sundyata, the legendary king of old Mali.[20] The economic aspect of his activity will not, in this case, appear in the form of money earned but in the gifts and favours that the master of the house will heap upon him. It is not only for these gifts that the 'griot' sings well and draws wonderful sounds from the 'kora'; but it is because he sings and plays so well he is laden with presents. For the prince, the fame of the 'griot' is the mirror of his own prestige, and the magnificence of his gifts is the outward symbol of his own power.

In the same way one can analyse the offering of a priest to his god, or the gifts of the faithful to this priest, or the presents given by a clan that receives wives to a clan that gives them. In each of these social relations, whether or not money plays a part, the economic aspect is that of the exchange of a service for goods and services.[21] Thus, *provided* we do not reduce the significance and function of a service to its economic aspect,

[20] V. Monteil, 'Les empires du Mali', in *Bulletin du Comité d'Etudes historiques de l'A.O.F.*, 1929, Vol. XII, pp. 291–447.

[21] When a professional singer sings at his brother's wedding, for the pleasure of the guests, his behaviour has no economic aspect. If he sings at a 'charity' function and waives his fee, his behaviour does have an economic aspect.

or deduce that significance and function from this aspect, the economic can be defined, without risk of tautology, as the production, distribution and consumption of goods and services. It forms both a domain of activities of a particular sort (production, distribution, consumption of material goods: tools, musical instruments, books, temples, etc) and a particular aspect of all the human activities that do not strictly belong to this domain, but *the functioning of which involves the exchange and use* of material means. The economic thus appears as a particular field of social relations which is both external to the other elements of social life and also internal to them, that is, as a part of a whole that is at once external and internal to the other parts, a part of an organic whole. The economic anthropologist's task is to analyse both this external and this internal aspect, and to penetrate to the depths of the domain, until the latter opens on to other social realities and finds there that part of its meaning that it does not find in itself. The more complex a society's economy the more it seems to function as a field of autonomous activity governed by its own laws, and the more will the economist tend to concentrate on this autonomy, treating the other elements of the social system as mere 'external data'. The anthropological viewpoint, however, as Dalton emphasizes,[22] forbids description of the economic without showing its relation to the other elements of the social system.

The idea of a 'system'

Now that the economic domain has been recognized, we must account for one of its 'properties', that of appearing as a 'system'.[23] Other domains of nature and culture possess this same property, since we speak of a nervous system, a political system, a philosophical system. We must therefore define this property that is common to any and every system of possible 'objects'.

[22] George Dalton, 'Economic theory and primitive society', in *American Anthropologist*, 1961, no. 63, pp. 1–25.

[23] For many economists, the existence of 'economic systems' is a belated historical fact characteristic above all of the Western world in its recent phase. A. Marchal, in his textbook *Systèmes et structures économiques*, P.U.F., 1959, p. 210, writes: 'Patriarchal economy seems too primitive and unorganized to deserve the description of "system". In it, the father distributes tasks among the members of the family, enlarged by polygamy and slavery. Cattle-raising is the dominant activity, and exchange is restricted to mutual gifts of a ceremonial nature (potlatch) or a silent barter'.

I propose to understand by a 'system': 'a group of structures interlinked by certain rules (laws)'. We are thus referred back to the idea of 'structure', by which we mean: 'a group of objects interlinked by certain rules (laws)'.[24] I will explain later this mysterious doublet 'rule (law)'. By 'object' I mean any reality whatever: individual, concept, institution, thing. By 'rules' I mean the *explicit* principles whereby the elements of a system are combined and related, the norms *intentionally* created and applied in order to 'organize' social life: rules of kinship, technical rules of industrial production, legal rules of land-tenure, rules of monastic life, and so on. The existence of these rules allows us to suppose that, in so far as they are followed, social life already possesses a certain 'order'. All anthropological investigations, undertaken from the angle of history, economics, ethnology, etc., lead us to the assumption that no society exists without organizing its different activities in accordance with the principles and logic of a certain willed order. The task of the social sciences is to compare these rules with the facts, so as to bring out 'laws'. Before dealing with the idea of the 'law' of a system's functioning, let me go back to the idea of 'system' and 'structure', so as to bring out an essential characteristic of their definitions from which I shall draw my first methodological principles of scientific analysis.

These definitions are actually 'homogeneous' in two ways. They both refer to combinations of objects in accordance with rules, that is, realities such that one can dissociate only by abstraction the objects-in-relation from the relations between the objects. Unrelated objects constitute a reality deprived of meaning, and objectless relations a meaning deprived of existence. Thus, all systems and all structures have to be described as 'mixed', contradictory realities made up of objects and relations that cannot exist separately – such, in other words, that their contradiction *does not exclude* their unity.

Both ideas refer to relations between a whole and its parts. A structure and a system are wholes in relation to their parts. A structure is thus both a whole in relation to its parts (objects plus relations) and a part in relation to the system (structures plus relations) to which it belongs. The same is true of a system in so far as it is included in a totality larger than itself.

[24] Among the innumerable studies devoted to the idea of structure, let me mention: *Notion de structure*, XXe Semaine de synthèse, Albin Michel, 1957; the articles by Granger and Greef in the *Cahiers de l'ISEA*, December 1957; *Sens et usages du terme structure*, Mouton, 1962.

An economic system is thus an element of the social system, or, to use Parsons'[25] expression, a 'sub-system' of the social system. These remarks bring us to the point where we lay it down as a principle that we must distinguish *levels* in every domain of 'objects', and carry out our analysis of a level (structure of system) in such a way as always to be able to see its links with other levels, to see it as part of a whole, even if, at the start, for convenience of study, such connexions have been 'abstracted', 'left out'. The need to take seriously both the specificity of the levels and the relations between them within the same totality forbids us to analyse them in such a way that one level can be *reduced* to another, or *deduced* from it. We must therefore tackle the problem of the laws of correspondence between structures without allowing ourselves to be affected by any implicit philosophy of causality in the social domain, any pre-conceived ways of approaching each level, such as the idea that the non-economic can be reduced to the economic, or deduced from it – or the other way round.[26] Armed with this principle we are able, since a system is an organic totality of objects in relation, to make clear what is meant by studying the laws of the functioning of a system.

The laws of the functioning of a system

When he studies a system, the investigator is faced with a twofold task. He has to find out what the elements of this system are and what their relations are, at a given time (t) in the evolution of this system (synchronic analysis). He has also to find out how these elements and their relations have been formed and have evolved during (*dia*) the time that this system

[25] Parsons and Smelser, *Economy and Society*, Routledge, 1956.

[26] The impossibility of reducing the different structures of social life to just one of their number, whether material or spiritual, rules out any linear, simplifying conception of causality in the sphere of the social sciences. Each type of society seems to be marked by a distinctive *relation* between the different social structures, and this relation determines the specific weight, in this society, of the economy, kinship, religion, etc. This relation between the social structures thus acts through and upon all the aspects of social life without it being possible to locate its efficacity anywhere, in any particular structure. Consequently, the influence of the overall social structure always enters in between one event and another, giving to each of them all its dimensions, whether conscious or not– in other words, the field of its effects, whether intentional or not. Between a cause and an effect there always lie the properties of the social structure, as a whole, and this rules out any simplified conception of causality.

has lasted (diachronic analysis, which is theory both of the origin and of the evolution of a system).

The use of the terms 'synchronic' and 'diachronic' has the advantage of putting in the forefront the *fact* of time (*chronos*)[27] and avoiding the impression that a structure can really be analysed without analysing its evolution. In this way one gets rid of the old ambiguous manner of talking that contrasted a 'structural analysis' with a 'dynamic analysis', as though one could exist without the other; as if time were a variable external to the functioning of a system which could be introduced into this functioning 'after the event'.

The study of a system, then, should enable us to know its 'laws'. What is meant by a 'law'? The moment has arrived to take up and clarify the relation between 'rule' and 'law'. While there are laws of social life, these cannot in my view, be confused with the 'rules', that is, the explicit, willed principles of organization of a society. To do so would presume that consciousness governs completely the movement of social reality. Conversely, experience forbids us to suppose that the social world functions without consciously willed norms playing a part. The investigator's task is to compare norms and facts so as to bring out *through their relations* a certain necessity that is expressed in the laws of the synchronic and diachronic functioning of the system.

To move from description of the rules to establishment of the laws, by way of knowledge of the facts, means passing from the intentional to the unintentional and analysing the relation between them: it means theoretically conceiving social reality as it manifests itself and as everyone experiences it, as a reality that is both willed and not-willed, performed and suffered, as a 'mixed' reality, to employ the expression Plato used[28] when referring to this world of ours.

If social life is subject to certain laws, these must make themselves felt in practice. This happens through the successive readjustments that a society makes in its own 'rules' of functioning when the situation, or in other words the facts, demand that this be done. By these readjustments,

[27] For the problem of analysis of the different historical times appropriate to different social structures, see M. Halbwachs, 'La mémoire collective et le temps', in *Cahiers Internationaux de Sociologie*, 1947, pp. 3–31, and, especially, F. Braudel, 'Histoire et sciences sociales: la longue durée', in *Annales ESC*, Dec. 1958, pp. 725–53. See also J. Le Goff, 'Temps de l'Eglise et temps du marchand', in *Annales ESC*, June 1960, pp. 417–23, and G. Gurvitch, 'La multiplicité des temps sociaux', Paris, C.D.U.

[28] Plato, *Timaeus*.

which take over and modify the relations between the rules and the facts, a society submits to its own laws without necessarily having a completely explicit or adequate theoretical awareness of them.

Scientific cognition strives to become explicit theoretical awareness. But this does not depend only upon a rigorous theoretical problematic. It presupposes no less the existence of a certain quantity and quality of information about the process of becoming of the societies concerned, so as to try to reconstitute their functioning with an adequate approximation to reality and for a sufficiently long period. Without a certain quantum of information, especially about the origin and transformations of a system, a scientific undertaking cannot be accomplished. It is possible, if one has collected a few rules and a few facts about a society, to rough out a synchronic analysis, to sketch a 'model' of what this society 'might' be, and if one has a number of successive pictures of this society, to attempt a diachronic analysis by offering diagrams of 'transition' from one state to another of the reconstituted system.

Thus, despite the shortcomings of their methodological equipment, prehistorians, historians, and ethnologists occasionally prove capable of completing the investigation and establishing of 'laws'. Perhaps the history of France between 1760 and 1815[29] has been sufficiently explored for this undertaking to be attempted. Perhaps Firth's work on Tikopia,[30] carried on during more than a quarter of a century, will provide a similar 'opportunity' in ethnology. The small number of these 'favourable' cases at once shows the imperative need to multiply historical work and ethnological investigations on the ground.

I have suggested abstract definitions of the nature of a system and tried to clarify somewhat the ultimate objective of all scientific knowledge, which is knowledge of laws. I must now apply these definitions more closely to the specific domain of economics. Two paths are possible for such an 'application'. One could describe the concrete elements of an actual system, supported by adequate information, and find the most probable 'explanation' of its functioning, the 'logic' that shows most respect for the sequence of events running through its evolution. In the context of our present study, this path is barred, for it is that of the specialist in a particular society and epoch. There is, however, another path, the one which explores not an actual system but a 'possible' one, the path of formalism.

[29] Cf. the works of G. Lefebvre, Labrousse, Soboul.
[30] Firth, *We the Tikopia*, London, 1936, and *Social Change in Tikopia*, London, 1959.

The formal model of a possible economic system

What do we mean by a 'possible system'? The representation of the element that is common to every possible case of the kind of system under consideration. The reconstitution, for example, of the 'totemic operator' that Lévi-Strauss[31] gives us is the representation of the formal element common to every possible system of totemic thinking. A common formal element is an 'invariable' that persists all through every one of the possible varieties and variations of the system envisaged. Formalism is an 'eidetic'[32] approach, by which thought is detached from every *actual* system so as to give us all the *possible* systems, and to rediscover the actual in them as a 'realized possibility'.

To the extent that, in order to construct the formal model of a possible economic system, thinking 'ignores the difference' between actual systems, the formalist approach does not, strictly speaking, give knowledge of *any* actual system, but rather an explanation of some of the *conditions of possibility* of this knowledge, through revelation of the *formal structures* of all possible economic systems. The formalist approach thus belongs to the sphere of epistemological reflexion by economic science upon itself, through the formal properties of its subject-matter.

Edward Leclair's[33] mistake lies not in constructing a model of this kind but in believing that in doing so he has produced a 'general theory' and proved, in opposition to Dalton, that the laws of political economy, worked out for our system of capitalist commodity production, constitute the heart of this general theory, thereby acquiring universal validity. Only the study of real systems will enable us to 'decide' whether the laws of one system are applicable to another, and to work out a typology, first, of the different varieties of a given system, and then of the different varieties of system. We may assume that, stage by stage, the conditions will eventually be assembled for the creation of a 'general theory' that will not be 'formal' in character. At the beginning of the road, the formal approach will have enabled us to prepare a series of questions to be put to the facts, in order to guide investigation towards the discovery of certain information – in

---

[31] Lévi-Strauss, *La Pensée sauvage*, 1963, chapters 5, 6. English trans., *The Savage Mind*.

[32] Using Husserl's expression, when he defines phenomenology as an 'eidetic' science, in *Logische Untersuchungen* and *Ideen I*.

[33] E. Leclair, 'Economic theory and economic anthropology', in *American Anthropologist*, 1962, no. 64, pp. 1187–8.

other words, to avoid falling into the rut of empiricism and to establish a 'problematic'. This will likewise enable us to avoid the vain speculative illusions of *a priori* deduction. For, if the general theory is not the formal theory of systems, this is because it is not possible either to 'deduce' the actual from the formal or to 'reduce' the actual to the formal. These precautions having been taken, what are the formal components of an economic system?

Since we have defined the economic activity of a society – the totality of *operations* whereby its members obtain, distribute and consume the material means of satisfying their individual and collective needs – an economic system is the combination of three structures, those of production, distribution and consumption.

If *what* is produced, distributed and consumed depends on the *nature* and *hierarchy* of needs in a given society, then economic activity is organically linked with the other activities – political, religious, cultural, family – that along with it make up the content of the life of this society, and to which it provides the material means of realizing themselves: for instance, the 'cost of living' of the dead among the Etruscans[34] and the Egyptians, the means of ensuring the prosperity of the lamaseries of Tibet,[35] etc.

The structures of production

Production is the totality of the operations aimed at procuring for a society its material means of existence.[36] So defined, the concept of production opens out on to all possible forms of operation of this kind, those that are characteristic of economies of food-gathering, hunting and fishing, in which a territory is 'occupied' and the resources needed are 'found' there, and also those that are characteristic of agricultural and industrial economies, in which what is needed is 'produced' by 'transforming' nature. An economic system may, moreover, combine food-gathering, hunting, agriculture and craft work. Historically, many societies

---

[34] R. Bloch, *Les Etrusques*.

[35] Stein, *La Civilisation du Tibet*, 1962, chapter on 'Economy and society'.

[36] Wedgwood, 'Anthropology in the Field: A "Plan" for a Survey of the Economic Life of a People', in *South Pacific*, August, 1951, pp. 110, 111, 115. Productive activity is not, of course, restricted to 'subsistence'. Cf. Steiner and Neale, articles referred to; also R. Lowie, 'Subsistence', in *General Anthropology*, pp. 282–320.

have evolved from an occupying economy to an economy that transforms nature.[37]

Comparing these economies makes it possible to outline a typology of forms of material life which is both chronological (historical) and functional (logical). Formally, the forms of production resemble each other in that producing signifies combining, in accordance with certain technical rules (T), resources (R), instruments of labour (I) and men (M) so as to obtain a product (P) that can be used socially. Production, the functional combination of three sets of variables (the factors of production $R - I - M$) assumes different forms depending on the nature of the variables and the possible ways of combining them. The relation between the variables is reciprocal. The raw materials used (R) depend on the instruments of labour (I) and the knowledge and skill (M) that make it possible to use them. Reciprocally, the instruments of labour and the knowledge and skill available reflect adaptation to a certain type of usable resources. There are thus no resources as such, but only possibilities of resources provided by nature in the context of a given society at a certain moment of its evolution.

All exploitation of resources thus presupposes a certain awareness of the properties of the 'objects' and of their necessary relations under certain 'conditions', and the application of a body of technique which 'uses' these necessities in order to produce an expected result. Productive activity is thus an activity 'governed' by technical 'norms' which reflect the necessities to which this activity has to submit in order to succeed. Hunting techniques, for example, imply a detailed knowledge of the habits of the animals being hunted,[38] their relations with the fauna and flora of their *milieu*, in other words, a 'science of the concrete'[39] that is hard to reconcile with the 'pre-logical'[40] mentality that only yesterday was ascribed to primitive hunting peoples.

Every production-process thus constitutes an ordered series of operations, the nature and succession of which are based on the necessities that are submitted to in order to obtain the expected ultimate product.

[37] Cf. I. Sellnow, *Grundprinzipien einer Periodisierung der Urgeschichte : Ein Beitrag auf Grundlage ethnographischen Materials*, Berlin, 1961. It must be remembered, however, that, in a hunting economy, for example, operations take place involving the transformation of nature: making tools, weapons, clothing, means of transport, etc.

[38] Cf. Birket-Smith, *Moeurs et Coutumes des Eskimo*, Payot, 1955, ch. 4.

[39] Lévi-Strauss, *La Pensée sauvage*, chapter 1.

[40] Lévy-Bruhl, *La Mentalité primitive*, pp. 39–47, 85, 87, 104, 107, 520.

These operations thus develop on the basis of a given natural *milieu* and of the given social realities which form the 'constraints' to which the technological system of production is subjected, constraints that 'limit' and determine the 'possibilities' of the system, its effectiveness.

The less complex its production structures, the more the effectiveness of a technological system will be dependent on the diversity of the natural conditions in which it operates.[41] The productivity of a system will be the measure of the ratio between the social product and the social cost that it implies. In so far as production operations combine quantifiable realities (resources, instruments of labour, men) and require a certain time to be completed, qualitative, conceptual analysis of a system leads on to numerical calculation.

Combination of the factors of production is carried out within the setting of what are called 'production units'.[42] These may be the small family holding, the village community, an industrial enterprise, etc. The setting thus depends on the nature of the work undertaken and of the means available (I, M) to undertake it. In 'primitive' economies some work requires the co-operation of all the men in the village community – e.g. the clearing of a field by the Siane of New Guinea – or, even, for tasks exceeding the power of separate communities, the mobilization of the whole tribe, or of even wider groupings. The construction of huge irrigation systems, or the undertaking of terrace cultivation by the great agrarian civilizations of Egypt[43] or pre-Columbian America[44] presuppose complex division of labour and centralized control of it. Hunting economies, such as that of the Blackfoot Indians,[45] knew forms of co-operation on the

[41] Daryll Forde, 'Primitive economics', in *Man, Culture and Society*, ed. Shapiro, 1956, p. 331.

[42] Dalton, in his article: 'Traditional production in primitive African economies', in *Quarterly Journal of Economics*, 1962, Vol. LXXVI, no. 3, pp. 360–77, rejects the general use of the expression 'production unit' (p. 362), on the grounds that this means only the Western 'firm', an economic organization without any direct link with the political, religious and kinship structures of society, and that its use obscures analysis of primitive societies by distorting them. This point of view is connected with the theses of Karl Polanyi on economies that are 'embedded' or 'disembedded' in the social organization, theses that I discuss later. Nevertheless Dalton alleges the universal existence of 'production groups' (pp. 362, 364).

[43] Hamdan, *Evolution de l'agriculture irriguée en Egypte*, UNESCO, 1961.

[44] P. Armillas, 'Utilisation des terres arides dans l'Amérique pré-colombienne', in *Histoire de l'utilisation des terres des régions arides*, UNESCO, 1961, p. 279.

[45] D. Forde, *Habitat, Economy and Society*, 1934, ch. IV.

tribal scale. They practised two types of hunting, depending on whether the bison were grouped in huge herds (spring and summer hunts) or scattered in small groups (autumn and winter hunts). The summer hunt required the co-operation and concentration of the entire tribe, the winter hunt that of much smaller groups operating over traditionally-fixed territories. The regrouping of the whole tribe in the spring opened the season of major political and religious ceremonies. Thus, close adaptation to the habits of the animals they hunted entailed a vast systole-diastole movement of economic and social life. The technical relation with nature is achieved through a division of roles among the economically active individuals, that is, through the relations between the 'economic agents' of this society within the setting of the production units. This setting must be compatible, to a certain degree, with the pursuit of the production-objectives. For example, mechanization of agriculture usually presupposes the existence of large-scale agricultural enterprises, owned either by an individual or by a community (the state). In the case of the great works carried out by the Incas, a more complex compatibility is to be seen between economic and political structures (centralized government). To show the possible ways in which non-economic social structures may function in the social organization of production, here is an abstract example. Let us assume that, in an agricultural village community, there is a lineage who live by their rights to use a certain number of plots of land, which are cultivated successively year by year. It is of little importance whether these cultivators produce for their own subsistence or for a market. We will merely assume that the family's labour-force and means of production (M, I) are insufficient to carry out certain production-operations of the agricultural cycle: clearing, enclosing, etc. In order to obtain the necessary complement of factors of production, the head of the family then calls upon his relatives by blood or marriage, or upon a certain age-group, upon persons dependent on him, perhaps upon wage-labourers. Consequently, the productive work is organized with the aid of personal services rendered (either spontaneously or, sometimes, under coercion) by these workers who are additional to the members of the family, for the sake of their kinship, political or religious relations with this family. The work is at one and the same time an economic, political and religious act, and is experienced as such. Economic activity then appears as activity with many different meanings and functions, differing each time in accordance with the specific type of relations existing between the different structures of a given society.[46] The economic domain is thus both external and internal to the other structures of social life, and this is the origin and basis of the different meanings assumed by exchanges, investments, money, consumption, etc., in different societies, which cannot be reduced to the functions that they assume in a capitalist commodity society and that economic science analyses.

Our example has shown us the economic aspect of the functioning of non-economic relations, but if we proceed further we find that the economic is not to be reduced to the functioning of these relations, and cannot be wholly understood on the basis of these relations. It is not at the level of these relations that we grasp the necessity of combining the factors of production in a certain way so as to obtain the products needed, in the given ecological (R) and technological (I) conditions. Economic science is neither ecology nor technology, nor is it dissolved in the study of kinship, religion, etc.

It begins with study of the social relations that operate in production and also, as we shall see, in distribution and consumption. This opens up several directions for investigation. One may note that the more complex the division of labour, the more does the kinship group or local community lose part of its economic function.[47] A part of production develops outside the family or village framework, in different organizations that depend on wider social groupings (the tribe, the state, etc.)[48] In new economic conditions, the kinship relations and the political and religious relations play a new role. It is the logic of the reciprocal modifications of the elements of the social structure that forms the object of the scientific

[46] Because of this, economic activity takes on the functions of social 'integration', to use the expression of P. Steiner, 'Towards a classification of labour', *Sociologus*, 1957, Vol. 7, pp. 112–30. Cf. also P. Bohannan, *Social Anthropology*, 1963, ch. 14, 'The economic integration of society', pp. 229–45.

[47] Cf. Neil J. Smelser, 'Mechanism of change and adjustment to change', in *Industrialization and Society*, report of 1960, Chicago, symposium edited by Hoselitz and Moore, Mouton, 1966, pp. 32–54. Sociology has raised the question of the typology of forms of grouping, by making the distinction between 'Association' and 'Community', which has occupied the central place among the fundamental categories of sociology since *Gemeinschaft und Gesellschaft*, by Tonnies (1887), and Max Weber's *Wirtschaft und Gesellschaft*, 1922, Part I, chapters 1 and 2 and right down to MacIver, *Society, its Structure and Change*, New York, 1933, pp. 9–12, quoted by Dalton.

[48] On tribal authority and the tribal economy, see Sahlins, 'Political power and the economy in primitive society', in *Essays in the Science of Culture*, ed. Dole and Carneiro, 1960, p. 412.

study of societies. In the setting of Western capitalist society, the economy seems to be governed wholly by its own laws. Polanyi bases himself on this appearance in distinguishing societies in which the economy is 'embedded' in the social structure from those in which it is said not to be, in which it is 'disembedded', as with commodity societies.[49] This distinction seems to me to be a questionable one, since the term 'disembedded' could suggest an absence of internal relation between the economic and the non-economic, whereas this relation exists in every society. Actually, the conditions characteristic of the functioning of an industrial commodity economy confer on the economy (during the 19th century, at least) a very extensive autonomy in relation to the other structures (the state, etc.) and lead to the disappearance of direct control over the product by the direct producers or the owners. In this particular historical context, in which the factors of production are commodities that are appropriated individually, the optimum combination of these factors appears to their owner as that which maximizes his profits in money terms. It is at this very point that we encounter the problem, which I shall analyse later, of the nature and possible forms of economic 'rationality'.[50] Maximizing an individual profit in money appears as the particular social form of economic rationality that is characteristic of capitalist commodity societies. This rationality is that of competing individuals who may or may not be owners of the factors of production. It cannot be reduced to 'purely' economic significance, because it also means a particular way of functioning of the family, the state, etc., in these societies, and because its aim, the accumulation of wealth in money form, creates possibilities for the individual of playing a role in the political, cultural, etc., structures of his society. In other societies, at other moments of history, economic rationality would have a quite different content. The prodigality in giving that is shown in potlatch contests will prove to be the best form of saving in other societies, ensuring for the givers security for the future and social and political prestige in the present. We shall discover this internal relation between social structures when we analyse forms of distribution.

[49] K. Polanyi, *Trade and Market in the Early Empires*, 1957, pp. 68, 71.

[50] J. R. Firth, *Human Types*, 1958, chapter 3, 'Work and wealth of primitive communities', p. 62; W. Barber, 'Economic rationality and behaviour patterns in an underdeveloped area: a case study of African economic behaviour in the Rhodesias', in *Economic Development and Cultural Change*, April, 1960, Vol. 8, no. 3, p. 237. See the critique of Hoselitz's *Sociological Aspects of Economic Growth*, 1960, by Sahlins, in *American Anthropologist*, 1962, p. 1068.

The structures of distribution

Distribution operations are those that determine in a given society the forms of appropriation and use of the conditions of production and of its outcome, the social product. Appropriation of these 'objects' is subject, in every society, to explicit rules which define the rights (written or unwritten) that the various members of this society possess in relation to these objects.

The first category of rules governing appropriation and use relates to the factors of production (R. I. M). The rules governing the appropriation of resources – land, raw materials – can assume a variety of forms, such as those analysed by the theory of systems of ground rent.[51] One may instance the collective ownership of a hunting territory by a community of hunters,[52] the common ownership of the land by the Inca *ayllu*, with right to periodical or hereditary use of plots, the collective ownership of the sub-soil in a socialist state, alienable private property, the *dominium eminens* of Pharaoh over the lands of the village communities, and so on. Ownership may relate to water, as with the rules about use of the reaches of the Niger among the Bozo and Somono fishermen, or the rules about using the irrigation canals in the *huerta* of Valencia. The rules may relate to tools, canoes, machines, *daba* (hoes) or anything else, including men.[53] Thus, the Greek or Roman slave-owner owned the labour-power of his slave and also his person, whereas the modern employer buys the use of his workers' labour-power but has no claim on their persons. The private owner of the land may not be the same person as the owner of tools and of labour-power with whom he associates himself in order to constitute a unit of agricultural exploitation (tenant-farming), and so on.

In a society, the rules about appropriation and use of the factors of production may differ for each type of object, and combine into a complex and coherent whole. Thus, among the Siane[54] of New Guinea the rules

---

[51] See, e.g. *African Agrarian Systems*, ed. Biebuyck, Oxford, 1963.

[52] See R. Lowie, *Primitive Society*, chapter ix; Herskovits, *Economic Anthropology*, chapter xiv; and the dispute between Speck Hallowell, Schmidt and Leacock regarding the priority of private property or collective property among the Algonquin Indians – Aveskieva, 'The problem of property in contemporary American ethnography', in *Sovetskaya Etnografiya*, 1961, no. 4.

[53] Cf. 'De jure personarum', in the Institutes of Justinian (in *Elements de Droit Civil Romain*, J. Heinnecius, 1805, vol. 4, pp. 90–107).

[54] R. F. Salisbury, *From Stone to Steel*, Melbourne, 1962. For a detailed analysis of this book, see M. Godelier, *L'Homme*, Vol. IV, ch. 4, pp. 118–32.

about appropriation of material objects (land, axes, clothing) or of non-material ones (knowledge of ritual) are of two kinds:

(1) A person has rights over an object that are like the rights of a father (*merafo*) over his children. He is responsible for them before the community and before his ancestors. This is the rule that applies to appropriation of the land, of sacred flutes, and of knowledge of ritual, goods that are under one's protection and cannot be transferred.[55]

(2) A person has rights over an object if he is like the shadow (*amfonka*) of this object. Such objects may be articles of clothing, pigs, planted trees, axes, needles. These goods are appropriated personally and may be transferred.

There is a relation of order between these two types of rules. If someone stands in *merafo* relation to the land, then only the work carried out in planting trees confers the right to individual appropriation (*amfonka*) of these trees. The existence of this relation of order between these two types of right reveals membership of the group as the foundation of the system of rights, and control by the clan over other dependent groups (men's houses, lineages), and over the individual, as the directing principle of this system. The system as a whole harmoniously combines the interests of the group and those of the individual, limiting, through the absolute priority of the former over the latter, the contradictions that could arise in connexion with control of scarce resources.

The second category of rules of appropriation and use concerns the effects of production, the ultimate product, whether in the form of goods or of services. This category itself includes two types of rules, depending on whether the motive of distribution is directly or indirectly economic. For directly economic motives, a share must be taken from the social product in order to renew the factors of production (R, I, M) and ensure continuity of production and of the material conditions of social existence. If this share during one period (t_2) is greater than it was in the previous period (t_1), then society, all other things being equal, has carried out an

---

[55] The idea of ownership has a field of application that extends considerably beyond the economic field. Cf. R. Lowie, 'Incorporeal property in primitive society', in *Yale Law Journal*, March, 1928, p. 552. It is significant that among the Siane the land is included in the category of inalienable sacred goods, the property at once of living people, their dead ancestors, and their descendants yet to be born. See also Hamilton and Till, 'Property', in *Encyclopaedia of the Social Sciences*, pp. 528–38.

'investment' and expanded its possibilities of production. If the share is less, it has reduced these possibilities. At this level we can see outlined certain forms of the dynamic of an economic system. Thus, it is necessary to take from a year's agricultural product the grain and seed for the following year, and to store these. Another reason for building up reserves is the fact that agricultural production is often seasonal, and months have to pass before the fruits of labour can be harvested. In some economies that produce sweet potatoes and *taro*, cultivation and harvesting are continuous operations, both for agrotechnical reasons and because of the lack of methods of storage. This is the case with the Chimbu of New Guinea.[56]

Also, in every society, it is necessary to care for those who are not yet producing (the children) and for those who are no longer producing (the aged and the sick).[57] Part of the product is set aside for their use, the amount depending mainly on the productivity of labour and the margin of surplus exceeding the producers' mere subsistence needs. Here we are at the intersection of rules with a direct and rules with an indirect economic motive.[58] The maintenance of chiefs, of gods, of the dead, of priests, the festivals that mark birth, marriage and death, warlike expeditions – all these social activities presuppose the use by society of material resources and of part of disposable time.

[56] P. Brown and H. C. Brookfield, *Struggle for Land*, Oxford, 1963.

[57] The rules of distribution of the product need to be studied in their relation to different conjunctural situations: (1) plenty ($+$), (2) satisfactory position ($\pm$), (3) shortage ($\mp$), (4) famine ($-$), and this over an annual cycle, as with the Eskimos, or over long cycles including whole years of plenty or of famine. Rules of distribution need to be distinguished in accordance with the nature of the goods (food, tools, luxuries, territory, etc.). Among the Eskimos, in situations of plenty or of famine the rules laid down for situations 2 and 3, which are the most usual, cease to apply. In a famine situation the group sacrifices the non-productive and reserves all its resources for the productive, upon whom the group's survival depends. This raises the problem of the relation between economic institutions and 'scarcity situations' (scarcity of game or of land, temporary or permanent scarcity, etc.). Cf. Smelser's criticism of Polanyi in 'A comparative view of exchange systems', art. cit., p. 177.

[58] Herskovits, *Economic Anthropology*, p. 12. On the rules among the Chins for dividing up and distributing meat in accordance with kinship relations and the other social relations, see the festival of Khuang Twasi described by H. Stevenson in *The Economics of the Central Chin Tribes*, Bombay, 1944. In Samoa, pigs were divided into ten parts, destined for ten categories of persons of different status (Peter Buck, *Samoan Material Cultures*, Honolulu, 1939).

Thus, among the Incas,[59] the lands of the village communities were divided into three groups: those left at the disposal of the members of the *ayllu*, those reserved for the Inca, and those reserved for the gods, and in particular for Inti, the Sun God. The lands of the Inca and the gods were cultivated collectively, by virtue of the *mita*, labour-service in which every married man had to take part. The product of these lands was stored in state granaries and serviced to maintain the nobility, the clergy, the army, the workers who built the roads, the irrigation systems, the temples, etc. A body of specialized officials, the Quipu-Kamayoc, drew up statistics to evaluate the wealth of communities and households and calculate the quantities of agricultural and craft products and the size of labour-force necessary for the maintenance of the 'ruling caste', the carrying out of large-scale public works and the waging of war. The framework for these statistics was a division of the entire population into 'ten categories, approximately defined by apparent age and aptitude for work'.

One could also cite the forms of ground rent, in labour, in kind and in money, levied by the feudal lord.[60] The amount of this rent generally depended on the unstable relation of strength between lords and peasants. Depending on this relation, the peasants were able to enlarge to a greater or less extent the share of their own labour that they appropriated, and to improve their agricultural holding. Another example is provided by the forms of share-cropping and tenant-farming lease which lay down how the product is to be shared between the owner of the land (R) and the owner of the instruments of labour (I) and of labour-power (M). Similarly, through the mechanisms of the formation of wages and profits, the national income is distributed among the classes and social groups of an industrial capitalist country.

If we analyse distribution operations as a whole, we note that some of them distribute to the non-economic activities of social life – politics, religion, culture, etc. – the material means necessary for the practice of these activities. Here, too, the economic is internal to all non-economic activity, and constitutes *an* aspect of *every* human activity, and, reciprocally, the non-economic activities are linked organically with the economic

[59] A. Métraux, *Les Incas*, Paris, 1961. On the Aztecs, see the important article by A. Caso, 'Land tenure among the ancient Mexicans', in *American Anthropologist*, August, 1963, Vol. 65, no. 4, pp. 862–78.

[60] Cf. Duby, *L'Economie rurale et la vie des campagnes dans l'Occident médiéval*, Vol. I, p. 115.

activities to which they give meaning and purpose. At the same time, the development of non-economic activities presupposes the existence of an economic surplus – meaning not what is 'redundant',[61] an absolute surplus, but what exceeds the level that is socially recognized as necessary for the subsistence of all members of a society. In his book *From Stone to Steel*, in which he describes the conditions and effects of the replacement of the stone axe by the steel axe among the Siane of New Guinea, R. F. Salisbury calculates that the subsistence activities that took up 80 per cent of the labour-time of men equipped with stone axes required only 50 per cent of this time when they used steel ones. The time 'gained' was devoted by the Siane not to increasing their material means of subsistence but to increasing their extra-economic activities – festivals, wars, travels. This choice between different uses of their time reflects the hierarchy of the values attributed by the Siane to their various activities.[62] An example such as this, resembling that of the Tiv, as described by Bohannan,[63] confirms

[61] Dalton, 'A note of clarification on economic surplus', in *American Anthropologist*, 1960, no. 62, pp. 483–90, replying to Marvin Harris: 'The economy has no surplus', in ibid., 1959, no. 61, pp. 185–99, and also: 'Economic surplus once again', in ibid., 1963, no. 65, pp. 389–93.

[62] E. Fisk, in his article: 'Planning in a primitive society', in *The Economic Record*, Dec. 1962, pp. 462–78, points out, on the basis of Salisbury's research, that the Siane, even before the introduction of steel axes, produced what was economically necessary for their subsistence and their social life *without* having attained the *maximum* productive possibilities of their system. They were thus able to put up with a growth of population and an intensification of production without causing a crisis of their system. Fisk calls this objective possibility a 'potential surplus'. Carneiro has shown the existence of such a surplus among the Kuikuru: 'Slash and burn cultivation among the Kuikuru and its implications for cultural development in the Amazon Basin', in *The Evolution of Horticultural Systems*, 1961, pp. 47–67.

This potential surplus must be distinguished from the idea of a potential surplus *already appropriated* by the landlords from the industrial capitalist, as propounded by Ricardo and Marx. For them, the already-appropriated surplus can serve development on condition that it is taken away from the landlords and invested productively.

Cf. the critical analysis of Paul Baran, *The Political Economy of Growth*, 1957, and by C. Bettelheim: 'Le surplus économique facteur de base d'une politique de développement', *Planification et croissance accélérée*, 1964, pp. 91–126. The analyses by Fisk and Bettelheim show clearly that the objective possibility of a surplus does not necessarily or automatically entail any economic and social development. For this, definite social conditions and stimuli are needed. If this is not seen, the idea of surplus explains nothing, and on this point Dalton is quite right.

[63] Bohannan, 'Some principles of exchange and investment among the Tiv', in *American Anthropologist*, 1955, no. 57, pp. 60–70.

certain analyses made by Polanyi and his followers Pearson[64] and Dalton, but refutes their essential thesis, which makes of the idea of surplus an analytical assumption that 'explains' social arrangements *ex post*, like a *deus ex machina*, and is condemned to remain without empirical proof or disproof.

Pearson and Dalton are quite right in seeking to ascertain the precise circumstances and nature of the existence of a surplus – is it accidental or permanent, is it recognized as such, and so on – especially in emphasizing strongly that what the consequences of the existence of a surplus will be depends entirely on the given institutional framework. In the case of the Siane, these people have appreciated and measured perfectly well the time that they have gained through the diffusion of the steel axe among them, and have devoted this time to the pursuit of those ends which are most highly valued in their eyes, because they ensure the prestige of individuals within the clan community. But this intensification of the most highly esteemed activities, which already constitutes a change as compared with tradition, even if it does not affect the overall structures, has been made possible by a technological change. It is in this sense that it is assumed that the appearance of a surplus makes possible – which does not mean 'necessary' – structural transformations in a society. And there is no relation between this statement and the claim that economic activity historically *precedes* other human activities and *must* necessarily be *valued more highly* than they are. The contribution made by Dalton and Pearson is, in fact, to bring out the errors of a crude materialism which postulates a mechanical causality between social facts the dialectic of which it cannot grasp. When, however, Dalton and Pearson allege that the idea of surplus is a mental construction that lacks any practical implications, the whole of economic practice and theory cries out against their view.

Before our eyes, the rapid transformation of the 'underdeveloped' countries underlines the priority of productive investment in development, in other words, the need to withdraw from immediate consumption the means for increasing future consumption. And by consumption we mean the ending of mass illiteracy, the training of skilled workers, the multiplication of services, as well as the infrastructure of agriculture and industry. For industrialization, a labour-force is needed that will be made available by the increase in agricultural productivity. This logic of facts,

[64] Pearson, 'The economy has no surplus: critique of a theory of development', in *Trade and Market in the Early Empires*, ed. K. Polanyi, 1957.

guided by the strategies of (forced) saving and investment, does not differ in kind from the 'take-off'[65] of industrial capitalism and its gigantic growth during the 19th century. From the analyses of Smith, Ricardo and Marx[66] to the statistics of historians like Mantoux[67] and Labrousse, the mechanism of the 'accumulation of capital' is described as a phenomenon of forced saving on the part of the working people and of investment in 'capital goods' by the bourgeoisie. These economists and historians, supporters of the idea of surplus, were the first to point out that institutional transformations in the spheres of law, the state and culture stimulated economic changes, and did not see in this role played by institutions any proof that the idea of surplus was essentially metaphysical. Actually, the metaphysics is to be found among those who were looking for a 'surplus in itself' and who do not know what to do with the idea of surplus when they come upon what actually exists, namely, 'relative' surpluses.

Furthermore, the idea of surplus is still obscured by the notion that many people still hold that there is a necessary causality between the existence of a surplus and that of the exploitation of man by man. This raises the general problem, not of the mechanisms but of the 'principles' of distribution, since the latter can be either equal or unequal among the members of a society. One and the same society may, moreover, follow different principles, depending on the objects that are to be distributed. The Siane ensure equal access for everyone to the use of the land and to subsistence foodstuffs. Luxury goods, however, such as tobacco and salt, depend on the initiative of each individual. As for actual wealth – feathers, shells, pigs – the material basis for ceremonial acts and for access to women, these are controlled by the elders of the families and the important men (*bosboi*), whose prestige and power they symbolize. But this inequality does not signify at all that there is exploitation of some by others.

Similarly, in a community divided into specialized and complementary groups – cultivators, fishermen, craftsmen – the exchange of their products enables everyone to have access to the totality of resources without there being any phenomenon of exploitation. From this standpoint, the sharing of products between those who have produced them and the individuals who are consecrated to the affairs of politics and religion is at

[65] Rostow, *The Stages of Economic Growth*. Cf. the symposium of 1961 on *Social Development*, under the direction of R. Aron and B. Hoselitz.

[66] *Capital*, I, chapters 26 to 33; III, chapter 47.

[67] Paul Mantoux, *La Révolution industrielle au XVIIIe siècle*, Paris, 1961.

first a form of exchange between manual workers and mental workers without any exploitation of the former by the latter. This exchange corresponds to a service rendered to the community, a communal function that has been taken upon themselves by particular persons. Exploitation of man by man begins when this service ceases to be rendered, and products go on being levied by the non-producers without anything being done in return for them. It is generally very difficult to determine where the authority of function stops and the authority of exploitation begins, in societies in which social contradictions, conflicts between groups, are not highly developed. This was the case with the kingdoms of Ghana and Mali, where an aristocracy carried out religious, political and military functions on behalf of the whole tribe, and slightly exploited the free men of the village communities.[68] Often the development of the power of a minority is a powerful factor in economic and social development, at least for a certain period. The unification of Egypt under Menes, the first Pharaoh, made possible the control of Nile irrigation, to the benefit of the village communities.[69]

Karl Polanyi, drawing his inspiration from Marcel Mauss,[70] has attempted to subsume the mechanisms of distribution under three principles: recriprocity, redistribution, exchange. An illustration of the first of these is the game of gifts and counter-gifts, the *potlatch*, of the Kwakiutl; of the second, the redistribution of products by order from above in the Inca Empire; and of the third, the universal circulation of the commodities land, labour or other objects in capitalist economy. This thought-provoking analysis would be more fruitful if it sought to isolate the different criteria of the 'value' that is attributed to the objects given, redistributed or exchanged, for these criteria would enable us eventually to analyse the differing forms of social equality and inequality.[71] On this point, analysis

[68] Mambi Sidebe, *Notes sur l'histoire de l'ancien Mali*, Bamako, 1962. See also Mauny, *Tableau géographique de l'Ouest africain au Moyen Age*, Dakar, 1961.

[69] Willcocks-Craig, *Egyptian Irrigation*, London, 1913.

[70] M. Mauss, 'Essai sur le don', in *Année sociologique*, 1925, pp. 30–186.

[71] The organization of the redistribution of goods by a minority within a tribe creates the *possibility* of a certain exploitation of the majority of the members of the community by this minority, and through this process the possibility of the emergence of a dominant social 'class' in a tribal society. While performing religious and political services to the community and favouring an expansion of the production and circulation of goods, this minority controls the social product to some extent (Trobriand) and sometimes controls part of the factors of production (the land in Pharaonic Egypt, under the Incas, the

of the different categories of structures of distribution has shown us the strategic role played in the functioning of societies by the operations and norms of the distribution of the factors of production. It is these that control, in the last analysis, the possibilities of action that a social system offers to the individuals and groups who operate it and are subject to it – possibilities, equal or unequal, of power, of culture, of standard of living. As we shall see in our conclusion, it is these possibilities of different systems that are contrasted in the arguments about economic 'rationality'. When the French bourgeoisie abolished, in the course of revolutionary struggles, the structures of the *ancien régime*, it did this in the name of 'reason', aware that it was opening for itself and for the other classes of society possibilities of economic, social and cultural development that could not flourish under the *ancien régime*. Ultimately, it is the rules of distribution that govern the structures of consumption.

The structures of consumption

Consumption of the factors of production – resources, equipment, labour – is nothing other than the actual process of production, the existence and continuity of which it ensures. It is thus subject to the technical rules of production and to the social rules governing appropriation of the factors of production. It operates within the framework of the production units. Personal consumption, in its individual and social forms, operates within

---

Imerina of Madagascar, etc.), and manipulates them to its own particular advantage. The problem of the appearance of permanent social inequality and of the transition from a classless society to a class structure does arise here, but neither Polanyi, nor Sahlins nor Bohannan raise it when they analyse how the principle of redistribution works. Preoccupied, with justification in Sahlins' case, with rejecting the mistaken interpretations by Bunzel, Radin and others who 'found' 'capitalist' exploitation of man by man among the Chukchee or the Yurok, or, as in Murra's case, with challenging 'feudal' or 'socialist' interpretations of the Inca Empire, these writers see in redistribution a simple extension of the principle of reciprocity that presides over kinship and marriage relations. In doing so, it seems to me, they hide the real oppressive nature of the aristocratic authority – as indeed do the myths justifying this authority which present it as merely a special feature of the old mechanism of reciprocity. See R. Bunzel, 'The economic organization of primitive peoples', in *General Anthropology*, pp. 327–408; J. Murra, 'On Inca Political Structure', in *Systems of Political Control and Bureaucracy in Human Societies*, 1958, and 'Social Structure and Economic Themes in Andean Ethnohistory', in *Anthropological Quarterly*, no. 34, April 1961, pp. 47–59; I. Shapeta and J. Goodwin, 'Work and Wealth', in *The Bantu-Speaking Tribes of South Africa*, pp. 150 et seq.

the framework of consumption units,[72] which may sometimes coincide with production units, as in the case of an agricultural small-holding.[73] Often the basis for the establishment of consumption units is kinship. The nuclear family, the enlarged family, the clan, the tribe, all may provide the framework of consumption, depending on circumstances. Among the Siane the wife prepares the food and takes it to her husband, who distributes it among all the members of the men's house. Another part of the food is consumed by the wife, her unmarried daughters and her sons who have not been initiated. Thus, all the 'values' of the social system are expressed in consumption, through the preferences and prohibitions affecting food, for example. Once again, 'the economic' does not possess all of its meaning and purpose entirely within itself.

With the process of consumption we conclude the description of the formal components of every possible economic system. This 'model' provides the guide-lines for a 'problematic' of economic analysis, that is, a series of questions giving direction to one's interrogation of the facts. What are the technological methods employed by a society? What is their effectiveness? What are the rules governing the appropriation and use of factors of production, and of products? What are the units and forms of consumption? What is the inner unity of these structures, their relation with the other structures of social life?

In the end we see that all production is a twofold act subject to the technical norms of a certain relation between men and nature and to the social norms governing the relations between men in their use of the factors of production. The organic solidarity of the structures of an economic system appears through the complementary and circular character of the processes – production making consumption possible and consumption making production possible.

Synchronic and diachronic analysis of economic systems can now be defined with more precision in the context of this problematic. Synchronic analysis will seek to reconstitute, at a certain moment in the evolution of a system, the functioning of the structures of production, distribu-

[72] The consumption unit for a product is the last social link at which the ultimate distribution of this product takes place before it enters into final consumption, whether individual or social. The consumption unit is not an empty social 'framework', as it is governed by a definite social *authority* (the head of a family, etc.), who has power to distribute and attribute.

[73] Often, though, there is no coincidence. Cf. Daryll Forde, 'Primitive economics', art. cit., p. 335.

tion and consumption. Diachronic analysis will seek to reconstruct the genesis of the elements of the system and of their relations, and then to follow the evolution of their functioning through a series of synchronical pictures of the system. By comparing the rules with the facts it will then try to determine the conditions under which the system changes or remains constant, and to work out the laws by which it functions.

I shall use this problematic in order to deal briefly with the two problems that have loomed at the intersection of all the paths we have followed hitherto. Why is a formal theory not a general theory? And has the idea of 'economic rationality' any scientific content?

2. THE PROBLEM OF A 'GENERAL THEORY' AND OF THE RIGHT TO 'EXTEND' THE CATEGORIES AND LAWS OF POLITICAL ECONOMY

In building my formal 'model' of a possible economic system, I deliberately *ignored all the differences* that exist between the actual systems. This method enables one to isolate the formally identical elements that are common to all these systems. 'Formally', however, does not mean 'really'. At the level of a formal analysis which, on principle, proceeds by ignoring real differences, no 'criterion' is available for *deciding* whether two systems are really identical or different. To decide this one has to analyse the systems as they are, so as to find out whether they belong to the same actual kind of system. This analysis therefore proceeds by subjecting itself to the concrete facts, which cannot be deduced from formal principles. By this road progress is made towards a genuine general theory that undertakes to picture both the identity *and* the difference between systems.

Using this method one can hope to be able genuinely to decide whether the laws of one system 'apply' to others, and whether there are 'real' laws common to all the systems.[74] This shows well enough that the

[74] It is hardly necessary to point out that this problem faces those historians who are constantly tempted to project upon ancient or non-Western societies the categories of 'slavery', 'feudalism', 'capitalism', etc. As regards Antiquity, see the well-known controversy about 'capitalism' in the ancient world, and the views of E. Meyer and Von Pölmann analysed by E. Will: 'Trois quarts de siècle de recherches sur l'économie grecque antique', in *Annales E.S.C.*, March, 1954, pp. 7–22, and the addresses by M. Finley and E. Will on 'Trade and politics in the ancient world' at the World Economic History Congress in 1962, at Aix-en-Provence. As regards feudalism, let me recall the

elaboration and the actual content of a general economic theory are identical with the ultimate aim of economic anthropology as R. Firth once defined it:

> What is required from primitive economics is the analysis of material from uncivilised communities in such a way that it will be directly comparable with the material of modern economics, matching assumption with assumption and so allowing generalizations to be ultimately framed which will subsume the phenomena of both civilized and uncivilized, price and non-price communities into a body of principles about human behaviour which will be truly universal.[75]

If, as ordinary experience indicates, economic systems are both identical and different – as, for example, in our own day, the capitalist and socialist systems – representing their reality cannot mean reducing or eliminating their contradictions. If we see only the difference between systems, we perhaps respect their singularity, but while this is preserved, intelligibility is lost, for thought is then left confronted with a diversity of radically heterogeneous realities, opaque to any attempt at comparison. If, on the other hand, we see only the resemblances, intelligibility seems to be preserved, but singularity is lost in a homogeneous totality in which only slight shades of difference can be discerned. By depicting reality as it is with all its contradictions, economic theory can hope to escape from this ceaseless and inescapable to-ing and fro-ing between two half-truths that when brought together, do not even make one – in other words, it can hope to cut the Gordian knot of the old paradoxes of the kind of historical thinking that was unable to conceive the structure and the event together, to conceive time.

The predominant attitude among economists and anthropologists, however, is to reduce or deny the differences between economic systems and, as they imagine, to rid their domain of its contradictions. This attitude seems to find firm support upon facts that have been collected empirically. In primitive economies we find division of labour, external

---

criticisms made by M. Bloch and R. Boutruche concerning the alleged 'exotic' feudalism of ancient Egypt, the Hittites, etc. (Japan being excepted). Cf. Boutruche, *Seigneurie et féodalité*, 1958, Vol. II, chapters 1 and 2. Similarly, in ethnology, it is customary to talk of 'African feudalisms' in connexion with the ancient states of Africa. E.g. J. M. Maquet, 'Une hypothèse pour l'étude des féodalités africaines', *Cahiers d'Etudes Africaines*, 1961, no. 6.

[75] Firth, *Primitive Polynesian Economy*, 1939, p. 29.

trade, money, credit, calculation, just as in our modern commodity economies. Consequently, Herskovits, or Leclair, seems to have every right to postulate that:

> Practically every economic mechanism and institution known to us is found somewhere in the non-literate world. . . . The distinctions to be drawn between literate and non-literate economies are consequently those of degree rather than of kind.[76]

The general theory appears to have been found before even being sought for, since it was there already. If there is no difference other than one of degree between all the economies known to us, then the laws of commodity economy discovered by classical political economy have universal validity and are 'found again' in every possible system. The higher explains the lower, the complex is the development of the simple, in which it was already pre-formed, in germ. The conclusion was firmly drawn long since by Goodfellow – economic anthropology will be either 'liberal' political economy or it will be nothing at all:[77]

> The proposition that there should be more than one body of economic theory is absurd. If modern economic analysis, with its instrumental concepts, cannot cope equally with the Aborigine and with the Londoner, not only economic theory but the whole of the social sciences may be considerably discredited. For the phenomena of social science are nothing if not universal. . . . When it is asked, indeed, whether modern economic theory can be taken as applying to primitive life, we can only answer that if it does not apply to the whole of humanity then it is meaningless. For there is no gulf between the civilized and the primitive; one cultural level shades imperceptibly into another, and more than one level is frequently found within a single community. If economic theory does not apply to all levels, then it must be so difficult to say where its usefulness ends that we might be driven to assert that it has no usefulness at all.[78]

I shall have no difficulty in showing that in trying to deny the 'real'

---

[76] Herskovits, *Economic Anthropology*, 1952, p. 488. See also Walker, 'The study of primitive economics', in *Oceania*, pp. 131–42.

[77] Goodfellow, *Principles of Economic Sociology*, London, 1939, pp. 4–5.

[78] Frank H. Knight, following Robbins, has taken this view to its logical conclusion: 'There are many ways in which economic activity may be socially organized, but the predominant method in modern nations is the price system, or free enterprise. Consequently, it is the structure and working of the system of free enterprise which constitutes the principal topic of discussion in a treatise on economics' (*Economic Organisation*, New York, 1951, p. 6).

differences between economic systems and rid this domain of its contradictions, Herskovits and others have brought their thinking into flagrant contradiction with the facts and with itself. Their attitude is ultimately based upon a prejudice relating both to the nature of primitive economies and to the Western market economy, and this prejudice sanctifies *a certain way of seeing* (or not seeing) the Western economy, and the other economies *through this conception*. Despite his efforts, Herskovits, having already set out side by side the two definitions of the economy, formal and real, asserts and questions at the same time that the laws of political economy apply to every system, renouncing through this double compromise the task of undertaking a real theoretical elaboration of the facts.

Let me resume my argument. In the first place, to allege, as Goodfellow and Rothenberg do,[79] that political economy applies to every economic system because the theory of prices applies to every such system means willfully to reduce political economy to the theory of prices which, to be sure, was dominant from Malthus to Marshall. It means cutting off from political economy a number of fruitful developments like Keynes's theory that full employment does not automatically prevail in a decentralized market economy. The basic reason why this amputation is made is, as Dalton has pointed out, that anthropologists are well aware, even though they do not admit it, that the essential pre-condition for Keynes's doctrine to 'apply' is missing, because the income of a primitive economy is not mainly derived from or dependent on the sale of products on a market.

Reducing classical political economy to the theory of prices means shutting oneself up in the practical helplessness of economists to analyse the mechanisms of our own Western economy when these are based on exchanges of goods and services that do not go through a market and are therefore not 'measured' by a price. As Burling has emphasized, the economist is obliged to leave out of his statistics of the national economy the domestic work performed by housewives.[80] An anthropologist, on the contrary, will see in the work done by women in the home in a 'primitive' society a reality that belongs to the economic sphere. Reducing political

[79] Rothenberg, review of *Trade and Market in the Early Empires*, in *American Economic Review*, no. 48, pp. 675–8.

[80] P. Bohannan, *Social Anthropology*, p. 220. More generally, it is hard for the Western economist to set out the national balance-sheet of an 'underdeveloped' nation, for 90 per cent of production is self-consumed and it is impossible to know what 'price' to attribute to it. Cf P. Deane, *Colonial Social Accounting*, Cambridge, 1953, pp. 115–16.

economy to the theory of prices thus means taking things 'as they appear', or as they are dealt with empirically, and not as they are, even in our market economies. A reality may be economic without being a commodity. To think otherwise is to make a theoretical fetish of the commodity. Already we can see how the anthropological perspective enables political economy to see itself better, through being subjected more faithfully to social reality in all its singularity and concretcncss.

Besides, even if, in our societies, the giving of a price to goods and services *seems* to be the criterion that defines the latter as economic facts, in other societies the giving of a price is a rare and limited fact that cannot constitute the decisive criterion by which economic activity is to be distinguished from the other activities of a society. For Burling, if economics just means price-theory, then it is an incredible contradiction to talk of primitive 'economics', since the latter uses money in a very limited way, or even uses it not at all, and especially because, as Moore has pointed out, land and labour are never, or hardly ever, the object of transactions through a market mechanism. Nevertheless, even in face of these facts, some economists do not lay down their arms, and in order to 'save' the right to apply to primitive economies the corpus of principles of the market economy, describe these economies as being marked by 'inelastic' supply and demand, and so subject to the particular group of principles of the theory of prices that apply to situations of inelasticity in a market. Dalton shows that thereby analysis of the facts is guided by the prejudice that the market structure, or its functional equivalent, exists universally.[81] For the theory of elasticities to be applicable and varifiable, however, it is further necessary that the inelastic resources and products be bought and sold through a market mechanism, which does not exist in a primitive economy.

Ultimately, the controversy is resumed again and again around the way in which most of the economists and anthropologists manipulate the master-concepts of political economy, those of *capital* and *money*. The definitions they give to these form the essential justification for the 'right' that many of them claim to extend the laws of commodity economies to every possible economy, as proclaimed by Salisbury:

The traditional western economic concept potentially most applicable and useful in understanding the Siane material is that of 'capital'.[82]

[81] See, e.g. Salisbury, *From Stone to Steel*.   [82] Salisbury, op. cit., p. 4.

Now, what is the nature of 'capital'? Three definitions seem to emerge from the plentiful and contradictory economic literature. First we have Thurnwald's (1932):

If by 'capital' is meant commodities which, by their own inherent nature, can not only maintain themselves but increase themselves, . . . [this] occurs in two main forms: capital in plants and capital in domestic animals, especially cattle.[83]

The second is that given by Firth and taken over by Salisbury:

Firth [in *A Primitive Polynesian Economy*, p. 273] stressed that capital is a stock of goods and services which is used in the productive process by being 'immobilized' (i.e. not used by the entrepreneur for immediate consumption) and 'used . . . to meet any . . . changes in the productive situation' (Salisbury, *From Stone to Steel*, p. 141). 'In real terms, then, capital will be defined as a stock of goods, present before a productive act is performed, used in production, and "immobilized" from direct consumption while the act is in progress' (Salisbury, op. cit., p. 142).

The last, in the line of classical thought, is given by Max Weber:

'"Capital" is the sum of money in terms of which the means of profit-making which are available to the enterprise are valued.'[84]

In all these three definitions capital is defined as an object – cattle, plants, tools, money – and this object possesses the property of growth. Capital is thus taken as it 'appears' in the most diverse material forms and in its apparent 'functioning'. A theoretical attitude like this gives rise to a whole sheaf of paradoxes. The fact that thinkers in Antiquity described the use of money as capital *by analogy* with the relations between certain elements of nature, animal or vegetable species, gives no-one the right to take this analogy for an 'identification'. If money was called in Latin *pecus*, from a word that also meant, and had meant for a longer period, 'herd' or 'flock', or if *tekhos* means in Greek the 'interest' on capital lent, and also the 'little one', the young offspring of an animal, this is merely a way of describing a 'cultural' object by analogy with a structure observed in nature. For an animal to become capital it must be bought and sold, that is, *a certain social relation*, a certain type of exchange, must be established between persons through the intermediary of the exchange of things – flocks, money, etc. To the first paradox, taking an analogy for an

[83] Thurnwald, *Economics in Primitive Communities*, 1932, pp. 108–9.
[84] M. Weber, *The Theory of Social and Economic Organization*, 1947, p. 192.

identification, is added a fundamental inability to see in capital more than a set of things, instead of essentially a social relation.

The consequences are logical and absurd. Since capital is a thing, or a property of certain natural objects, any society which uses these things (plants, animals) uses capital. Capital, a fact specific to societies with a commodity and money economy, thus turns up in every agricultural or pastoral society. Here indeed is a paradox, for an anthropologist to be unable to see a social relation beneath its material appearances, and so to transform something social into a 'fact of nature'.

In the case of Firth and Salisbury the thesis is a more complex one. Capital is still a set of 'things', but now they are withdrawn from consumption and so used in a 'social 'process; but, alas, this definition actually belongs to another concept, that of 'factors of production'.[85] And this concept, as we have seen, applies to any form of economy, commodity or not, that needs, in order to produce, to use material and human means (R, I, M), without these necessarily having to assume the particular form of capital. The concept of capital has thus been 'extended' and maintained for the analysis of every society, after its distinctive monetary character and the specific social relations of commodity exchange that it implies have been taken away from it. At this cost it becomes applicable to every society, without defining any of them, and obscuring all of them. One may well wonder what the underlying reason can be for this obsessive obstinacy in introducing the idea of capital into every kind of society.

If capital presupposes the existence of money and commodity economy, is Max Weber's definition fully satisfactory? No, if money is regarded as something that brings in profit by virtue of its mere existence; yes, if money is used as capital only through certain social relations. To summarize the problem briefly, for a thing to be used as capital, two conditions are needed:

The first, necessary but not sufficient, is that this thing be bought and sold. Anything can become capital if it becomes a commodity for its owner. When land, labour and goods become commodities, the production

---

[85] Daryll Forde recognizes this explicitly in 'Primitive Economics' (with Mary Douglas), ch. XV of *Man, Culture and Society*, ed. Harry J. Shapiro, New York, 1956, p. 340: 'The simplest definition of capital, and one which is significant for any primitive economy concentrates on the tools and equipment for production.' Firth, in *Human Types*, p. 79, restricts the idea of capital to: 'certain types of goods [devoted] to facilitating production', but stresses that capital is rarely invested 'with the definite idea of getting a return from it'.

and circulation of commodities become general, and money takes the form of all-purpose currency, a currency in universal use.

But not all money functions as capital. It may serve as a mere means for the circulation of commodities. Money functions as capital when the using of it brings its owner something more than its initial value – a surplus-value, a profit.

If we separate these two conditions we restrict ourselves to the appearance of things and fall into Thurnwald's paradoxes. In its essence, capital is not a thing but a relation between men realized by means of the exchange of things. It is a social fact.

From this angle, Marx, following Ricardo,[86] analysed the circuit of the 'metamorphoses' of an industrial capital[87] and showed that under the different successive appearances of a capital there lay one process only, the development of an invested capital. Before it is invested, a capital appears (1) as a certain amount of money, M. This money is transformed (2) into factors of production the use of which creates (3) commodities of one kind or another, the sale of which (4) brings in a profit, $\triangle$ M. By way of these four stages, M has thus become M' (M $+ \triangle$ M). If we compare M with M' we recognize Weber's definition of capital; if, however, we consider stages 2 and 3, capital appears as means of production, *à la Firth*, or as some sort of commodity to be sold; thus, under the diversity of successive material forms, there is the functional identity of one and the same capital which is fructifying, and this presupposes that labour and the other factors of production can be bought and the product sold – that is, it presupposes the existence of certain social relations, and it is within this social structure that material things become capital.[88]

The classical economists showed that all the forms of capital – financial, commercial, industrial – presupposed the existence of exchange and of a currency of some kind, used in different ways (loan of money, buying and selling of commodities, productive investment) in order to make a profit (interest, commercial profit, entrepreneur's profit). They also pointed out that the financial and commercial forms of capital had an antediluvian

---

[86] Ricardo, *Principles*, chapters 5 and 6.

[87] *Capital*, II, chapter 1.

[88] Marx, in *Wage-Labour and Capital*: 'A Negro is a Negro. He only becomes a slave in certain relationships. A cotton-spinning machine is a machine for spinning cotton. Only in certain relationships does it become *capital*. Torn from these relationships it is no more capital than gold in itself is *money* or sugar the *price* of sugar.'

existence, in some cases going back to very ancient times in certain Asiatic societies, whereas industrial capital, typical of modern capitalist societies, had become a dominant economic fact only late in history.

These already old-established analyses illuminate two apparently paradoxical features that are often mentioned by anthropologists when they describe 'primitive' societies: the absence of capitalism animated by a 'spirit of enterprise'[89] (even when the existence of capital in the given society is alleged – meaning means of production) and the presence in economies where there is exchange, with or without the use of a currency, of certain forms of behaviour that are formally very close to that of a financier who seeks to maximize the return on his loans (the potlatch, among the Kwakiutl, and interest-bearing loans on Rossel Island) or that of a trader who makes money by 'bargaining' over his purchases and sales. (Cf. the Gim Wali of the Trobrianders, the exchange which accompanies the Kula but is distinct from it by the nature of the objects exchanged and the bargaining that takes place in connexion with their exchange.)

But this resemblance, as we shall see, has limits based on the very nature of the exchanges and of the circulation of goods and currency (when this exists) in primitive societies, and these limits forbid us to mix up these phenomena with those of developed commodity societies, or to interpret them entirely on the basis of classical political economy. In primitive societies, goods are classified in distinct and hierarchically ordered categories, and their exchange and circulation are strictly compartmentalized. It is in general impossible and unthinkable to exchange one article for *any* other article *at all*, regardless. The economic structure of primitive societies is thus, as Bohannan puts it, 'multicentric',[90] unlike capitalist economies centred upon a market. The 'multicentric' character of the economic structure is determined by the particular relation that

---

[89] This lack of the 'spirit of enterprise' is often regarded by the economists as proof of the 'irrationality' of the primitive people, their lack of 'economic principles' (Cf. R. Firth, in *Human Types*, p. 62). Other economists, inspired by Schumpeter's views, in *The Theory of Economic Development*, chapter 2, on the entrepreneur, present this lack as the most serious psychological obstacle to the rapid development of under-developed societies (Cf. Baumol, *Business Behaviour, Value and Growth*, New York, 1959, p. 87); Easterbrook, 'La fonction de l'entrepreneur', in *Industrialisation et Société*, 1962, pp. 54–69; and Leibenstein, *Economic Backwardness and Economic Growth*, 1957, p. 121, on 'requisites of an entrepreneur'.

[90] P. Bohannan, *Social Anthropology*, chapter 15; also P. Bohannan and G. Dalton, *Markets in Africa*, introduction.

obtains between the economic and the non-economic in primitive societies, and expresses this relation. The compartmentalizing and hierarchical arrangement of goods arises from their use for the functioning of distinct social relations – kinship, politics, religion – relations that each possess a distinct social importance. In entering into the functioning of these many and various relations, goods and currency acquire *utilities and significances* that are multiple and hierarchically ordered.[91] Consequently, currency and other economic phenomena, being directly determined by the relation between all the structures of society, constitute a reality that it is a more complex task to analyse theoretically than the economic realities of capitalist societies, because it is socially *pluridetermined*. The compartmentalized and hierarchical classification of goods thus expresses the specially dominant role played in a particular society by relations of kinship and marriage (e.g. the Siane), or political and religious relations (e.g. the Incas) – that is, it expresses the dominant aspect of the social structure. These observations enable us to appreciate better a number of features of the economic mechanisms of primitive societies.

The hierarchy of goods is organized in accordance with increasing scarcity. The category of scarcest goods contains those that enable men to attain the social roles that are most highly valued and for which competition between members of the society is keenest, because they procure the maximum of social satisfaction to those who obtain them. The restricted number of these dominant roles necessitates that social competition, in its economic aspect, shall be effected through possession of the scarcest goods. On this basis one could analyse theoretically the existence of scarcities that seem to be 'artificial' in certain societies: some shells brought from far away, pigs' teeth that have been artificially made to grow in a spiral shape, the existence of *limited* series of shells (Rossel Island)

[91] Maurice Leenhardt has listed in his article: 'La monnaie néo-calédonienne', in *Revue d'ethnographie et des traditions populaires*, 1922, no. 12, eighteen situations in which currency in the form of shells was used, and P. Métais took up the problem again in 1952: 'Une monnaie archaique: la cordellette de coquilages', in *Année sociologique*, pp. 3–142. I think it is worth pointing out that historians studying ancient Greece have raised the problem of the multiple significances of currency – religious, ethical, etc. – starting with B. Laum's book *Heiliges Geld: Eine historische Untersuchung über den Sakralen Ursprung des Geldes*, 1924. See Will, 'De l'aspect éthique des origines grecques de la monnaie', in *Revue historique*, 1954, pp. 212–31, and the most recent restatement of the question, by C. Kraay, 'Hoards, small change and the origin of coinage', in *Journal of Hellenistic Studies*, December 1964, pp. 76–91.

and of coppers (Kwakiutl), each item having its own name and history,[92] and so on. Everything happens as though society had 'instituted' a scarcity by choosing unusual objects for certain exchanges.

This would also explain the principle behind the exclusion of subsistence goods from the field of objects that enter into social competition. By excluding these goods from competition and ensuring relatively equal access by everyone to the use of them (the land being, moreover, excluded from any competition between the members of the group), the group safeguards the survival of its members and its own continuity.[93] Competition within the group begins beyond the level of problems of subsistence, and involves not the loss of physical existence but only the non-attainment of social status. Consequently one might seek to explain that subsistence goods, when they enter into social competition on the occasion of ceremonial feasts, must acquire the 'scarcity needed' for them to play this role, and that this scarcity is created by an exceptionally large accumulation of them that must inevitably result in their destruction, their economic non-use. This 'purposeful waste', far from being 'irrational' economic behaviour, would then possess its necessity in the actual content of social relations.

Similarly, the fact would be explained that in certain complex primitive societies (Tiv, Trobriand, Kwakiutl), whereas subsistence goods can hardly ever be converted into anything else, certain rigorously defined possibilities are allowed for converting among themselves the goods belonging to other categories, so as in the end to command those goods of the highest value that give access to women, to political or religious authority, and so on.[94] At the same time, since these scarce goods bring prestige, or the satisfaction desired, only if they are generously redistributed or ostentatiously destroyed, social competition can continue to operate, and social inequality remains relatively limited and can be challenged continually. The theoretical problem is therefore to know how, in societies of this type, inequality becomes more serious and firmly

[92] H. Codere, *Fighting with Property*.

[93] C. Dubois, 'The wealth concept as an integrative factor in Tolowa-Tutunni Culture', in *Essays in Anthropology*, 1936.

[94] Franz Steiner has sketched a theory of these principles of conversion (*Uebersetzung*), both negative and positive, in his article: 'Notes on comparative economics,' in *British Journal of Sociology*, 1954, pp. 118–29. P. Bohannan distinguishes between the principle of conversion of goods within the same category ('conveyance') and the principle of convertibility of an article from one category into an article from another ('conversion').

established, how it actually ceases to be challenged (except ritually and symbolically when the ruler dies), how a social minority is able to benefit *permanently* by an *exceptional* situation, even if it continues to redistribute part of its possessions. This is the problem of the conditions for the transition to the state, of the birth of a class structure within a tribal society, the problem that was raised, and mis-presented, by Morgan in the 19th century, but which today dominates all political anthropology.

There is another possible consequence, economic this time: it seems that if subsistence goods enter only indirectly into social competition within primitive societies, there is no need for production of these goods to be carried on by the members of these societies beyond the limit of their socially necessary wants. The functioning of the social structure, which does not require maximum use of the available factors of production determines the intensity of the incentives to developing the productive forces involved in the production of subsistence goods. This social limit on incentives to develop the productive forces explains the generally slow pace of development of these forces in such societies[95] and the absence of individuals animated by a 'true spirit of enterprise' – in other words, the motivation of an industrial capitalist.[96] This absence and this limitation, far from being 'irrational', express once again the logic of social relations and are neither a 'psychological' problem nor a problem of human 'nature', whether savage or civilized. On the contrary, this situation expresses the *conscious control* that 'primitive or ancient societies' habitually exercise over themselves, a control that quickly disappears with the development of commodity production.[97] The *optimum* of production of subsistence goods in a primitive society thus does not correspond, here any more than elsewhere, to the *maximum* of possible production, but this optimum expresses the 'social necessity' of this production, its relative 'social

[95] Each type of society has its own rate of evolution, based on the social structure itself. Historians have noted that, with changes in the type of society, there occur changes in rates of evolution (the flow of innovations, etc.).

[96] Shea: 'Barriers to economic development in traditional societies', in *Journal of Economic History*, 1959, 4, pp. 504–27, and M. Nash, 'Some social and cultural aspects of economic development', in *Economic Development and Cultural Change*, 1959, pp. 137–51.

[97] Regret for the passing of this control finds expression in Aristotle's violent criticism of 'money-making', the striving – absurd in Aristotle's view – for money for its own sake, which was in contradiction with the Greek ideal of family autarky, and was a source of many ills for the Greek community. Cf. *Politics*, 1257 a–b.

utility', compared with the utilities of the other purposes, accorded different values, that are recognized as 'socially necessary' and are based on the actual structure of social relations.[98]

The economic optimum here appears as that organization of economic activities (production, distribution, consumption) which is most compatible with the realization of socially necessary objectives, and so that which is best adjusted to the functioning of the social structure. The economic optimum thus appears, for the moment, as the result of an intentional organization of economic activity (allocation of resources, combination of factors of production, rules of distribution, etc.) directed towards the better functioning of all the social structures (kinship, politics, religion, etc.), and this result is meaningless unless reference is made to the functioning of these structures.[99] The economic optimum is thus the economic 'aspect' of a wider, 'social' optimum.[100] This intentional activity, which is aimed at achieving the best possible combination of means to attain alternative ends, is strictly what I shall call the conscious, intentional aspect of economic rationality, to be later distinguished from

[98] This is stressed by Fisk and Carneiro when they show that there is a potential surplus in the Siane and Kuikuru societies. In this sense Pearson and Dalton are right in showing that the existence of a potential surplus does not automatically entail a transformation of the social structures. Among the Siane, after the introduction of steel axes, the production of subsistence goods was not expanded, but instead war, matrimonial exchanges and festivals were all conducted on a larger scale.

[99] It is in this sense that Max Gluckmann analyses the structure of the tribalization and detribalization process in Africa, and shows the logic of the attitude of the African worker who has to leave the subsistence sector and at the same time retain it, in order to possess security against the ups and downs of urban employment ('Tribalism in modern British Central Africa', in *Cahiers d'Etudes Africaines*, 1960, pp. 55–72).

[100] Cf. J. Lesourne, 'Recherche d'un optimum de gestion dans la pensée économique', in *L'Univers Economique*, *Encyclopédie Française*, 1960. When recalling the idea of the optimum in Pareto's sense, as meaning a 'state defined by the impossibility of simultaneously improving the situation of all the individuals', many economists consider that this definition is a 'sociologically empty' form. It applies to any and every economic organization, capitalist or socialist (to confine ourselves to modern industrial societies). Mathematically, the problem is that of a 'bound' maximum, the solution of which is found by associating with each constraint of the form 'Fi' = constant a variable, 'fi', called the Lagrange multiplier. Lesourne shows that economic optimum is a 'restricted' optimum dependent on a 'social optimum'.

On this problem, see the writings of Allais, Lerner and Pigou, and especially Koopmans, *Three Essays on the State of Economic Science*, 1957, Essay I, section 2, 'Competitive equilibrium and Pareto optimality', and J. Rothenberg, *The Measurement of Social Welfare*, 1961, pp. 92–3, 95, 97.

'unintentional' rationality. Thus the 'rationality' of the economic behaviour of the members of a society is seen as an aspect of a wider,
fundamental rationality, that of the functioning of societies. There is
therefore no economic rationality 'in itself', nor any 'definitive' form of
economic rationality.

This confirms my analysis of the theoretical inadequacy of the formal
definition of what is economic that is currently accepted by economists.
In every society the 'intelligent' behaviour of individuals appears 'formally' as the organization of their means in order to attain their ends. It
is clear that if this attitude is described as one of 'economizing' their
means, then all purposive activity becomes 'economic', or has an economic
aspect. The 'formal' properties of 'rational' economic behaviour therefore
do not suffice either to distinguish economic from non-economic behaviour or to define the real content of economic rationality proper to each
type of society, a rationality that is only an aspect of a wider, social, overall
rationality. As it is not possible either to *reduce* the economic rationality
of a society to these formal principles or to *deduce* it from these principles,
the formal definition of what is economic is not only incapable of defining
its object but also remains practically useless for analysing the real problem it presents – that of the best *form of organization* of the economy in
the framework of a given society. This analysis presupposes a scientific
explanation of the *raison d'être* of the ends that are socially recognized as
necessary, of what their foundation is in the structure of the societies in
question. This scientific explanation is still only in its infancy.

If we return from this analysis of the intentional aspect of economic
rationality, to our starting-point, the critique of the notion of capital, the
existence of compartmentalized categories of goods, currency and forms of
exchange and their significance in the working of competition within a
primitive society, we can assume that in every society, whether primitive
or not, there is a definite field open to social competition, a field structured
by the dominance of certain social relations over others (kinship, religion,
etc.). It is this field that offers individuals the *possibility* of acting so as to
maximize those determined and hierarchically ordered social satisfactions the *necessity* of which is based upon the particular way the social
structure functions.[101]

This would illuminate both the fact that one can regard the formal

[101] Cf. the critique of Hoselitz by Sahlins in *American Anthropologist*, 1962, p. 1068;
also Firth, *Elements of Social Organization*, pp. 137, 142 and 153.

principles of the rational attitude as being universal and the fact that the real content of economic rationality differs from one type of society to another. To put forward, as do so many economists, the maximizing of the money gains of individuals as the sole rational attitude possible, an absolute and exclusive model, is to forget that this form of economic rationality is the product of a special historical evolution[102] and is characteristic of developed capitalist societies in which the control and accumulation of capital constitute the strategic point of social competition. Furthermore, the capitalist form of economic rationality differs fundamentally from the forms of rationality of primitive societies in that in it the structure of the field open to social competition is such that the struggle for control of the factors of production plays the decisive role, so that quite a different content is given to social inequality.

[102] Numerous Marxists, claiming to find support in Marx's ideas, continue to think that the idea of economic rationality came in with capitalism. Cf. O. Lange, *Political Economy*, chapter V, 'The principle of economic rationality'. Lange is content to make a few allusions to 'the customary and traditional character of economic activity under the conditions of natural economy', and rapidly refers to Herskovits, Sombart and Weber before affirming (p. 193) that 'the principle of economic rationality is the historical product of capitalist enterprise'. On Lange's views see Angelo Pagani, 'La razionalità nel comportamento economico', in *Antologia di Scienze Sociali*, Il Mulino, 1963, pp. 97–148; K. W. Rothschild, 'The meaning of rationality: a note on Professor Lange's article', in *Review of Economic Studies*, Vol. 14 (1), 1946–1947.

As a rule, the problem of economic rationality is confined to study of the forms of behaviour, decision and organization that are most likely to procure for individuals the maximum of expected satisfactions. It is generally assumed, for reasons of convenience of calculation, that the society being studied possesses an economy either of perfect competition or of centralized planning. The problem of rationality then seems to revolve entirely around psychology, the mathematical theory of probability, and the theory of information. In no case, however, has the idea of rationality ever been worked out and criticized theoretically, and the problem of the basis of socially necessary wants is evaded, by means of vague statements about the arbitrary nature of subjective preferences.

The task is then restricted to seeing if the actual behaviour of the producers and consumers conforms or not to the principles of rational behaviour. If it does not, then the actual and the ideal are contrasted, and the irrationality or rationality of the individual and of the social world are discussed. In another direction an attempt is made to estimate the chances for a decision which is assumed to be rational to be followed by the expected effects, taking account of the degree of information possessed by the economic subject, the value of his forecasts. Then a 'science' of the organization of enterprises is hastily constructed, such as to enable the entrepreneur to possess the motivations and the information needed if he is to take the best 'management' decision – the rational decision.

The assumption can be made that the development of new possibilities for production in tribal societies shifts the strategic centre of social competition from the domain of the distribution of the most highly valued elements of the social *product* to that of the distribution of the *factors* of production among the members of society – without competition over the distribution of the product ceasing to play a part.[103] Social inequality becomes greater, and may become permanent when a minority has exceptional rights of control over the conditions of production: control of land and hydraulic arrangement among the Egyptians or the Incas, rights over the labour of slaves in Greece, labour-services rendered by peasants, and so on. All possible combinations of unequal distribution of the product and of the factors of production need to be explored by economic and political anthropology in order to explain how the transition has taken place from primitive tribal societies to new forms of society including a class structure, whether embyonic or well developed, and in which the old principles of reciprocity and redistribution either disappear or no longer play the same role.[104]

Thus, the explicit content of the idea of economic rationality is that of the problem of the basis for the organization of production and distribution in different types of society. Within this dual content the organization of distribution (of the products or of the factors of production) plays the dominant strategic role. On the epistemological plane, these analyses enable us to define more closely the conditions for working out a 'general theory of economic systems'. Since, as we have seen, it is not possible to deduce from formal principles the content of different economic rationalities, nor to reduce this content to these principles, the general theory will be neither a formal theory nor the projection into all societies of the structures and laws of functioning of capitalist societies (or of any other type of society taken as *absolute* term of reference). Neither a formal theory nor an extension of political economy, this general theory in process of construction would be *the theory of the laws of functioning of the economy within different types of possible social structures, and of the basis of these laws,* and this scientific knowledge is bound up to a large extent with

[103] D. Forde, 'Primitive Economics', art. cit., p. 338.

[104] E.g. the control of the trade routes for gold, salt and slaves by the Sarakole artistocracy of the kingdom of Ghana in the 11th century, and the control of water and land by the King among the Imerina of Madagascar in the 18th century. Cf. G. Condominas, *Fokon'olona et les collectivités rurales en Imerina,* chapters 1 and 2.

theoretical knowledge, at present very unevenly developed, of the bases of the other social structures – kinship, religion, politics.

In order to see for a last time the sort of paradox to which a certain use of categories of political economy can lead us in the study of primitive societies, we will analyse the practical consequences of Salisbury's use of the idea of 'capital', before setting out the conclusions of L. Lancaster on the functioning of currency and credit on Rossel Island, which seems formally very similar to the working of financial capitalism.

Having defined capital as Firth defines it, and resolved to discover the 'capital' of the Siane, Salisbury still had to 'measure' it, since there is no science without measurement. Now, he had no price-indicators he could use for this task, since neither land or labour, nor the bulk of the products, were exchanged on a market. One criterion alone was left to him, a single analysable datum: the amount of social labour that the production of goods and services had required. He calculated, for example, that making a stone axe took on the average six hours of labour, a needle one day, a large 'men's house' five days' labour by a team of thirty men, one day's labour by a team of six men, and one day's labour by a team of thirty women, or 186 days' labour altogether. . . .

This information is very useful, but what it measures is the productivity of the Siane system of production, not its 'capital'. Salisbury was thus *really* measuring the productivity of the system while *believing* that he was measuring a capital, without criticizing his own concepts. Long since we have been taught by physics, for example, to separate science from belief, to isolate the positive achievements of Newton from the ideas that Newton held regarding the existence of an absolute Space and Time, and to explain both the real achievements and the mistaken ideas. The misadventures of Salisbury's method illustrate the dangers of an uncritical attitude in theory. In measuring the social cost of goods, Salisbury, somewhat horrified at what he was doing, took the path of doctrinal *lèse-majesté* in relation to the 'prevailing ideas' of the economists. For to measure the 'value' of goods by the social labour necessary to produce them is to go back to the fundamental theses[105] of the founders of political economy and of Marx,[106] who was their disciple on this point, theses long since rejected as useless by the economists of the marginalist inspiration.[107]

[105] Ricardo, *Principles* . . ., chapter I.   [106] *Capital*, I, pp. 4–5.

[107] M. Godelier, 'Théorie marginaliste et théorie marxiste de la valeur et des prix', *Cahiers de planification*, Ecole des Hautes Etudes, no. 3, 1964. P. Bohannan firmly

By a strange fate, the thesis of labour-value, formerly the basis for analysis of modern commodity societies, has become 'good' for analysing a primitive non-commodity society. The paradox is that every economy presupposes the combination and consumption of factors of production, and only labour realizes this combination. Thus the value theory of the classical economists possessed in principle a capacity for universal, anthropological explanation, and could be applied to every society, ancient or modern, commodity or not, liberal or planned. Unfortunately, the idea that this principle of explanation is outdated and obsolete has prevented many from recognizing one of the universal theoretical assumptions of political economy. Nevertheless, I do not think that the labour theory of value explains by itself how prices are formed in a market economy. The category of 'price' is much more complex than that of value and expresses both the cost of production and the social utility of an article, measured through the working of supply and effective demand. It is this last point that marginalism has developed. However, as Marshall pointed out long ago, in the long run the evolution of prices does follow the line of evolution of costs of production. One might perhaps be tempted to find a relation between the social utility of goods, their exchange-'value', and the labour necessary to produce them, or to produce their equivalent, in a primitive society, when they are obtained in a regular exchange (cowries, etc.). Actually, the most highly valued goods are the scarcest, and possess a status equivalent to luxury articles in our societies. Often it has required a considerable amount of labour to obtain them or to accumulate their equivalent. Steiner has analysed the Yap currency, in the form of huge stones, as described by Furness in 1910. Others have estimated the amount of labour and foodstuffs needed for breeding pigs in New Guinea. These goods represent an exceptional direct or indirect levy upon the society's resources in labour and subsistence goods. At the same time, owing to their scarcity, they are called upon to play an essential role in social competition, in which they acquire their manifold significance and their exceptional social utility.

Actually, it seems to me, political economy cannot be, or is not adequate to form, a general theory, because the economic phenomena in a primitive

---

rejects the labour theory of value: cf. *Social Anthropology*, chapter 14, p. 230. R. Firth, in *Human Types*, p. 80, takes up a much more subtle attitude. In the same line of thought as mine is L. Johansen, 'Some observations on labour theory of value and marginal utilities,' art. cit.

society, though simpler than the economy of a modern society, are *socially more complex*, and consequently have *neither the same significance nor the same content*.

In order to finish with this essential point I will take up again the analysis of the ultimate master-concept of political economy, the last excuse for discovering the laws of political economy in primitive societies: the concept of money. We find examples of 'primitive money'[108] in the writings of Armstrong, Bohannan, Guiart, Lancaster, Salisbury and Wilmington.[109] These examples present great differences but they bring out one negative characteristic common to all these 'primitive moneys': they cannot be exchanged for absolutely anything whatsoever – they are not 'all-purpose currencies'.

Bohannan[110] has shown the existence among the Tiv of Nigeria of three categories of objects: subsistence goods, prestige goods (slaves, cattle, metal), and women. Within each category one object can be exchanged for another. Between the second and third categories certain principles of conversion make possible access to women on the basis of brass rods, but goods of the first category cannot be converted into those of the second – nor, and especially not, into the third. There is thus no money serving as common denominator between these three categories, and labour and land remain outside them.[111] When European money was introduced, its role of universal equivalent was seen as a threat to the traditional social structure, and the Tiv tried to save the 'model' of their exchanges by adding a fourth category to the other three, in which European money was exchangeable for goods imported from Europe, or for other European money. This attempt soon collapsed.

[108] Cf. on this problem the works of P. Einzig, *Primitive Money in its Ethnological, Historical and Economic Aspects*, 1949; Quiggin, *A Survey of Primitive Money: The Beginnings of Currency*, 1949; R. Firth, 'Currency, Primitive', in *Encyclopaedia Britannica*.

[109] Wilmington, 'Aspects of Moneylending in Northern Sudan', in *Middle East Journal*, 1955, pp. 139–46.

[110] Bohannan, 'Some principles of exchange and investment among the Tiv', in *American Anthropologist*, 1955, Vol. 57. By the same writer, 'Tiv Markets', in *New York Academy of Sciences*, May, 1957, pp. 613–22, and introduction to *Markets in Africa*, 1963.

[111] Moore, 'Labour attitudes towards industrialization in underdeveloped countries', *American Economic Review*, 1955, no. 45, pp. 156–65, and his article, 'Industrialisation et changement social', in *Industrialisation et Société*, Paris and The Hague, Mouton, 1964, pp. 293–372.

Salisbury's work on the Siane enables us to get closer to understanding the properties of a primitive currency and to present a theoretical interpretation of it.

Among the Siane, goods were divided into three heterogenous categories: subsistence goods (products of agriculture, food-gathering, the crafts); luxury goods (tobacco, palm oil, salt, pandanus nuts); and precious goods (shells, bird-of-paradise feathers, ornamented axes, pigs) forming part of ritual expenditure on the occasion of weddings, initiations, treaties of peace, religious festivals. No article in one category could be exchanged for an article in any other. Substitutions were effected only within a category. There was not one currency, but several currencies, not a general exchange of goods and services, but limited and compartmentalized exchanges. When European money appeared, the principle of non-convertibility of goods was applied to it: coins were placed in category 2, notes in category 3. The reciprocal convertibility of coins and notes, correlative of the convertibility of money into any other article at all, was neither understood nor accepted by the Siane for a long time. I am going to try to explain why this had to be. It seems to me that the absence of a universal currency among the Siane was due, on the one hand, to the limited character of exchanges, the lack of real commodity production (this was the negative reason), but also, on the other, to the need to regulate access to women within a clan and to balance the circulation of women among the clans (this being the positive reason). This second reason, arising from the kinship structures, made it imperative, it seems to me:

(1) To *choose*, among the available resources, certain types of goods, in order to make these correspond to women, and these goods had to be limited in quantity, so as to correspond to the scarcity of women, and to demand greater effort and be more difficult of access than other goods:

(2) To *sever* the mode of circulation of these goods (pigs, shells, etc.) radically from the mode of circulation of other goods, which means setting up a scale of goods arranged in several heterogeneous and non-substitutable categories.

The absence of an all-purpose currency thus appears doubly necessary. An analysis inspired by classical political economy would grasp only the negative reason, the absence of commodity production: an anthropological analysis adds the positive reason. This twofold way of looking at the situation clarifies both the fact that, for a Siane, the significance of an all-purpose currency could not be spontaneously recognizable, since it had neither meaning nor necessity in his own social system, and the fact that the introduction of this currency entailed a threat to his social system.[112] Here we come to the general problem of the relations between economic structures and kinship structures, and one may ask what modifications are made in the long run to the axioms of a kinship system as a result of the development of generalized commodity production and all-purpose currency.[113]

The existence of a currency thus has not the same meaning in a primitive economy as in a Western commodity economy. One and the same reality may take on different and unexpected significances through belonging to different social wholes. Once again, the structure gives a meaning to the elements that compose it, and if one's method is a good one it is not the same element that has to be sought in several structures, in order to prove functional identity, but *the same relation between the elements* of one structure and those of another. My interpretation leads to the same conclusion as that of Dalton. The differences between economic systems are no less important than the similarities, and the differences are due to the different social structures within which the same element functions.

To complete this argument, let us look at the system of currency and credit existing in Rossel Island, as described by Armstrong[114] and interpreted by Lancaster.[115] On Rossel Island there was a currency made up of two series of shells, the Ndap and the Nkö. Each series contained a limited number of coins, arranged in 22 categories in the case of the Ndap and 16 in that of the Nkö. No value was a multiple of a basic unit. The Ndap series had the highest value. Values 1 to 18 were used in ordinary transactions, but those from 19 to 22 figured in exceptional transactions

[112] Cf. P. Bohannan, 'The impact of money on an African subsistence economy', *Journal of Economic History*, 1959, no. 4, pp. 491–503. On the destructive effects of European money upon the potlatch of the Kwakiutl, see Steiner, 'Notes on comparative economics', art. cit., p. 123.

[113] Cf. Smelser, 'Mechanisms of change', art. cit. Morgan had already pointed out that kinship systems are stable elements that evolve very slowly in comparison with the changes that occur in the role of the family.

[114] W. E. Armstrong, *Rossel Island*, 1927, and 'Rossel Island Money, a Unique Monetary System', in *Economic Journal*, 1924, pp. 423–9.

[115] L. Lancaster, 'Crédit, épargne et investissement dans une économie non-monétaire', *Archives européens de sociologie*, III, 1962, pp. 149–64.

only, being handled by the chiefs in accordance with a certain ritual. Coins of category 22 were handed down in the male line of a family of powerful chiefs. Through the intermediary of this system of values a complicated credit system was established. The island's life revolved around a set of social obligations involving transactions in money. In order to carry out a certain transaction it was necessary to possess a certain kind of coin. If one did not possess it then it had to be borrowed, and at the end of a certain period one had to pay it back. In order to do this one could hand over either a coin of the same value, plus some coins of an inferior value, or else a coin of a higher value. Thus there existed an interest, related to time, the rate of this interest being fixed in ritual discussions. Each individual sought to invest his coins, so as at the end of a certain time to obtain coins of a higher value. A financier, the *ndeb*, borrowed and discounted the coins of owners of 'liquid' assets, and took care of the repayment rituals. Everyone thus sought to derive profit from the circulation of money and acted as though he wished to maximize his individual advantages. With this example (and with that of the Malekula currency described by J. Guiart),[116] we seem very close to the modern idea of financial capital. Everyone competes with everyone else to maximize the profits that he draws from the use of a currency. However, Lancaster has shown that this closeness is deceptive. Actually, in the society of Rossel Island, the accumulation of wealth in the hands of certain individuals *did not lead* to an increase in the overall wealth of society, unlike what happens in a Western economy where the credit mechanism is directly a factor of growth through the role it plays in the financing of productive investment.[117] This money and this credit are imbricated in a system that is closed in upon itself and is based not upon commodity exchange but upon a system of 'giving' dominated by the principle of reciprocity. Unlike Mauss,[118] who took Armstrong as his authority for alleging that the operations of credit and giving were identical, Lancaster sees them as two distinct manifestations of the same principle: whoever is in possession of certain goods at the end of a transaction that calls for an eventual 'return'

---

[116] J. Guiart, 'L'organisation sociale et politique du Nord Malekula', in *Journal de la Société des Océanistes*, VIII, 1952.

[117] Daryll Forde says: 'Money of itself does not give a closed economy any link between the present and the future. . . . A community can only be said to save to the extent that durable goods are produced. . . .' ('Primitive economics', art. cit., p. 342).

[118] Mauss, 'Essai sur le don', art. cit., p. 199.

is in the situation and under the obligations of a beneficiary, and this is socially a state of dependence. The cycle of the transaction is closed by the repayment of the debt, with interest, but in the meantime a social relation is created which, in a primitive economy, belongs to a social dimension that goes far beyond the relation between debtor and creditor in a Western economy and gives it a different meaning (social obligations and ritual requirements on the occasion of funerals, weddings, successions – the debt conferring, so to speak, authenticity upon the event).

Lancaster's conclusion regarding Armstrong's materials is thus the same as mine in relation to Salisbury's. The theories of political economy are insufficient to explain a primitive economy, because the latter is socially more complex, and the *uncritical* application of these theories *obscures* the primitive economy more than it illuminates it, as it provides only superficial resemblances while concealing significant differences. Indeed, even the greatest anthropologists have not been able to avoid the snares of deceptively obvious words and apparently 'explanatory' analogies. Boas expressed himself in these terms in his well-known description of the potlatch:

> The economic system of the Indians of British Columbia is largely based on *credit*, just as much as that of civilized communities. In all his undertakings, the Indian relies on the help of his friends. He promises to pay them for this help at a later date. If the help furnished consists in valuables, which are measured by the Indians by blankets as we measure them by money, he promises to repay the amount so loaned with interest.[119]

Such words suggest a close equivalence between potlatch and credit, but Dalton, relying on Boas himself and on Irving Goldman,[120] has shown that here too the differences were more important than the similarities. In the market economy, credit has a variety of functions, the most important being the financing of 'enterprises' through short-term and long-term loans. The borrower uses this all-purpose currency in a materially productive way so as to be able to pay back the loan together with the interest charge upon it, while still retaining some profit. This is not the

[119] Boas, *Twelfth and Final Report on the North-Western Tribes of Canada*, 1898, *British Association for the Advancement of Science, 1891–1898*: quoted in Marcel Mauss, *The Gift*, Glencoe, 1954, p. 100).

[120] Goldman, 'The Kwakiutl of Vancouver Island', in *Co-operation and Competition among Primitive Peoples*, ed. M. Mead, 1937.

case with the Kwakiutl. In a market economy, the apparatus that creates debt and credits is an element in the institution of the market. Rates of interest are variable, depending on supply and demand on the money market. There is no law in a market economy that 'constrains' anyone to borrow, and to borrow only from the group to which his family belongs. Among the Kwakiutl, blankets are a currency of very limited usage. The sphere of the potlatch is that of transactions in certain goods and with special currencies that are not used in other spheres and remain distinct from the sphere of everyday life. In our economy the essential elements of every-day life are acquired through the market, and to the same market belongs the mechanism of debit and credit. The mechanism by which the debt is created, the conditions for repayment, the penalties for failing to repay, are entirely different from what they are among the Kwakiutl. In our economy the debtor always takes the initiative in contracting the debt, but in the potlatch it is the 'creditor' who takes the first step, obliging his rival to accept his gifts. And, most important, the chief motive of the pot-latch is the seeking of honorific prestige, not the accumulation of material wealth, and the ultimate conclusion of the potlatch code of honour is the destruction of wealth in order to show one's worth and thereby to crush one's rival.

Through the analysis of these four examples (Tiv, Siane, Rossel, Kwakiutl) we can perhaps make out a sort of general law. The more complex the division of labour, the more do economic activities acquire relative autonomy in the social totality and the easier is it to define ele-mentary economic categories, that is, categories and laws that are 'simply' economic. Contrariwise, the simpler a society is, the less possible is it to isolate the economic from the other elements in social life, and the more complex will be the analysis of an apparently economic mechanism, since the entire social configuration is directly present at the heart of this mechanism. In a certain way, the simplicity of the categories of thought seems to be in inverse ratio to the complexity of the structures of social reality. In this sense it is because it produces 'simple' concepts that 'the higher explains the lower', that political economy is the *starting-point* of economic anthropology. At the other end of the journey, however, economic anthropology finds that political economy is not enough for its purposes, and that it can itself provide political economy with the angle of vision that the latter usually lacks, in order to mark out its limits, its field of theoretical and historical validity, and perhaps to suggest to it the need to clear up its *terrae incognitae*, its uncultivated areas, to explore its own world in the manner of an ethnologist.[121]

By wishing to see political economy[122] as already the general theory of 'what is economic', one ends up losing sight of the sociological and historical dimension of the facts, transforming a social fact into a natural one, denying or distorting the facts found in primitive societies, even deceiving oneself about the actual functioning of our own economic system, and eventually one forgets that good rule of method that allows for one and the same element to take on a different meaning in wholes that are structured differently. Facts, method, science, all are lost, and this because one has lost the anthropological point of view, the comparative point of view, because one is following the 'natural' bent of a culture by taking one's own society as 'absolute' point of reference. Uncritically, one is taking the rationality of Western economy as the only possible rationality. In other words, one is *justifying* it while analysing it, something that is characteristic of ideological thinking. Can the concept of economic rationality escape from the realm of ideology and possess a scientific content? Is there even such a thing as *an* 'economic' rationality?

3. TOWARDS A RENOVATION OF THE IDEA OF 'ECONOMIC RATIONALITY'

'The Greeks lived formerly as the Barbarians live today' – (Thucydides, I, 6, 6)

I will limit myself to taking a little further the problematic that I have already outlined for this idea – the most difficult of all, and calling for very extensive development. Science, as we have seen, is lost where ideology begins, and ideology begins when a society takes itself as the absolute point of reference and as centre of perspective, whether initial or ultimate. To take one's own society as one's centre of perspective is, indeed, the

---

[121] See Eisenstadt's article, 'Anthropological studies of complex societies', and the discussion with Banton, Barnes, Gluckman, Meyer Fortes, Leach, etc. in *Current Anthropology*, June 1961, Vol. 2, no. 3.

[122] Arensberg, 'Anthropology as History', in *Trade and Market in the Early Empires*, ed. K. Polanyi; and Fusfeld, 'Economic theory misplaced: livelihood in primitive society', in *ibid.*

procedure followed spontaneously by every consciousness; but scientific knowledge begins when the affirmations of spontaneous awareness are challenged and transcended.

Economic science itself was born when the generally-accepted and 'obvious' idea that the *ancien régime* must be upheld was challenged, and when the rules of functioning of an industrial and commercial capitalist economy were taken as the object of analysis and seen as the principles of a 'rational' society. From the beginning, political economy was involved in criticizing, explaining and justifying. And this criticism and this justification were held to be absolute, this explanation was seen as decisive, since the rules of the new economy were, it was believed, in accordance with the principles of 'natural Reason', transcending every historical contingency. History had been led astray through ignorance of the true principles: now that these were known, the reign of Reason would begin.

In this way the mechanisms of commodity economy were both described and 'given value'. Facts became 'norms'. The new economic system was presented and 'felt' as being a 'model' before which the rules of the *ancien régime* and of other societies were indicted, judged and found guilty of 'irrationality'. Very soon after this, with Fourier and Saint-Simon, later with Marx,[123] and nowadays with the upheavals of decolonization and the confrontation between systems on a world scale, criticism of the principles of free enterprise developed, producing as evidence the exploitation of the workers, the wastage of resources, crises, colonial imperialism, etc. It is no longer obvious that the pursuit of private interest automatically promotes the public interest. With the same idea of conferring value upon a 'model', the ancient Greeks treated foreigners as 'barbarians', and only yesterday the sociologists discovered that primitive peoples had a 'pre-logical' mentality. In discussing the subject of rationality are we doomed to compile a doxography of the prejudices of men and societies?[124] Is there nothing but prejudice, ideology, illusion, in this

[123] Marx, *Economie and Philosophical Manuscripts of 1844.* See Part II, section 1 above.

[124] See the famous passage by Alfred Marshall: 'Whatever be their climate and whatever their ancestry, we find savages living under the dominion of custom and impulse; scarcely ever striking out new lines for themselves; never forecasting the distant future, and seldom making provision even for the near future; fitful in spite of their servitude to custom, governed by the fancy of the moment; ready at times for the most arduous exertions, but incapable of keeping themselves long to steady work. Laborious and tedious tasks are avoided so far as possible; those which are inevitable are done by the compulsory

perpetual motion of complementary and successive ascription and denial of value to different forms of behaviour? Can there be scientific knowledge of the rationality characteristic of a particular system, and can this be compared with other systems?

What meaning is accorded implicitly to the idea of economic rationality? To find the answer, I will proceed *a contrario*, by recalling the content that underlay the charge of 'irrationality' brought against the *ancien régime*: briefly, that system was accused of *being an obstacle to technical and social progress*.[125] Thus, the idea of economic rationality is organized around two poles of significance. By a 'rational' economy is meant one that is 'efficient' and 'just'. 'Efficiency' relates to the technical structures of production, in other words, to the greater or less domination by man over nature, while 'justice' relates to relations between men in their access to resources and to the social product. If we compare these two fields of meaning with the state of our present theoretical knowledge, we observe a dissymmetry between them. Technical efficiency is the subject-matter of thorough-going research, aided by processes of calculation. Operational research provides some of these methods, which make it possible to raise the productivity of various combinations of factors of production. 'Social justice', however, is a sphere of apparently insoluble conflicts, and it is not easy to see when the equation between justice and welfare will be satisfactorily settled, despite all the 'welfare' theoreticians.[126] Nevertheless, we can see that these two fields of meaning are in fact one. The best

---

labour of women' (*Principles of Economics*, 1890, Appendix A: 'The Growth of Free Industry and Enterprise': 1946 edition, pp. 723–4).

[125] The idea of progress, like that of rationality, cannot be deduced from *a priori* principles, but assumes many different contents, determined socially and historically. There is no 'true essence' of man that must be recovered, or gradually built up, and constituting both the driving force and ultimate purpose of the evolution of societies, and also the court before which the philosopher or the theoretician summons societies in order to 'judge' them. A speculative attitude such as this has nothing in common with science, and is characteristic of all the 'philosophies of history'. Thus, Morris Ginsberg 'summons economic development before the principles of a rational ethic', in 'Towards a Theory of Social Development: The Growth of Rationality', p. 66. See also E. Seifert, 'Le facteur moral du développement social'. For a discussion of Ginsberg's view see R. Aron. 'La théorie du développement et l'interprétation historique de l'époque contemporaine', in the UNESCO symposium on *Social Development*, 1961, in which the contributions by Ginsberg and Seiffert appear.

[126] Cf. I. M. D. Little, *A Critique of Welfare Economics*.

combination of factors of production is not sought after merely in order to maximize the personal profit of their owner. If the question of rationality relates to these two themes, productivity and justice-welfare, then clearly it lies at the heart of everyday life as an inevitable and permanent question, which calls for an answer not only in theory but also in practice. A closer analysis reveals that the question of the technical and social efficiency of a system is the question of this system's potentialities – more precisely, of the *maximum potentialities* that this system has for bringing about the economic and social changes that are necessarily imposed upon it. It is not possible here to analyse the potentialities of all actual systems known to history, past and present, but it is possible to tackle the problem 'formally', that is, to outline the 'problematic' of such an analysis. How does one tackle the analysis of a system's 'potentialities'? I think we have to distinguish between two planes – the plane of consciously created, willed potentialities, and that of potentialities that are submitted to, whether consciously or not – and two levels of rationality, the intentional and the unintentional.

Willed rationality is seen first in the use that a society makes of its environment. Every technique, as we have seen, makes use of the potentialities of a *milieu*, and assumes a knowledge, whether rudimentary or complex, of the properties of the objects forming this *milieu*, and of their relations. Schlippe[127] has shown, for example, that, behind the appearance of chaos presented by the itinerant agriculture of the Azande, there lies a rigid, hidden order. The scattered arrangement of cultivated plots, the different forms of association for purposes of cultivation, represent close adaptation to ecological possibilities. The work of Conklin,[128] Viguier[129] and Wilbert[130] has shown that the ratio between cultivated and fallow land among practitioners of extensive agriculture revealed an exact knowledge of the regeneration cycle of the fertility of soils. G. Sautter has shown that the ratio between land cultivated continuously and land cultivated discontinuously, as expressed by the concentric arrangement of the cultivated land in West Africa, depended on the possibilities of pro-

[127] Schlippe, *Shifting Cultivation in Africa*, 1955, Part 3.

[128] Conklin, *Hanunoo Agriculture in the Philippines*, F.A.O., 1957, and 'Study of shifting cultivation', in *Current Anthropology*, Vol. 2, Feb. 1961, pp. 27–61.

[129] Viguier, *L'Afrique de l'Ouest vue par un agriculteur*, Paris, 1961, p. 29.

[130] Wilbert, *The Evolution of Horticultural Systems in Native South America, Causes and Consequences*, Caracas, 1961.

ducing manure and the means for transporting it. The potentialities of a *milieu* thus constitute alternatives that can be exploited under certain conditions and which always necessitate a conscious effort if they are to be exploited.[131]

Hackenberg[132] has studied the economic alternatives offered to the Pima and Papago Indians by their territory, situated in the central desert and the south-west of Arizona. He classifies these alternatives in accordance with an increasing gradient of technological intervention in the given facts of the *milieu*, a gradient that arranges in logical order: (1) Hunting and food-gathering, (2) Marginal agriculture, (3) Pre-industrial agriculture, (4) Industrial agriculture. In the 17th century the Papago, living in dry mountain valleys, drew 75 per cent of their resources from hunting and food-gathering, whereas for the Pima, in the basin of the Gila River, the corresponding figure was 45 per cent. The rest of their resources was obtained – to a greater extent by the Pima than by the Papago – from marginal agriculture which exploited with a very simple technique, the fertility of the soil maintained by the rain and the natural irrigation of the Gila River. Among the Pima, in contrast to the Papago, the fields were permanent and the way of life was that of fixed settlement. The differences became much greater when the Pima went over to pre-industrial agriculture. By co-ordinating their efforts they improved their hydraulic system. The introduction of wheat, a winter grain-crop, by the Spaniards completed the cycle of harvests and ensured the subsistence of the communities, thanks to agriculture, all through the year. Consequently, the Pima were now completely freed from their former dependence on hunting and food-gathering. The Papago, on their more arid territory, were never able to produce agricultural resources in sufficient quantity to replace hunting and food-gathering. The white men introduced industrial agriculture, producing cotton. They brought the Gila River under control by building dams and big reservoirs. This meant effecting a far-reaching

[131] G. Sautter, 'A propos de quelques terroirs d'Afrique de l'Ouest', in *Etudes Rurales*, 1962: Godelier, 'Terroirs africains et histoire agraire comparée', in *Annales E.S.C.*, 1964, no. 3.

[132] Hackenberg, 'Economic alternatives in arid lands: a case study of the Pima and Papago Indians', in *Ethnology*, 1(2), April 1962. Archaeology has begun to provide information of use on the evolution from marginal agriculture to intensive agriculture in pre-Columbian Peru and Mexico, in the ancient Middle East, etc. E.g. D. Collier, 'Agriculture and civilization on the coast of Peru', in Wilbert, op. cit., pp. 101-9, and the commentary by Eric Wolf.

change in the *milieu*, which presupposed the use of machines and a market economy to give an outlet for the produce. This potentiality the Pima, and *a fortiori* the Papago, had been unable to realize.

The potentialities of a *milieu* are thus actualized or developed through the techniques of production. It seems that the lower the technological level of a society, the simpler the economic system, the fewer 'alternatives' exist for an economic 'choice' and the smaller is the maximum production that the society will be able to attain. The fluctuations of this maximum depend very much more upon the variations in constraints external to the system than upon internal variations within it. If, for example, we analyse the units of land measurement that were used in the Middle Ages – the acre, the ploughland and so on – we see that they express the largest area that could be cultivated by a plough-team in one day or one year. This maximum depended on the conditions of the terrain – valley, hill-slope, heavy soil, light soil – and the agrarian metrology adapted itself flexibly to these variables.

Maximization of production is meaningless, however, without reference to the hierarchy of needs and values that are imposed upon individuals in a given society, having their basis in the nature of the structures of this society. The maximizing of production is only one aspect of the overall strategy of maximizing social satisfactions which is imposed upon individuals and groups within this society. In connexion with Amatenango, a community of the Indians of the State of Chiapas, in Mexico, Nash[133] has shown that none of them is unaware of the rules for maximizing monetary gain, but that the ends that each one seeks to maximize are objectives to which value is accorded otherwise than in accordance with this economic magnitude. Every man endeavours to pass through the entire cycle of communal offices, civil and religious, that will confer on him an important rank in the group's hierarchy. Every man therefore practises a complex set of forms of behaviour, co-operating and competing with the other members of the group, allowing for the prestige and wealth of his family and marriage-connexions. These examples show us that the intentional rationality of a social system is revealed in the form and through the purposive acts by which individuals combine means in order to attain their ends. But this 'formal' analysis says nothing about the nature of these means and these ends. Above all, it does not allow us to analyse

---

[133] Manning Nash, 'The social context of economic choice in a small society', *Man*, November 1961, pp. 186–91.

certain properties of a system that are neither willed by nor, often, even known to its agents, an unintentional level of rationality.

When theoretical consciousness arrives at knowledge of this level, it has passed from rules to laws, from the known properties of a system to those of its properties that were unknown at the start. We will deal with this delicate point by means of a few examples. Hackenberg points out that when the Pima adopted the cultivation of wheat and went over to a system of permanent agriculture, they greatly transformed, without wishing to, and, probably, at first without knowing it, the wild flora and fauna of their environment, the basis of their old economy of food-gathering and hunting. After a certain time, any return to these old forms of economy became, first difficult and then impossible. The Pima had thus destroyed one of their economic possibilities, and cut off all retreat in that direction.[134] Furthermore, population increase, connected with the development of agriculture, made such a path fundamentally inadequate to their needs. Thus, by adopting a new economic system, a society acquires some new possibilities, while depriving itself of others. All determination is negation, as Spinoza and Hegel said. And this deprivation is not aimed at by any consciousness, anyone's intention. It is not the deliberate act of any person taken separately, but the unconscious work of all. At the same time, however, the new possibilities that a society opens to itself have their own objective limits, their own shutting-off mechanism.

Conklin, Viguier and many others have shown that, in a system of extensive agriculture on patches of denshered land, there was a *necessary ratio* between land cultivated and land left uncultivated, in order to ensure maintenance of the fertility of the soil and reproduction of the productive system at the same level of efficiency.[135] When this ratio is exceeded, the 'equilibrium' of the system is upset,[136] a process of defertilization and deterioration of the soil sets in, yields decline, social difficulties begin. If no solution is found, the vicious circle of extensive cultivation sets in: when yields fall, cultivated areas expand, and when cultivated areas expand, yields fall. The functioning of the system is thus incompatible

[134] If all further development is blocked for certain reasons, such situations can create the conditions for the appearance of 'false archaisms'.

[135] Carneiro points out that the nomadism of the crops is not necessarily due to exhaustion of the soil but to the difficulty of working them after a few years of cultivation, owing to encroachment by weeds. Cf. art. cit.

[136] Cf. Leeds, *The Evolution of Horticultural Systems*, p. 4.

with certain rates of population growth, or with the necessity of extending cultivated surfaces so as to produce industrial crops and obtain income in money form. The problem then arises of how to change the system so as to break the vicious circle it engenders and resolve the contradiction between production and consumption,[137] means and needs. This example throws up a number of theoretical problems, and offers some light for their solution.

Sometimes, as we have just seen, the very success of a system creates the conditions for its failure. Extensive agriculture makes possible in general a higher rate of population increase than is offered by an economy of food-gathering or hunting, but beyond a certain point, this density of population is incompatible with the maintenance of conditions for the proper functioning of the system, or at least the rules that yesterday were effective and rational are no longer so in this new situation. Thus we obtain the hypothesis that there is a functional correspondence between the working of a system and a certain type and a number of external and internal conditions for this working. There is thus no economic rationality 'in itself', definitive and absolute. The evolution of a system may, in certain conditions, develop contradictions that are incompatible with maintenance of the essential structures of the system, and reveal the limits to the possibilities of the system's 'invariance'.

What is meant by the 'invariance' of a system? Not the invariance of the elements combined in the system but the *invariance of the relation* between these elements, the invariance of its fundamental structures. The hypothesis can be advanced that, beyond a certain point, variation in the variables of a system dictates variation in the functional relation between these variables. The system must then evolve towards a new structure. In this connexion an objective dialectic of the relation between 'structure' and 'event' becomes apparent. A structure has the property of tolerating and 'digesting' certain types of event up to a certain point and time when it is the event that digests the structure. A social structure can thus dominate an evolution and contradictions both internal and external up to a certain point which is not known in advance and is not a property of the 'consciousness' of the members of the society defined by this structure but a property of their social *relations*, both conscious and unconscious. The

---

[137] Leroi-Gourhan, *Le Geste et la Parole*, 1964, p. 213, 'Le Territoire': 'The relation between food, territory and density of population ... is an equation with variable but correlative values'.

conscious action of the members of a society to 'integrate and neutralize' the event or the structure that threatens or injures their social system has been strongly emphasized by anthropologists, and shows the inner bond between the intentional and unintentional rationalities of the system.[138] We have seen, for example, the Tiv and Siane seeking to integrate European money and the new commodity exchanges into a supplementary category and thereby to preserve, while giving it a wider field of action, their traditional system of circulation of goods. We have also seen these attempts fail after a certain time. The contradiction that developed here did not come from inside the system, like the contradiction between population growth and extensive agriculture, but from outside it. Nevertheless, it also reveals what the internal possibilities of this system are. There is thus, when it comes to forming a science of societies, no theoretical superiority of non-acculturated societies as compared with acculturated societies, or vice versa. The former are needed in order to understand the latter, and the latter throw light on the former. This reciprocity enables us to attempt an analysis of the possibilities of invariance of the different social systems.

The resolution of a contradiction that is incompatible with the invariance of a system does not necessarily result in the mutation and destruction of this system. When a crisis breaks out in a community of slash-and-burn cultivators, if there is plenty of land available around this community, it can break up and, so to speak, expel the contradiction by hiving off daughter-communities around it. This solution maintains the economic system and multiplies it, while endowing it with great stability

---

[138] Awareness of the limiting conditions for balanced functioning of an economic system is perhaps expressed in certain myths of the Siberian hunters, or Tupi-Guarsani, in the idea of an original pact between the different species of animals and man, by which man undertakes not to kill the animals *without necessity*, without needing to do so, on pain of terrible vengeance by Nature against the human community. Cf. E. Lot-Falk, *Les Rites de la chasse chez les peuples sibériens*, Paris, 1953, ch. IV, 'Les Esprits-maîtres'.

In another context, Richard-Molard suggested that the economic and social role of the 'master of the land' in the archaic agricultural societies of Black Africa should be analysed in connexion with the need for systems of extensive agriculture to ensure the maintenance of equilibrium between man and the land by vigilant supervision of the periods when land is cultivated or left to lie fallow. 'In the evolution of the tropical agricultural areas of Africa and of their density of population, of their conservation or of their erosion, there are two thresholds, one above the other and quite different, of technical and demographic optimum, separated by intermediate stages that are more or less critical' (J. Richard-Molard, 'Les terroirs tropicaux d'Afrique', *Annales de Géographie*, 1951).

of evolution. When hiving off is impossible, the contradiction has to be resolved on the spot by producing more from the same area and going over to more intensive forms of agriculture. Some writers, such as Richard-Molard[139] and G. Sautter explain in this way the presence of intensive agriculture among the Palaeo-Negritic peoples of Africa, who were probably driven from their original area by invaders and confined to their places of refuge, where, in order to survive, they were obliged to exploit a limited territory intensively.[140]

Besides, the existence of contradictions within a system does not mean that this system is doomed to paralysis. Some contradictions are constituent features of a system, and give it its dynamism for a certain period. Thus, under the *ancien régime*, peasants and lords were both opposed to each other and in solidarity with each other. The contradiction between them *did not rule out* their unity like the contradiction between a master and his slaves. The struggles between peasants and their lords, far from weakening the system, gave it a stronger stimulus. When the peasants succeeded in forcing their lord to reduce labour-services and rents, they then had more time and means available to develop their own resources. The peasant communities became richer, exchanges became livelier – and the lords benefited from this prosperity. Some have supposed that the economic, social, cultural and demographic dynamism of feudal Europe between the 11th and 13th centuries had its source in the possibilities of growth that were contained in the contradiction of the lord-peasant relationship, at least so long as the lords were still 'entrepreneurs of production' and had not yet become almost exclusively mere 'drawers of ground-rent' and a parasitical class.[141] There are thus contradictions that act as

[139] art. cit.

[140] When the 'Pax Gallica' unclamped the grip that enclosed the Kabre of Togo, they invaded the plain and once more practised an extensive agriculture that was much less 'advanced' than the intensive system of their mountain period. Carneiro puts forward the hypothesis that the contradiction between population and production creates the conditions for new socio-economic systems to appear when the area of cultivable land is strictly limited, as in the narrow valleys of the Peruvian coast or in the mountains of the Andes or of New Guinea. This hypothesis seems confirmed by Brookfield's important study of 31 localities of New Guinea with varying ecological conditions, where six forms of agriculture are found, increasing in intensity in proportion to the increasing density of population ('Local study and comparative method: an example from Central New Guinea', *Annals of the Association of American Geographers*, 1962, no. 52, pp. 242–254).

[141] Duby, op. cit.

driving forces of economic and social development, or periods when the social order and the economic system can evolve rapidly without being held up by acute contradictions. Perhaps the difference between the contradictions of a primitive community – the unity of the working of competition and co-operation – and those of a class society is that the former do not entail economic and social changes *directly*, or at the same pace as the latter. In order to verify this point, exact investigations and statistical inventories would have to be made. In any case, however, if a system functions only under certain conditions, the optimum of its functioning corresponds to a 'state' and a 'moment' of the evolution of this system in which its internal and external contradictions are best 'dominated' – which does not necessarily mean 'excluded'. For, while excluding the surplus population of a society of slash-and-burn cultivators means resolving its contradiction, destroying the relation between master and slave, or between lord and peasant, does mean really 'changing' the system, abolishing it, in the way that the night of 4 August, 1789, saw the 'abolition of privileges and of the *ancien régime*'. But we ought not to consider the optimum functioning of a system in the manner of Montesquieu seeking the date of the highest 'grandeur' of the Romans before they fell into irremediable decadence, or Toynbee describing the death-throes of civilizations strewing the arena of history with their remains. At each moment of a system's evolution there is an optimum practice that can be employed in order to dominate the contradictions of that moment, and those who are called great leaders are precisely the men who find the 'necessary' transformations. One may assume, however, that a system is at the optimum of its functioning during the period when the compatibility of the social structures that compose it is at its maximum.

Thus the idea of functional compatibility and incompatibility leads us towards an operations research and cybernetics of economic systems, towards a logic – not formal but 'real' – of the evolution of systems which is the proper theoretical task of economic anthropology.[142] Our last analyses, however, may have left the impression that an 'economic' rationality capable of isolation does exist. The analyses of Nash and Lancaster gave us a glimpse of individuals pursuing a wider, social rationality, which covers and organizes the totality of social relations. This sets us on the

[142] On the relations between cybernetics and economics, see Henryk Greniewski, 'Logique et cybernétique de la planification', *Cahiers du séminaire d'économétrie*, C.N.R.S., 1962, no. 6.

path to a compatibility much broader than the compatibility between an economic structure and an event or a structure that is also economic, on the path to a functional 'correspondence' between economic and non-economic structures.

Hackenberg has shown that the development of a pre-industrial agri-culture among the Pima resulted in the development of six features that were unknown to the Papago, and created a difference that was now a difference of 'kind' between their two social systems. The habitat of the Pima became concentrated and definitively settled. Co-operation devel-oped between several villages, for organizing water-resources. The econ-omy was finally liberated from food-gathering and hunting. An agri-cultural surplus could be exchanged with other tribes. The employment of a labour-force from outside (the Papago), which had become necessary, had begun a process of social differentiation. Finally, and above all, the political and social structure had become much more complex within the extensive Pima communities than it was among the Papago. A tribal authority had been formed, headed by a single chief.

This example raises the general problem of intentional and uninten-tional correspondence between all the structures of a social system, of 'social' rationality. Ember[143] has tried to show, by a statistical analysis, the general relation of correspondence between economic and political development. For primitive or pre-industrial societies the indicators of economic development cannot be direct, since we have no prices with which to measure the value of goods and services. Economic specializa-tion is a valid indicator, but is hard to pin down in usable form, amid the materials provided by ethnographic and historical writing. Ember, follow-ing Naroll,[144] selected two indirect indicators of both economic specializa-tion and economic development: the larger size of the social community (connexion between productivity and population-growth), and the relative importance of agriculture as compared with hunting, food-gathering and stock-breeding. As indirect indicators of political development he selected the degree of differentiation of political activity, measured by the number of different functions connected with the task of government, and the level

---

[143] Melvin Ember, 'The relationship between economic and political development in non-industrialized societies', in *Ethnology*, April, 1963, pp. 228-48. See the old work of L. Krzywicki, *Primitive Society and its Vital Statistics*.

[144] Naroll, 'A preliminary index of social development', in *American Anthropologist*, 1956, no. 58, pp. 687-715.

of political integration of the society, measured in terms of the most extensive territorial groups on whose behalf one or more activities of government were carried on.

He took at random a sample of 24 societies from the list drawn up by Murdock[145] of 565 cultures, contemporary and historical, and studied the correlation between his four indicators. It emerged as a strong one, in a non-linear relationship. The complexity of social systems seems, to employ Naroll's expression, to increase in geometrical progression, like the complexity of biological systems. Ember interprets the relation between economics and politics by adopting the assumption that politics plays a necessary and decisive role in a society as regards control of resources and of the product, or, in other words, in operations of redistribution. And this role increases with the importance of the surplus that the economy produces. In a society of food-gatherers the distribution of products is direct. It is no longer the same in a more complex economy. But examination of the deviant cases in Ember's sample shows us that we must not seek a mechanical, linear connexion between economic and political systems, and that the nature of the economic system counts less than the dimensions of the surplus that it can produce, in other words, its productivity. Among the Teton Indians, who were bison-hunting horsemen, community sizes were relatively large, despite the absence of agriculture, and political complexity and integration had also reached a high level. In fact, at the period when the high plains of the North were relatively underpopulated, bison-hunting on horseback obtained more resources than primitive agriculture. In a different set of conditions, a fishing economy like that of the Kwakiutl of British Columbia could provide a production per head greater than that of an agricultural society.

These deviant cases bring out the fact that it is not possible mechanically to deduce a political system from an economic one, nor to reduce a political system to its economic functions, for a political system assumes other functions, too, such as defence, which do not belong to the economic sphere. Thus, among the Pima, at the moment when they were going over to permanent agriculture, the menace of the Apaches contributed to hasten the regrouping of the habitat and the political integration of the villages under the authority of a single chief. It is in a complex and subtle context like this that the idea of surplus has been taken up by the

[145] Murdock, 'World ethnographic sample', in *American Anthropologist*, 1957, no. 59, pp. 664–87.

prehistorians[146] in order to explain the appearance of the great Bronze-Age societies,of the Near East, or the great pre-Columbian empires of Mexico and Peru.

Through the hypothesis of a correspondence between economic and political structures[147] we meet again the idea of a wider rationality, a correspondence between all the structures of a social system – kinship, religion, politics, culture, economics. There is thus no strictly economic rationality, but instead an overall, totalizing rationality – an historical, social rationality. Max Weber already in his day attempted to show a correspondence between the Protestant religion, merchant capitalism, and modern forms of law and of philosophical thought. This task demands, if it is to bear fruit, the organic collaboration of different specialists in social facts, and such collaboration implies a methodology that has not yet been elaborated.

On the basis of this overall social rationality revealed by anthropological analysis, the economic mechanisms can be reinterpreted and better understood. A kind of economic behaviour that seems to us 'irrational' is found to possess a rationality of its own, when set in its place in the overall functioning of society. Nash showed that the Amatenango community, while not unaware of the rules of monetary gain, was unable to experience real economic expansion owing both to the low technological level and to the lack of land that dragged down the whole society, and also to the fact that accumulated wealth was periodically drained away in the carrying out of the religious and secular functions of the community instead of being invested for productive purposes. The absence of 'spirit of enterprise' and incentive to invest is therefore not explicable by a merely economic necessity but also has its *raison d'être* in the actual structure of the Indian community. The economic behaviour of this community may seem 'irrational' to us, but this view reflects two attitudes – one, ideological, due to our taking Western society as absolute centre of reference, and the other which notes an objective limit to the Amatenango social system's ability to ensure continued technical progress and an evolution of its members' standard of living. It is clear that these two distinct attitudes

---

[146] Steward, 'Cultural causality and law: a trial formulation of the early civilization', in *American Anthropologist*, 1949, no, 51, pp. 1–25; Braidwood and Reed, *The Achievement and Early Consequences of Food Production*, 1957, Harbor Symposia, pp. 17–31; V. Gordon Childe, *Social Evolution*, chapters 1 and 2.

[147] Cf. Sahlins, 'Political power and the economy in primitive society', art. cit.

reinforce one another, so far as the uncritical spontaneous consciousness is concerned.

By way of all these analyses and distinctions some theoretical conclusions can be gathered together. There is no rationality 'in itself', nor any absolute rationality. What is rational today may be irrational tomorrow, what is rational in one society may be irrational in another. Finally, there is no exclusive economic rationality. These negative conclusions challenge the preconceptions of 'ordinary' consciousness and are remedies against the 'temptations' that these present. In the end, the idea of rationality obliges us to analyse the basis of the structures of social life, their *raison d'être* and their evolution. These *raisons d'être* and this evolution are not merely the achievement of men's conscious activity but are the unintentional results of their social activity.[148] While there is some rationality in the social development of mankind, the subject of this rationality is not the isolated and absurd individual of a timeless human nature and psychology, but men in all the aspects, conscious and unconscious, of their social relations. Synchronic and diachronic analysis of past and present social systems would enable us to get an inkling of the 'possibilities' of evolution inherent in these systems, their dynamism; it would illuminate retrospectively the particular circumstances of the *uneven development* of these societies, and would give us a new conception of the contrasts that exist between societies today. The history of societies is not accomplished in advance, today any more than yesterday. The idea of a linear evolution leading all societies mechanically through the same stages by the same paths is a dogma that has quickly foundered, despite Morgan's[149]

---

[148] Unintentional does not mean lacking in 'meaning'. Beyond the field of his conscious activities, the domain of the unintentional is not, for man, a silent desert in which he suddenly petrifies into a 'thing' like the rest, but is the other face of his world, in which all his behaviour finds part of its meaning. The unintentional is not merely that part of man that is made up of the sediment of all the 'non-willed effects' of his undertakings, it is the place where the hidden regulators are organized that correspond to the deep-lying logic of the systems of action he invents and practices. The unintentional is not just that which it 'seems' mainly to be, a reality that Sartre describes to us as the 'practical-inert' reverse side and effect of our living projects, it is the hidden aspect of our social relations where part of the 'meaning' of our behaviour is actively organized. It is the elucidation of this meaning that the anthropological sciences undertake to carry out, by revealing the relation between the intentional and the unintentional, discovering the 'laws' of social reality. Cf. Sartre, *Critique de la Raison Dialectique*, 1960, Vol. I: 'De la "praxis" individuelle au pratico-inerte'.

[149] Morgan, *Ancient Society*, 1877.

authority, in the insoluble quarrels of dogmatic Marxism.[150] It seems to me that the assumption of a certain unintentional and intentional rationality in the evolution of societies leads to a 'multilinear' evolutionism that seeks, in that laboratory of social forms called history, to reconstitute the precise conditions for the opening or the closing of different possibilities.[151] And this multilinear evolutionism that will come into being seems to be nothing else but the general theory of economic systems, the ultimate task of economic anthropology.

*

[150] Engels's successors forgot that *The Origin of the Family, Private Property and the State* (1884) began with advice to modify Morgan's 'classification' of the facts in the event that 'important additional material necessitates alterations' (FLPH edition, p. 33).

Marx's text presenting the first Marxist general outline of the evolution of societies is still unpublished in French, having been found only in 1939 ('Formen die der kapitalistischen Produktion vorhergehen', published in the *Grundrisse der Kritik der Politischen Ökonomie*, Berlin, Dietz, 1953 [now available in French as *Fondements de la critique de l'économie politique*, Paris, Anthropos, 1968. The section specially mentioned is available in English as *Pre-Capitalist Economic Formations*, London, Lawrence and Wishart, 1964]). It is to be observed that in this document Marx does not assume, as his successors did, that all societies must pass through more or less the same stages. On the contrary, Western history seems to him to have evolved in a 'singular' way. See my discussion of this work: M. Godelier, 'La notion de mode de production asiatique', in *Temps modernes*, May 1964.

[151] Cf. on certain points, J. Steward, *Theory of Culture Change*, 1955, chapter 1. Most often, a schema of the evolution of societies was a speculative construction whose author peopled it with his 'ideas' about the word, and in particular about his own society. Depending on whether he admired the latter or was critical of it, the author either made history advance along the paths of progress and civilization or caused mankind to fall from its original goodness. Good or bad, primitive man remained what he was, a theoretical puppet made up of cultural elements taken from among contemporary 'primitives'. Cf. K. Bucher, *Die Entstehung der Volkswirtschaft*, 1922, chapters 1 and 2, who attributes to the original savage living in a pre-economic stage all the vices that contrast with the alleged virtues of civilized man (egoism, cruelty, improvidence). Cf. O. Leroy, *Essai d'introduction critique à l'étude de l'économie primitive*, 1925, p. 8.

The evolutionists, instead of studying societies as they found them, seeking in their actual struggle the logic of their functioning, analysed them hastily so as to construct an alleged origin and a pseudo-history for them.

In order to save the the facts, evolutionism had to be rejected, and from Goldenweiser and Lowie to Radcliffe Brown the slogan became 'Sociology versus History'. On the basis of the information gathered, diachronic analyses can now be attempted that are free of all preconceptions about the evolution of mankind.

I have tried to bring out some methodological principles for critical use of the categories of economic science. These are only hypotheses, needing to be checked. But economic science, like the other social sciences, is still caught in the labyrinth of a method that is incapable of conceiving the identical *and* the different, the intentional *and* the unintentional. It will need to find the Ariadne's thread of its future by getting as close as possible to the literal content of the empirical material provided by anthropology and ridding itself constantly of any temptation to project upon history the phantom of our modern societies, transforming the relative into an absolute. If this is done, scientific consciousness will become what it should be, both internal and external to its object.

(*L'Homme*, V, no. 2, Sept. 1965)

Index

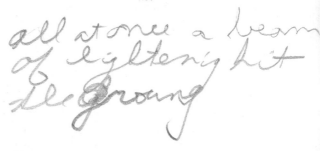